SHADOWS OF THE SUN

─────────●─────────

THE DIARIES OF HARRY CROSBY

Edited by
EDWARD GERMAIN

────────●────────

Santa Barbara
BLACK SPARROW PRESS
1977

Cover photograph by Ray Hartman.

LIBRARY OF CONGRESS CATALOGING IN PUBLICATION DATA

Crosby, Harry, 1898-1929.
    Shadows of the sun.

    Includes index.
    1. Crosby, Harry, 1898-1929 — Diaries.
2. Poets, American — 20th century — Biography.
I. Title.
PS3505.R883Z52   1977   811'.5'2 [B]   77-2869
ISBN 0-87685-304-1
ISBN 0-87685-303-3 pbk.

TABLE OF CONTENTS

A Selection of Photographs follows page 148.

ACKNOWLEDGEMENTS

I am grateful to Harry T. Moore, Professor of English at Southern Illinois University and literary executor of the Estate of Caresse Crosby, for permission to edit and print the complete text of *Shadows of the Sun* and, together with his wife, Beatrice, for encouragement and hospitality. John Martin of Black Sparrow Press suggested this project to me. Andreas Brown of Gotham Book Mart in New York City, who initially planned to publish these diaries, kindly made available his copy of Volume I annotated for the printer by Caresse Crosby. Kenneth Duckett and his resourceful staff at the Morris Library of Southern Illinois University aided me. My wife, Sara, who became as engrossed with Harry Crosby as I, helped identify the characters in the diary. I want to thank Graham Mackintosh for his typography and page layout. Sasha Newborn, who set this book in type, ingeniously broke the codes on pages 133 and 222. Seamus Cooney and Judyl Mudfoot did the arduous proofreading. Alysse and Ashley Weeks of Ann Arbor, Michigan, and Lynn and Bob Bassler of Northridge, California, let me turn their homes into studies while the manuscript progressed through its stages. Thank you all.

E. B. G.

INTRODUCTION

It is almost impossible not to read these diaries as a poet's eight-year romance with death, consummated late in the afternoon of Tuesday, December 10, 1929, in a borrowed New York apartment in the Hotel des Artistes. Harry Crosby and one of his mistresses took off their shoes and lay on the bed together, fully clothed. Then Harry pressed a .25 caliber Belgian automatic pistol to Josephine Rotch Bigelow's left temple and blew her head apart. For two hours Harry may have lain alive beside her with his arm beneath her head. Then he pointed the pistol at his own forehead and pulled the trigger.

Josephine Bigelow may have goaded him into it. The day before, she had sent Harry an impassioned poem that ended with the words, "Death is *our* marriage." But Harry had talked of suicide for years. In 1921 he had written to his love, Caresse, who was then still Polly Peabody and married to another man, ". . . If worse should come to worse and you couldn't get a divorce . . . I'll come down and kill you and then myself so that we can go right to Heaven together and we can die in each other's arms and I'll take the blame so you won't have to worry, Dear." He filled his diary with references to death and evaluated techniques of suicide: jumping from a plane, poison, even leaping into Mt. Vesuvius. The previous Sunday he had tried to persuade Caresse, now his wife, to jump out of their hotel window with him—but she hadn't been ready to die. Josephine was. One of Harry's other mistresses, the "Lady of the Golden Horse," called her "that poor demented girl," and was sure that Josephine had called Harry's bluff: "She put the idea in his head and he could not back out."

Josephine Bigelow had as much nerve as Harry Crosby—and Harry's daring impressed everybody. Hart Crane, describing him enthusiastically to Malcolm Cowley in 1928, marvelled that Harry would do anything and everything that entered his mind. But so might Josephine. Like Caresse, Josephine had committed adultery with him, and like Caresse, she had betrayed a blue-blooded, Back Bay, Bostonian husband. Harry must have loved that; he hated the prudery of "The City of Dreadful Night." He and Caresse had fled Boston when they married in 1922. "Christ what a narrow escape, far narrower than escaping the shells at Verdun," Harry wrote in his diary when they reached Paris.

But Josephine had not run away. She was living in Boston with her new husband, Albert Bigelow, and seeing Harry when he and Caresse came to visit his family. The lady had nerve, and no common sense. But she had power—psychic, sexual power over Harry.

They had met in the summer of 1928 when Josephine was visiting Europe to buy her trousseau. They had made love and it had been overwhelming. "Fire Princess," Harry began to call her. She became a figure in his dreams and in his imagery of the Sun:

> I wake up dreaming of aeroplanes and orchids whirling in circles around two figures the Sorceress and the Fire-Princess and it is nine months ago to-day (long enough for me to have had a fire child) since we have seen each other but my heart still writes sonnets to her eyes my body still blazes into fire at the thought of her and I still look out my library window every day at sunset towards the west* and to-night after a thirty-one day drought it began to rain—the sound of the roulade of the rain upon the roof come out of the rain dear Yes Dear into my heart where I shall penetrate you with Fire.

Harry had married the first woman he had known this passionately. His early letters to Caresse are more ingenuous, equally ardent:

> I know absolutely and feel it in my heart and soul that our love can never change no matter what the circumstances. I swear to never doubt anything that you have told me and I have never doubted for one instance your love for me since that afternoon last November in The Factory where you gave me your soul forever.

Harry knew that Josephine evoked dangerous powers. He half didn't want to see her when he and Caresse arrived in New York in November 1929. But he wanted somebody. He had told the Lady of the Golden Horse that if she would come out with him, he needn't see Josephine before the Harvard-Yale game on November 23. But the Lady had other plans.

And so Harry had kept his appointment with Josephine and those that followed. The lovers spent half of their last two weeks together. They took a train to Detroit, registering in the Book-Cadillac as Mr. and Mrs. Harry Crane. There, they swallowed opium pills "and all night we catapult through space J and I in each other's arms vision security happiness."

Four days later, death was on Harry's mind. His last diary entry is terse: two parts of a syllogism.

One is not in love unless one desires to die with one's beloved.

There is only one happiness it is to love and be loved.

Still, he had always written about killing himself and his beloved. What made it different this time? That he was depressed? That by May he had lost 19,000 francs on the races which had deepened into a $2500 loss by the

---

*i.e., towards Boston.

Introduction

end of October? That on October 29 the stock market crashed?

Harry suffered no serious shortage of money. In October, when his luck temporarily returned and a horse he dreamed about won $500, he lavished his winnings on a watch. Earlier in the year "in one of my moods," Harry had sold $4000 worth of stock *before* the crash. His father, Stephen Van Rensselaer Crosby, a Boston investment broker, was wealthy. His uncle, J. Pierpont Morgan, was far wealthier. No, Harry was not badly off.

Harry had gone looking for a gun on the first of September, but he had bought guns before. He once gave five to the guests at Count Armand de la Rochefoucauld's dining table, so they could punish him for being late to dinner. And though he admits to depression in the fall of 1929, he also records exhilaration at having finished his best book, *Sleeping Together*. In fact, he was to present a copy to his Uncle Jack Morgan that Tuesday, when he met Josephine instead.

So we come back to Josephine. Could she have drawn it all out of him, all the death-wishes and the suicide plans and the romantic ideal of dying with the one he loved? The Lady of the Golden Horse wrote to Caresse, "He would do anything on a dare you know."

What might the dare have been, to kill them both? Or to commit suicide together? Josephine, her wide sensuous mouth smiling at him, lying on the bed pressing the gun against her own temple with Harry watching her; what must he have felt when she did it, if she actually did it? He waited two more hours to follow her, but he never backed out.

It is fascinating, almost impossible not to read the diary like this.

. . . . .

Ezra Pound read it differently. "Crosby's life," he writes, "was a religious manifestation. His death was . . . a death from excess vitality. A vote of confidence in the cosmos."

Caresse thought Pound closer to the truth than Eliot, Stuart Gilbert or D. H. Lawrence, who also wrote prefaces to volumes of Harry's poems. Gilbert's preface is sentimental. Eliot's is a pro forma piece that soon exhausts the reader's patience. Lawrence, however, elaborates an extraordinary metaphor:

> Man fixes some wonderful erection of his own between himself and the wild chaos, and gradually goes bleached and stifled under his parasol. Then comes a poet, enemy of convention, and makes a slit in the umbrella: and lo! the glimpse of chaos is a vision, a window to the sun.
>
> But after a while, getting used to the vision, and not liking the genuine draught from the chaos, commonplace man daubs a simulacrum of the window that opens onto chaos, and patches the umbrella with the painted patch of the simulacrum. That is, he has got used to the vision, it is part of his house-decoration . . .
>
> The joy man had when Wordsworth, for example, made a slit and saw a primrose! Till then man had only seen a primrose dimly, in the shadow of the umbrella . . .

Shadows of the Sun

Chariot of the Sun . . . is a glimpse of . . . the chaos alive . . . of the living, untamed chaos . . . It is poetry at the moment of inception in the soul, before the germs of the known and unknown have fused to begin a new body of concepts . . .

It is poetry of suns which are the core of chaos . . . chaos has a core which is itself quintessentially chaotic and fierce with incongruities. . . . There is . . . the elusive gleam of the sun of livingness, soft and gold and strange as the lion's eyes . . .

On the part of the poet, it is an act of faith, pure attention and purified receptiveness . . . It is the impulse of the sun in chaos . . . the sun within us, that sways us incalculably . . .

Agreeing, with Lawrence, that Harry's poetry was an "act of faith," Pound concludes forcefully, "There is more theology in this book of Crosby's [*Torchbearer*] than in all the official ecclesiastical utterance of our generation." Pound, also, finds Harry strongest when he is most nearly a seer. Of *The Mad Queen* Pound concludes:

Anybody but a blighted pedagogue subsidized to collect washlists and obstruct the onrush of letters will feel an ass in trying to concoct a preface to the magnificent finale:

"PREHENDERE TO CATCH HOLD OF YOUR SOUL AS A TALENT OF PURE FIRE ENTER INTO ABSOLUTE POSSESSION OF THIS FIRE MAKE A CHAIN TO PRESERVE THIS FIRE ATTACK TO DEFEND THIS FIRE."

These words are Harry's creed; *Shadows of the Sun* is a history of that creed.

There is a naive and desperate authenticity to the sun-fire images in Harry's diary. Pound comments on this while exhibiting one line from Harry's poems: " 'I can *hear* fire' is evidence for the cognoscenti," he writes, and wonders if the "general reader" will know that it refers to something quite different from the crackle of some mundane object burning. That is, it is Harry himself burning:

I feel my eyes filling with fire . . .
I feel the taste of fire in my mouth . . .
The Sun is the sound of burning in my ears.

Harry patiently tried to expand his sun imagery into a myth system. The results, in individual instances, can seem contrived. But the accrued images retain their obsessive authenticity as they record profound aspects of Harry's psyche. They show deep traumas, unresolved Oedipal patterns, great inner violence, and a surprising lack of true self-understanding.

Malcolm Cowley, for one, thinks that Harry's experiences as an ambulance driver during World War I turned his libidinous fire back on itself, so that in the years that followed it became self-consuming. From a tiny pocket notebook that Harry kept during the war come fragments of that story:

Introduction

Friday, September 21, 1917. Decided definitely to go to Paris and sign up for the duration of the war. Over the Top with the Best of Luck and give them Hell!!!!!!! Left for Paris. Hectic night on the train. Typical French trains . . . Went to bank. Saw Galetti. Took my physical exam. I signed up for the duration of the War!!!!!!!

Harry saved a photograph of the American recruiters who roamed Paris in jeeps signing up volunteers for the American Ambulance Corps. On the back of it he scrawled "They Got Me!!!"

Two months later, Private 1st Class Henry Grew Crosby, American Expeditionary Force in France, drove through fire at Verdun:

Thursday, November 22, 1917 . . . Most exciting day ever. This P.M. in going up to Haudremont went through hell. The Boches were shelling the road—tremendous ones right near me came in. "For whosoever calleth upon the name of the Lord shall be saved." Shell hit 10 yards away in "abri." Eclat . . . Mashed 741 to pieces. Thank God with all my heart for saving me. Spud Spaulding wounded. Barrage . . .

"741" was Harry's Ford ambulance. The shell blew it apart around him, leaving him miraculously untouched.

One entry sums up Harry's experiences at war:

Saturday, March 1, 1919. Won Oh Boy!!!!!!! THE CROIX DE GUERRE. Thank God.

For Harry, Verdun signified "the ride through red explosions and the violent metamorphose from boy into man." For Malcolm Cowley, analyzing the event in *Exiles Return*, "There was indeed a violent metamorphosis, but not from boy into man; rather, it was from life into death." Cowley didn't meet Harry until 1929. But he studied *Shadows of the Sun* before writing *Exiles Return* in 1934. He decided that the war had traumatized Harry, and that the trauma had grown like a cancer until it killed him, twelve years after the event.

Harry's father, Stephen, wanted to agree that Harry died from what was then commonly called "shell shock." Harry's mother wrote Caresse that

A doctor who is a specialist on diseases of the nerves sent for Steve and told him all about shell shock . . . and that the sex complex is very over-developed in these cases. And he assured Steve that it was bound to get worse as time went on so that comforted Steve for no one could want any one we loved to go to pieces and I felt that was happening . . .

No matter how disorienting Harry's war experiences, it is unlikely that, by themselves, they could wring Harry to death over a twelve-year interval. Other answers lie deeper in Harry's personality. As a boy he liked best to swim when the beaches were closed, the surf high, and the undertow strong. As a young man he constructed naive but powerful connections between religion and sex and death and salvation. When he first slept all night with Caresse in 1920, he told her that death and pure love were inseparable. After he meets Josephine, in 1928, the violence always incipient in him begins to break through. He starts to associate Josephine with fire. Unusually violent passages from his reading stick in his mind:

> that he who has had connection with a Guru's wife shall cut off his organ together with the testicles, take them in his joined hands and walk towards the south without stopping until he falls down dead . . .

He becomes obsessed with escapes, often to the point of unconsciousness. He drinks excessively and uses more and more opium—even though he writes that he ought to stop. Buying a hammer, he blurts out: "a marvellous thing with which to kill someone." Flying over a cemetery, he thinks suddenly: "It must be nice to drop bombs."

He begins to have terrifying nightmares. His parties become filled with "mad words and drunkenness and bottle-breaking and rape."

When Harry symbolically kills himself, shooting his portrait, burning and shooting at his poems, he splits apart without understanding the consequences of what has happened:

> The inward nerves of my vision are beyond the sentiments of my heart and have no communication with the operations of my intellect. I boast of having affected this . . .

Finally, the singular relationship he has had for ten years with Caresse deteriorates. She had been his "Sun Queen," he her Sun King, religious, romantic-mythical figures like the Guru and his wife. "We are no longer in love," he writes in his diary—a phrase that Caresse omitted in her posthumous edition.

Now there is Harry and Josephine instead of Harry and Caresse.

Harry's poem, "Assassin," recalls the self-destruction in the passage about the Guru. "Assassin" destroys everything Harry hates. The poem ends:

> I shall cut out my heart take it into my
> joined hands and walk towards the Sun
> without stopping until I fall down dead.

· · · · ·

The act of suicide is so strong in its demand for our attention that it makes itself seem a full climax to whatever events preceded it. Yet it may not be so. Harry had determined to "Die at the right time"

> no matter where you are in the depths of the coal-pit, in the crowded streets of the city, among the dunes of the desert, in cocktail bars or in the perfumed corridors of the Ritz, at the right time when your entire life when your soul and your body your spirit and your senses are concentrated are reduced to a pin point the ultimate gold point the point of finality, irrevocable as the sun, then is the time and not until then and not after then . . .

But was that Tuesday really the right time? At noon, Harry had lunch with Gretchen Powel, an old friend, who heard him complain that Josephine was

Introduction

"pestering" him: "she had threatened to kill herself in the lobby of the Savoy-Plaza if he didn't meet her at once. He agreed to see her, reluctantly."

The coroner's report confirms that Harry waited an hour or two after Josephine died before killing himself. One clerk at the Savoy-Plaza imagined that he saw Harry wandering about the lobby during this time.

Reading *Shadows of the Sun* makes one try to puzzle out those hours. Even if he merely lay beside Josephine's body, what was Harry thinking? Did this suicide seem the apotheosis of his ideals? Had his whole life led him here?

. . . . .

Harry Crosby did not need to die to verify or validate in any way the symbolism in his diary. Anyone but Pound's "washlist collector" will understand the ferocity of his images, occasional visions through a slit in the umbrella of conceptual knowledge, glimpses of his chaos. In the eight years of *Shadows of the Sun*, they form a complex calculus increasingly integrated with death, increasingly self-conscious ("I am an Arrow Arrowing into the Sun"), though hardly more self-aware. Whether Harry looked into himself too narrowly or too deeply is open to speculation. But surely he centered himself too completely around his sun visions. "Chaos has a core which is itself quintessentially chaotic and fierce with incongruities," Lawrence perceived. Yet through his slit, Harry saw only sun-fire.

He had a religious sensibility in an age that found no religion to embrace. He studied the Bible systematically from Genesis to Revelations, but found no spiritual teacher. He sought out arcane references to the sun in Plato, Nietzsche and Schopenhauer. In Egypt he had the sun of Ra painfully tattooed on his back. In France he branded himself with coals. He finished the fifty volumes of the *Sacred Books of the East* and learned only marginalia.

He recorded all this alongside the other events in his daily life:

> April 3, 1928. Terrific day. D. H. Lawrence appears to be sculpted by Caresse. Frieda appears with Aldous Huxley and the typewritten sheets of *The Escaped Cock* and there is a discussion about Joyce. C and I pro-Joyce Lawrence and Huxley anti-Joyce . . . but it is a friendly discussion this time . . . and then C and I rushed off to the lawyers on the Place Vendome where we met Joyce and drew up the contract for us three to sign. How I despise lawyers—they waste so damn much time and their bird-brains are spotted with technicalities. Afterwards Joyce went with C to the Black Sun Press (he didn't want to meet Lawrence—said his eye hurt him—he is very timid) and I went home and the Jolases appeared and we discussed the future of *transition* and I agree to stand back of it and become an associate editor.

Harry knew everybody: counts, princesses, artists, explorers, actors, surgeons, lion-tamers, "poets and painters and pederasts and lesbians and divorcees and Christ knows who." But though they appear in his diary, few of these people live or breathe there. Harry doesn't focus on them. We learn what they do, what they wear, but not what they feel or fear.

In those few entries when he does observe people closely, he is apt to describe best those he knew least, or who were most unlike himself: for example, the Rubens woman in the cafe at Rambouillet:

> ponderous, strong, loud-laughing giving suck from an enormous mammal to a sturdy, delighted child (who at the same time was watering the floor) and her heavy husband was watching her and at his feet a big dog lay asleep . . . the woman primitive, naive, proud of her tremendous breasts (and rightly so) the child sucking in ecstasy, his legs widespread . . .

More often, Harry is looking at objects, landscapes and events—the frenzy of New York as the depression begins; the delirium of a Paris nightclub binge. He can observe events with unusual clarity: how a horsefly that he has tried to kill exhibits courage; how a camel undulates across the desert. He excels at observing the explosive metamorphoses that occur whenever his mind alters the visible world; for example, looking through a train window after an overdose of hashish:

> . . . a flock of birds became a flock of comets the telegraph poles were women burning at the stake the clickety click of the train going over the rails was the bursting of firecrackers. Suddenly a sharp severing of a cord "the flash of what a tongue could never tell" the sudden touching of a match and my head cracked open and I exploded into Sun.

. . . . .

Harry was born into Boston and banking and started to write seriously only when he left them. He broke his final ties in 1923 when he resigned from the Morgan-Harjes bank in Paris. He had quit the Boston Morgan bank a year earlier, but only to accept the job in Paris that his mother had arranged for him through Uncle Jack Morgan. In this strategic move, timing had been critical.

Caresse, at Harry's urging, had finally received her divorce, and had decided to visit relatives in London "to straighten myself out." Harry transferred to Paris before his parents, who opposed the match, could learn of Caresse's plans. He flew to London and swept Caresse away, first to Paris, then to Italy—where they registered in Venice as the Vicomte and Vicomtesse Myopia—and then on to romantic Étretat:

> Sunnygolden and a solitary beach sunk between two abrupt cliffs. Silver and gold with the seagulls overhead in the Sun and the gentle sound of sun-waves. Je ne sais plus rien au monde and naked into the sea of sun while a lace parasol watched from the beach.

Back in Paris, a row with the mother of another of Harry's girlfriends sent Caresse steaming to Boston. Harry threw himself into dissipations "pour me distraire," which didn't. Broke and lovesick, he finally cabled Caresse:

Introduction

Enough of this hell. Sailing steerage Aquitania. Have engaged bridal
suite for return trip. Say Yes. Signed Harry.

When the Aquitania redocked at Paris, Harry debarked with his new wife,
her children ages 7 and 4, and her maid. "Harry and I were actually escapists
from the society in which we had been brought up and I wanted my children
to be escapists too," Caresse recalls, in her autobiography, *The Passionate
Years*. But Harry, who had piled presents on the children when he courted
their mother, had slight use for them now. So Caresse sent her maid home,
hired a *Petite Mère*, and as soon as the children were "tall" enough, packed
them away to boarding schools.

That summer of 1922, Harry and Caresse lived in a "romantic balcony
apartment" overlooking the Seine. From there, at 8:15 A.M., dressed in his
dark banker's clothes, Harry would paddle to work in a red canoe. Caresse
in her bathingsuit paddled bow. At the Place de la Concorde, Harry got out,
leaving Caresse to paddle home against the current "cheered on by whistles
and applause from the bridges overhead."

For 21 months Harry worked at the bank—in between holidays, affairs,
excursions, balls, parties and the horse races. With the encouragement of his
cousin, litterateur Walter Berry, Harry finally abdicated the bank for poetry
on New Year's Eve, 1923. In the next seven years, he published six volumes
of his poems at Black Sun Press: *Sonnets for Caresse* (1925), *Red Skeletons*
(1927), *Chariot of the Sun* (1929), *Transit of Venus* (1928), *Mad Queen:
Tirades* (1929), and *Sleeping Together, A Book of Dreams* (1929). Caresse
published his seventh volume, *Torchbearer*, posthumously in 1931.

"We knew that someday we must see our poems in print," Caresse writes,
thinking about the summer of 1925, when she and Harry had lived at Étretat
in a deserted gun emplacement with lace curtains and had written poems for
each other. "It did not occur to us to submit them to a publishing house—the
simplest way to get a poem into a book was to print the book! What we
needed [was] . . . a printer." They found him on a ramble through the maze
of tiny streets in the Latin Quarter: Roger Lescaret, a scruffy, nearsighted
man whose print shop was crowded with birth announcements, handbills
and marriage invitations. He had never printed a book, but he was not
lacking in skill. And Harry had a plethora of energy and imagination.

"I've met the most wonderful poet!" Harry would tell Caresse at lunch.
"He's going to come for dinner tonight. We have to get a bottle of Cutty
Sark. That's what he likes to drink." And the poet would arrive, in this case
Hart Crane accompanied by Eugene Jolas. Jolas believed, correctly, that
Harry was "the one man in the world with the good taste, energy, money,
and enthusiasm to bludgeon Crane into finishing *The Bridge.*"

He was also the man to publish D. H. Lawrence's *Sun* and *The Escaped
Cock*, and the *Einstein* of his friend Archibald MacLeish, *Short Stories* by
Kay Boyle, poems by Jolas, and sections of Joyce's *Work in Progress*—all
making the transformation from manuscript to book in the jumbled
printshop of M. Lescaret, now *Maître Imprimeur*. After Harry's death,

Shadows of the Sun

Caresse continued the press until World War II, publishing works by Ezra Pound, Dorothy Parker, William Faulkner and James Joyce.

. . . . .

The account of Harry Crosby's relationship to the expatriate writers of the twenties in Malcolm Cowley's *Exiles Return* provokes the following thoughts: If there was an expatriate generation, then Harry Crosby had a special place in it. It is true that he had more money than most, and that he lived more like a playboy than a bohemian. Nevertheless, Harry had gone through all the "Lost Generation's" rites of passage; in Cowley's words:

> the separation from home, the effects of service in the ambulance corps, the exile in France, then other themes, bohemianism, the religion of art, the escape from society, the effort to defend one's individuality, even at the cost of sterility and madness, then the final period of demoralization when the whole philosophical structure crumbled from within, just at the moment when bourgeois society was beginning to crumble . . .

Harry believed that something in the generation that made him was dying. "Race Ruin" he called it. What he looked for in literature was a reason to live. He was fanatically literary; recalls Archibald MacLeish, "he was drowned in it."

When Harry died, the "Lost Generation" ended. The other exiles, if they were that, committed suicide or went home—to the Depression, to the slow rallying of the stock market, to the gradual reopening of the chastened banks. Some of the writers moved to Hollywood, others sought colleges. The twenties became romanticized—all the more after World War II. Now Harry Crosby's diary is again being published, a remarkable window to that frail, glittering interlude. It should purge nostalgia.

Aside from its ubiquitous but personal symbolism of sun-death, the dominant metaphor in *Shadows of the Sun* is flight—appropriate to the psyche of an exiled generation. Its pages are filled with sudden departures—to Deauville "Taximeter broke at four hundred francs," south at 88 miles per hour, to a new nightclub, to Italy, to Spain to rendezvous with Hemingway, to Egypt, to "Orleans and on through Blois past Chaumont . . . past Amboise and on through Tours and Poitiers . . . and on at seventy miles an hour along the road to Angouleme . . ."

Jazz is flight. Whiskey, pot, cocaine, hashish and opium are flight. Sex is flight.

The single hero in this book is Charles Lindbergh. He flew like Daedalus out of the night into the Paris airport in 1927, where an exulting, hysterical crowd tore at his plane and where Harry vowed to learn to fly.

Harry began lessons, flying with an instructor—"France below like a pack of cards flung at random upon a table."

He grew irritable if a lesson was rained out. He marvelled at the illegal aerobatics of one of the pilots.

Introduction

Finally, on Armistice Day, 1929, Harry soloed for the first time, a flight into the sun.

His pilot's license is in the Crosby archives at Southern Illinois University. It arrived at his home in France after he killed himself and has no entries on it.

Edward B. Germain
Dublin, New Hampshire
October, 1976

SELECTED BIBLIOGRAPHY

Anthology. Ed. Harry Crosby. Dijon: Maurice Darantiere, 1924.

Bushee, Ralph. *Catalogue of the Black Sun Press Archives,* Special Collections, Morris Library, Southern Illinois University, Carbondale, Ill., unpublished.

Cowley, Malcolm. *Exiles Return: A Narrative of Ideas.* New York: W. W. Norton, 1934.

Crosby, Caresse. *The Passionate Years.* Carbondale, Ill.: Southern Illinois University Press, 1968.

Crosby, Harry. Unpublished notebooks, letters and memorabilia in the Black Sun Press Archives, Morris Library, Southern Illinois University, Carbondale, Ill.

———— *Sonnets for Caresse.* Paris: Herbert Clarke, 1925.

———— *Red Skeletons.* Paris: Éditions Narcisse, 1927.

———— *Chariot of the Sun.* Paris: At the Sign of the Sundial, 1928.

———— *Shadows of the Sun* (First Series). Paris: Black Sun Press, 1928.

———— *Transit of Venus.* Paris: Black Sun Press, 1928.

———— *Mad Queen.* Paris: Black Sun Press, 1929.

———— *Shadows of the Sun* (Second Series). Paris: Black Sun Press, 1929.

———— *The Sun.* Paris: Black Sun Press, 1929.

———— *Sleeping Together.* Paris: Black Sun Press, 1929.

———— *Shadows of the Sun* (Third Series). Paris: Black Sun Press, 1930.

———— *Aphrodite in Flight: Being Some Observations on the Aerodynamics of Love.* Paris: Black Sun Press, 1930.

———— *Collected Poems of Harry Crosby* (four volumes, boxed). Paris: Black Sun Press, 1931:
> *Chariot of the Sun.* Introduction by D. H. Lawrence.
> *Transit of Venus.* Preface by T. S. Eliot.
> *Sleeping Together.* Introduction by Stuart Gilbert.
> *Torchbearer.* Notes by Ezra Pound.

———— *War Letters.* Preface by Henrietta M. Crosby. Paris: Black Sun Press, 1932.

Jolas, Eugene. "Harry Crosby and *Transition.*" *Transition,* June 1930, pp. 228-29.

Kahn, Sy. "Hart Crane and Harry Crosby: A Transit of Poets." *Journal of Modern Literature,* I, pp. 45-56.

Unterecker, John. *Voyager: A Life of Hart Crane.* New York: Farrar, Straus & Giroux, 1969.

Wolff, Geoffrey. *Black Sun: The Brief Transit and Violent Eclipse of Harry Crosby.* New York: Random House, 1976. Contains an extensive bibliography.

A NOTE ON THE TEXT

Harry Crosby wrote his diaries passionately and informally, scrawling in pencil in a looseleaf notebook. Although later he carefully copied and edited these rough entries for publication, he inserted very little punctuation and used no italics to indicate book titles or foreign words and phrases. The present edition preserves his stylistic idiosyncracies and inconsistencies, including spelling errors, which I have refrained from decorating with "sic."

Shadows of the Sun was originally published in three volumes by the Crosbys' Black Sun Press. The diary entries for the years 1922-1926 were published as the "First Series," 1928. The years 1927-1928 form the "Second Series," 1929. Harry's final year's entries were published posthumously as the "Third Series" in 1930. The colophons identify each edition as limited to 44 copies.

Entries for the "First Series" are reproduced verbatim in this present edition, accompanied by a few explanatory endnotes, mostly reporting notations that Caresse Crosby made in the margins of a copy submitted to a London publisher. Differences in the entries for 1928 and 1929 between the published editions and Harry's holograph notebooks make a textual comparison useful. It suggests both how Harry went about writing his diary, and what Caresse did to it after he died. However, I have not tried to produce a variorum edition, which would require picayune adjustments. I have tried to restore entries that are of uncommon interest, or that show aspects of events otherwise obfuscated.

The last entries present a dilemma. Harry had gathered his diary notes for 1929 through November 11 and had begun to edit them. Then on November 16 he, Caresse and the Lady of the Golden Horse sailed for New York. Subsequent entries survive in a looseleaf holograph notebook. But where the entries through November 11 are arranged chronologically, the ones thereafter frequently are not. I have done my best to puzzle out the sequence, and have indicated where my version differs from that made by Caresse in 1930. Of Caresse's intentions, there can be no doubt. She censors certain references to Josephine, forging an entire line rather than admit the two in bed together. Earlier in the entries for that year, it was Caresse who struck out Harry's statement that he and Caresse were "no longer in love." It was also Caresse who added the word "wholly" to his entry of the next day, "now we are in love again."

Further explanation of my editorial decisions for these entries may be found on pages 167 and 226 of this edition.

E. B. G.

SHADOWS
of
the
SUN

ONE : 1922/1926

1922

I

January 1. New York and all day in bed while the snow falls silently outside and all night on the train alone to Boston.

4. Went over last year's accounts. Discovered I had spent seven thousand dollars—more for charity than for gambling, more for flowers than for clothes, more for her than for myself.

27. Watertown. Or is it because I have the fox's fear of being trapped?

February 7. Eva Le Gallienne in Liliom. The play would have been gold had it consisted of only the first scene in the first act—the park bench scene. Many lives the same. Many soldiers fortunate to have been killed in the war. "Those whom the gods love die young" (cliché) But what is youngness? One may live to eighty and still be young. Invisible Youngness.

Today Momma gave me a hundred dollars for going a month without drinking. Wasn't worth it.

9. Ashamed and unhappy and owe it to her to be a thousand times more dignified and gave the Burnier Landscape I inherited from my grandmother to the Museum.

10. Relentless remorse on my part; infinite weeping on hers.[1]* Snowstorm and the low sighing of the wind and a walk across country and darkness and a souper à deux and togetherness (and the low sighing of the wind).

12. Confession. Darkest Day. The world is upside down. Blackness

13. No need to wonder why I have always been frightened by 13. Dreary day at the bank (usual) and then the Black Letter. And all my illusions are strewn on the ground like rose petals after a storm. The long, long battle up the hill—up the hill of defeat. Boomerang. I forgive her I forgive her but who am I to forgive and who is she to be forgiven?

28. Tossed my sun-cross into the air to see whether to fight on or surrender. Fight on as it falls upon the floor sun upwards.

March 6. Dark day of doubt.

8. Her preciousness. Yet thrust deep into my heart is the sharp knife of despair. Adios. Shall never forget her eyes. Encountered my father. Pathetic attempt at sympathy. "Will give you a Rolls-Royce" and "People would never never have approved." Whiskey and to bed. Cried all night.

12. Have not been to the Bank for five days.

14. Resigned from the Bank.

21. Mamma has secured for me a position in the Bank in Paris. Happier—One of my wild days where I threw all care to the wind and drank

---

*Notes for Volume One begin on p. 134.

to excess with 405—Result of being happier. At midnight drove old walrus' new automobile down the Arlington Street subway until we crashed slap-bang into an iron fence. A shower of broken glass, a crushed radiator, a bent axle, but no one hurt. Still another rotten episode to add to my rotten reputation.

March 22. Remorse and the usual gestures: a letter of apology, a cheque for damages, a gold resolution for the future.

April 17. New York. "Ma Jeunesse" to quote Baudelaire, "n'est qu'un ténébreux orage, traversé ça et là par de brillants soleils." H half dressed is shaving, 405 in a Japanese kimono crosslegged on the floor sewing lace underthings, and I stirring gin and iced orange juice in a pewter teapot, But the Sun is three thousand miles away.

May 1. Paris. Tossed the sun-cross to see whether to go to Constantinople to join the Armenian Relief or go to work at the Bank as I had promised Mamma. Verdict said stay. Instead flew to London [2] And all night the coal fire burned in the grate.

4. Together [3] to Paris in a Mammoth Aeroplane. Wings of the Sun.

12. Under the sun trees in the Bois. Under the moontrees in the Bois.

17. Noon and Apéritifs chez Bodega. Gay, gayer, gayest and we hail a taxicab "Quelle adresse, Monsieur?" "Deauville, s'il vou plait." Taximeter broke at four hundred francs.

24. To the Battlefields, and the Fort de la Malmaison and the memory of that October four years ago. And how I have changed but the land itself is little changed since the war and it is still The Waste Land. Prayed into the Red Sun. For what? I do not know. At Soissons, in the Lion Rouge, in the enormous bed, suns within suns, and cataracts of gold.

27. Morning at Notre Dâme and our vision soaring up a sunbeam through the stained glass window to the Sun.

June 4. To the Chateau de Madrid. Changed clothes with a waiter (tenue de soirée est de rigueur) so that I could dance. Dancing and then to bed in the Château and the plaintive music of the tango and the coolness of linen sheets—and I am twenty-four years old to-day and we bathe in the forest and at midnight gaze into the Red Sun. C'est Kefalin qui gagne!

July 12. The Simplon Express after going to the wrong station. Pauvre petite fille. Resolved first last and for all time to close my Book of Wild Oats. Amen. All night towards Venice.

14. Venice and quietness. Gondola to the orange-red Casa Petrarca by the Rialto on the Grand Canal and the vision I imagined when I was here two years ago. And all evening long, beneath an opiate moon, serpentining noiselessly in a long black gondola, through a labyrinth of unfrequented canals out to the Giudecca and again into the darkness of deserted waterways. It is late, long after midnight, when we reach the Casa Petrarca. The Vicomte and Vicomtesse Myopia.[4] (the Sun-Count and Sun-Countess Myopia)

July 18. To Etretat to walk through the drizzling rain up the great cliffs and from here we watched the black fishing barques sail slowly in and saw the fishermen haul them by means of creaking windlasses. High upon the rocky beach a small circle showed where the fish were being auctioned. Darkness and always the dull pounding of waves upon the shore.

19. Sunnygolden and a solitary beach sunk between two abrupt cliffs. Silver and gold with the sea-gulls overhead in the Sun and the gentle sound of sun-waves. Je ne sais plus rien au monde and naked into the sea of sun while a lace parasol watched from the beach.

22. Sharp knives to be withdrawn. Why did I let her go [5] why why why O Sun-God tell me why. At last our wounded love has healed, has grown strong again, is solid gold, gold as the gold sun. But there are sharp knives in the heart (to be withdrawn).

31. The most unbalanced, unsettled, unforgiveable month. Pinned a chart on the wall. Each evil I wish to conquer I have named. Thus Cigarettes (Smokeplume), Gambling (Pyramid), Girls (Masked Marvel), Drink (Ritz Bar), Extravagance (Extravagance), Late Hours (Nocturne), Talkativeness (Chatterbox). Each day is represented by a square. The race from start to finish is a hundred squares. Each day I abstain I shall advance the name (or horse) one square.

Tortured to think we are three thousand miles apart in Body even if we are One in Thought. "It is not good that the man should be alone." And though I see Joan everyday, I am as much alone as if I were alone.

August 9. Pour me distraire organized a fiacre race. Four partners in four fiacres? A prize of five hundred francs. Down the Champs-Elysées bound for the Ritz-Bar, about a mile in all. At the Concorde the four hacks were well grouped and it was not until after the Rue de Rivoli that Joan and I were defeated in the final sprint by half a length, the others trailing behind. Brandy for the coachmen, cocktails for ourselves, and a brimming bowl of champagne for broken-down Marguerite. To make of life a race; to "run the straight race through the Sun's good grace."

12. Joan left for Africa. Not even there to say goodbye to her. Another closed book. She was like an appendix. Now she has been removed I feel strong and unafraid. The breast and the womb.

15. Elaborate luncheon at the Ritz (Extravagance moves back a square). then drove a virgin called Jeanne (she works in the Bank) to Deauville (Masked Marvel moves back a square) where I left her with her cousins and all night it rained and all night I gambled (Pyramid moves back a square) in

the Salle de Baccara. What a spectacle! What avarice! What hunted faces! What folly! Smoked and drank and went to bed at five in the morning. (Smokeplume, Ritz Bar and Nocturne all move back a square) But I was morose and silent and Chatterbox advanced.

August 17. Drove the virgin back to Paris through the rain. On the way stopped for a bottle of wine at an inn and to dry our clothes. She was very desirable in front of the fire. But for once loyalty stronger than desire (Masked Marvel moves up a square). The breast and the womb.

18. A holiday in the city. Bottles of wine uncorked in the garret and with friends from the Ritz Bar indulged in a high stake baccara game. Onlookers. Empty bottles out the window. An accouchement in the room next door. Our door barred against the trying-to-interfere proprietor. Wilder and wilder, higher and higher the stakes; twenty louis a hand, thirty louis, forty, fifty and the last few hands at a hundred louis. Won double what I lost at Deauville. Lucky in cards, unlucky in love. The hell you say. Where is she? Where is she? [6] Cocktails at the Ritz, soup at the Sacré-Coeur, fish chez Prunier, meat and vegetables in the Latin Quarter and dessert at the Pré Catelan in the Bois, a novel and extravagant meal. And a mad, absurd gramophone dance in a brothel (same name as 405) on the Rue Brey and a plump Yvonne and we all left without paying and to the Montmartre to dance away the night. More money spent, more health ruined, more remorse. All the horses move back a square.

19. Bank at eleven and sat there in a stupor all day, not even having the energy to go out for luncheon. What would Jay say? Or Mamma? Or most important C? At four rejoined them at the hotel, all of them still in bed. Targets for Disgust.

22. To Deauville with N and five Zelli girls (Masked Marvel moves back two and a half squares) whom we had invited when much intoxicated last night. A run up the beach, horses, champagne and baccara and so back to Paris by the evening train. Still another mad day, always tortured deep deep deep down by the Image. She haunts me.

23. Fever and chill. No wonder. Seventy days before I sail. N and three others also sick.—too much dissipation and together we all sat upon a balcony in the Sun. The little femme de chambre tried to make us eat, and gentle Jeanne climbed the garret stairs and sat by my bed but I was too miserable to care. I love only the *real* Her.

30. Can't stand it any longer! In desperation bet N a hundred dollars I could reach New York before he could (he is sailing day after to-morrow). Dragged myself out of bed, borrowed a hundred dollars at the bank and bought a steerage passage on the Aquitania. Morale from E to B. But I seek A.

1922

August 31. Cherbourg and gazing with eager eyes over the Atlantic into the setting Sun. And why shouldn't the Sun carry my heart to her and why shouldn't she send hers back by the Moon?

September 1. Told I must remain a week in quarantine. Uncontrolled rage and ran up and down not knowing what to do. At the last moment tried bribery and spent a last franc obtaining a laissez-passer. Five minutes later the steerage tender cast loose her moorings and slipped out into the harbor. No need to be confined behind iron bars or stone wall to know what prison is. For an hour tossed about in the bay, but as the copper-colored Sun sunk beyond the horizon the giant liner hove in sight, black smokeplumes pouring from red funnels. Aquitania! Aquitania! (A fight getting aboard, a fight for cabins.) Sirens shrieked, the ship vibrated, headed straight out to sea and I was off across the Atlantic an arrow seeking its target! (Target for the Flaming Dart.)

4. Am on deck H below the water line and next the engines. Hotter than hell and it smells. Decided to sleep on deck. A red blanket and the stern deck and sleep under the stars. "Pleasures deferred maketh the heart sick."

5. Hadn't a sou, needed money badly, so into the first class and soon a desperate game of cards. *Had* to win and won and retreated to the steerage with forty dollars which I was fool enough to spend on giving champagne to a crowd of unfortunates (you can keep only those things which you give away) The popping of corks and at midnight under the light of the moon vague recollection of flicking empty bottles with a drunken adroitness through the portholes of the first class staterooms. Sudden darkness but the Moon slept with the Sun in my heart.

6. Seven in the morning. Bathed in the first class swimming pool. Only way to a bath.

Seven in the evening. Dined with Mrs. Oswald and her two daughters (pincushions). Evening clothes, hair immaculately parted, shoes polished, gold-tip cigarettes, contrast to four days on the bow deck in an undershirt and a pair of torn trousers. Caviare and mock turtle soup and humming birds on toast—pleasant relief after the canned beef and boiled potatoes of the steerage. Unfortunately during the café noir a steerage inspector appeared and tapped me on the shoulder. What right had I to be in first class. Would have replied "love" had it not been for the pincushions. Thanked my hostess and departed without mortification. (I had eaten.)

7. Carlotta (gold hair and soft eyes) lowered me (in a basket) figs, bananas and a bottle of benedictine. Madonna of the Promenade Deck. Regretted the champagne party for I could have sent her orchids. To-morrow we should see land. The too-great excitement of love.

8. A gold-grey mist like a city of the Arabian Nights. Out of my head with excitement. Will to-morrow never come?

September 9. Outside walls but within the newborn Sun. The battle is over, the race is run.[7] Thank the Sun, Thank the Sun the race is won. Felt like a marathon runner who has breasted the tape but who is on the verge of collapse. To the docks to meet N and how amazed he was and the hundred dollars, and the grayness of a gray day. So glad it is a gray day   so glad for our small gray bed, so glad for C, so glad for sleep (Sun Sleep.)

21. Read Les Désenchantées. Am I?

October 7.[8] I love the shortening days, the pale autumn sun, the falling leaves, the smoke from brushwood fires, and the horses galloping down the racecourse at Longchamp. And I love drawing into my shell. One expands too much in summer.

27. Last day at Longchamp and a pouring rain and Ksar est battu.

November. Armistice Day and violets on the grave of the Unknown Soldier and four years now since that morning at Harsigny when our dug-out door burst open and a poilu shouted: Finie la guerre!

15. Bought a bronze racehorse, but when shall we be able to buy a real one? and sent the A. D.[9] a Chinese porcelain bull and the Comte de Civry for luncheon and to the races and recovered all we lost in October.

24. Vincennes and the trotting races and of all places the most sordid and lost two hundred dollars and returned home in the subway downcast and discouraged. Resolved never to bet again.

25. Resolved to regain what we had lost. To Auteuil and in the big hurdle race plunged heavily on Abri who came from behind in the last few strides to win by a neck. Won three hundred dollars (qui ne risque rien ne gagne rien) and C is delighted. All night galloping horses whirled through my brain.

28. Rose up in my wrath and fired all three servants and there is nothing like a drastic policy when the occasion demands and Goopy Pohlman gives us a lottery ticket for a case of whiskey. An original wedding present!

Thanksgiving Day and I have much to be thankful for and today in the Bank was promoted to Les Etudes Financières and I have a large desk and a stenographer and a bell-boy at my beck-and-call and comparative freedom. (Christ) and I said prayers to-day visualizing the links at Essex, with the stone cavern to the right of the green, the tall fir-trees, the curling smoke from the brushwood fire, and the vision into Sun.

December 17. A copper-colored sun sinking down behind the black bare trees of the Tuileries and the ground hard and covered with frost. C'est l'hiver.

Christmas and went to Bodegas where I sat by myself sipping hot portos and thinking of Jacqueline[10] and of the Sun, the red-gold winter Sun.

1923

II

January 4. A fairytale princess,[11] rosecolored cheeks, eyes of gray blue, bobbed hair, gray squirrel coat and her gray toque and her large gray muff (Little Muff) and Prayers on the Essex links, the rock cavern, the dark firs and an ascending in gray smoke through the gray day into the gray-gold of Sun.

17. Every morning past the Unknown Soldier and so down the Champs Elysées strong-gazing into the copper-orange sun that rises like a monstrous flower from the rose-gray garden of mist behind the Grand Palais. Then the frost-covered paths of the Tuileries, and the Place Vendôme and the Bank.[12]   A hard walk especially— [13]

Lunched to-day with Goldenhair (Clos-Vougeot) and afterwards to the morgue (closed) to the catacombs (closed) to a tattoo shop (closed). Absurd.

23. We bought a Henner painting and C wrote "soft is thy skin as mist at morn." and I say "soft is Thy . ." and I finished reading Pericles and have now read all Shakespeare. The sadness coincident with the ending of a phase of one's life counteracted by the joy of a definite accomplishment. Same might be said of first love (physical).

24. Fed up with banking and the bank and if only I could summon enough courage to resign, only my family would strenuously object with sound, practical, commonsense New England arguments. Encouraged by Meredith "that genius is the taking of infinite pains" for if I have nothing more I have at least a stubborn perseverance (shades of my Grew ancestors—give them credit where it is due).

February 3. "As one who long in poplous city pent, Where houses thick and sewers annoy the air," but now Switzerland and already invigorated, with eyes sparkling like suns. Climbed alone above the timber-line to pray into the setting sun. Then down, down to where a shadow (Carlotta) waits below, and together we snowshoed through the dark and down and down to the frozen lake and on through the darkness towards the myriad lights of the hotel. Told me her life history (not interesting). Must be of a sympathetic nature for so many people have confessed to me their sorrows and, what is more important, their joys. Or do all people confess?

March 18. Spring is in the air and the birds are singing in the trees of the Tuileries and the green buds are sprouting and the air is fragrant and everywhere fountains are playing, and the tops of the taxicabs are thrown back and all the little midinettes are wearing their peek-a-boo shirt-waists and their filmy skirts. Spring is in the air. La Primavera.

27. Have begun to neglect work at the bank in order to study words in the dictionary (do you know what·an aardvark is, or a xebec?) to write letters in order to acquire style (Pascal often re-cast letters twenty times before being satisfied with them) to read (whenever the opportunity offers), and as the

31

head of the class used to do all my Greek for me at school, and as Goopy used to look after my ambulance for me during the war, so now Vicomte du Mas (deux mots if you please) occupies himself with what work I am supposed to do Thus the day is devoted to books.

Three letters—from X, Y and Z. X to marry Y and the Vulture is the outcast. But in the long run who knows, and if there is often an Evening Wolf perhaps there is also an Evening Vulture. Far-fetched? I don't think so. On second thought. Perhaps. But then all life is Perhaps. We think as we run in the forest in a circle.

April 1. Won seven hundred dollars last month on horse-racing. Sergeant Murphy in the Grand National ("why didn't you ride your own horse Mr. Sanford"), l'Yser at Auteuil, and old Canadian in a flat race at St. Cloud. Four requisites necessary: nerve, coolness when in adversity (which is the art of pulling down one's flag), a prearranged system, and a strong capital to work with. But the races are making me nervous and I am playing too high. Nor must I let racing interfere with books. As for banking it can go to H E double L.

18. Evening that ended by my escorting Carlotta (at her request let it be said) into a bordel where we sat upon the sofa drunkenly trying to decide which of the eleven daughters of joy was the least joyless. Angry at them, angrier at Carlotta, angriest at myself ("wine is a mocker, strong drink is raging: and whosoever is deceived thereby is not wise.")

May 1. Told me I had strong, angular, mediaeval features, a beautifully-shaped head, the look of an old man with a young face, and the appearance of having suffered. Also told me I was unexpected. Enjoyed his studio —the large sofa stuck in the corner opposite the entrance and protected by a red iron stove, the heaped-up cushions and half-darkness through which one could vaguely distinguish the bronze Buddha that sits upon the black-lacquer cabinet among the Chinese wood-carvings and the jades. And the small piano whereon fantastic dragons breathe their darts of flame. A tiled floor and tea in old porcelain teacups that have no handles and an unbroken silence save for the monotonous snoring (like the French 'ronfler' better) of the agèd tabby-cat who with her master reposed upon the window seat—and so alike were their faces in the waning light that from where I lay ensconced on the sofa I could scarcely tell them apart. Outside in the deserted garden the shadows of the evening crept slowly along the ivy-covered wall (de la littérature.)[14]

8. Christ isn't life complicated yet. it all begins so simply. Must exert thought control and bannish all such ideas from my mind. Still the shepherd of desire leaves the flock (of unsatisfied desires) to seek the lost sheep.

14. Morning. Heard from Lionel that he had had a son.
Evening. Heard from Lionel that he had lost his son.
But (to-day is S.V.R.C.'s birthday) what a disappointing son I have been.
There can be only one Sun. (Voilà la réponse!)

"Wake? For the Sun, who scatter'd into flight
The Stars before him from the Field of Night,
Drives Night along with them from Heaven, and strikes
The Sultan's Turret with a Shaft of Light."

May 22. Bank banquet. A dismal affair. Poor people trying to enjoy themselves are more pathetic than rich people trying to have a good time for the poor are utterly defenceless whereas the rich are sheltered by their cynicism. Utterly defenceless. Why. Because they come with illusions.

To-day my m-in-l departed. Crocodile tears.

I am glad France has taken the Ruhr, glad too that Pharaoh killed Lord Carnavon.

27. C is sketching every day at the Grande Chaumière and I have begun to run every day over the grass track at the Racing Club and we bought two Zorn etchings one of a reclining Nude called Elin (the strength of her body and the asking of her eyes) and we moved from the Belles-Feuilles to the Hotel de la Gare d'Orsay over the trains.

June 1. Moved into the littlest nest on the Quai d'Orléans, Ile Saint-Louis looking out over Notre Dame and the Seine. As we went to bed chimes of the Cathedral were chiming and a great moon of solid gold was rising above the towers. And always a river like a liquid ribbon, black-gold.

4. Twenty-five years old. The half-way mark. Ran a mile. Before going to sleep I told C. This was important.

9. Bought two love birds, two white kittens, two tortoises and four goldfish. The birds live in a cage, the kittens in a basket, the tortoises in a salad bowl and the goldfish in a miniature aquarium. The birds are Tristan and Isolde, the kittens Sagesse et Promesse, the tortoises Cloaca and Sloth, the goldfish Sunwarm, Sunnygolden, Sunbeam and Sunbow. The love-birds escaped and flew off into the Sun, the kittens were a nuisance and we gave them to the littlest girl, the tortoises were uninteresting, and we gave them to a small boy, and only the goldfish remain. All this in the course of a day!

10. The orchids at the horticultural show. Almost as beautiful as C.

Introduced to Paul Rainey, African game-hunter. Hunts lions with hounds. Remember years ago when I was a little boy hearing him lecture on lion-hunting. Remember too even before "Where are the lions? Where are the lions?" The littlest boy—and the frailest.

Dreamed of Jacqueline on the shores of a sea submerged in gray fog with somewhere an invisible Red Sun. If invisible how did I know it was Red?

18. There are too many people in the world and Mount Etna is erupting and thousands of lives are lost. Let them be lost. Let them be lost.

Have grown to believe Monday is the best day of the week. Monday with me corresponds to the number 7 and to the letter T. All three are silver-gray.

Love the two little yellow satin chairs in the den, love the bathroom opening into the dining room, love our balcony overlooking the Seine.

Barges coming up the river, barges going down the river. Thus do our lives wax and wane.

June 20. Gave C a diamond wrist watch, the one we saw together in a little pawn shop as we were coming home from the Rendez-vous des Mariniers. She left for Versailles. The Bal des Quatz'Arts. Innumerable glasses of brandy, and home stark naked in a taxicab! My Roman toga and even my drawers to which I had pinned a hundred francs were gone!

21. Bed and no Banking and no running at the Racing to-day and C returns from Versailles and a vague mal du pays for Singing Beach and Myopia Links and Essex Woods and the Apple Trees [15] in the Fog.

24. The Grand Prix and Sir Gallahad threw his jockey before the start and came to grief in a brook and Filibert de Savoie a gray horse won and the heat was intense and Geraldine almost fainted and was forced to retire to the ladies toilet (hate the word toilet) from the window of which she watched the race and afterwards tea-dancing at the Cascades.

28. To Chartres and the Cathedral and the stained glass windows (prayer through their colours) and we burned a cierge (to the Sun) and on to Tours quaint old Tours, still smelling faintly of isoloires, still dead as the Moon, still unchanged since Kitsa and I were there en pension fifteen years ago. And always the Loire flows past on its way to the sea! Alluvial.

29. Catherine de Médicis and Diane de Poitiers in the Chateau of Chaumont. No stronger than the castle of my soul (Caresse and Jacqueline.) [16]

July 1. Invested in a brand-new bright-red canoe (Red Arrow) which we launched from the Ile Saint-Louis to the curiosity of a crowd of hangers-on who shouted erroneous advice from the parapet of the bridge. With the current past the Ile de la Cité, past the Conciergerie (Vision of Eben) past the Louvre and under the Pont Royal as far as the Place de la Concorde. [17] Towed back upstream by catching hold, with our boathook, to the tender at the end of a long string of barges. Left the Arrow tied to a lavoir. Left to-morrow tied to the Red Arrow.

4. The ceremony of the unveiling of the statue to Alan Seeger (soldier-poet) and the reading of his Rendez-vous with Death (translated) and, at the end, to the triumphant sound of trumpets, troops at attention defiled past the grandstand: Foch, Pétain, Joffre, Mangin, Poincaré, Millerand, and our uninspiring ambassador. Very impressive, very significant as all such things are to those who went to war. Stood with the small contingent of members of the Field Service, and afterwards we were invited to the Elysée Palace where we were introduced to Millerand and Mangin (How the poilus used to shake their fists at him and call him Le Boucher.) Felt sorry for the old white-haired gentleman who came all the way over from America on a pilgrimage to his son's grave

and
ran three long miles in the noonday sun
then
tea and supper with Geraldine. (Frivolité.)

July 8. Seventeen ran in the Grand Prix du Racing Club (distance a mile) A gruelling race on the hottest of afternoons. Took the lead at the three-quarter mark but could only finish third. All for a silver papercutter! And now for cigarettes and cocktails and other more intimate diversions!

10. Calamity. Our race system on which we had banked such extravagant hopes crashed and we are poorer by two thousand dollars. Unpleasant awakening! What a bitter lesson! What a débâcle! Proves that one should never be over-optimistic (Where are the lions? Where are the lions?) Nothing is sure, save Sun alone, and even Sun, is it always sure? *Yes.* Always. Held with C a mock symbolic funeral by filling my magnificent gray derby (the one I wear at the races) with ordures from the kitchen and hurling it from our balcony into the Seine. Felt chastened and resolved to read the Bible Old and New Testament, from Alpha to Omega. Shall sell our etchings (poor little Elin) and shall not gamble any more and shall not take any vacation. Fortunately une plaie d'argent ne tue jamais (even when starving?) but from this day I am a fatalist. Mektoub.

12. An enormously fat cousin (Phoebe) to stay and it was scorching hot and there were cold cocktails and we took her out in the canoe and would it be fun to make love to a girl as corpulent? At any rate not in this weather.

14. A hard paddle in the Sun tormented by thirst (too many cocktails last night) and the banks of the Marne and noise and crowd and consequent discouragement and no wind and no sequestered place to bathe and orchestras and firecrackers and a longing for the cold cold sea (chasteness of sea-girls). Had come to enjoy a peaceful weekend in the country but we were infinitely worse off than if we had been Place de l'Opera. Began to paddle back at seven o'clock (taking turns) with the idée fixe of home at all costs. Cooler and a sluggish current, and at last the Seine and darkness save for the distant display of fireworks over Paris (a year ago the distant display of fireworks over the Giudecca—wished we were in the gondola) and more herculean efforts and a glimpse ahead of the twin towers of Notre Dame. One last laborious mile and we slid among shadows to the dark lavoir and somewhere it was midnight. Twenty-five miles in twelve hours, and C is the bravest as well as the loveliest, and the darkness of our bed and long untroubled sleep.

24. Began to read the Bible and wish my name were Chedorlaomer Crosby.

28. Began to lay the foundation for my castle of philsophy (not to be confounded with my inner or *inmost* (to be exact) Castle of Beauty): life is pathetic, futile save for the development of the soul; memories, passionate memories are the utmost gold; poetry is religion (for me); silence invariably has her compensation; thought-control is a necessity (but is disloyal in affairs of love), simplicity is strengthening (the strength of the Sun); fanatic faith in the Sun is essential (for the utmost Castle of Beauty). Must have vision, must acquire the power to sift dross from gold; must be gentle (gentle as a gentle girl) and loyal; must cultivate poise; must exercise, not for pleasure but for health; must give away a tenth to the poor ("and of all that thou shalt give me I will surely give the tenth unto thee"). Out of the evil ashes of this race ruin there has been born a phoenix of good.

August 10. C is away at the seashore and Paris is hot and I am homesick for the North Shore: basking on gold sands, surf-bathing, invigorating air, golf, tennis, the happy-go-lucky crowd and lovely Goldenhair—all these I miss. To-day I hate the French and their unhealthiness, hate the dead city, hate the endless honking of the taxihorns, hate the lifelessness of the bank.

14. Cabourg and no money left and we decided to leave the hotel and at sunset we strayed down the beach and found the hull of an old rowboat stuck in the sand and with this as shelter we built a fire of driftwood and cooked a supper of baked potatoes and toasted crackers and drank down a bottle of the darkest wine. Then we curled up in the hull of the boat and tried to go to sleep but were soon besieged by myriad black-beetles that crawled out from the rotten wood of the hull. And we were forced to move. And it was very dark. And there was the weird sound of seagulls and there was eelgrass and the sound of the tide creeping in over the wet sands and it was cold and a heavy fog came drifting in from the sea and it was long after midnight and it began to rain and we took shelter in the eelgrass behind the dunes, forlorn and miserable.

25. Geraldine and champagne orangeades at the Ritz and afterwards to dance in the Bois and to dance in the Montmartre and finally at dawn to Les Halles where we were the only dancers. Seven o'clock and the end of the last bottle of champagne and a crazy bargain with a sturdy peasant to haul us to the Ritz in his vegetable cart and thus we reclined Geraldine in her silverness I in my blackness, upon the heaped-up carrots and cabbages while our poor man strained in the harness. A memorable ride with the strong summer Sun streaming through the streets, she frivolous and gay, I pale as her dress, with champagne eyes and tousled hair. The Ritz, and a gift to the cuisine of our vegetable cargo, and a paying off of our man (too early to eat at the Ritz) and then she to a warm bath and I home to a cold one. After which in a taxi-cab to the Bank. Is it to-morrow or yesterday? That is the way I feel.

29. Compare the Old Testament in its elemental simplicity to the crude cumbersome barges that I watch for hours from our balcony. Yoked oxen give me the same reaction. All three impart strength to the soul.

Luncheon with the daughter of a woodcutter. Believed in God (God is the Sun) simply because religion is the only thing in life that does not disillusion. (I believe in the Sun because the Sun is the only thing in life that does not disillusion.) Returned to the Bank without even asking her name.

Banking is so dreary—dull and men and women were not made to be shut up in a cage and what a cage, the enormous cage (apologies to whom it may concern). And Paris is hot and enervating and I miss the cool crisp autumn nights on the sleeping porch at Manchester. I feel so lifeless, haven't even the courage to go out in the canoe, too weary to work at stocks and bonds or even to read the Bible. All I am good for is to drink champagne orangeades with Geraldine in the garden of the Ritz, the only oasis in this stagnant August Paris.

August 30. The Aquarium and Yellow Roses and a Letter. P.S. The maid never returned to turn down the bed.

September 1. C is de retour and I thank the Sun, and we eat our three meals out-of-doors; breakfast in the garden of the Ritz (raspberries and cream) luncheon at Laurent's in the Champs Elysées (raspberries and cream) and dinner at the Pré Catelan in the Bois (raspberries and cream).

5. A to stay and luncheon with her and Paul Rainey at the Escargot (snails pheasant and burgundy but no raspberries and cream) and he is in love with her and she is not very nice to him and he is going away to-morrow and he *gives* me an automobile and he has invited us all to come out in January to his ranch in Africa and I heard myself asking again "Where are the lions? Where are the lions?"

Down the Seine in the Red Arrow to watch the big swimming race, mermen and mermaids and what mermaids! Unchasteness of Seine-girls. Banks and bridges black-blocked with spectators and afterwards we hooked on to a barge and were towed back to the lavoir.

7. From the Quai d'Orléans to the Princess B.'s [18] apartment, Faubourg Saint-Honoré, which we have taken (with A.). Love the Princesse's blue-wood bathroom and I dozed in a hot bath and out of doors it is Autumn and the days are growing shorter. The Princesse's bedroom has a soft 'protected' bed built into the mirrored wall, a soft pearl-gray carpet, rose-colored wallpaper and hangings of pale green. Richness and soft beauty. As we are on the ground floor it is possible for us to gaze from our bed into the little garden: We now have two maids and a cook, a governess, and a chauffeur who earns more money than I make at the bank.

9. One Year (Paper).

14. Golf at Saint-Cloud and the invigorating air and the autumn sunset and the enormous rose-gray moon that rose above the dilapidated barn where I always pray, and I love the melancoly of this time of the year.

Finished the Old Testament and liked Ecclesiastes best, much the best, Vanitas, vanitatum and all is vanity, the philosophy of the Rubaiyat. "For who knoweth what is good for man in this life, all the days of his vain life, all the days of his vain life which he spendeth as a shadow? For who can tell a man what shall be after him under the Sun?"

September 17. A radio "Paul had stroke. Buried at sea" So dreary, so desolate, so lonely—and the sharks "I would fain die a dry death" and be "dust unto dust and under dust to lie" The unforeseen and unannounced ways of death. How infinitesimal we are. How peu de chose devant l'immensité du monde. Buried at sea, and the horror the thought implies. Told A and she fainted. So it seems she loved him after all, so it seems, she too must have a broken heart. Unsuspected, for she always treated him with indifference and the realization of this has doubled her anguish.

Something unnatural about his death. He had said it was to be his last voyage to Africa. He had refused to take his valet with him remarking that he did not wish to bring back another corpse (his first valet having been brought back in a coffin). And he had remarked he was going to see a doctor in London before sailing. Were these presentiments of death or is Wilde right when he says that there is no such thing as an omen "Destiny does not send us heralds. She is too wise or too cruel for that". He was the fairest man I ever knew (a rare quality nowadays) a man with the heart of a boy, and the greatest hunter of his age. Lionhearted too from the lions he hunted and if we hunt for beauty can we be Beautyhearted? or for Sun Sunhearted?

29. And it appears that there was someone who wanted to kill Rainey (a man on board disappeared the day of his death) and there was a Hindu fortune teller (also on board) who predicted that Rainey would not be alive when the ship reached Cape Town. Was he murdered? Was it suicide? Was it really a stroke of paralysis? Or is it possible in spite of the cable that he is still alive?

October 10. L'hiver approche (as we grow older winter comes sooner and sooner until at last all the year is winter). Love late autumn best. Autumn Sunsets.

A has a nouveau-riche friend who never wears the same dress twice. Pleasant for her friends and A who dined with her last night returned with a dozen dresses—each dress having a hat, a purse, a pair of silk stockings, a pair of slippers, a chemise and a nightgown to match. She must never wear drawers for there weren't any! Estimated that the clothes were worth fifty thousand francs.

11. One's innocence deteriorates rapidly: in kindergarten was amazed to hear of kissing; at boarding school was shocked at lewd stories, during the war felt a revulsion on hearing of perversion; now worry very little about morals.

Like being definite about things; to know without hesitation who I like most (in what order they come), what drinks I like best, what books I enjoy most. This banishes indefiniteness and argues for strength. But as far as the bank is concerned I am ambitionless.

12. The nouveau-riche friend for luncheon with three exquisite dresses (too bad the husband is away or I might have had some suits and neckties, only he has gone to America to see about his income tax) and what

·

is the story about the time she was showing some of the English nobility over her London house "Here is my room, and J's is on the floor above" and as an afterthought "That doesn't mean we dont sleep intimate." But she is really very harmless and her generosity is genuine and she says she likes poetry (which with me atones for a multitude of sins) and if she enjoys social-climbing, why in Christ's name shouldn't she social-climb?

My mind has emerged from its midsummer lethargy and I feel creative (body as well as soul) But self-expression in a bank, it needs the forest of freedom if it would flourish. I want to be individual and move in a sphere of my own. I am in revolt. But I am in the hands of the Sun-God (or the Sun-Goddess?)—"et s'il me faut marcher beaucoup?"

To-day Goldenhair is being married and I see silver sand and a stone bench among dark fir trees and a midnight supper in a haystack and a winning of lace garters at a whippet-race, and a rose-colored boudoir, and the tall dark trees of Cathedral Wood ("grands bois, vous m'effrayez comme des cathédrales")—a dark sun-box of memories to remind me that one grows up and that childhood vanishes forever.

October 14. A Sunday and a beautiful lost lady. [19] Dressed in red, with a small black hat with a black lace veil which concealed her eyes so that she looked mysterious. She wore a jade pendant and her rings were of jade. Nails hennaed and dark red lips. Chinese. And her voice (I shall never hear voices again) low, very sad, very weary, almost whining at times. Chinese. And it was a gray afternoon (but once I caught a glimpse of the orange-winter sun low in the sky) and all the leaves in the Bois were falling and the trees were already very bare while overhead a flock of wild duck were hurrying south in V formation. Absorbed the gray melancholy of Autumn and there was a crackling fire and pink marble steps into the sunken bath and it was like the Roman Bath (callidarium) and I was bewildered and confused and lost in a dream.

16. Still in a daze and no more of Goldenhair and life can be very unexpected "since no mån's eye can pass beyond the Sun."

E se le fantasie nostre son basse a tanta altezza, non è maraviglia, chè sopra il sol non fu occhio ch' andasse.

17. Rose Prince at 25 to 1 won the Caesarewitch. A profit of twelve thousand francs. Orchids to the Sun.

19. Bostonians hate her (the lost lady) so I hate Bostonians

20. Letter in Gray.

24. The fourth day of heavy fog and Paris is like a city of the dead.

25. There is a dirigible—silver-gold in the Sun, for to-day the fog has lifted: The birth of freedom! Sun-Freedom!

26. Caviare and Château-Yquem (Chez Philippe) and to the races at Maisons-Laffitte and I should have been at the bank working and I remembered nothing about the horses—only the warm wind blowing down the straightaway as we stood by the rail gazing into the Sun.

A leaves saying that I have driven her away and this is partially true and I am glad and sorry (contradictory feeling so frequently experienced in life); glad we shan't have to see her any more (or what is more to the point her friends—story of Mrs. P. and the five hundred francs), sorry that I have not looked after her the way Rainey would have wanted. Forgive me O Sun for my sins.

November 4. To Longpont for the Bell Ceremony, the bronze bell in honor of Davis. How natural to be once more in the great forest of Villers-Cotterets. How natural to be again in ruined Longpont! And how natural to be drinking brandy from a flask! It was pouring with rain and there were fifty people for luncheon including the Bishop of Soissons and all the clan of Fezensacs and C had the Bishop on her left and a Marquis on her right and I was between the sheets (imaginaire) with a Duchess, and a sumptuous repast with a great deal of wine and a speech by Fezensac and a blessing by the Bishop. Then into the Chapel for the benediction of the bells. And the villagers came en masse, ignorant, curious, superstitious, pious, unspoiled by modern life—just as they were centuries ago, and there were three sermons pronounced in memory of Davis for there were three bells (ours and two that the Fezensacs gave) and I thought of Davis (five years now since he was killed in the Argonne) and of our friendship in the dawn of our youth when life was sunnygolden and war a myth. And the rain, always the rain pattering upon the roof and it was very dark with here and there a candle burning and the sing-song voices of the priests as they intoned their oraisons and incense fumed upon the altar and the air was warm with the breath of worshippers. And we had had so much wine—Drowsiness—Then to strike the bells with a small iron hammer (formality which ended the service) and then the distribution of dragées to the children according to the custom of France. And a pale woman with glasses (unwiped) and straggly hair (damp) who asked me if I remembered her and who said (when I said I was afraid I did not) "Je suis Geneviève." So this was the voluptuous girl of sixteen, the girl with the sun in her eyes, the girl of the passionately red lips with whom I had once sat on a gravestone all one long afternoon!

And now the manor house for hot chocolate and brandy and so back to Paris in the car, holding hands in the rain, and I smoked my pipe and thought of Davis (it must be cold in the grave to-night) while behind us in the dark rang the three bells.

5. C has revolted against anyone sharing with her the queenship of my heart [20] and she is tragic and unbalanced and I am nervous and erratic —The fact of A having gone is but an incident and life is a Tempest. Walked for exercise in our tiny garden around and around and around like the proverbial squirrel in his cage—saying prayers, darkly praying, softly praying inner thoughts. Wasted days for the most part except for the gloriousness of the Letters in Gray. Knights and Ladies and Castles.

November 7. In the Barn I say prayers and I am a mystic and religion is not a question of sermons and churches but rather it is an understanding of the infinite through nature (Sun, Moon and Stars) through Color (Sun, Moon and Stars) and through soul (Sun, Moon and Stars).

8. "I shall be waiting for you when you are ready to come."

9. Any phase of life can teach one qualities which may be applicable to all of life: thus horse-racing teaches one to be a good loser, the army how to judge men and how to be self-sufficient and evil how to eschew evil. But a hell of a lot of good this does me this morning. It is a gray dog, the gray dog which is not accepted and I too refuse to take it back and so it becomes the property of the butler ("yet did not the chief butler remember Joseph, but forgat him").

10. Invitation to dinner and drew lots whether to accept, and accepted and drank seven cocktails and telegraphed I was coming to London and went out to dinner. More cocktails. "And in his half-bewildered heart he played at being king." And I went to the Rabbit Bar (two whiskeys) and to the New York Bar (two whiskeys) and to the Casino de Paris (two whiskeys) and I broke the ring of jade trying to put it on my finger. Sent for my chorus girl friend and took her out dancing and we danced and drank champagne and I left abruptly without even saying goodnight to her (most ungentlemanly performance) and so to bed drunk and exhausted.

13. Last night dreamed a dream wherein I was being sucked into a bottomless quagmire. In a last desperate effort I reached out arms for help, a brief moment racked by the torture (perhaps the worst torture of all) of Uncertainty and then instinctively reached out towards C and in the same moment we became a rose-gold oneness. (into Sun)
Awoke late, and breakfastless, coatless, hatless started for London. A book, a flask of brandy, and my pipe. By driving at breakneck speed in a taxicab caught the noon aeroplane less than a minute (her propellors were already whirling) before she left the aerodrome. And away, up up like some gigantic bird, but half an hour later, engine trouble and we were compelled to come down in a stubbled field ("red cattle on the stubbled year") A nearby farmhouse and wine, bread and cheese and at four the engines roared again, the passengers climbed into the cockpit and off we went hurtling through space towards England. Darkness as we approached the Channel and we were soon lost in the fog. It seemed as if we were outside the world. Steady drone from the engines and brandy from the flask. Sleepiness. Far below, now, the sparkle of a lighthouse, like the sparkle of a cierge in a cathedral of Fog and the red and green lights of a coaler butting against the tide (Masefield). Then a thin white thread of waves and the vagueness of the English coast. A sudden drop down and down, (to the frozen lake) a sharp angle over a stone wall past a flock of sheep and we had alighted (orders not to fly by night). Resulted in a long tedious drive in a taxicab to London—darkness, the suspicious silence of travellers and fleeting glimpses

of hedge-rows. London and champagne and caviare and a tremendous re-statement after contrast.

November 23. Paris. My heart is a racecourse whereon four sunhorses gallop. Horses of the Sun. (Erythous Acteon Lampos Philogeus—H and C and J and C—Gold and Rose and Grey and Jade)

27. To a christening in a sordid part of Paris out by the walls where I stood godfather for the son of a man in the bank. A squalid wooden church that looked like a cardboard box and we could hear the rain pattering upon the roof and the dark and sinistersounding words of the priest, and there was a smell of unwashed bodies, and the hero of the occasion snivelled and cried and drooled (I hate children) while I answered the questions of the priest. Afterwards on foot through the rain along a muddy alleyway, past dreary buildings to the uninviting entrance to a tenement house. A winding flight of stairs and a barren room and cooped up for three hours among food and smoke and bottles of beer. A Zola scene. The suckling of a child and more beer and at last a delighted escape and back again to the security of the Princesse's.

30. Heavy fog over Paris and cold dampness and lights on all day and only one more month at the bank. Thank the Sun-God. And the storm has been weathered in safety and the city is very still and we walked together in the garden.

December 7. Read the Ladybird (D. H. Lawrence). Perhaps the best short story I have ever read. "To her softly. Now you are mine. In the dark you are mine. And when you die you are mine. But in the day you are not mine, because I have no power in the day. In the night, in the dark, and in death, you are mine. And that is forever. No matter if I must leave you, I shall come again from time to time. In the dark you are mine. But in the day I cannot claim you. I have no power in the day and no place. So remember. When the darkness comes, I shall always be in the darkness of you.

"Nothing can ever separate us, unless we betray one another. If you have to give yourself to your husband, do so, and obey him. If you are true to me, innerly, innerly true, he will not hurt us. He is generous, be generous to him. And never fail to believe in me. Because even on the other side of death, I shall be watching for you. And you will be at my side. You will never leave me anymore, in the after-death. So don't be afraid in life. Don't be afraid. If you have to cry tears, cry them. But in your heart of hearts know that I shall come again, and that I have taken you forever."

9. At the Autumn Salon a Japanese print in blue-gray of a stupid peasant with a pitchfork, prodding a yak with crooked horns and a game of laughing landhockey in the garden.

17. Read Marie Stopes on Married Love; that for married people it was natural to make love three times a week. Liked her quotation from Meredith "The speeding of us, compact of what we are, between the ascetic rocks and the sensual whirlpools, to the creation of certain nobler races, now very dimly imagined." (Sun-Races). "Nor will she deprive him of the natural joy of knowing that he is giving her delight." And "This mutual orgasm is extremely important," and "The Queen of Aragon ordained that six times a day was the proper rule in legitimate marriage." Dieu!

December 18. A long walk in the Bois and we came upon a stone house half-hidden by the trees, a house with a garden enclosed by a stone wall and guarded by a great iron gate. A handful of silver to the old crone and the gate was swung open. The Cimetière de l'Abbaye de Longchamp (had never heard of its existence) and we wandered among the graves, and the grass was tall and unkept and weeds everywhere and moss growing upon the wall and tombstones all leaning awry and by our side the aged crone mumbling and muttering. With her lean forefinger she indicated the grave of a danseuse du roi. Cypress trees grouped in a corner and the place overrun by cyclamen. A *real* burying place. We must be buried there.

Christmas and for me a purple handkerchief ("and all that there is of beauty in me to give") and the day is very clear and cold and after prayers at the Madeleine and after luncheon at the H's where everyone drank hot punch from a great wassail bowl, we walked out to the Bois to the Cimetière de l'Abbaye de Longchamp where the old woman greeted us. The Cimetière and the Soul. Dead leaves and the frost on the ground and the sentinel fir tree watching over the dead. Over the top of the stonewall a red-gold winter sun had almost set. The air was cold and damp and in the underbrush we saw a leaning tombstone with an archaic urn carved upon it. Nearby a simple stone cross enclosed by four low stone pillars these linked together by a rust-corroded chain. Among the trees a white goat browsed and under the dark wall. Soul in Eternity dreaming and praying prayers into the departing Sun. It was dark when we reached Paris and to bed to read the Lettres Passionnées de Ninon de Lenclos. Would be easy to fall in love with her and natural ("Il était dans la destinée de Ninon d'avoir eu pour amants le mari, le fils, et le petit-fils de Madame de Sévigné.") A red, sun-gold Christmas.

30. Went aboard the boat for Corsica but at the last moment as the hawsers were being unloosed we dashed down the gangplank, turned in our tickets, and entrained for Italy. A dreary day in spite of Lancelot and Elaine and the olive trees and the blue Mediterranean. At night reached Vintimille and successfully evaded the passport officials (ours we had forgotten in Paris) and there was a wretched hotel.

31. Forded a shallow river to avoid frontier officials and then walked for two hours in the hot sun. At noon, discouraged, we boarded a slow train and rattled all afternoon along the seacoast towards Genoa which we reached, after many dreary hours, at supper time. Bed and prayers and the year is at an End.

III

January 1. To Pisa. Pisa lifeless, a dead city silent in the cold grayness of late afternoon and the just-before snow feeling and the hooves of the horses on flat cobblestones and the mud-colored Arno and along a street and no sidewalk and no pedestrians. Clear and empty and frozen. The leaning tower. Like a soul that has been hurt by love. And so on foot together towards Florence!

2. Empoli bathed in rust-gold sun and the magnificence of cities at sunset, "la gloire des cités dans le soleil couchant" to quote Baudelaire.

3. Along the Arno towards Florence and a picturesque landscape with the old tow-path curving ahead of us, the ragged fishermen fishing in the river from the grassy banks or from frail green-and-brown skiffs, the woodchoppers hewing down trees from the opposite mountain side, the fleet of white ducks paddling and drifting with the current; and loveliest, a group of thatched cottages clustering together to form a large farm building orange and pink and bird's-egg blue, the color of the walls reflected in the river: gray-blue smoke ascending through gray stillness.

Towards evening Brozzi and here, exhausted, hired a two-wheeled cart and jogged and jounced into Firenzi by night, warming our hands over a brown earthenware pot filled with red ashes.

4. A circular marble bathtub built into the floor and entered by unlocking a grilled gate and descending two marble steps. Belonged to Marie-Louise but was she the only person to ever bathe in it? The grilled gate suggested how pleasant it would be to have a bathtub or a bed or a book all to oneself, unshared. Disheartening to consider the ugly bodies that have washed in one's bathtub, to imagine the people who have been born, who have made love, or who have died in one's bed, or to know that myriad unclean fingers have soiled the pages of one's favorite book. Was reminded of the pink marble bath on the Quai d'Orsay. And to-day is her birthday.

5. In a hot bath at Turin (no grilled gate) reading aloud to C. "It is mentally and morally injurious to man to do anything in which he does not find pleasure" (at this point a blushing maid appears with coffee and eggs) and "Selfishness is not living as one wishes to live, it is asking others to live as one wishes to live. And unselfishness is letting other people's lives alone, not interfering with them." Shall lay flowers on his grave. Oscar O'Flahertie Wills Wilde.

8. Not a good omen for the step after Queen should be Goddess. Answered it—a wife the Moon to her husband; a husband the Sun to his wife, but there is a state expressed by a star and a Letter in Gray is a star and Jacqueline is a star, but there are no other stars. But there are flowers.

11. Bourdelle at the Chaumière: "C'est la précision encore une fois—ce n'est pas autre chose." Of C's work "Plus de peinture que de sculpture, mais très fine et très fraîche. Il manque un peu de proportion." Said that the relation of the parts of a statue to its entirety must be the same as the isolated pieces of an orchestra to the whole of the orchestra. A leg must be more than a leg, an eye more than an eye. "Il faut chercher la vérité, il faut chercher dedans les choses, il faut travailler pour la postérité."

January 12. Elle est à la fois ma femme et mon enfant.

13. Color schemes for our racing silks: a rose heart on gray, a black star on white, a white star on black, a pink sun on gray.

With A to the Conservatoire. He is studying with Vincent d'Indy. Needs to be tortured by chaotic emotions. But Paris will do for him what Boston never could. Liked in particular the "Symphonie Fantastique" (Berlioz) with the idée fixe and the vagues de passions et de mélancolie.

15. Bored by politics ("full of sound and signifying nothing") and in the future I shall always wear a black tie and "la vie c'est une affaire d'âmes impériales" and what of the accidental collision of motes in the Sun?

16. Donned mouldy track regalia and ran over the spongy grass covered now with dead leaves. There was a brume and the woods were mysterious and cool. The glow of health.

To the Caveau des Oubliettes Rouges, Rue Saint-Julien-le-Pauvre. "Far from the lights and noise of the Grands Boulevards in a squalid quarter of Paris that was old in the Middle Ages, is a low red door feebly lighted by a lantern, dangling on a rusty chain." This Caveau, now a Latin Quarter drinking haunt, was once part of the bloody prison of the Petit Châtelet. Villon was imprisoned here.

> "En l'an trentiesme de mon aage
> Que toutes mes hontes j'ay beues—"

The moon to-night is a silver bird above the black towers of Notre Dame. (the Sun a gold bird within the black tower of the soul.)

17. To the Grande Chaumière for C and to hear Bourdelle talk and to gaze upon the nakedness of Tina and which of three inscriptions shall I write upon the picture in my gold locket. Played the horse-game to decide.

18. Smell of damp dead leaves and smoke of brushwood fires. And yet the smell of under-arms. One unchanging, one depending.

Tea with our pederast friends and they have a maid who has a mouth like a camel.

Overgaveaway books, clothes, chattels, following the precept of Diogenes "that a man's wealth should be judged by the things that he can do without." This evening wore a hat to please my mother.

20. A rock of gold. Within is the rose-gold shadow which is us, as water and the wave, gold and the bracelet. Vices, virtues, pleasures, pains, enemies, friends, fears, hopes—nothing but particles of dust, star dust perhaps, but dust, upon the impenetrable outer surface of the rock. Already a part of Infinity. Sun-Infinity.

January 24. Laurence Hope wrote:

> "Men should be judged not by their tint of skin
> The Gods they serve, the Vintage that they drink,
> Nor by the way they fight or love or sin
> But by the quality of thought they think"

and when I die I should like to have these lines for epitaph. (Sun-thoughts)

Ran a mile jumping over stone walls and hedges, and it was a sunnygolden morning and I breathed the gold of the gold sun, with soul as gold as the body of a girl.

25. Intense pleasure from getting cold and then luxuriating in a hot bath. This evening wore both a hat and an overcoat to please Mamma (but not a stiff collar).

Before going to sleep read Baudelaire

> "Alors, ô ma beauté: dites à la vermine
> Qui vous mangera de baisers,
> Que j'ai gardé la forme et l'essence divine
> De mes amours décomposées!"

26. Have learned to speak for myself and not to say what other people would like to have me say (not to be a slave.)

27. A gold racehorse with diamond eyes a horse out of and into the land of beauty, and this evening reminded me of what Wilde says: "Most personalities have been obliged to be rebels. Half their strength has been wasted in friction."

28. The horrors of Boston and particularly of Boston virgins who are brought up among sexless surroundings, who wear canvas-drawers and flat-heeled shoes and tortoiseshell glasses and who, once they are married, bear a child punctually every nine months for five or six years and then retire to end their days at the Chilton Club. Christ what a narrow escape, far narrower than escaping the shells at Verdun.

Switzerland and the gold of the Sun on frost and the sound of the snow crunching under our feet.

29. From the security of the inner towards the insecurity of the outer and that is why I am happy.

Consider Jesus-Christ as the prophet of God. But I pray only to the Sun-God.

February 1. Colors permeate the rock of gold and in beauty of color we live and die. To merge into the color of the Sun. But the color of the sunset was ruined to-day by a girl (sunsets are so often created by a girl) by Miss Shields of the running nose. Dress-shields. Damp. Lost Sunset.

4. Sun-gold snow-bath and naked together in the softness of snow, into the softness and coldness of snow, and before supper, for contrast, a hot bath.

Dislike the hemmed-in feeling one has in the mountains. Was never meant for a cage. "From the restricted and fenced, man's instinct is ever to escape."

February 6. Blizzard and the security of bed, and ping-pong, and cocktails and duchesses and divorcées and débutantes and until to-day have always finished every book I began. It took Antic Hay to break the bad habit. Yet Crome Yellow is charming.

8. Branches burdened with the weight of snow, the last faint sunrays filtering through the fir-trees, interveining my trail with gold shafts like bars across a score of music. Primeval pure is the last sunray, pure as a dark shadow, pure as the snow on snow.

Thought of B while I was undressing and of the night he sat in the fireplace and struck a match to the kindling wood and announced he was Joan of Arc. I wonder if she suffered any more than he did? And the cotton cocoon on top of his head, as big as an egg (result of diving on to a marble floor instead of into the water). And the day he fired revolver shots into the books in the library or else the time he jumped naked into a tramcar. And then the day of his real suicide (not to be a slave)

9. The Trail again and there was a high wind blowing across the lake so that on the return from my wanderings into the dark wood my tracks were obliterated. "Just as the sand-dunes, heaped one upon another, hide each the first, so in life former deeds are quickly hidden by those that follow after." (Marcus Aurelius).

For Thoughts the Gold of the Sun. Not to be a slave nevertheless a slave to the Sun.

10. Credo, I believe—that a bronx cocktail is the best drink, that newspapers are an abomination, that the sea is marvelous from the vantage point of the beach and horses marvelous from the vantage point of the ground, that violets and gardenias are the most perfumed, that woman is the slave to man and also all his "joye and blisse," that life is a black sadness powdered with suns of gold.

Must converse in a more modulated voice, must be much less nervous and not wear myself out with unnecessary excitement, but above all I must be as gentle as a girl to the Queen and to the princesses of the inner Centre, hard as nails to the outer world.

Am apologized for for my appearance. Annoyed. Nevertheless donned a stiff-bosomed shirt to please my mother, but on returning to the hotel it went out the window cuff links and all. And why shouldn't I share with C the same brosse à dents?

21. Mimi to see Mamma and she works chez un notaire and has two hours for luncheon with always an hour to spare. The weather is cold, her apartment far away, so instead of walking through the streets (no fun to walk through the streets if one cannot afford to shop) she goes, almost every day, into a fashionable church adjacent to where she works, to sit in the warmth and quiet, and listen to the funeral services of the rich!

Shadows of the Sun

Met a Mrs. Tola to-day. Told me she had been a virgin, a mother, a wife, a divorcée and a wife again within a year! But is this any queerer than to own the manuscript of Dorian Gray and never to have read it?

Why is it that white swans have black beaks and black swans red?

February 25. Vieux Colombier and was disappointed in Copeau and read de Quincey all through the play. "I have sat, from sun-set to sun-rise motionless, and without wishing to move."

March 8. London. Collected twenty pounds from a dishonest bookmaker but have lost twenty times that sum since I began.

Sold old jewelry for four pounds and bought with the proceeds four bottles of absinthe.

> "I wonder often what the Vintners buy
> One half so precious as the stuff they sell."

Turner's fiery suns (after absinthe) (sunsets on the brain) but the play to-night (Galsworthy) will leave no footprints upon the sands of the brain.

15. Paris again and Jasper invented Enosinthe, half-absinthe, half Eno's Fruit Salts and then he drank four of them and went out to the races and was pickpocketed. Breadcrumbs for Carp.

16. Lost C's string of pearls. In a taxicab? In a bar? Encouraged by Marie Bashkirtseff "Rien ne se perd en ce monde." Discouraged too. There are so many things one would like to lose.

April 5. Removed a skull from the Catacombs ("horrible est la mort d'un pêcheur"). Is it the skull of a man or a woman, of a boy or a girl; is it the skull of a warrior or of a courtisane; of a princess or a thief? A princess perhaps whose hair was of sun and whose eyes were of fire. When did she flourish, what were her intimate thoughts, where did she die and how did she come to be buried in the Catacombs of Paris?

> "Why, if the soul can fling the Dust aside
> And naked on the Air of Heaven ride
> Were't not a shame—were't not a shame for him
> In this clay carcase crippled to abide?"

Astounding to consider that if everyone in Paris were to fall dead to-day the number of corpses would not equal the number of skulls interred in the catacombs.

Climbed afterwards to the top of the Tower of Notre Dame (376 steps) and after having crawled like snails through the dark dampness of underground, it gave me a certain splendor of the Sun, and the bridges this afternoon were like pearls upon a silver chain (where is the lost string of pearls) and there was a diminutive tug (a black smoke-plume issuing from her smokestack) towing a long line of low-lying, coal-burdened barges, coming upstream, butting against the current. And there was a red dory fastened to the rear barge that bobbed up and down like a cork, and afterwards we saw the gargoyles and no wonder C preferred the doves who fluttered in and out or else perched upon the rafters of the belfry.

April 7. Supper Au Canard Amoureux run by Jules and Juliette (on vient de poser le linoleum pour le dancing) characteristic "boîte" honeycombed with salons intimes each with its divan and its bidet. Discussed costumes for the Quat'z Arts—isoloires in the form of robe de style for the girls, tables de nuit for the men! From the Canard Amoureux, past Little Home a house of red lights, past an electric plant where turbines purred and on past "à la destruction des animaux nuisibles," to a square and boarded a double-decked tram-car and from here we watched the night life of the poorer districts—lovers strolling and kissing, restaurants flooded with light, long lines of creaking carts loaded with vegetables, snailing in from the country, heterogeneous bistros crammed with workmen. With a certain amount of dexterity unhooked the enormous tin number plate from the top of the trolley and took it home to the Saints-Pères.

8. Bought underdrawers, a remarkable event, but I have been wearing C's black lace pretties for a week. Never like spending money on clothes.

At fourteen Marie Bashkirtseff wrote "C'est affreux! affreux! lorsqu'on n'a rien au fond de l'âme." Yes, and I imagine that is the tragedy that lies back of most people's lives "lorsqu'on n'a rien au fond de l'âme." Thank God for C and the Sun.

"Ce qui dominait tout l'oeuvre de Zorn est la femme souveraine, impudique, consciente de la puissance victorieuse de sa chair, l'être passionné et mystique qui ne peut pas penser mais seulement sentir." Should never have sold Elin.

But if I ever find the etching Dimanche de la Bergère I shall buy it coûte que coûte for it is Jacqueline.

New York—le boudoir à travers les âges; Paris—le bidet à travers les jambes and the cable I sent the Vulture yesterday is returned to me with this cryptic message scrawled in red ink across the back "Arrêté par New York à cause d'indécence." I think the word was "bastard."

15. The garret is reached by a rope ladder. Ladders to the Soul. Ladders to the Sun.

Four hundred louis (over twice the year's rent) on Sir Gallahad. A length to spare.

Nicolas Alfan de Ribera, Marquis de Villanueva de las Torres for supper and some of the fresh paint came off on his dress suit.

May 15. "Il existait à Paris, sous la République, des clubs de suicidistes. Leurs statuts identiques, obligeaient les membres à se tuer successivement; le suicidé annuel était désigné par la voie du sort." And Montaigne says "la plus volontaire mort, c'est la plus belle."

17. To Rue Gît le Coeur to see a miniscule apartment perched like a nest on the roof of the house (stork's nest) looking out over Notre Dame and the

Seine, ideal for lover and mistress, but not large enough for children (impedimenta.) Unless Children of the Sun.

May 18. The Cluny and its Mediaevalness and I like the old suits of armor, the pikes and the lances, and the curious battlegear, and I like the old coaches and the frail Venetian glass, and the Dame à la Licorne, woven in gentle faded colors, and the Dutch faïence, and the carved woodwork, and the old-fashioned musical instruments, and the iron caskets; but above all the Sun that filtered through the stained glass windows in waves of yellow satin to color the precious metals and the faded embroideries. And afterwards to the chapel to say sun prayers and to the deserted garden to wander among the moss-covered statues

19. Early supper at the Rendez-vous des Mariners favorite haunt of Alan Seeger before his Rendez-vous with Death

> "God knows 'twere better to be deep
> Pillowed in silk and scented down"

and in glasses of red wine one silent toast

> "Be mindful of the men they were, and raise
> Your glasses to them in one silent toast"

Then the Red Arrow out of winter-storage and washed it and launched it at the foot of the Quai d'Orléans. There were fishermen but never a catch. Perhaps they are like the Chinese philosopher who fished in a pond where there were no fish merely for the joy of fishing.

Later there was a gold moon, a pool of gold (almost a sun-moon) into which I prayed. Wilde is right "one can realize a thing in a single moment only to lose it in the long hours that follow with leaden feet." Yet even a spark of perfection, a spark of pure gold creates within the soul a strength of beauty to store away (as squirrels store away nuts) for Eternity in the Forest of the Sun.

20. A Bohemian supper: Gretchen took a bath during the meal, C retired to bed, Croucher and Kittredge threw cream puffs out the window and I read the Paris-Sport. Everyone had a good time for everyone did what they wanted to.

Bashkirtseff says "le milieu dans lequel on vit est la moitié de l'homme." (The Sun.)

21. Party au Canard Amoureux and a great sugar-crusted cake and little flags to announce seven different nationalities and in front of each girl's plate rose-bud garters and in front of each man's plate a silk handkerchief and the table was freighted with bottles, and there was a man who played the guitar and a man who played the banjo and there was a girl who sang songs, and there was Sato who with tears in his eyes sang a Japanese tragedy, a weird, weird song which held Blanche and Tina spellbound. And when he had concluded he ate four helpings of chicken, gobbled lettuce from an enormous salad-bowl (which he held poised on his knees) drank everything in sight and shouted "Banzi" (whatever that meant) at the top of his lungs; "Première fois content à Paris . . ." and then gazing on the naïve Tina "Je deviens senti-mental et féroce." Everyone went home together in a taxicab—eleven of us crammed pell-mell—a network of arms and legs.

May 22. After the races, in the Bois, a herd of frightened deer huddled together in startled suspense for around them roared the machinery and through the woods tramped hideous people. How incongruous in their setting, how delicately beautiful (yet not as beautiful as the sun-deer of the soul). To-day C wore her passionnate Yteb dress the one with the huge bow behind.

White narcissi before the gate of the tomb of Marie Bashkirtseff (a stone edifice enclosing her atelier just as she left it in the year of her death 1884.)

Began reading Le Suicide dans l'Antiquité et dans les Temp Modernes, "Moi je considère que le regret causé par la mort d'une personne chérie est toujours une cause légitime pour le suicide. Nous voyons dans l'histoire romaine de nombreux exemples de femmes ne voulant pas survivre à leurs maris, et il est certain que leur suicide fut regardé comme légitime."

25. And there were three priests and I was asked to lay my hand on the Bible and to swear that I was telling the truth and verbally I swore and mentally I did not and they asked me many questions and I told many lies and said whatever came into my head and they were very nice about it, but if it had not been for a gold horse with diamond eyes I would not have perjured myself.

27. A mess moving! Crates, trunks, impedimenta of every description and the bed was pulled up through the window by a rope, and I ran out and bought a magnificent old Holland desk for a thousand francs (it has secret drawers and a bowling scene carved on the outside) and by supper time I have raked the garden and have unpacked all our belongings (including the skull from the hat box) have removed our trunks one to the garret, one to the cellar, have kindled a fire in the library, have put books in the bookcase, tacked down the carpet and opened a bottle of Scotch whisky for the occasion. A wood fire and cool sheets and a curving of a darkness into light.

28. Read from seven until seven (exception made for luncheon) Les Métamorphoses d'Ovide and I liked best the tale of Pyramus and Thisbé "et leurs cendres reposent dans la même urne" and after supper friends appeared and we played a game which consisted in tossing pebbles down a drainpipe and I forgot to say that I bought yesterday a Persian battle-axe, a brass bell and an iron lantern at the Foire Saint-Germain in the Place Saint-Sulpice.

31. Vienna is hot; Vienna is dull; Vienna is sad; and I have nostalgia for Paris, but I liked the famous salt-cellar wrought in gold by Benvenuto Cellini for Francis the First. No cheap bric-à-brac in those days. Ours is an age of things perishable. Liked also the collection of armour.

Dinner with Prince Lubomirski and the Baron de Wullerstorff at an open air café-chantant where we drank the new wine, and they all went on afterwards (I was depressed and went back to the hotel and cabled the Vulture I would not go to Constantinople with him this summer) to the Chapeau Rouge.

Why is the letter A white, B black, C silver, H red? (Yet C is rose and H is gold)   And why are F, T, O and Mondays significant? And do I prefer rose-gray or silver-gold? And why all these questions? ("that, like Acestes arrows, catch fire as they fly")

Gentleness, barge, forestial, orchidaceous, sadness, Sun, these are gold; blouse, happy, bosom, cigar, these are dross.

June 1. Napoleon, "he cast a doubt on all past glories, he made all future renown impossible," so quotes S.V.R.C. and we saw the Blue Danube and four remarkable statues in bronze by Kolbe and we sent post-cards to Paris (two thousand kronen or $400 for a stamp at the pre-war rate of exchange) and there is a general aimlessness in Vienna, and the men carry their hats in their hands (and their hearts?) and Berni gave a farewell party and there was mah-jong and the Austrians hated us and there was a baroness who had a Rubens body (and Berni lay with her that night?)

3. The Orient Express (thank God) and prospects of Paris. Tolstoy is reading Uncanny Stories, S.V.R.C, Heu Heu the Monster, C Pepys and I Benvenuto Cellini and here is what he wrote about his colossal statue of Mars: "Il faut que je rapporte un fait qui donnera une idée de la dimension de ce colosse; il y a vraiment de quoi rire.—J'avais expressément défendu à tous les gens qui étaient à mon service d'amener des femmes dans mon château, et je veillais strictement à ce que cet ordre fût observé. Mon élève Ascanio s'était amouraché d'une jeune fille extrêmement belle qui n'était pas moins éprise de lui, car un soir elle s'enfuit de chez sa mère pour venir le trouver. Elle ne voulut plus le quitter, mais il ne savait où la cacher; enfin, comme il ne manquait pas d'esprit, il imagina de l'introduire dans mon colosse et de lui arranger un lit dans la tête même de la statue. Elle y resta longtemps. Ascanio la faisait seulement sortir pendant la nuit. Cette tête était fort près d'être achevée, par vanité il la laissait découverte, de sorte que presque tout Paris la voyait. Les voisins commencèrent par monter sur les toits mais la curiosité se propagea et amena une foule de gens."

4. Birthday in Paris and told no one and drank a toast to myself in a glass of red wine and I have Benvenuto's desire to merge myself in the gold of the Sun   ("Oh, let me escape thither, (is it not a little one?) and my soul shall live.")

7. Must "renoncer aux choses inutiles." Hate to waste time, yet all morning was spent about town and all afternoon in receiving callers. Discouraging. One hour a day wasted means forty-eight days a year thrown to the winds.

Sold our canoe for a thousand francs and it leaks like a sieve and drank red wine at the Rendez-vous des Mariners and bought a "bague ayant pu servir à empoisonner" in an old curiosity shop Rue du Vieux-Colombier (I have sat, from sun-set to sun-rise motionless, and without wishing to move), and from a ragamuffin a sling ("instruments of cruelty are in their habitations") with which I succeeded in hitting the cat that prowls at night among the shrubbery of the garden.

June 14. Bought a racehorse, Bucentaure, a two-year old by Or du Rhin out of Sans Frusques, for twenty thousand. He belonged to Max Dearly and has never run. Vierge. Our trainer is Eugène Pantall at Chantilly and our advisor the Count. Our colors are casaque gris-perle, croix de Malte rose, toque noire.

15. Words: arctic, absurd, bleak, barbaric, coarse, crude, chaos, couch, desolate, defenceless, disconsolate, disillusion, envenomed, emerald, embers, entangled, fragrant, feudal, fragment, gnarled, gracious, grandeur, hazardous, hawk, heraldic, illustrious, illusion, icicle, irresolute, impregnate, idolatry, ineffectual, imaginative, knight-errant, labyrinth, littleness, loveliness, loyalty, legend, lurid, leviathan, mediaeval, mysterious, mushroom, macabre, merciless, massacre, nostalgia, noon, nakedness, obsolete, orchid, overarch, owl, oasis, primeval, posterity, perfume, pagan, phantom, pool, pronged, peacock, python, provocative, preposterous, pregnant, quaint, quagmire, quarry, queenliness, royal, refractory, restrengthened, remote, reverberate, ruin, rust, rocking-horse, stronghold, sacred, sunnygolden, sadness, skeleton, sunembroidered, Sun, smoke, softness, seer, sorceress, shipwreck, stallion, steppingstone, turquoise, tapestry, tempest, turbulent, tea-chest, toadstool, tigress, thrust, tortoise, traceried, triumphant, unfrequented, unmuzzled, urn-shaped, untangled, unicorn, unquestioning, uncoffined, unchaste, unanswered, unchallenged, virgin, vampiric, vagrant, veil, vastness, vagueness, weariness, wistful, wagon, watch-fire, wayward, yoke, youngness, yield, zodiac.

17. Quat'z Arts Ball. Timbrels and dancing and uncircumcised lips. Got in by saying I was painting a nude for the Prix de Rome. An enormous room and the blare of trumpets and the mad pounding of toms-toms A riot of color. And much dancing, until, exhausted, wandered out into the street and in the cool of the morning rocked home in a fiacre and there was a thick darkness in all the land of the soul.

21. Erotic books (is this the result of the Quat'z Arts?) La Princesse de Babylone, The Decameron, Le Jardin Parfumé (with the 69 different positions for making love), Les Courtisanes d'Athènes et de Corinthe, and two historical tales by Guillaume Apollinaire: La Rome des Borgia and La Fin de Babylone.

24. C leaves with the Wretch[21] for America and a man without a woman is a forest without a tree. Or rather a tree without a forest.

25. A stained-glass window.

Shadows of the Sun

June 28. Through which flames the Sun.

29. Crazy friends at three in the morning on their way home from the Montmartre. Uncorked champagne and having drunk it they departed stumbling over flower-beds in the dark and knocking into trees. In the morning found a pair of lace pretties in the hammock! After supper hoed up weeds and raked the gravel path watered the flowers and thought about C.

30. "Mais je ne vous connais pas, Monsieur" (at the races). Didn't ask her name but called her Mademoiselle Fragile (black satin dress with white cuffs and white collar) but she wasn't. Why should we both be reading Les Oraisons Funèbres?

July 7. With Mademoiselle Fragile and a quiet supper at the Ritz and there was cold milk instead of champagne. Lost my hat and from now on decide to go hatless. And to-morrow I will stand on the top of the hill with the rod of the Sun in my hand.

14. Wild dancing in the streets all last night, grotesque couples whirling madly about to mournful dance music while paper lanterns swing to and fro between the drab buildings silhouetted against a lemon-colored sky. Departing day. The tragic sadness of the pleasures of the poor. Two boys revolving like tops, the earnest face of a man manœvring his woman through the crowd (Zorn), urchins upgazing in open-mouthed astonishment, two craintive maidens who cling to each other on the outskirts of the group and who timidly point to the pirouetting couples, and a crone, wizened and stooping, her white cap a patch of cleanliness among the dark shadows, and the old world face of the organgrinder,—glimpses of the underworld, the restless, sweating underworld, the rabble seeking after happiness ("O Jesu make it stop") and how much more beautiful the full moon turning to silver the garden of the pavilion or the red Sun turning to autumn the garden of my soul.

17. A dream last night. Not to be interpreted. I was standing at the prow of a swift-sailing ship, far far out at sea and the sky was dark. A leviathan with redgold eyes and nostrils snorting flame, plunged past bent on some terrible errand of destruction. As it disappeared beyond the horizon the black sea grew calm but not less black. In a rainbow upon the water I saw a nymph ride past widespread upon a dolphin. She *is* Beauty. And I was aware of battleships painted silver and gold (in the form of suns) of bulky junks flying the skull and crossbones (in the form of stars) and of diminutive soot-colored fishing-smacks (urn-shaped). Icebergs of the Moon floated past. With a gold pen I traced upon a sheet of silver emerald-colored words and enclosed this chronicle in an iron casket blacker than the sea and with black ropes lowered it into the sea until it was engulfed in blackness. Then, suddenly, for no apparent reason, I found myself sun-entangled with C. Sun-nymph in the forest of the Sun and is she the nymph who rode widespread upon the dolphin?

1924

July 18. Finished l'Assommoir and was horribly depressed "le nom de Lantier lui causait toujours une brûlure au creux de l'estomac comme si cet homme eût laissé là, sous la peau quelque chose de lui." If Gervaise felt that way about Lantier . . .

19. "It is true greatness to have in one the Frailty of Man and the Security of a God" (the sun) (Bacon).
Saw G. That perfume of hers (Narcisse Noir) would undermine a saint.
Bought a bottle of Benedictine and drank a toast to the sun-nymph (C).
Read Dorian Gray (second time). Its sparkling cynicism, its color idealism and its undercurrent of dangerous philosophy. "The mutilation of the savage has its tragic survival in the self-denial that mars our lives. We are punished for our refusals. Every impulse that we strive to strangle broods in the mind and poisons us. The body sins once and has done with its sin, for action is a mode of purification. Nothing remains then but the recollection of a pleasure, or the luxury of a regret. The only way to get rid of a temptation is to yield to it." (tempest of applause).

21. The sun is streaming through the bedroom window, it is eleven o'clock and I know by my dirty hands, by the torn banknotes on the dressing table, by the clothes and matches and small change scattered over the floor that last night I was drunk. Disgusting! And there is a cable on the mantelpiece (how long has it been there?) and it is from C and I am unworthy. This the result of reading Wilde. Blanche. Rhymes with Avalanche.
And I long for the sunbasking on Singing Beach, for the smell of the woods around Essex, for the sunsets at Coffins Beach, for the friendliness of the Apple Trees. Paris palls in summer and I crave hard exercise and sea-bathing and I would even like (for me tremendous admission) a small farm near Annisquam with a stone farmhouse looking out over the flat stretches of sand towards the sea. The hell you say.

22. The Marquis sends his picture signed Nicolas Alfan de Ribera, Bazan Y Godea, Marquis de Villanueva de las Torres, Des Duques d'Alcalà, Grands d'Espagne! Jesus Christ insignificant in comparison!
Paid out to-day (typical day this summer) cierge at Notre-Dame 5, stamps 5, charity 10, tips 10, (are tips charity?) bottle of port 20, taxi-cabs 30, luncheon chez Philippe 200, Ritz Bar 40, cable 80 (total 400.)
"Ta gueule et fumier" shouts a waggoner at my taxi-driver.
Brandy for colics, sherry flips for breakfast, champagne for sparkle, port for passion, évian cachat for damn fools. Did I buy port for passion?
Finished Bacon's Essays at one minute before midnight "There be Monkes in Russia, for Penance, that will sit a whole Night, in a Vessell of Water, till they be Ingaged with hard Ice." Damn Fools. Prefer hedonist theories to ascetic.

23. C writes that she is desperately bored and that her mother objects to her letting her hair grow under her arms. Ye gods!

Eglantine (Christ what a name for a man) for supper. No wonder everyone says he is a pederast. We drank four bottles of red wine.

July 24. In the Paris-Sport "Bucentaure, Golden Wood, Désio, Radziville et Louiset sont restés ensemble presque sur la même ligne jusqu'à mi-parcours où Bucentaure avait une légère avance, devant Golden Wood que suivaient Désio et Radziville. A la distance, Oleg, un instant attardé, venait très vite attaquer Bucentaure, mais sans parvenir à l'inquiéter." And a radio to the Leviathan for C is on her way home!

Rain in the evening and a hot bath and to bed naked. One always sleeps better that way (except in the war or in winter or on boats). Perhaps after all one doesn't sleep better that way. ("ayant peur de mourir lorsque je couche seul")

28. Saw Joan now married. Is the only girl I have ever been ashamed of.

Read to my taxi-driver from La Rochefoucauld: "On n'est jamais si heureux ou si malheureux qu'on se l'imagine."

Mademoiselle Fragile dressed in white. Said I reminded her of Dorian and later on sprained my wrist falling off a table on which I was performing acrobatics for a lady in green. And where are the wise men and the sorcerers?

30. Virgins are like cigarettes: they leave one unsatisfied and this applies spiritually as well as physically. Finished Les Oraisons Funèbres and then finished Les Saints Désirs de la Mort: "Ceux qui durant leur vie, ont eu le coeur et l'esprit attachés au ciel (au Soleil) montent au ciel (au Soleil) après leur mort. Mais ceux qui ont eu leur âme attachée à la terre, descendent sous la terre." Why not?

August 1. Leviathan on the horizon and with C alone to the Mont Saint-Michel and a room at the Cheval Blanc, and the sea was sad and the houses slate-gray but the window-box was filled with red geraniums and at the very end there was a sunset—gold clouds upon a background of steel over the grayness of the sea. And so to bed and sleepiness filled with visions of the day's journey, the demolished, deserted farmhouses, the arched bridge of stone and the stone cross by the cross-roads, the low-roofed chaumières, the meadows boxed in by green hedges, the "fumiers d'où naissent les roses sublimes" and all the tragedy and sadness of the land. Below our window a tavern and we are vaguely aware of fishermen drinking and chanting seasongs, and aware too of the great Monastery standing guard above. Then deep deep Sleep.

3. The cloisters and the slender pink columns and the miniature hanging-gardens and the battlements to serve as protection against the enemy and the sea. And beyond Tombelaine. But where are the monks bending over their manuscripts by the light of candles (while log fires burn in the fireplaces carved out of the solid rock—"The True Religion is built upon the Rocke") and where are the prisoners deep in dark cells, cold and alone, and where is the winter fog, and where is the sound of the bell ringing at the turning of the tide to warn the fishermen to run for safety? But there was Lobster and Benedictine at La Sirène (a tavern constructed in the fourteenth century) and there was a Sun that plunged this evening like a red arrow into the breast of the sea and there were seagulls upon the rim of a floating buoy like pearls upon a black coronet, and there was the tide in one continuous incoming wave sweeping over the sands faster than a man can run. Imprisoned here one might write something—

> "Oh that my words were now written!
> Oh that they were printed in a book!"

August 4. A remarkable old woman with a white lace cap tied on by an enormous white bow. She is a Madame Victoire guardian of the privies and she stands before the door of the retreat haughtily holding Monsieur's coat or Madame's parasol and gazing defiantly at the passers-by. She is wizened and her skin is like yellow parchment. Her eyes are halfclosed like a crocodile's. She wears black sabots which clank on the cobble stones when she walks. She solicits her clients. She is a mumbling, maundering sort of person. I enter the retreat in order to have the pleasure of giving this worthy creature ten francs which so overcomes her that she crosses herself and hands me a lady's parasol instead of my coat!

On foot, Granville to Le Repos, two hours through quiet countryside powdered with thatched cottages and gardens and meadows where cows browsed, until we came to the hamlet and the dull hotel by the railroad track. And she became his wife; and he loved her.

5. Breakfast at Beauchamp in an old house: crisp omelette, tumblers of cold milk and a large hunk of bread and there were peasants drinking cider from a stone jug and there was the pretty daughter of the house (the fairest of the daughters of the land)

> "Full many a flower is born to blush unseen
> And waste its sweetness on the desert air."

And there was a great shaking of hands and we went up a long hill and it was gray and C sang and I smoked my pipe and we went past chaumières from whose chimneys rose smoke plumes blue and gray (morning along the Arno) and there was a creaking of cart wheels and the occasional crow of a cock and barnyard oders mingled with the perfume of flowers. Little cottages with glistening pots and pans and stone flanges and niches in the outside walls for little statues of the Virgin (prayers to the Virgin) (the Virgins of the Sun in Peru) and certainly these cottages in Normandy inspire chaste thoughts more than do the advertised churches of America.

6. A forgotten hamlet off the highroad and eggs and beer and sleep beneath a hay-rick, and the drone of myriad insects and the babbling of a brook and the sun flaming in a cloudless sky, a ship of gold across a sea of blue. Supper at Tessy and afterwards along a tow-path in company with a lame peasant girl with the Vire on our right, past Fervaches and the Moulin de Fervaches, reflecting itself on the imperceptibly moving water (why should the water in the middle of the river seem higher than near the banks?) and on for another mile to La Chapelle-sur-Vire where innumerable stone crosses scattered over the opposite hill-side were like thoughts (unbeautiful) upon a brain.

A garret room, a glass of brandy, a crawling into bed, a blowing out of the candle and a falling asleep soothed by the ceaseless swish-swishing of a mill-wheel.

August 9. One may or may not be glad to leave Paris but one is *always* glad to return. Paris is the City of the Sun. Breakfast of raspberries and cream and bacon and eggs in the sunny-golden garden of the Ritz and I believe that luxury like prayer is purifying.

The house without C was dirty and desolate, now it is bright and delicate. No more cold meals, no more untidiness, no more disorder. She supervises the Ox, paints the bathroom and gardens in the sunshine while I continue reading about suicide (he who desires peace wages war.)

Smoked my blackened pipe and drank brandy from a flask with the Vulture (just back from Constantinople) and he told me he slept last night with a lady he met on the train (Cerulea) and it is nice to know there are a few hounds left and later on we invented a game of ball to play against the wall of the lumber shed.

The bracelet C pawned at Deauville (most horrible of towns) is returned. C très artiste in her black silk dress which buttons up the back. It has a lace collar and lace cuffs with black ribbons.

20. Chantilly and they are burning charcoal in the forest (a burnt sacrifice to the Sun) and we had tea (in Paris) with Black Bess and she has enormous mammals, and perhaps Jasper was right after all (this has nothing to do with Black Bess) when he said there was no such thing as a friend. Not to be a slave.

27. Says [22] that it is ridiculous for me to write poetry that the days of Shelley and Byron are over. "The idea of you writing poetry as a life work is a joke and makes everybody laugh" and "You will be a dismal failure and laughing stock if you take poetry writing seriously." Lastly, "I'm not cross with you (not very!) but think it very stupid and shows that after two years you are still in the clouds and just as much a visionary as ever." Best praise he ever gave me and doesn't the Bible say: "Where there is no vision there the people perish."

31. The Sun-God is a harmony of colors which break off into particles to float earthward like colored snowflakes. Each color-flake has a soul. When two of them merge into one, the Sun-God draws them back to live Forever in His Inner Color in the form of a star or a moon or a sun. But the majority of the flakes fall to the ground unmerged and melt without ever having merged. These are lost souls. But once two souls have merged it is Irrevocable, it is for Eternity in the Color-Kingdom of God. In the Color-Kingdom of the Sun.

September 1. My pipe is the tent, the tobacco the days of my life, and the smoke is the soul ascending through ceilings and bridge tables and pots and pans and roofs and darknesses and stars into the Sun. Birth the lighting of the pipe, marriage the smoking of it, and death the knocking out of the ashes.

2. Cobras and tarantulas and opium and a tale of the Foreign Legion, tale which reveals the âme impériale ("la vie, c'est une affaire d'âmes impériales") of the French soldier. King was in a company made up of men from the Midi and it was the morning of an attack. The Captain saw that one of his men was trembling and "why are you trembling?" he asked, and back came the answer proudly spoken "Sire, je tremble de courage!" Immortal words of some forgotten soldier of France. (Elisabé).

3. Bucentaure ran and was beaten but I saw only the gold of the sun as it shone on the Croix de Malte rose (with its background of grey)—the colors of my soul.

5. 　　　　"And all men kill the thing they love
　　　　　By all let this be heard
　　　　　Some do it with a bitter look
　　　　　Some with a flattering word
　　　　　The coward does it with a kiss
　　　　　The brave man with a sword!"

Whom have I injured?

6. In Paris one looks at women from the point of view not of face but of contour. What was the remark in Crome Yellow about "women being always practically the same; shapes vary a little that's all." Flowers of the garden but there are thorns also and thistles.

Read in Plutarch an important passage. Zeuxis is replying to Agatharcus who is proud of his facility and speed in painting. "Et moi au contraire" says Zeuxis "je me glorifie de demeurer longtemps à les faire, parce que ordinairement la soudaineté et la facilité ne peult donner une fermeté perdurable ni une beaulté parfaite à l'oeuvre: mais la longueur du temps ajouter à l'assiduité de labeur en la manufacture d'un ouvrage, lui donne force et vigueur de longue durée." Flaubert.

16. "l'adorable inconnu des robes qu'on soulève."

17. Books Books Books and how one was clothed in a binding fashioned from the skin of a courtisane, how one was abandoned to rot in the rain, how another was rongé par les rats, how still another watched over a sleeping princess (il faut être celui-là).

18. Gave our summer address as Sakis Persia to the Boston Social Register. Might have said Tonga, Samoa or the Radak Isles. Might have said Reykjavik Iceland. But never could have said Manchester-by-the-Sea.

Bought a blackjack from Tunti. Better to give than to receive (certain things)

Should have bet on the Le Roi to-day, stupid of me not to ("qui ne risque rien ne gagne rien.") Oxen and Asses.

Picked up a newspaper (rare event) and read: "In the following position, East is the dominating wind, you are South playing the one-double game. East's first discard is the Seven of Characters. What will you do with it and why?" Answer: Kiss pretties. Recall Gautier (in his preface to Mademoiselle de Maupin) "La lecture des journaux empêche qu'il y ait de vrais savants et de vrais artistes."

Every night to see which side of the bed we shall sleep on we roll dice. C won and chose the side nearest the window. Window to the Sun.

September 28. Children have a picturesque façon de parler, thus the Wretch says: "someotherbody" and "do I disturv you?" and asks "what part of us goes to heaven; is it our thinks?"

October 7. Wish I had been born in October. Wish I had been married in October. And now I wish to die in October. (only not this October)

11. The trees in the Bois are red-gold or should I say the leaves of the trees in the Bois are red-gold. And the Sun and at night there is a great October moon.

Won a wager from C she holding that Sunday was the last day in the week. But if she thinks it *is* the last day then for her it *is* the last day, just as if I should think the Mauretania was the Queen Yseult, why then the Mauretania (for me) *would* be the Queen Yseult. All of which is quite evident.

"Schools" remarked Amy Lowell "are for those who can confine themselves within them. Perhaps it is a weakness in me that I cannot."

Burnt up my flimsy pale-blue sweater (it was torn and spotted) which C gave me long ago, as I never want anyone else to wear it.

16. The Cimetière de l'Abbaye de Longchamp; entangled foliage, gravestones leaning awry, moss-covered stone walls,

Perhaps it is here I shall kill myself.

Must live in colors. A red-gold sun flames westward with my inmost color-prayers. ("et leurs cendres reposent dans la même urne")

17. Autumn grayness with a fog creeping in over the quarter and the taxi horns sound far away, and there is stillness and the yellow leaves softly fall and the log fire burns to red-gold in the soul.

18. Fear of ridicule ruins many a generous deed. Add to this fear of being refused. (Whom have I injured?)

Vicomtesse de S for luncheon and she claimed that if a woman abstained from making love for seven years she would become a virgin again. She (the Vicomtesse) couldn't (I am sure) remain seven days without making love!

October 19. Bucentaure runs in a claiming plate at Longchamp and after having led almost all the way finished second in a field of fourteen and he was bought by a German and it is an October night and it is raining.

29. The Count for tea and he told us how he won a wager (Sunday is the first day of the week) by entering the leopard's cage at the Circus. Could only do this for C. And for Jacqueline?

November 5. Zola in his preface to l'Assommoir says: "L'Assommoir est venu à son heure, je l'ai écrit, comme j'écrirai les autres, sans me déranger une seconde de ma ligne droite. C'est ce qui fait ma force. J'ai un but auquel je vais." Wonder if the majority of the artists of the Autumn Salon could say as much. Arrow into Sun.

Sold a beach picture (it used to be the painting of my soul of five years ago) and C sold both her diamond bracelets (to Cartier). Then we bought a Corot "Lisière du Bois le Soir."

11. Six years ago to-day and the unknown soldier feels the finger of the Sun.

17. Bourdelle at the Chaumière. A rock among a sea of nonentities. (brokers and bankers take notice) And the eight commandments—

"Il faut travailler pour la postérité."
"Chaque fois un peu plus loin."
"Pas de grand art sans chiffres."
"Quand vous voulez faire une grande chose tous les détails doivent être grands."
"Il faut avoir de temps en temps de mauvais caractère."
"Il faut observer de près, il faut comprendre l'extérieur et l'intérieur."
"Rien ne se fait sans effort" (even children)
"Il n'est pas que l'architecte au monde."

Then he corrected the work: to one jeune fille "Il faut exister un peu Mademoiselle;" to another "Il faut être plus sauvage;" to an Australian "Il y a dans ça du vrai tempérament;" to a weak-looking individual (gigolo or pederast) "Ça, Monsieur, c'est trop gentil."

Bourdelle despises cleverness. He admires what is solid, strong, sharp, well-defined. Never be timid, he says, and always seek la grande qualité, the soul of the work ("la vie c'est une affaire d'âmes impériales).

Showed us an Aztec head observing that a piece of stone no larger than this has sometimes saved empires from oblivion. Are we or are we not afraid of oblivion? Yes we are afraid of oblivion.

19. Notre-Dame, oasis in a desert of discord. Grey-black, gold-gray, rose-grey are the colors of the columns and of the arches and of the walls, and are the colors of the columns and of the arches and of the walls of my soul. Ran my hand over the stone columns. The coldness of stone and the burning of a cierge. It twinkled like a lighthouse (flying over the channel at dark a year

ago) To warn of what? Or to welcome to what harbor? The Harbor of the Sun.

No money to give the young nun at the door so gave her the two books I was carrying: Lawrence's Ladybird and Renée Vivien

> Les Tombeaux sont encor moins impur que ta couche
> O Femme! Je le sais mais j'ai soif de ta bouche."

Too bad not to have had Les Oraisons Funèbres or Les Saints Désirs de la Mort.

November 23. The tyranny of things is the bête noire of the artist. The tyranny of the lingam is the bête noire of the yoni. (Boston Transcript please copy) See Joyce Potaaaym 287.

Wrote an essay De Laudibus Virginitatis "Fasting maids whose minds are dedicate to nothing temporal."

Supper (Oysters and Anjou) and home in a hack and our cocher was a vrai type and I owed him five and gave him twenty and wish now it had been a hundred. Le Favori.

The Encyclopedia Britannica (thirty-two volumes) a gift from Mamma. Immediately looked up Hero and Leander, Pyramus and Thisbe, ("et leurs cendres reposent dans la même urne") Tristan and Yseult. H and C

24. Two Americains for luncheon. One thought that every gentleman should knock down every negro he meets (And every negress? Knock up?) and the other considered love a form of indigestion—(it certainly would be with him). Glad I am déraciné. Ubi bene, ubi patria.

> "Such wind as scatters young men through the world
> To seek their fortune further than a home
> Where small experience grows."

December 7. Somehow to-day I am the Sea and C (Sea) the Red Arrow (not the canoe but August Third)

10. To buy Christmas presents and in characteristic fashion began by first buying one for myself "La Boussole des Amants," a small exquisitely-bound, lemon-colored volume (Amsterdam 1670) from the library of Robert Hoe. The Ex-Libris suggested the idea for one of our own.

We went to look at wigs—white wigs, pink wigs, lavender wigs, bobbed hair and long-haired wigs—but all impossibly expensive.

Luncheon at Walter Berry's the prayer shell from Tibet and the Egyptian stone cat imperturbable upon her haunches, and the Aztec death mask and the Bible from Siena (which he bought for a 'rien' in a New York Y.M.C.A.) and the Indian and Persian colored prints and the Gauguin landscape and the Marie Laurencins and the Houdon bust (which I dislike) and the small Burne-Jones lent by Berenson and the books books books books books and the bindings and the colors of the books. But best of all the Degas in the dining room (where Ethan Frome was written) the little Degas nude to whom I should like to make love. "And a flaming sword which turned every way to keep the way of the tree of life."

December 11. Studied Sufism "Towards the end of the second century we find the doctrines of mystical love set forth in the sayings of a female ascetic, Rahiao Basra, the first of a long line of saintly women who have played an important rôle in the history of Sufism. Henceforward the use of symbolical expressions, borrowed from the vocabulary of love and wine becomes increasingly frequent as a means of indicating holy mysteries which must not be divulged.

—The human soul belongs to the spiritual world and is ever seeking to be re-united to its source (the Sun). Such union is hindered by the bodily senses but though not permanently attainable until death, it can be enjoyed at times at the state called ecstasy when the veil of sensual perception is rent asunder and the soul is merged in God (in the Sun)"

12. A beautiful woman is a gift from the Sun sent upon earth to protect and inspire the souls and bodies of men and it is more beautiful almost than individual color to be in a woman's thoughts, within her body (and the softnesses thereof) ("and my covenant shall be in your flesh for an ever-lasting covenant") within her soul (color of the rainbow) to almost *be* that woman. But then again it is devastating.

Bourdelle autographs two books for us, (under the name C "J'écris sous ce nom qui me trouble. Voilà une vérité. La vérité est, mais hélas nous pouvons que la pressentir", and under mine "Travaillons pour ceux qui nous suivent et nous vivrons plus longtemps.")

Sea-Lions is impossible. Served steak in a soup bowl, left all the windows wide open, forgot to sweep the parlor, upset a pot of boiling water, scalded herself, and bustled about disarranging and breaking things. Her excuse is that she is sixty-five years old and "Mon Dieu, c'est vrai, mais je ne peux ni lire ni écrire (as if that had anything to do with it). She is an inveterate gambler at the races and I have to read her the results from the Paris-Sport. I like her best when in the afternoon she croons old lullabies to the Wretch. But how I hate her in the morning!

Christmas and the Cimetière de l'Abbaye de Longchamp and orchids and gardenias on the grave of the danseuse du roi. The Gate to the Sun.

Last day of the year and into the red-gold of the Winter Sun. Arrow into Sun.

IV

January 2. W.V.R.B. at tea-time "What fun you will have là-bas au soleil" and saw Gerald Murphy and he is going to Bâle to paint locomotives.

5. Pompeii and the unburied city and the frigidarium and the callidarium and the house of the balcony (its stone beds and its obscene frescoes) and the Cave Canem and the Ionic columns (the temple of Isis, the temple of Apollo) and the cobblestoned streets with the marks of the chariot wheels. Must read Bulwer-Lytton. Came out by the Via Marina after seeing the Museum where the stonified corpses of those who suffocated and were buried alive in the lava can still be seen in the positions in which they died—a courtesane lying on her stomach with her chemise rolled up, a man in agony with a towel wrapped round his mouth, a dog gone mad, sinister proof of the power of Lady Vesuvius.

—Into Naples and the dark green and the dark orange of the orange trees and the black-blue of the Bay of Naples and urchins along the tracks who scrambled for coppers.

—In a wagon to the wharves through the picturesque disorder of traffic and there was a beautiful Italian peasant-girl with a sprig of gardenia, and a donky-cart carrying a corpse, and beggars everywhere, and then the maze of masts and the steamboat for Tunis and the shore-lights, the lights of Naples, dwindling dwindling into Nothingness.

6. Palermo at dawn and Trapani at dusk and a hand in hand through narrow streets and quietness and a vast plate of macaroni and a vast bottle of Chianti. Footsteps echo through the paved streets, the strains of a hurdy-gurdy penetrate the deadness of the heart and the raucous cry of street urchins brings sadness of despair. As the ship sails a star rises over Africa. Prophetic.

7. And the docks of Tunis and the coldness of Tunis and the indefiniteness of plans and the weariness of travelling: the itineraries, the tickets, the no-privacy, the gloomy rooms, the expense, the need of a guide.—Cous-cous and bugs in the dates (discovered too late) and the knowledge of bugs inside. And then the Souks. What silks and satins! What an aroma of the East! What a conglomeration! And Arab tea in the Souk des Femmes and for C a rainbow-colored sash and a pearl-gray jacket with gold brocade. Beggars and Spahis and Arabs in white burnouses sipping black coffee and smoking hashish, and the Place Sidi Bahi and the femmes publiques who sit on their doorsteps (warming their hands over smoking braziers) furtively watching the men as they stroll up and down. Courtyards and walls of bird's-egg blue and earthen jars and dark doorways from whence comes hoarse laughter, and dusk and a cold wind down the street and the women huddling over their braziers (a bed and a colored rug and a grated aperture for window) and we bought four jars of the best brand of opium.

1925

January 8. And the coldest, dreariest journey from dawn till late at night to Constantine. Australia could not have been more desolate and there was Zagha a rug merchant who talked of Persia and of the perfume of Bulgaria and who showed us a flask of concentrated Attar of Roses (worth $100) and there was an officer of the Foreign Legion which is quartered in the town of Sidi Akba.

9. And we passed through El Kantara and came into the Sun and then Biskra and basking, and in the evening to an Arab café and to the street of the ouled-nails and to a dervish dance where a fanatic stuck pins through his cheeks and put a red-hot iron in his mouth and danced with a flaming torch fastened to his scarred body; and apparently he has never been near a woman and apparently he spends his days reading the Koran, and when he dies he will be regarded among Arabs in the same light as Christians regard a saint, and the money he gains goes to the poor, and there was a black priest who supervised the proceedings which included an exhibition of scorpions taken out of a bag and promenaded along a man's arm. And afterwards the chasteness of a full moon.

10. And the Sahara Express (painted white)—and here we are in Africa in the Sahara on our way to Touggourt. And we have seen scorpions, Arab dances, snake-charmers, little girls (eleven years old) for pleasure, and les mangeurs de choses immondes.

—Indigène villages and no more mountains and arid plains and at noon the real dunes of the desert stretching as far as the eye could see, rolling into Infinity.

—Touggourt and the end of the railroad and two sand-white burnouses and the beginning of the caravan: Hadrassi Ben Ahmed (guide) the modern young Musulman (valet and cook) in a palm beach suit and dancing pumps and a red fez; the chamelier and his two sons Mohamed and Hahmed to drive the camels, and lastly two musicians (a flute-player and a tom-tom player) with little Zora to dance. Sand dunes and on our left the mud-caked walls of Touggourt. Gold in the Sun. A deserted street, a camel-pen then past the Tombs of the Touggourt Kings. Nomad campfires and the sun disappeared and the sands grew cold and tents were pitched and there was a great orange moon that rose over the fringe of palm-trees. And the chamelier (like a Tartar) with a pan of hot camel's milk (for me superior to cow's and certainly more strengthening—it is purported to be an aphrodisiac when mixed with honey) and we sat on top of a dune and there was a camp fire and hay was thrown to the camels and the tents were banked with sand and we ate in a tent while outside the musicians made barbaric sounds—plaintive, insistent, poignant—it seems here that people have never altered, but are always, from time immemorial irrevocably the same. Smoke and a chilled dampness and through the open tent flaps the black form of an Arab at prayer—a sad litany and a rocking backwards and forwards—and from Touggourt the sound of dogs barking and from far away over the sands the howling of jackals.

"All night the hungry jackals howl together
Over their carrion in the river bed,
Or seize some small soft thing of fur or feather
Whose dying shrieks on the night air are shed"

and there was a steaming platter of couscous and a goodnight to Zora and a snuggling into burnouses (which are houses in themselves).

January 11. Little by little to unfreeze and it is not hard to understand the worship of the Sun.

—Westward over undulating dunes and the disdainful majesty, the unruffled demeanor of the camels (large hornless ruminant long-necked cushion-footed quadruped with one hump or two) and how they seem to be a combination of horse, of cow and of giraffe, and the usefulness of these ships of the desert whose milk is nourishing, whose thirst can endure, whose backs can bear heavy cargoes, and whose meat even is edible. Ours a sorry-looking lot (only the baby camel seems thoroughbred) dungcovered, with half their fur rubbed off (by the leather thongs) and their noses pulled out of shape (by the iron rings of the leading cord). But the most marvelous part of a camel are his eyebrows—how remarkably bushy, how haughty, how feather-lustrous.

Under a hot sun our caravan advances. The feeling that all this was once the sea—the ripples in the sand, the monotony of the dunes, the vastness of the waste stretches, the cloudlessness of the sky, the dreary music of the musicians. At noon a sun-pool of sand between high dunes and the sun in the Sahara is strong and when we awake our faces are flaming red. Nu pieds in the afternoon up and down dunes and into the Sun and this is the halfway mark, the furthest point from home (but is not real home inside the soul or rather inside the Sun) and now towards Paris! Paris City of the Sun!

—Buried things in the sand—a bronze medallion with our sun-cross on it and two bottles with self-addressed post-cards.

—Azure-blue and sun-white at noon but in the late afternoons shadows slant and turn purple, and dunes turn from white to gold to rose to gray and the sun is otherwhere and the moon beyond Touggourt is an enormous lavender pincushion into which I thrust the pins of my desire. Straying camels are herded, hobbled and fed. The musicians emerge from their stupor and squat upon their heels around the fire and the Assyrian smokes hashish and the camels low and the two children huddle in silence while the guide stands upon a dune searching the desert (for he is afraid of the Nomads) and the sands grow cold and the jackals begin to howl and there is a wind and always the feeling of the sea and there is hard, dry bread and a handful of dates for the camel drivers and the children (tout le désert mange comme ça) and I notice that the children never speak and that the little dancing girl is almost asleep. Hashish and Arab tea and all the strange unreality so utterly different from home and I am glad we have shared this Beauty.

January 12. High overhead shines the cold moon no longer lavender-luscious but arctic like a frozen sea and over the dying embers crouch the musicians and little Zora and the children are nowhere to be seen and the camels are ghosts and the coldness of the sand is the coldness of snow and there are cups of coffee and we mount our camels and towards the east a grayness announces another day. Towards Touggourt with the sky an inverted ocean of scudding wave-clouds and near to our left a caravan of camels bringing in wood swaying like trees in a wind (Dunsany Wood). A heap of bleached bones and the sand is tattooed with the footprints of jackals. As we approach the town we see camels appearing and disappearing behind the dunes and from nowhere an oasis emerges and the palm-trees are parasols and far off the reflet rose of the sun strikes a white minaret.

"And strikes the Sultan's Turret with a Shaft of Light." Standing upon a dune three Nomads in white against the dawn and behind them, in a hollow, five black tents. A mongrel snarls and barks and then the cemetery and the tombs of the kings and the earthen walls of Touggourt. Where are the snake-charmers (Where are the Lions? Where are the Lions) but for three years the snake-charmers have not come to Touggourt.

The train and Djama with its roofless mudcracked walls and its multitude of beggars—three thousand they say—and what a rabble of rags and tatters —patriarchs and ragamuffins, crones and virgins, the halt and the blind gathered together for copper coins. An impression of scrawny arms, of hands clutching, of famine faces (by reason of the famine)—in open combat. There was a squaw-woman with a horrid baby papoose-fashion on her back and a bastard-wretch with no hair and eyes clogged with dirt, and there was a young Arab with teeth of hard snow who played upon a flute and there was a tattooed lady and a saintly person with watery eyes whose garment was a torn piece of sackcloth and there were black boys from the Soudan and there was The Little Girl of the Pink Ring. As the train turned the corner the last thing we saw were two boys in combat (they had run down along the track) over the last coin.

And plains powdered with sage brush and at Stil curious graves like the menhirs of Brittany. As we drew into Oumache the sun set. Three Arabs oblivious of the train were prostrating themselves upon the station platform. A dying dog basking against the wall looked up at us with the knowledge of death in its eyes. Back of the station a low line of mud-walls, then darkness, then Biskra.

14. An agèd Arab tattooed us—with crosses on the soles of our feet but he was not an expert and to have Lions and Gazelles and Suns and Slavegirls we shall have to seek elsewhere.

Naked all day on our sunpiazza and slow turning from ivory to brown and I worship the Sun and I am entangled in the Sun.

15. Vieux Biskra built of earth and the gold-brown of the walls and narrow streets and palm trees and children in the sun and through open doorways Arabs reclining on mats sipping coffee and playing dominos. A

mosque and a young man reading aloud the Koran and the top of a minaret and everywhere color of gold and the life has not changed since the time of the Bible and there is the grave of a marabou and in a courtyard a woman is washing (Bathsheba) and there are Arabs coming into town on diminutive donkeys (not coming into town in diminutive Fords) and there is a tiny Tofla tending her goats in a deserted palm garden and there are crumbling walls and sun-baked houses and a certain sluggishness and it never rains and the sun gives health and all one needs are dried dates and bread and coffee (and of course hashish) [23] and a straw mat in a bare room of stone ("a man's wealth should be estimated by the things he can do without") and we walk to the Café Maure and smoke hashish (to the amusement of the indigènes) and we see the village sheik in a black and white burnous and a little negress accroupie in his path (no self-consciousness here) and there are more walled gardens and date trees and troughs of brackish water to irrigate them.

And on our way back to the modern Biskra we enter the gates of the native cemetery—an arid field of innumerable dried mounds of clay. No inscriptions mark the mud blocks which serve as gravestones and the Arab rests here until he becomes an unnamed handful of the surrounding dust. The only distinction in this strange buryingplace is that the graves of their women are marked by a block at the head and at the foot while the graves of their masters have but one.

—After supper, Eastern beverages, more hashish and the gyrations of the dancers to the sound of tom-tom and wind instrument (most proper dances) and there are the sword dancers and afterwards through a hashish den, through a low stone doorway, up a dark alleyway and into a small room to see our little Zora "dans une danse du ventre toute nue." Two gaunt musicians and beer and hashish and little Zora removing layer after layer of the most voluminous garments, the last piece being a pair of vast cotton drawers, such as clowns wear, and which was gathered about her slender waist by a huge halyard. Then she begins to dance, slownesses at first with curious rhythms of her ventre and then convulsive shiverings (two matchless breasts like succulent fruit) and wilder the music and more serpentine her rhythms and her head moves forward and backward, and her body weaves an invitation and we went home to the hotel and O God when shall we ever cast off the chains of New England.

January 16. And the chains of New England are broken and unbroken but the death of conscience is not the death of self-consciousness and there is something Montaigne said and would it be so terrible to marry someone who was deaf and dumb (provided she was beautiful?)

17. To hunt the jackal and an hour before dusk on desert ponies out across the dried riverbed straight into the setting Sun, through an abandoned Senegalese village and past the black tents of the Nomads.

> " 'Tis but a Tent where takes his one day's rest
> A Sultan to the realm of Death addrest;

The Sultan rises, and the dark Ferrash
Strikes, and prepares it for another Guest."

An hour later we dismount and so down a rocky ravine to a cache prepared in advance and we picket a goat upon the opposite ledge and we load our rifles and we begin to wait and we wait and we wait (Where are the Lions? Where are the Lions?) and the hills turn to rose-copper to copper to black and the Nomad fires kindle one by one like eyes in the dark and across the valley towards El Kantara the forlorn whistle of a freight train and the terror-stricken goat bleats and through my field glasses I think I see two shadowshapes. The fear of night and then a star-bed of stars (inverted garden of the sky) and we wait in vain for our quarry and someone said there was a hyena and we saw nothing and finally we untied the goat and rode back into Biskra and the Nomad dogs never stopped barking.

January 18. Snake charmers in the garden of Allah and the great Cobra that sways like a fountain in the wind and the hornèd viper that squirms sideways over the dust and the monotonous beating of tom-toms and the relationship of Cobra to Zora (or is she Viper) and would I were a Snake-Charmer!

19. Goodbye to Vieux Biskra and to the Café Maure and we see the school (bare room open to the sky) and all the children in red fezes and in the hand of the professor a long bamboo rod ("to-morrow I will stand on the hill with the rod of the Sun in my hand") to tap offenders and all they learn is the Koran.

I am ready for the North.

20. And a last morning of basking and soul into Sun and little Zora for luncheon (all three of us in the bed) and we put the earrings upon her ears, and the bracelets upon her hands and C gives her a pair of lace pretties and I perfume and she is wearing all her amulets and has added new tattoo marks in our honor and I wonder what the people in the hotel think. And the last we see of her is a small bronze hand waving goodbye from the foot of the avenue and we are glad to go and there is El-Kantara rose-gold in the sun and then darker and darker and darkness!

21. Algiers and it is a sordid city filled, like Tunis, with the riff-raff of Africa, and no boat until to-morrow, and sherry and chicken hash on toast and gazelles in the tennis court and a bottle of whiskey to make the time go.

23. Marseilles and after buying tickets to Paris ten francs left and we eat supper and the bill is fifteen francs and we promise to pay from Paris and they are not as condescending as they would have been in America.

24. Paris, and all other lands and cities dwindle into Nothingness. Paris the City of the Sun.

27. Flaubert took six years to write Madame Bovary, four years to write Salammbô, seven years to write l'Education Sentimentale. I quote the Encyclopedia: "This ruddy giant was secretly gnawn by misanthropy and disgust of life. This hatred of the bourgeois began in his childhood and developed into a kind of monomania. He despised his fellow-men, their habits, their lack of intelligence, their contempt for beauty, with a passionate scorn which has been compared to that of an ascetic monk. Flaubert's curious modes of composition favoured and were emphasized by these peculiarities—He worked in sullen solitude, sometimes occupying a week in the completion of one page; never satisfied with what he had composed, violently tormenting his brains for the best turn of a phrase, the most absolutely final adjective. It cannot be said that his incessant labors were not rewarded. His private letters show that he was not one of those to whom easy and correct language is naturally given; he gained his extraordinary perfection with the unceasing sweat of his brow. One of the most severe of academic critics admits that in all his works, and in every page of his works, Flaubert may be considered a model of style. Less perhaps than any other writer, not of France, but of modern Europe, Flaubert yields admission to the inexact, the abstract, the vaguely inapt expression which is the bane of ordinary models of composition. He never allowed a cliché to pass him, never indulgently or wearily went on, leaving behind him a phrase which "almost" expressed his meaning. Being as he is, a mixture of almost equal parts of the romanticist and the realist, the marvelous propriety of his style has been helpful to later writers of both schools, of every school—The degree and manner in which, since his death, the fame of Flaubert has extended, form an interesting chapter of literary history—Flaubert is a writer who must always appeal more to other authors than to the world at large, because the art of writing, the indefatigable pursuit of perfect expression, were always before him, and because he hated the lax felicities of improvisation as a disloyalty to the most sacred procedures of the literary artist."

January 30. Visit to Bourdelle's Atelier in the Impasse du Maine and the gigantic figures full of underlying strength and in particular the head of a serpent and also the plan for a tombstone he is going to sculpt for us.

Afterwards to A's where we found him discussing the Russian Ballet with two young musicians. How much more interesting than a talk on auction bridge or the stock market!

Burned a great candle before the Sun-Cross and burned incense before the Buddha. Am trying to find a giant candle which will burn for a week (or perhaps a wick floating in oil would be better) "The fire shall ever be kept burning upon the altar, it shall never go out."

February 1. Finished Les Croix de Bois. And above all else we who have known war must never forget war. And that is why I have the picture of a soldier's corpse nailed to the door of my library.

Wrote

SHADOW SHAPES

A log burned low within the fireplace
And friendly books upon the table lay
Around a bowl where orchids in display
Nodded their lovely heads with charming grace
At their sweet mistress dressed in filmy lace
Of gold and silver, perfumed disarray
That to the weary soldier brought dismay
And caused his boyish heart to beat apace.
Where were his friends, how envious they must be
Of him among this sheltered warmth and light
While they accursed were crawling through the wire
Cringing down downwards in the sucking mire
Or running in the rain with horrid fright
Lost in the monstrous darkness of the night.

February 4. Decided on the poison—laudanum, the name given by Paracelsus to a famous medical preparation of gold and pearls and it is ruby-colored and "one who has swallowed a toxic or lethal dose of laudanum usually passes at once into the narcotic state without any prior excitement. Intense drowsiness yields to sleep and coma which ends in death from failure of the respiration."

24. Looking down from the Pont Royal saw a man on a barge whose entire back was tattooed—a knight holding a spear astride a charger. Must have a Sun tattoed on my back but where in Paris am I to find a tattoer?

The pursuit of knowledge more adventurous than the pursuit of big game but not, no a hundred times not, as adventurous as the pursuit of Beauty (Sun-Beauty).

—Began Les Paradis Artificiels. "Toute débauche parfaite a besoin d'un parfait loisir."

March 13. Burgos before dawn and an arctic wind and the giant cathedral dark against a gibbous moon.

—The Cofre del Cid, the famous trunk which he filled with stones and sand and took to a jew usurer who lent him money believing it to be full of treasure, and there was the tomb of a man and a woman lying together in a large niche in the wall, the Lady on the inside protected, the Knight on the outside, facing outwards, protecting. And there was a Mary Magdalene attributed to Leonardo, the soft roundness of her arms, the softness of wavy hair clinging to her breast, and the voluptuousness of her ecstasy—all her soul, all her body abandoned to God. (I wonder why the Spanish do not varnish their paintings). And the marble slab in the floor in honor of the Cid (were it not for his wish to be buried with his horse Babieca, he would have been buried in the cathedral) and there were the choir stalls (dolphins and dragons, fabulous birds, gladiators, dancing girls and two little boys "ne buvez jamais d'eau.") 'As Théophile Gautier so well expressed it, these choir stalls present "unité dans l'aspect et variété infinie dans le détail, voilà le difficile problème que les artistes du moyen-âge ont presque toujours résolu avec bonheur.") Ascended to the Dome, Dome which the people of Burgos paid for by going a year without butter, and a windswept rooftop and a stone balustrade and brandy from a flask.

—To the Cartuja de Miraflores and a monk (Frey Jacinto) and his expression of horror when I asked him if he ate meat (carne). They live in stone cells and can only converse with each other three hours each week. Good place for Chatterbox Fern.

March 14. and Madrid and the Ritz and the Velasquezes (Infanta) and the Goyas, (La Maja Vestida La Maja Desnuda) and the Breughels (El Triumfo de la Muerte).

And the collection of armor at the Real Arméria and the little suit of armor for a dog to be used in boar hunting and it is a better collection of armor than at Vienna and my heart is a battle-field of pikes and helmets and gauntlets and peacock plumes and huge horse armor and shields and chain armor.

15. The Plaza de las Toros, and a parade and fanfaronnade and a red door and the bull black, farouche, who blinked for a moment at the sun, then plunged head lowered, at a crimson scarf. Four periods: the waving of the scarfs (matadors) the goring of horses (piccadors) the infuriation (banderillos) and the period of death (espada). About twenty minutes from the defiant entrance of the bull until his ignominious dragging away. Like a musical composition: allegre, andante, capricioso, fortissimo—a great symphony of color. The butterflies and the bull, and the horses and the bull (a crushing against the wall, entrails in the dust and a dagger stabbing into the brain—this is the fate of the hard-working cabhorse of Madrid) and now the attacking bull is attacked the hornèd grasshoppers thrust their colored prongs into his back—two blue, two green, two red—colored pins sprouting from a black pincushion (an enormous lavender pincushion into which I thrust the pins of my desire) and now thin streaks of blood red-black in the sun and where are the cows of the pasturage now and what is the roar of the jeering throng and who is he who advances with a red cloth? It is the Espade Lorenzo de la Torre and under the red cloth he holds a sword and to his right and to his left flutter the gorgeously-colored scarf-wings of the butterflies. And with the naked sword he sights the tired beast as a gunner sights his gun and there is a quick step forward as he plunges the sword deep into the monster's back so that only the hilt is visible in the form of a cross and there is a streaming of blood from the mouth and a final twitch of the head and a toppling over and four mules (magnificently caparisoned) drag the dead beast from the ring. And the red door swings open again and the new black bull in the center of the ring is the axle of a gorgeously-whirling wheel whose spokes are yellow and red, green and blue, orange and mauve, salmon and seagreen, fawn-colored and silver, fugitive and faëry-like weaving like dervishes, into danger, out of danger, an enormous embroidered butterfly-wheel, and then ponderous piccadors astride their bony blind-folded horses and the bull's horn dug deep to the hilt as a pin perforates paper and the banderillos again whirling like autumn leaves and the espada and the coup de grâce, and the twisted mouth like a dead fish, and the pouring of sand upon the bloodstained sand ("just as the sand-dunes heaped one upon another, hide each the first, so in life the former deeds are quickly hidden by those that follow after.")

And the third bull and the ditch-delivered, lion-hearted son of Spain who jumped from the crowd and flaunted a red cloth in the most approved-of-style and the burst of applause as he climbed back over the wall and the twelve thousand white handkerchiefs breaking like whitecaps on a black sea and the last bull and the crowd as they jumped over the wall to swarm like myriad flies around the blackblood carcass of the bull and so to the Ritz putting away bloodstained images, barring from my brain the bloodyeyed bulls (hence the word bull's eye) the bloodstained arena, the bloody entrails of butchered horses and the blood-guilty brutality of the lusting spectator. Spain I see boasts two soul sides, one represented by Frey Jacinto and the Monastery, the other by Lorenzo de la Torre and the Bull-Ring.

March 16. Segovia and the desolate granite campagna, the lonely road, the deserted villages, the chain of lowlying mountains. The austerity and sternness of Northern Spain, a sterile land without trees, without vegetation, and the porcelain and pottery factory at Segovia, and it was here that Zuloaga painted the Uncle Danielli that hangs in the Boston Museum. Would have liked to have pilfered an illuminated manuscript from the Library of the Cathedral, manuscript that contained a strange macabre painting of insects devouring a corpse. But it was chained to an iron ring in the wall.

Later in the day the Escorial built with blackgray granite, sinister, like some giant sanatorium, a sterile monument set in a rocky desert—no beauty—only a monotonous, granite mournfulness and as we approached the great entrance gate I caught a glimpse of a huge stork flapping wearily over the roof. A glacial, sepulchral coldness and a morose guide who conducted us through interminable bare rooms, along dark granite corridors, across cold and deserted courtyards. Sombreness. Once I stopped to look out a window (there are said to be eleven thousand) and gazing out I saw a solemn, colorless garden in keeping with the solemnity of the building. But the gloomiest part was the descent into the crypt (Panteon de los Reyes) where lie the buried Kings of Spain, down a long granite staircase, into the small octagonal burial-vault built directly under the high altar of the church so that when the priest elevates the host he finds himself standing directly above the dead kings (Tombs of the Touggourt Kings). Black sarcophagus and the empty tomb of Alphonse XIII (vision of Deauville and cocottes and the salle de baccara) and how many times he must be haunted by this chamber of horrors. How different this chamber which oppresses, which smothers, from the sunshine and moonlight and chaste disorder of the Cimitière de l'Abbaye de Longchamp.

And as we ascended the interminable flight of stairs I felt invisible octopus arms groping blindly in their desire to enlace and suck us back from the Sun (God spare us from being buried after the fashion of the monarchs of Spain) so that once more on sea-level I was glad of my flask and glad to omit a visit to the skulls of the martyrs and to enter instead the Library where the vellum-bound folios were turned inwards so that the gilded edges on which the titles were stamped faced outwards (le roi Dagobert a mis ses culottes à l'envers).

And at last escape from prison and the granite soul of Philippe II and out again into the Sun and the same reaction as from the bull-fight,—the damned-glad-to-be-alive feeling. Escorial in Spanish signifies refuse and it is well named and the Ritz, after this forlorn edifice, was like a faëry palace (and full of faëries). Like the word pederast better.

March 18. Toledo and the Cathedral and the House of El Greco, and the narrow streets (se prohibe el transito de coches) and the autograph of Charles the Fifth (yo rey) and Ulysses ("kiss and delighted to, kiss to see you") and a little femme de chambre who to judge by her screams was ravished during the dark hours of the night.

19. In the shadow of the cathedral and gigantones and the upper cloisters where priests and acolytes, cobblers and housewives, carpenters and tailors live in little niches giving on a large courtyard forming part of the cathedral, and down below beneath the cathedral a treasure room of gold but in the shops no Toledo blades.

20. Cordova and the courtyard of orange trees and fragrance of orange trees and the enormous mosque and the impression of an endless sea, of a slender, rose-colored sea of marble columns and the unreligiousness (from a northern point of view) of things Moorish and a tumbledown house where Columbus may have stayed and the old Roman gate and the great Guadalquivir and the old Moorish flour mills and the eating of navaranjos plucked by ourselves in the town park and the yellow genestia and the mimosa and the almond trees and towards evening the clustering whitewashed houses of Seville from whose roofs sprout grass and weeds.

21. And a warm sun-morning in the gardens of the Alcazar: fountains and flowerbeds and the touching of roses and the fragrance of oranges and restraint is an evil (why not a plunging naked into pools, why not a oneness in some sun-filled arbor?) but we did race our way through the topiary (new word for me) work of the maze and we did kiss in the sun-center and we did toss coppers to the gold-fish and afterwards we found the fountain where Maria de Padilla used to bathe while Don Pedro's courtiers showed their gallantry by drinking the water and there was the Court of the Maidens (doncellas) where in summers long ago nude ladies of the harem bathed in silver fountains or lay among the roses and there was the Doll's Court with huge blue and green vases and there was an old cedar tree enlaced by rose vines which crawled and clung even to its topmost

branch so that it looked like a tall tree of roses (white and red) but there was no war of the roses but only the gold ripples of the Sun.

—A Zurburan in which he painted himself not once but twice, then up inclined planes to the tower-top of the cathedral and the sexton tolled the bell and when I asked him why, he replied that someone had died in the city, but the Guadalquivir still continued to pour its silver through the gold of the fields ("in Heine's case, at least, poured the wine of translation from the golden into the silver cup. O. W.") and below, black specks still crawled and scurried as if nothing had happened. But there was a dove who flew into a cloud and perhaps this was the departing soul. And after tea with Alice Gould (she is making a minute study of Columbus) to the Bibliotheca Columbina and there were the signs of the Zodiac (best word in the Z's) in a book of hours, and ancient maps, and Columbus' autograph, and a curious treatise on Machina Tormentaria.

March 22. Alone to the Cock-Fight (Combatos Gallos) and rabble peering into a slit through the wall and se prohibe orinar scrawled in bold black letters on the white-washed wall and a broken chaise percée on a pile of bricks and a cripple with an enormous green waterpot watering the street and I invited my cab-driver to come with me and I was glad I had my brass knuckles. A balcony that looked down on a small ring and the weighing of game-cocks upon large scales (over the ring) suspended from the ceiling. A gong and the cocks were set down in the ring and bookmakers shouted odds and there were tense underworld faces and all the seriousness of a bull-fight and all the excitement. Gray and green, white and black, purple and yellow I was the only one there without a cap. There were no women. For perhaps a minute the combatants eyed each other, wings widespread, bodies elongated, and their heads not more than an inch apart (old English print). Both birds clipped for action, and one could see that they had gone through a long training for the momentous occasion. One white the other black, it was not difficult to wager a peseta with my cab-driver and another with a morose individual who informed me in broken French that he had been stoker on a tramp steamer. Chose Black. Peck peck peck a peck a peck peck like the tapping of a woodpecker ever searching for throat and eye and head until combs began to show red and the White was spattered with blood. Courage and speed—no longer crowing at the sun, no longer covering some squawking hen but attacking peck a peck peck and pinching of throat and coxscomb peck peck and a man garbed in black, one having high authority, and whose duty lay in regarding the tall sand-glass fastened to the iron rail of the ring and the fight was to last twenty minutes (about the time of a bull-fight) and when one thinks of prize-fighters and their intermissions every two or three minutes one wonders at the endurance and pluck of the birds who go at it from the beginning hammer and tongs peck a peck peck—but as the fight neared the finish they began to tire and instead of darting at each other they waddled like ducks to the charge and then the cruelty of the sport with the almost-blindness of the birds—strutting past each other, pecking at space, their heads not an inch apart, searching with bloodied, unseeing eyes. Then they would find each other and peck a peck peck like a trip-hammer and now body-weight began to count and often one bird and often the other was pushed into the rails. Unsteadily Black (a white feather stuck in his eye) sought White and unsteadily (a black feather stuck in his eye) White sought Black—like a game of blindman's buff, and the sand in the hour-glass had almost run out and White was groggy and sought shelter under Black's wing or leaned unsteadily against the rails until Black, his mouth full of white feathers attacked throat and head, coxscomb and neck until White sank like a limp rag upon the mat and Black was conqueror and Night has conquered Day and Darkness shall rule over Light.

March 23. From Seville to Granada along mountainsides powdered with gray-green olive trees, past the Rock of the Lovers, along fields of ploughed red earth, nine hours in the car made bearable by my flask and my pipe. Granada and the Alhambra with C at Sunset and the influence of the Moors and a run down a wood road into a hot bath.

24. And it has begun to snow and where are the poets and princesses in the Court of the Lions (Where are the Lions? Where are the Lions?) and the Hall of the Two Sisters (an arctic wind) and I draw my head snail-fashion into the warmth of my scarf, and can the heart thus be drawn into the warmth of the soul, or is the heart flame and the soul arctic, and there were arabesques (stone embroidery) and slender delicate columns (adolescent phalluses) and the Sultan and Sultana's bathroom (Paris architects please copy) and a tower and more wind and more snow and in the afternoon the cathedral and the tomb of Ferdinand and Isabella. ("et leurs cendres reposent dans la même urne")

25. To the Garden of the Generalife to toss a coin into a fountain (silver into gold, soul into sun) and the sunnygolden arches of crystal water swaying gently in the breeze (Zora and the Cobra) and there was a cypress tree (Cyprès de la Sultana) six hundred years old.

26. On the train to Madrid read Irving "In Murcia, Valencia, and other eastern provinces, men of the highest rank might be seen in public bareheaded. The warrior King, Aben Hud never wore a turban, neither did his rival and competitor Al Hamar, the founder of the Alhambra." Argument for my never wearing a hat (to-morrow I will stand on the top of the hill with the rod of the Sun in my hand.)

After crawling through Don Quixote country, Madrid and the Ritz, and once more in touch with the world.

28. Barcelona and the cloisters of the cathedral and swans in a large cloister fountain (why have white swans black beaks and black swans red?)

And a Stravinsky concert conducted by himself (he is at the Ritz) and the audience behaved atrociously and I forgot to say that to-day Mamma bought me a silver goblet (had she known for what purpose!)

March 29. Montserrat and as dreary as my childhood Montserrat was gay and I lit the giant candle in the monastery and performed rites to the Sun.

30. Spain arid and morne, France fertile and belle and Carcassonne a castle of gold and my soul is a castle of gold and C is Queen of the Castle and it is a Sun Castle.

April 1. The doddering guardian in the apse. "Voilà," he began pointing upwards "un supplicié les jambes repliées en arrière. Et au milieu un renard et à gauche un hibou. Ensuite à droite une salamandre et au milieu une truie allaitant sa portée et à gauche un ours, et là—Hercule qui exprime la force. A coté un prêtre qui exprime la douleur et ensuite deux anges qui portent une banderole et là un chien, et un loup là. Un chien en arrêt et un aigle à coté. Dans le coin, un prisonnier une chaîne au cou—il est assis sur un boulet. Là c'est un moine qui réfléchit—il a la tête sur la main. Voilà une espèce de je ne sais quoi. Au milieu un corps de boeuf et à coté un moine, et là un singe à queue de lézard. Dans le coin une femme qui cueille des glands et qui les met dans son tablier. Et là enfin, une soeur qui réfléchit" and am I the hibou or the wolf or the soeur qui réfléchit?

—The ramparts, and the sun is strong and lizards are basking in the crannies of the wall and I look down from the battlements over the new city and upon the steep, grassy slope, a girl is digging up dandelions while a dirty-faced tot ("a totty in her courses") clings tenaciously to her skirts hampering her labors. Red slippers and black stockings and the glint of a knife in the Sun and a herd of goats and a brushwood fire and the watching of her shadow and the mediaevalness of the ramparts and the strong interior feeling and Carcassonne perhaps the outward symbol of the soul.

6. Paris, and all other lands and cities dwindle to Nothingness. Paris the City of the Sun.

9. Baudelaire's Birthday and wrote in his honor a Sonnet

> I think I understand you Baudelaire
> With all your strangeness and perverted ways
> You whose fierce hatred of dull working days
> Led you to seek your macabre vision there
> Where shrouded night came creeping to ensnare
> Your phantom-fevered brain, with subtle maze
> Of decomposèd loves, remorse, dismays
> And all the gnawing of a world's despair.
>
> Within my soul you've set your blackest flag
> And made my disillusioned heart your tomb,
> My mind which once was young and virginal

Shadows of the Sun

Is now a swamp, a spleenfilled pregnant womb
Of things abominable; things androgynal
Flowers of Dissolution, Fleurs du Mal.

April 10. Bought two Dutch pictures (influence of the Prado) winter and snow on the ground and skating and gray-green for the ice and gray-white for the snow and gray-brown for the mill in the background and dull reds and dull blues for the skaters.

And after supper La Nuit Ensorcelée (Chopin) with the costumes and scenery by Bakst.

12. Taxicabs, telephones, typewriters, "and the thousand natural shocks that flesh is heir to" give no time for meditation—and we are like wind-swept insects clinging for a brief moment to a blade of grass only to be blown on again and on and on across the fields of life. And I am nervous and high-strung to-day as I scurry about here and there, doing this and that with feverish haste. To what purpose?

—But the Mazarin Library is an oasis in the heart of Paris. For a rendez vous. With whom? (Zora par exemple and I wonder if she is still in Biskra and I wonder.)

—Bought C a Persian bowl, pale blue with figures drawn in black. "And that inverted bowl."

—Ate a tomato to-day for the first time.

19. Noon. Good advice from W.V.R.B. to set aside regular hours for work and to stick to them religiously. And how Anthony Trollope when he had finished a three volume novel at eleven o'clock, instead of stopping work for the day, began immediately upon a new book until his allotted time was up. Suggested I read Rimbaud. Wish I could buy him the Baudelaire Letter.

Four o'clock. Bought W.V.R.B. the Baudelaire Letter and for C a Chinese Wood-Carving.

20. It is really too tremendously nice of you. The letter is wonderful. Think of poor Baudelaire offering the MS of Les Fleurs du Mal for 400 francs and not even getting an answer!— [24]

23. Rat day and the Rat [25] comes in from Saint-Cloud and at luncheon she suddenly asks: "What is the dirtiest piece of furniture in the house?" Answer: the bureau for it never changes its drawers!

But listen to Rimbaud at the age of eight: "—ces poètes-là, voyez-vous, ne sont pas d'ici-bas; laissez-les vivre leur vie étrange, laissez-les avoir froid et faim, laissez-les courir, aimer et chanter; ils sont aussi riches que Jacques Coeur, tous ces fols enfants, car ils ont des rimes pleins l'âme, des rimes qui rient et qui pleurent, qui nous font rire et pleurer: laissez-les vivre! Dieu bénit tous les miséricordieux, et le monde bénit les poètes!"

24. "It is rather difficult to write as there is a large green parrot sitting on my head" this from G and she is just back from India where she has been hunting tigers in the jungle and she described the funeral pyres by the sacred Ganges that burn day and night while the hungry crocodiles wait for the remains, and the English (f them, they are always interfering wherever they go) have forbidden the widows to fling themselves upon their husbands' pyres.

April 25. Baudelaire's grave is in the Montparnasse Cemetery three hundred yards from our door—"c'est le massif, là-bas, le long du mur" said the gendarme and not having any flowers we laid a gold coin at the foot of the grave.

Then across the City to the Père-Lachaise to the Tomb of Oscar Wilde (given by a Lady and the work of Jacob Epstein) and into the stone are cut these words from the book of Job:

> "Verbis meis addere nihil audebunt
> et super illos stillabat eloquium meum."
> (After my words they spake not again;
> and my speech dropped upon them)

and then four lines from The Ballad of Reading Gaol

> "And Alien tears will fill for him
> Pity's long broken urn
> For his mourners will be outcast men
> And outcasts always mourn."

And here we laid narcissi. (Marie Bashkirtseff)

30. Day ruined by the Sea-Lions. Gave her a bet to place on Black Sun but when the horse won and I asked for the profit she calmly stated that the bet had never been placed and when I asked her why she hadn't told me this before the race she said she had forgotten. Certain it was a "frameup" arranged by her and the bookmaker, dishonesty that cost us $100 or a flask of concentrated Attar of Roses (Zagha) and it proves again that in all business as well as in all pleasure one should deal with the *best* people and go to the *best* places (Signed S.V.R.C.) and I am furious and I bannish Sea-Lions from the pavillon henceforth and forevermore and fortunately "une plaie d'argent ne tue jamais."

May 1. Began Jane Austen: "The gentleman offered his services, and perceiving that her modesty declined what her situation rendered necessary, took her up in his arms without farther delay and carried her down the hill." How quaint after Rimbaud "Un grand vaisseau d'or, au-dessus de moi, agite ses pavillons multicolores sous les brises du matin. J'ai créé toutes les fêtes, tous les triomphes, tous les drames. J'ai essayé d'inventer de nouvelles fleurs, de nouveaux astres, de nouvelles chairs, de nouvelles langues."

12. X to marry Y. Beauty and the Beast again but if beauty gives herself to the beast it can only mean that she has a mixture of bestiality in her beauty.

May 13. In the morning sun to Vaux-le-Vicomte and the many-fountained gardens and green swards and we crossed an artificial lake in a scow and there was a flowered hillside on whose crest stood a gigantic statue of Hercules and down the hill again to undress and so head first into the coldness of a fountain and sun-gold into the gold of the Sun (at such times should like to be a girl for a girl is capable of giving herself more than a man).

If I lived in the Château I should dive from my bedroom window every morning into the moat and swim in sunripples around the building and climb back again by means of a rope ladder and at night I should have the drawbridge raised and to hell with a country where they are building glass-houses (people in glass-houses should not take baths in the day time) because glass is cheaper than lumber.

Then Fontainbleau and orange blossoms in the Sun and Courances and the Château of the Marquis de Ganay and the sadness of the stables: the empty stalls and the old stableman; and the late afternoon sun flickering into the harness-room—bridles and bits, reins and whips, the brass polished as in the vanished days and the smell of used leather—and there were the old coaching prints. The carriages stood in a sad row and there was a smart phaeton which in its hour must have made a great display behind high stepping steeds. But all that has faded and machinery has stamped its heel of ugliness upon the unromantic world.

And in the Château there was a boudoir with a tin tub on a raised platform beside a table à raser at which Monsieur could shave as he gazed upon the loveliness of Madame in her bath, and through a window I could see a flock of sheep and a tree reflected in a pool (C the tree reflected in the pool of my soul) and birds sang and so in the car back to Paris.

25. Bought two race-horses: Dom Luco and Catilina.

June 3. Bought a mongrel puppy from a washerwoman and he has no tail and he is six weeks old and we christen him Corydon.

7. Chantilly and saw Catilina who looked like a giraffe (Dom Luco was superb) and asked Steve Donoghue to autograph "Just My Story" before he won the Prix de Diane.

12. Read a book by Haraucourt on the Cluny. From the time of Charlemagne to the Seventeenth Century tout le monde couchait nu et rarement on couchait seul.

Au milieu du seizième siècle, Paris ne connaissait encore que deux carrosses, l'un appartenant à la Reine, l'autre à la Maîtresse du Roi. Plus tard, nous voyons Charles Neuf en interdire l'emploi dans les rues de Paris. Henri Quatre n'en possède qu'un seul et, par une lettre à Sully, il s'excuse de ne pouvoir sortir, la Reine ayant pris le carrosse.

Les gentilshommes étaient sans cesse à cheval et les dames continuaient à monter en croupe, comme au moyen-âge; souvent les plus hautes princesses se rendaient ainsi aux fêtes royales du Louvre.

L'usage des fourchettes est fort récent; au milieu du seizième siècle on mangeait encore avec les doigts et l'on se servait au plat commun; les personnes les plus considérables y puisaient les premières; avant le repas chacun se lavait les mains à la table même et ostensiblement, afin de donner à tous les convives l'assurance de sa propreté, à la fin du repas on se lavait de nouveau.

Les cartes à jouer nous ont valu l'invention de l'imprimerie; en 1392, le roi Charles VI était devenu fou, on essaya de le distraire avec des cartes, auxquelles il prit goût; aussitôt la fantaisie publique, par imitation, se passionna pour cet amusement, mais les cartes peintes coûtaient fort cher; on eût alors l'idée de graver les images sur des planches de bois qu'on noircissait d'encre et qu'on appliquait ensuite sur le vélin.

Généralement, et même dans les habitations princières ou royales, on se contentait de jeter les ordures par les fenêtres, ou même de les verser devant la porte. Dans les galeries du Louvre, grâce à leurs galeries de statues, dans les escaliers magnifiques, grâce à leurs paliers, dans les chambres, grâce à leurs amples cheminées, les seigneurs et les grandes dames de la Renaissance trouvaient leur retrait ordinaire.

Les Ceintures de Chasteté—

June 13. Fed Ula the female monkey three gin fizzes and she ran up and down a rope ladder, and the Clever Girl was christened by a Russian Princess I should have liked to have violated and there were strawberry gin fizzes and drunken dancing and I was fortunate to get home.

14. Read from Guillaume Apollinaire's Fin de Babylone: "Victrix examina curieusement le corps de la jeune fille. Il y avait, gravés des seins aux talons, des ornements divers, fruits, fleurs, profils humains. Ces derniers semblaient se concentrer vers le centre rond et poli. Là, parmi de gracieuses arabesques, trois jambes humaines étaient dessinées, orientées dans le même sens autour d'un point situé à une distance entre le nombril et le temple de la virginité;" and I am more than ever anxious to be tattoed, it has almost become an obsession. (Biskra didn't count.)

15. Jehanne d'Arc and a boyish girl in a suit of gold-link armour and more than ever I am a Mystic.

17. Etretat and a plunge in the sea and we take an absurd little house (it was a gun emplacement during the war and looks, from a distance, like a lump of sugar) on a little hill above the town and there were fishing-smacks drawn up on the beach and a tramp steamer out at sea (black insect crawling across the setting sun) and I began Chaucer's Legend of Good Women: Cleopatra, Thisbé, Dido, Lucretia—these four killed themselves.

18. Red-brown sails and a flock of sheep have more influence on the soul than churches and the word of preachers and on the highest cliff I build an altar to the Sun and call upon the name of the Sun.

Shadows of the Sun

July 1. I offer champagne and it is her first glass and she is nubile and I like candlelight at night and there is the sound of the sea and what is this dream that I have dreamed?

2. Basking naked on the roof and Nubile to tea and a reading about Arms and Armour and Asceticism in the Encyclopedia, and there is a lonely farmhouse made of stone standing across the valley on the golf links and around it browse sheep (brown stars around a grey moon) and it is an altar for strange prayers and after supper shyness and her brown eyes like marbles.

5. And we sat upon the roof and she has a delicate nuque and to corrupt the young is a temptation and there was a red-gold moon like a princess rising from her bed of gray fog and there was a prayer towards the farmhouse on the hill which passed through the farmhouse as sand through a sieve and entered the bed of the red-gold moon and entered the red-gold moon, and was this disloyal to the Sun?

8. Règlement de la Maison: (sign in the little hotel)

1° Le locataire qui laisse après son départ quelque objet redoit 0 fr. 10 par jour pour frais de garde.

2° On est prié de dire son nom, en rentrant le soir, après l'extinction du gaz.

3° Le tapage est formellement interdit, un locataire causant du scandale pourra être renvoyé sur le champ.

4° On est prié de parler à voix basse dans les chambres passé dix heures.

5° Il est defendu de faire entrer quelqu'un coucher avec soi—

The beach and a bathe and Nubile sat on the roof while I dressed and afterwards we danced and afterwards I dragged the mattress upon the roof and waved goodnight to her (she is at the villa below) and so to sleep under the stars under the sun (invisible) under the moon and the eleven stars.

9. And another goodnight from the roof-top and a disappearing under blankets and where is C and why is the world so desperately sad and why do the waves never cease beating against the beach?

10. And we danced after supper and home along the beach and there was a fog-horn and a heavy fog creeping in from the sea and up brick steps (and little Barbara-Jane to carry up the staircase in the rain) to the Villa des Rochers and it was black and behind us we could hear the waves sucking the stones on the beach and through fog across the silent garden and into the black house and where is C and why is the world so desperately sad (ce mal d'être deux) and why do the waves never cease beating against the beach?

11. Books from Quaritch: Serpent-Worship and Animals of No Importance and in the Encyclopedia Tree Worship and Phallic Worship and Serpent-Worship and Fire-Worship and Ancestor-Worship and the Worship of the Sun. I am a Worshipper of the Sun.

15. The Man from Siam describes fish-fighting in Siam: how these rainbow-colored fish are put in a huge bottle and how they fight to the death and how it is as cruel as the bull-fight or the cock-fight, but is anything as cruel as the fight between the body and the soul?

July 20. The remark is the knife penduluming across the open wound of my heart.

21. Between tea-time and midnight read Dorian Gray. "Nothing can cure the soul but the senses, just as nothing can cure the senses but the soul."

24. Sunmyth, sunworship, sungod, sunbox, sundried, sunfish, sunflower, sunbonnet, sunshade, sundial, sunbird, sunbath, sunbeam, sunrise, sunset, sundown, sun-ripple, sunlight, sunburied, sunsuffused, sunembroidered, sunblind, sunwarm, sunburst, suntreader, sunlike, sunwards.

Gave C a frail-gold Persian scarf embroidered with rampant lions and frail gazelles, all in gold, with a fringe of pale-gold roses.

25. Christened and launched the catamaran Caresse the real C breaking a bottle of champagne across the bow. (where is the Russian princess and Ula the monkey?) and it is painted bright orange with white suns fore and aft and it is built for two and it costs $15 and it is light as a feather and out at sea a tramp steamer tosses and plunges by, the sun shining on its red iron sides, and is my heart also a freight boat? (carrying gold to the Sun).

27. All last night the wind cried to the waves, all night the waves thundered upon the shore, all night the rain made tempest with the wind and bed was the inner centre of the world. And C the flower in the bed (hence flowerbed).

And this morning the fishermen pulled at the creaking windlasses and drew their fishing smack high and dry and from the Casino the red flag warned bathers not to bathe and L went in to the consternation of the lifeguards and I admired his folly (courageous as so many foolish things are) and it was for Miss Stone and did not Leander swim the Hellespont night after night to see the beautiful Hero? But L did not perish and his Lady did not have to drown herself in the sea. And we stood upon the beach and marvelled at the madness of the storm and the waves crumbled on the pebbled beach and with a sucking-sound the undertow sucked back and the surf was a white angriness between two giants (the cliffs) and at night a sheet of blackness covered the beach and men carrying lanterns ran up and down and there was the broad yellow beam of the lighthouse stabbing like a knife the black brain of the sea and faintly from the ball-room came the incongruous music of the dance (de la littérature again).

30. Sat next a pretty girl (she came in out of the storm in a white polo coat) and it was a dinner-party and I liked the way she used the word 'nakedness' and of stepchildren (she is a step-child herself) she made the wistful remark that they were the reminders, hélas, of the dreadful ogres and the fearful monsters of the past (like the Fairy-Tale stories) and her husband asked C where she had lost her virginity, and she told him at the Circus and everyone danced and we played (each person contributing 100 francs)

Marguerite where each person took a name "Mademoiselle" "Un peu" "Madame" "Beaucoup" and so forth and we took a daisy and plucked the petals and L won four hundred francs and it was late and I forgot Nubile.

August 1. Wrote a Sonnet for C

> Among the shadows in a forest dense
> The Druid priests came seeking sapience
> Beneath the sacred oak. And unafraid
> The ancient Hindus of the phallus made
> Their god. In India a serpent King
> Held sway and in the Persian rites they sing
> Songs to the Sun. The Christians mourn the loss
> Of Jesus Christ who died upon the cross.

> Each soul must have its god so I choose thee
> To take the place of sun and moon and stars
> To be for me the odor of the rose
> To be for me the turquoise of the sea
> To be for me the nectar in the jars
> Of magic love. In thee I seek repose.

3. S depresses me. If only women realized the charm of being chaste—how chasteness is almost as important as beauty and how it is the axle of the wheel of beauty.

"Who can find a virtuous woman? for her price is far above rubies."

4. In the boat two miles straight out to sea, and the sea entered my soul silver-green and the Sun is the gate to Infinity; and I read in the Bible: "Seeing that which now is in the days to come shall all be forgotten" and I drank a cocktail with the girl of the white polo coat and she has a charming way of using her hands when she talks (and when she . . .?)

6. Paris. As the little waif in the park-bench scene in Liliom, or kneeling (mystical) in gold armour (physical) in Jehanne d'Arc?

8. Champagne and Orchids.

9. and to the Saint Lazare to say goodbye to Little Nubile and "on est si peu de chose devant l'immensité du monde" and I go to A's and "il y a un monsieur qui dort" (if only we all could dort Always) and I hate summers in France and I drink a whiskey and all is desolation. (letter in gray)

10. Le monsieur qui dort is more depressed than I am and his philosophy of life is that we are put into this world to see how much punishment we can stand and that when we can't stand any more we die. Far wiser to pluck the rich dark clusters of the Vine of Death. (the one anodyne for torture and despair).

Read Chamber Music. Read Pot of Earth. Read Tulips and Chimneys.
Ary the Hound of the Baskervilles, Marie the Maid, and A, B and C

playing at the double piano and rose-petals scattered all over the floor.

August 14. Prayers under the graygreen water into a gray sun and Saint Claire for supper along the quiet country lane and there was the smell of milk and green trees and Corydon [26] is a dungdevourer. (I am a sundevourer)

Another day is over and I am glad.

Why is it that in spite of our mistakes we never wish to live our lives over again? Semper avanti!

20. And it is always better that the woman should reach safety before the man (beginning of a letter to M).

A basketful of flowers in our thoughts and because they are invisible they are everlasting (end of a letter to M.)

21. I wonder how many rainbows there are in the world at once? (I wonder how many sunbows there are in the soul at once?)

Billiards with the Count and a painfully slow walk to Saint Claire and more billiards and the Count in the sea looked like a Neptune his hair and his beard silver in the sun and C pretty and petite was a Nereid.

27. Wrote Fierté.

> And if I lie it is because I hate
> To bare my heart to those who desecrate
> The beauty of the world. I disapprove
> Of revelation and I seek to prove
> By secret rites a man may stand alone
> Need not depend upon the dull touchstone
> Of servile mobs. Silence is always best
> And I prefer a scornful, lonely quest.
> But should you care I would so crush for you
> This ungessed heart that you might take and taste
> With parted lips its dark and purple wine
> And fill your mouth with my mad love which drew
> Around your frailness, garments strangely chaste
> As silver moons and suns incarnadine.

29. Seven miles up and down cliffs to the Phare and back again and the wind shrieked and the tide was coming in and there was a sucking sound, and it was sunless and drear and desolate, and we were glad to get home again.

And there was Algebra and a Lady-Harpist and a vast amount of drinking and dawn was breaking as we climbed wearily up the hill to bed. How many dawns before the Real Dawn?

30. Last bask on the roof, last seabathe, and last supper at Saint Claire and there was 1811 brandy and the dogs gamboled and Corydon scoured for immondice (coprophagous) and so farewell to Grazer the cow and farewell to the red poppies clustering against the dark fir trees and to the dahlias and the phlox that reminded me so much of our garden at the Apple Trees and farewell to Le Manoir of Saint Claire and a kissing and a being kissed and sun-oneness into the setting sun. Sunsetcolored Hour.

September 3. A hot-water bottle and a purse ("tout est plaisir quand on aime") and it is all green and gold and I smoked my pipe in a hot bath. How many *real* things in life we have undone.

4. C comes back to-morrow and this morning I wrote

INSEPARATE

I am away, away-away from you
So far away, and yet it does not seem
The awful thing that oftentimes we knew
Before we knew that love was not a dream
But something more of more substantial worth
That mocks the pain of parting and believes
In everlasting oneness on this earth,
As in the world to come. No longer grieves
My soul. We are like water and the wave
Inseparate and though we travel far
Down everwidening ways yet are we brave
—I sometimes think that when we are apart
You lie more closely-cradled in my heart.

8. Installed for the Autumn at the Goya (Faubourg Saint-Honoré) and there is a miraculous bathroom (black and gold) and Spanish twin beds and an odor of richness and a balcony in the sun and we are high up and it is like being in a fortress.

12. My totem to-day is the wolf, the lone timber wolf baying his rune to the frozen moon (Maitab the Moon). Fiercer than the Evening Wolves. Vulture.

17. The Montmartre: Oysters and caviar, champagne and whiskey, cocaine and dancing, and at gray dawn Les Halles and the farmwagons and the wheelbarrows and the crates of fruit and the vegetables and the flowers and with a Faery Princess to the silver-tarnished Lac in the Bois.

18. And at four o'clock a hot bath and oysters and La Figlia Che Piange (T. S. Eliot).

"Stand on the highest pavement of the stair
Lean on a garden urn—
Weave, weave the sunlight in your hair
Clasp your flowers to you with a pained surprise
Fling them to the ground and turn
With a fugitive resentment in your eyes
But weave, weave the sunlight in your hair."

and Y and Z appear and take a bath together and B appears and smells salts and so another day is over and shall we thank the Sun-God?

September 21. As we were eating breakfast the telephone rang to announce "Catilina est mort à l'entraînement." (The only horse I was never afraid of—pauvre bête).

Dropped water bombs with the Wretch from our balcony and scored a direct hit. Red Umbrella.

October 3. To the Circus (first time since my birthday in 1907) and we were very bored until four of the prettiest Spanish girls came on for a song and dance and their costumes were very fresh and their songs very gay and it was a thousand times more fun than the dancing we saw in Spain and afterwards we went behind the scenes and invited them to go out with us for a drink and we all got into a taxicab including an aged mother and we went to the Café de la Paix and all drank hot chocolate and there was a little brother and they came from Valencia and their names were Adelia, Amelia, Carini, Marini and Antonio.

4. Vicomte de M (deux mots) here to tell me his woes and we drank Xérès and the telephone rang as usual and I didn't answer it and he couldn't understand and he couldn't understand why I never read the newspapers ("Charles X en ordonnant la suppression des journaux rendait un grand service aux arts et à la civilisation") and he asked if I still never wore a hat (et en hiver vous ne vous enrhumez pas?) and his woes were singularly uninteresting and after he left, C reappeared from a hot bath and we drank a bottle of champagne and went to bed.

8. A cold gray day with winter in the air and the days are growing short and there is a wood-fire crackling in my soul and I bought from Belin on the Quai Voltaire a little and very expensive volume Les Amours de Céphale et Procris—and there were dead leaves and old statues in sunken gardens and shadows in the Tuileries. Et toujours les fontaines qui jaillissent (pour se donner?).

11. Dead leaves underfoot and the smell of woodsmoke and the pale autumn-gold of the Sun and the security of the Goya.

24. Bought a Corot Letter and Lent D $250 to marry his Lady of the Harp. And to-day played a horse called Man in the Moon and he lost and if it had been called Girl in the Sun would she have won?

Wrote

CHINESE JADE

As I was strolling down the Rue de Beaune
I spied within an antique shop a horse
Elaborately carved in pale jade stone
Combien vaut-il? Dix mille. Pas cher. Of course
I only had a mille. I went away.

That afternoon at Longchamp in the rain
I played my thousand francs on Faraway
Who ran against Vierge Folle and Weathervane,
Bangor and London Fog and Flowerbed
The favorite. My choice at ten to one.
Now up the stretch they come, Bangor ahead
Now London Fog. Then Faraway. I've won!
So to the shop my pockets filled with gold
To find the horse of jade had just been sold!

October 25. At Longchamp played ten thousand francs on Tricard in the Prix Gladiateur and he was beaten by a neck and I wired to Strata to borrow a thousand dollars and again the saying "une plaie d'argent ne tue jamais" and if it is awful to consider the follies we have done is it not a hundred times more awful to consider the follies we are going to do.

27. Nineteen Rue de Lille. [27]

31. Gold and red and brown are the leaves on the ground and it is a gray day and our black Dom Luco gallops out to the post (Casaque Grixe, Croix de Malte Rose, Toque Noire) and twenty-two horses ran and we were twenty-second and afterwards to the Cimetière de l'Abbaye de Longchamp.

November 1. At W.V.R.B's after dinner opened a book on Italian Gardens (Edith Wharton) and read on the flyleaf "with the compliments of the author" with an exclamation mark and in that exclamation mark lies a Tale.

3. Naïveness in a Letter. [28] "There are at least ten girls in here trying to do some studying, and each one yelling at once, How do you do this, and how do you do that. It's quite hot. You know that expression, n'est-ce pas? See how good I'm getting in French. My roommate has just finished doing French for me so I guess I had better copy it. This doesn't happen every day, but to-day I had unusually a lot of studying, and the French was very hard.

All the windows are open and a skunk is just outside. I wish letters wouldn't take so long to get from here to you.

All the Sardines (that's me and my three other room-mates) go around with cigarette-pipes but not lighted in our mouths and white sailor pants and middies and blazers and you can see us a mile away."

4. Dom Luco runs in the sun, Dom Luco runs in the rain, but Dom Luco never wins. I only wish he would tomber mort à entraînement and then we could collect the insurance.

The painters and plumbers are still painting and plumbing, the graphaphone is playing (A Pretty Girl is Like a Melody) Madeleine is putting on rouge (what a way for a nurse to act) the Wretch is playing at dolls, the fire is merrying, the champagne is sparkling and C (A Pretty Girl is Like a Melody) is reading in bed and all is security and it is easy to forget the nothingness of Dom Luco and the rain splashes down in the Rue de Lille and I am strong in the stronghold of my soul. (A ringaround of weaving red-gold like the swirling hair of our Henner Nymph.)

November 5. (that damn mother of his ruined his life) came on for the wedding and he never spoke a word as her boat backed out of the pier and she could see his white face (her face like a pale gardenia against the blue background that was the night) (M.A. not M.O.) looking up at her from the crowd at the end of the wharf (il est dangereux de se pencher en dehors).

6. P and G (announced as the duc and duchesse de La Rochefoucauld) and L, and I was disappointed in L (six feet and sixteen not a happy combination) but she did say of Picasso "Yes, he paints what he thinks" and Absinthe was the order of the day ("use a little wine for thy stomach's sake.")

7. Chez Prunier and at the next table the loveliest child with long innocent hair and softest eyes and young goldenness and we drove all over Paris trying to find a box of candy for her and we finally discovered an enormous one and I gave it to the vestiaire (pour Mademoiselle Charmante) and we were an hour late to the theatre and all through the performance (Revue Nègre) I kept thinking of her and what a contrast between Joséphine Baker and Mademoiselle Charmante. Black and White. Peck a peck peck. "Imperthnthnthnthnthn. Haltyaltyaltyall."

15. Went out to buy silk pyjamas but came back with a first edition of Les Illuminations very rare as there were only two hundred copies edited by Verlaine and the price was five hundred francs.

And to-day with the Wretch I placed the Skull in the Donjon.

Seven years ago to-night, with other soldiers in a cave in Tartiers and I remember it so well how cold the moon was and how much rum we drank to keep warm.

16. Read La Folie Erotique: C'est ainsi qu'un jour, jouant au billard, il s'était oublié jusqu'au point d'uriner dans le paletot d'un de ses deux collègues.

Gilles de Retz se livra pendant quatorze années à des orgies abominables, dans lesquelles il fit massacrer plus de huit cents enfants? and he admitted in a letter to Charles VII how he *almost* killed the Dauphin who eventually became Louis XI.

And the Marquis de Sade qui prétendait que, dans les relations sexuelles, le plaisir de l'un se mesurait aux souffrances de l'autre, and his extraordinary conception and carrying out of the idea of "une chaîne interminable de pédérastes, franchissant un mur pour redescendre de l'autre coté, sans aucune solution de continuité." I quote twice more, the first would make a remarkable subject for a poem "il (I forget who 'il' is) suppose que de temps en temps, par une méprise du Créateur, une âme de femme se trouve incluse dans le corps d'un homme" (and I suppose vice-versa). This is of great interest.

The second "Périandre, tyran de Corinth, après avoir fait mourir sa femme Mélita, eut des rapports sexuels avec le cadavre. Ce nécrophile historique a eu des émules à toutes les époques."

If the wine has vanished from the urn is the urn any less chaste? If the shadows have vanished from the Sun (no past) is the Sun any less chaste?

November 19. Bought a first edition of Les Fleurs du Mal for twelve hundred francs from B and B showed me a letter from Goops a chef-d'oeuvre dated April 2 and postmarked late in July. "Dear B, I have just returned from Boston where S showed me a telegram saying you wished to come home. Why you dirty coal heaver, you counterfeit cook, you lousy bastard, you don't know when you're well off. If you want a change why don't you get yourself locked up in La Santé for a couple of weeks. That's the difference between Paris and New York. You can have a better time for a 100 francs in Paris than you can have here for $50. I know, believe me. Here I am willing to cut off my right arm to get get back again and you are spending money telegraphing for a job over here. That dough should have been spent in a bistro. This is the god-damnest country I was ever in. Nothing but mockies and bum grog. You'd be there about 2 weeks and then you'd get homesick. Anybody who has lived a couple of years on the other side never will be contented with life over here. Only the saps who go across for two weeks are glad to get back. Now let me tell you something for your own good—if you never come back it will be too soon, as you won't be able to work here the way you have worked over there. You might think you can, but I know better. I've tried it and made a failure of everything I've tackled. One can work 15 hours a day over there and not feel it as much as 8 hours here. There's a big difference, believe me. Everybody says you're a Mug to even try to come back. Even D says you're a chump, G III says you're crazy, and Vulture says you're a god-damn fool. I shall tell you what I think of you when I see you. Well I am getting tired of writing and will now hit the hay.
Yours with sincere affection Goops

22. Wrote a twin poem to the Young Queen (which is the soul) called Salammbô (which is the body).

To an exhibition of Léon Bakst. A great artist. Liked in particular a red water-color, a Salomé, and a Cendrillon. Not to forget the Nuit Ensorcelée (April).

All day in the street the hawkers hawk their wares "marchand d'habits, chiffons, ferrailles à vendre" and at night in a glass of brandy a toast in honor of the day (the day of the barrage at Verdun, the day S was wounded) and I smoked my pipe which has become almost a religious act, almost a prayer.

Black pyjamas and a white bunny coat (door-keepers for the ark—of the Sun bien entendu).

27. With C to the Tuileries and in one of the fountains an inventor was experimenting with a toy steamboat which ran by real steam. It was brass-plated, about two feet long, and real steam issued from a diminutive smoke-

stack. Cold gray water and red goldfish. The inventor turned towards us with a wonderful smile "voilà quatre ans que je travaille dessus." To hell with banking.

November 29. The Bois. Crumbs to the swans (why again have white swans black beaks black swans red and would red have white?) and there was a dark gold sun back of dark fir trees like a Redon eye looking over a hedge and there were dead, damp leaves underfoot and the aroma of smoke and the stark, naked trees and we met the Count and he came to tea (5-9) and five glasses of absinthe ("use a little wine for thy stomach's sake") and many stories heard before and the majesticness of his head with his silver hair and his square beard. Neptune. And the Nereid.

30. C called on the Comtesse de Noailles "Je vous dis franchement, j'adore mes poèmes" and "to be really great one must be understood by everybody" and Victor Hugo and Shakespeare are her two favorites and her hair was dishevelled and she sat propped up on lace pillows in a great bed, and the telephone never stopped ringing and it was very dark and outside in the street stood a line of limousines, and there were men waiting in the waiting room.

> "Si vraiment les mots t'embarrassent
> Ne dis rien. Rêve. N'aie pas froid,
> C'est moi qui parle et qui t'embrasse
> Laisse-moi répandre sur toi,
> Comme le doux vent dans les bois,
> Ce murmure immense, à voix basse."

December 14. Snow and walked across the gray-white Tuileries, and the poor naked statues and the flakes of snow disappearing into the cold water of the fountains and the sun-abandoned trees and with C (after champagne) to Pélléas ("plus longue que mon bras, plus longue que moi") and a Persian print "for the Radjah of the Sun and Roses from his adoring and his cunningest concubine."

17. With A in his Fiat for Nice and C in her red velvet robe waving goodbye from our bedroom window and the Barrière and Fontainbleau and snow along the roads, and the Gothic cathedral and a pair of waggoner's gloves at Sens, and through Avallon to Saulieu for the night and the trees were bare and black and the snow desolate and cold and I am lonely ("ayant peur de mourir lorsque je couche seul.") Bucentaure.

18. Saulieu to Valence, a long day, almost three hundred kilometers and there was the Côte d'Or with an old castle sleeping in the snow and there was burgundy at Mâcon and the afternoon was long and arctic and cold and I snuggled deep into my fur coat and composed a sonnet.

MONOTONE

Mile after mile across a pearl-gray land
Along a frozen road, past village spires
And on through breathless woods where brushwood fires
Smoulder beneath the naked trees that stand
Dreaming of springtime's viridescent hand:
A lonely farm, dogs bark, a white horse mires,
And chantecleer is crowing his desires
To empty skies that cannot understand.
And on I go, and on, always alone
With my embittered thoughts that like black crows
Startle the whiteness of the winter snows;
My once-enraptured heart has turned to stone,
Senseless to all save life's drear monotone
Which through me like a sunless river flows

and long after dark we came into Valence.

December 19. Valence to Orange (the Arc de Triomphe erected by Julius
Caesar two thousand years ago and the huge stone open-air Theatre) and to
Avignon "sur le pont d'Avignon on y danse, on y chante" (the old arched
bridge and the old city walls) and luncheon at the hotel where Alfred de
Musset had a room and a quarrel with George Sand and rain all afternoon
and Saint-Tropez, and just before Sainte Maxime we ran off the road into a
ditch and we had to walk and it was dark and there were palm trees and
angriness of waves along the shore and more black rain and Blackness.

21. Came back last night from Marseilles third class and glad to get back
to Paris. Paris City of the Sun—only to-day is a grey day.

And to A's where I found him playing a duet with old Madame C and T
was throwing clothes into an enormous bag preparatory to going to Florence
and poor Marie knelt on the floor and tried to fold things and was
blasphemed for her pains and Ary the dog drowsed on a bed (the Hound of
the Baskervilles) and Madame S appeared white and timid and I ate oranges
with her and later on talked poetry with A and all went well until I said I
preferred Pot of Earth to Shelley whereupon he smashed his tea-cup and
saucer on the floor, and on a lacquer table was a bowl filled with rotting
flowers (lessive) and they had been there for more than a month.

Christmas—and C is still away and it is a sombre grey day and out to the
Cimetière de l'Abbaye de Longchamp—one strong flame into the red-gold
Sun. And a gift to the Roux (they were there before I was born) and a glass of
wine with them and there was the dog and the parrot and the white goat.
Talked no English to-day and carried the Skull from the Donjon to the
Library.

26. E from Bordeaux and lent him $250 to get divorced ($250 to D to get
married) and to the Montmartre and there was a girl from Ajaccio

like our once-upon-a-time Zorn etching (Elin).

December 31. "Tout est dangereux et tout est nécessaire" and to bed to write

UNCOFFINED

How many things there are in my past life
That I regret, how many misconceits
How many hours of ill-considered strife
And drunken-dreary days of dull deceits?
How many maids unzoned to me their charms
While I persuaded them that love was truth,
How many are the harlots in whose arms
I've spent the shipwrecked night-times of my youth!
And as I sought to find excuse I came
Upon the fatal words of wise Voltaire:
Tout est dangereux et tout est nécessaire—
They whirled like autumn leaves within my brain,
Until I sought the Sun to disentomb
This long-dead foetus from my strangled womb!

V

January 8. Princesse Persane gray fur and gold eyes and she purrs and afterwards a lioness skin for a thousand francs. And the largest and loveliest bunch of violets and a cluster of hot house grapes and two red-gold oranges from Algeria.

16. Gosse says in Silhouettes: It would be an excellent thing for some young English poet to devote himself to a version of the Lusiad, which is not very long for an epic—What is wanted would be the power to transfer to English the mingled vigour and the voluptuousness of the Portuguese.

> "The Orange-Tree hat in her sightly fruit
> The Colours Daphne boasted in her hair."

And Frank Harris says in his life of Oscar Wilde "Strong men are made by opposition, like kites they go up against the wind."

The Count brought us a book called Vaillantes Chevauchées de la Cavalerie Française and I read aloud some of the pages he wrote so many years ago of the famous cavalry charge at Sedan in which he took part as an officer in the Chasseurs d'Afrique and I could see him living the charge again, seeing his friends fall, hearing the sound of the bugles, as they charged the Germans. (there will always be war).

Two lecture letters from the family to reprimand for extravagance. Cabled "Penitent." Nevertheless went this afternoon to Luichon, to Lafon, to Levitsky, and ordered many books to be bound.

All day it snows, very strange for Paris.

19. La protégée de Monsieur to call in her sabots which she removed to walk up stairs and I translated one of my poems for her and drank a glass of Madeira with her and gave her a hundred francs.

Bought a wooden ladder for Croucher to climb to the top of the mammoth armoire and I climbed up and watched him take photographs of C and afterwards borrowed his cutaway for the wedding and it was old and crumpled and camphor balls spilled out from the pockets. (Gretchen has done a damn good scene from Cyrano by pasting strips of different-colored paper upon a piece of card-board).

Post-card from the Lady of the Golden Horse with the Diamond Eyes of the Château of J Le Grand and the room where one of the J's locked up his wife (Hélène) for thirty years because she had been untrue to him. Last week she (the Lady of) tried to buy Frank Harris' Confessions and the man at Brentano's said: "No we haven't any more, for two days ago an old lady appeared and asked for the book and Harris himself was in the shop and offered to autograph it for her and the old lady was delighted and thanked him. Only the next morning she came back in a rage and asked them what right they had to sell her such a scandalous book and she made so much fuss that they took back the books and sent all the copies they had back to Harris." To hell with the lady and to hell with Brentano's.

1926

January 22. C suggests I write a book composed of the most curious authentic letters I have received (transposed of course) with my own real or imaginary answers to them and in Pepys read "So to Mrs Hunt, where I found a Frenchman, a lodger of her's at dinner, and just as I came in was kissing my wife, which I did not like, through there could not be any hurt in it."

24. A met us at Beaulieu and we presented him with a clock and on the card I quoted in Greek Réjouis-toi, épousée! Noble époux, réjouis-toi pleinement and there was a Rops drawing of Mademoiselle de Maupin that I would rather have had than the Sargents and someday perhaps I shall have it and I talked to L about Browning (he has a box full of his letters) and L I liked (he paints interiors) and told me he came from the Weaseley side of the family whatever that may mean and he has a white mustache and is unobtrusive and in the evening met the Vicomte Merveilleux du Vignaux and he and A and I drove over to Monte Carlo 'and dined chez Ciro—a full moon and myriad stars and a black sea—a black black sea—but no blacker than my heart and M said he thought there was only one beautiful woman in three thousand and though it sounded absurd at first I believe he is right and back to C (my heart less black, and silver as the sea which had also changed) sitting on the floor of the car gazing into the moon. Moon you belong to the Sun.

26. No hat and a winged collar and Croucher's camphorsmelling cutaway and a red prayer-book in my hand and yellow gloves in the other and C was charming in a frail black dress with lace and a black hat to match trimmed with lace which came down over her eyes so that she seemed mysterious (The Ladybird). Breakfast and brandy out in the Sun at the Villa Sylvia and birds were singing and there was a lovely garden and a playroom where there were old fairy-tale books and there was a rocking-horse, a reminder of long long ago days. And then every-one was ready and we went off to the church and here A was married to S and I officiated as best man and lost myself in a red-gold Sun and almost forgot to hand A the ring and after the ceremony into the vestry where I signed for A and the Duke of C for S. After the reception we rushed to the hotel paid an outrageous bill (in retaliation we put the nicelooking bed-cover in our valise to use at home in the guest room) gave the little Italian waiter a hundred francs to buy English books, and so by car at break-neck speed to see if we could overtake at Vingtimille the Express for Rome. We did overtake it with four minutes to spare and got the last compartment on the sleeper. Romewards.

27. The lady in ecstasy all night in the next compartment and her extraordinary love cries "the soft cries of love's delight" and I have never heard anything so demonstrative, so physical. (The old world can still teach the new) and in Rome three hours before the train to Naples and we had hot chocolate and muffins and then chartered a hack and saw the forum and the fish-market and churches and fountains so that we almost missed the Express.

January 30. Vesuvius windswept and full of fog. Down a rocky declivity and we could see the erupting volcano vomiting red blocks of lava which rattled and smouldered at our feet. The sound was the sound of a big shell bursting the reverberation of thunder, the clanging of an iron door, and I was reminded of the war. Sulphur steam rose everywhere, heavy clouds poured downwards and hot lava sizzled and grew cold. We waited for four or five of these tremendous explosions which occurred about a minute apart then a terrific climb back up the precipitous path, exhausting in the high altitude. We reached the rack and pinion in time to catch the last train down and we were the only two who came up in our car who did what we did (the others could not have possibly seen anything due to the fog). Suicide in the actual crater of Vesuvius would be impossible (unless there was absolutely no erupting going on) as one would in nine cases out of ten be maimed before reaching the rim.

In a little station on the main line from Pompeii to Naples we saw a poor boy with a wooden leg who asked if he might shine our shoes and I gave him five lire and some crackers and now I wish I had given him more. Le Favori.

February 1. The Museum and a red-bronzed hero and a Swinburne red-haired very pale lady and there was a torse of Psyche and then mirabile dictu I bought a hat, a wide cap done in black and white squares, this to please the family (a real sacrifice on my part) and so with C to the docks and O God I hate Naples (see Naples and die) and we chartered a rowboat and a strong boatman and off we went down the harbor to meet the Count Biancomano and there were fishing smacks and tug-boats hauling stone-filled barges, and dilapidated dories and ships at anchor. The Humilitas, a freighter, was taking on coal and as we reached the end of the long breakwater, the Solunto outward bound for Tripoli surged past. Our boatman rowed us out into the bay and the sea was gray-black and it was rough. And far off, a speck upon the horizon, and nearer, and it was the incoming steamer, the Conte Biancomano, smoke pouring from her funnels in a long black plume. But storm clouds scudded overhead and it grew rougher and we tossed about like a cork, and soon were forced to row in under the lea of the breakwater and an hour later we were waving silk scarves at the towering liner and I took the cap from my pocket and put it on my head (eight months). As we drew close to the boat a waving of hands and scarves but too far away to talk. Twenty minutes later we were on shore in time to greet them as they came down the gangplank and after a frightful hour of searching and fighting for trunks we all drove off to the Excelsior.

2. On the way to Pompeii left a letter with the station-master at Pugliano for the boy with the wooden leg (storpiate ragazzo) and on our way back saw the boy and gave him a hundred lire and with S.V.R.C. saw the Octopus fed at the Aquarium and the Octopus made me afraid of the Sun for as the tentacles of the Octopus search for food so the tentacles of the Sun search for souls.

February 3. Palermo. The fear of uncertainty is the most terrible of all fears. Blackest Day.

5. With S.V.R.C. to the Catacombs (escorted by a monk) and the skeletons were entirely dressed and whiskers and beards and eye-brows were often apparent and virgins wore tin crowns on their heads and there were babies and there were priests in red velvet and it was weird.

With H.M.C. to the Marionettes in a toy theatre, a room the size of the cock-fight room in Seville, a room divided into stage, pit and gallery (where we sat). The audience (about 150) composed of men and boys, H.M.C. being the only woman in the house unless we count the old hag who sold tickets (one lira each) at the entrance. Everyone wore caps and nearly everyone smoked. The pit was crowded and people sat on rude benches. Cobwebs hung from the faded blue ceiling (ciel de lit). The walls were white-washed. A mechanical hurdy-gurdy rendered dreary music and everyone talked. As the footlights went out the tawdry curtain (representing the Rape of the Sabine women) went up. A final crash from the hurdy-gurdy, then it ceased and a marionette appeared, a young knight clad in silver armour. He appeared to be trying to rescue a lady (also in armour) who was bound in chains and who was about to be decapitated. And there ensued a hand to hand fight between the knight and the executioners and there was much clashing of sabres and a great slicing off of heads and there were rival knights and more crossing of swords and at the end the young knight carried off the fair captive and it was all very quaint and primitive—the set faces of the marionettes, their strange gestures, the glimpses of the huge hands of the manipulators, the various tones of the ventriloquist's voice, the classic simplicity of the subject, and the breathlessness of the audience.

8. Girgenti. Never never never never want to see Palermo again. Here the Temple of Juno and the Temple of Concord and inside me the Temple of the Sun.

9. All day on the train to Syracuse and read Baudelaire and wrote a sonnet and endured.

NOSTALGIA

I care not for the almond trees in bloom
Nor for the sea that year on year enshrines
This stone-eternal isle. Nor for these wines
That cannot dissipate my songless gloom.
I care not for the peasant at her loom,
Nor for the gay Sicilian carts, the mines,
The lemon groves or painted wayside shrines,
This land is like my heart, a ghost-thronged tomb.

In dreams I seek the darkness of the north
The cruelty of wintersaddened days,
And ever and anon, and back and forth,

Shadows of the Sun

I wander unguessed down the Paris quays,
To watch the fog come creeping up the Seine
And feel the shrouded charm of city rain.

S.V.R.C. impossibly nervous, in a state of excitement when any of us got off for a breath of air for fear we should be left behind (we stopped at every wayside station) and he urged H.M.C. to drink and when she did and felt gay turned on her and told her she must never take a drink again and he is always worrying about What People Will Say (that is his *real* bête noire) and then he found a newspaper (a week old) and discovered that Continental Can had risen two points and then of course he was in a great humour and there was a lady in our car who had made that horrible seventeen hour journey from Tunis to Constantine and so I liked her. One has an instinctive penchant for those who have been through the same hells as oneself.

February 10. Syracuse. The Roman Amphitheatre, the Ear of Dyonisius and the Greek Theatre, the Amphitheatre for cruelty, the cavern-prison for ingenuity, the Greek theatre for thought, and here it was that Pindar sang his odes, here it was the multitudes watched the great battle in the harbor, and here it was that Timoleon of Corinth gave counsel to the people. The Ear of Dyonisius suggests a sonnet, the octave to show how the tyrant listened to the whispering of his prisoners, the sextet to compare a beautiful lady to him, listening to the prisoners of her heart. Think of this cavern dating from 400 B.C.! and yet that is not so very long as compared with the caves and the cave-paintings in the Dordogne that W.V.R.B. tells us about in l'Art Méditerranéen. On the way back to the hotel C lost her purse the pink one with two or three hundred lira in it (Nothing is ever lost. M.B.)

11. A tempest is raging in the Ionian Sea and I was disappointed in the Venus Anadyomene and I snatched a jaw-bone from a skeleton lying in an open sarcophagus (this for my dentist for the teeth seemed in good condition) and later on with H.M.C. in a painted boat up the Cyane where the papyrus grow in abundance, and before supper a walk in the ancient quarries and they reminded me of the Arabian Nights and there were orange trees (The Orange Tree hath in her sightly fruit   The colours Daphne boasted in her hair), and a grave and a statue and a tall cypress tree whose bark I touched and through whose branches I prayed. For what?—the Sun.

12. Train to Taormina. S.V.R.C. as usual counting his money, H.M.C. (indefatigable) as usual reading aloud from a History of Sicily, C as usual looking out the window and I as usual reading Baudelaire.

"Et des habits, mousseline ou velours,
Tout imprégnés de sa jeunesse pure,
Se dégageait un parfum de fourrure."

—Taormina and all Sicilian disillusions vanish and the shops are fascinating and the peasants are quaint, the streets and houses picturesque, and all the countryside is pink with almond blossoms. Scones in a tea shop and far down the valley the waves are thundering along the coast and there is a fog creeping down from the mountains. And there is a little cottage we would like to buy with a lantern hanging at the gate and a wayside shrine and a profusion of almond blossoms. And there was a Mr. Wood who once upon a time came to Taormina for two weeks and stayed twenty-five years and he paints water-colors and then it began to rain and there is a stove in our room at the hotel and more hot buttered scones.

February 14. Away to Messina and on across the straits of Messina (Reggio with a million gold lights low-lying to our right) to Italy. C and I on the deck of the ship searching through the darkness for Scylla and Charybdis.

16. Through the Campagna to Frascati and the Villa Torlonia. A stagnant fountain and a bullfrog and moss and maidenhair and wild violets and the golden singing of birds. Crawled inside a tree-trunk, an Arthur Rackham tree-trunk, and prayed to the Sun. Inside were cobwebs, ashes and the damp odor of leaves. It was a live oak, a gnarled ilex, green all the year round— And then the Villa Falconieri and the Lago de Cipressi: the song of the fountain, the reflection of the cypresses in the water, the moss-covered rocks, the dilapidated stone bench, the color of the water sky-blue, cloud-white, cypress-green. No wind and pale gold sunlight filtering through the trees and a grassiness and an inverted mirror, the stagnant green-black of the water, color of a soul and a floating leaf (device of the soul) and I could visualize nymphs dancing their ringaround under the silver of the Moon or the gold of the Sun.

17. Rome. To Saint Peter's (ugly, a dreary interior, no mysteriousness and a dwarf woman dressed in black.) At the Vatican S.V.R.C. nervous and unappreciative, H.M.C. interested in everything no matter what it was, and C and I hand in hand marveling at a marble, and there was the Vatican Library and Torquato Tasso's autograph and a manuscript page of his poetry (he rhymed fecondo with giocondo) and later to visit with C the graves of Keats and Shelley and we laid daffodils and violets on their graves and kissed in the Sun and she is sun-lovely and there was the Temple of the Vestal Virgins (and inside me the Temple of the Sun) and there was the Fontana Trevi into which we threw the littlest gold coin but I don't really know whether I ever want to return to Rome.

18. Baths of Diocletian (Museo della Terme) and there was a Nascita di Afrodite and a Nimfa Sorpresa Al Bagno (so often thought of and, sadly, so seldom done—your postal has come T) and the Ermafrodite Dormiente

> "Sex to sweet sex with lips and limbs is wed,
> Turning the fruitful feud of hers and his
> To the waste wedlock of a sterile kiss."

But most marvelous the Venus of Cyrene and the desire to kneel and kiss everywhere and all over and she is perfection. She *is* Beauty and her body is Soul and I understood marble and prayed into a marble Sun.

> "And all her body is more virtuous
> Than souls of women fashioned otherwise."

February 19. To the station one hour ahead of time (at S.V.R.C.'s insistence) and the Seven of Hearts in the Station (good omen) and the Parigi Celere, and so goodbye to many-fountained Rome and the last thing we saw was the big pyramid in the English cemetery. Goodbye Shelley. Goodbye John Keats.

Mild sunny afternoon along the shore of the sea and Livorno and Pisa at six o'clock with a glimpse of the cathedral and the leaning tower (like a soul that has been hurt by love) and the tow-path that runs along the Arno towards Florence. And there was a rose-brown, red-golden sunset and reflections in the water, and Genoa and Turin and after innumerable tunnels (are there tunnels through the mountains of the heart) Modane.

20. Paris. Telegramme from Rome: Rita Rushing Relentlessly, Rensselaer Reading Rubbish.

25. With C and S.V.R.C. to buy dresses at Tolstoy's "I lost my umbrella reading your poems." And a mannequin (Raymonde) (vision of the Venus of Cyrene) and I couldn't take my eyes off her [29] and I spilt my cocktail (after taking the last one on the tray) and S.V.R.C. bought two dresses (Caprice and Aphrodite) for C and Tolstoy has named a dress Caresse which Raymonde wore ("a thing of beauty is a joy forever") and S.V.R.C. kept saying Look at the workmanship, Look at the workmanship on these dresses and I kept thinking how much I should like to have a harem, and later on with C along the Quays in the crépuscule and there was a silver-gold moon rising above the Louvre and we bought a bed—a Louis XV bed—delicate and feminine, couleur vert et or with roses of gold. And this is the first real bed we have ever had. "Again, if two lie together, then they have heat: but how can one be warm alone."

28. Saw the Count and he showed us a letter in black (O Letters in Gray) he received yesterday and it was a friend of his announcing his (the friend's) own death, and to-day in the Figaro the Count read that his friend had shot himself and there were tears in the Count's eyes as he read the letter.

After supper everyone read around the fire, Mamma, the Life of Mrs. Jack Gardner; S.V.R.C., Poe's Murder in the Rue Morgue, C, her own poems and I began and finished Verlaine's Fêtes Galantes

> "et des désirs sans nombre
> Mon ombre se fondra à jamais en votre ombre."
> (Shadows of the Sun).

March 3. —Aunt Jessie left me a thousand dollars which I shall spend for Books.

And I gave Hargreaves the jaw-bone from the sarcophagus at Syracuse and had a tooth (of mine) photographed (physical in the negative) and on my desk is a picture and I look into her eyes and am inspired. Elle inspire toujours (Hôtel des Saints-Pères).

March 4. The Tea.

5. Sent a louis d'or "would you mind putting this louis d'or for me on Davis' grave?" and to-day in my wanderings found Rémy de Gourmont's Litanies de la Rose "Fleur hypocrite, Fleur du Silence," the de luxe René Kieffer Edition with colored plates by André Domin, and bound by Kieffer, and for it I paid three hundred francs but I would have paid a thousand had it been necessary. Have hunted for this book for one year.

> "rose aux yeux noirs, miroir de ton néant, rose aux
> yeux noirs, fais-nous croire au mystère
> fleur hypocrite
> fleur du silence"

6. Discovered that Roche who has our Corot is in prison. For what? Where did he leave the Corot? Has he sold it? Shall have to wait until Monday before finding out anything. We have had more trouble over that damned painting!

The chimney caught on fire but the pompiers arrived and the flames were quelled. Result of the fire: Two cracked walls. What would happen if the soul caught on fire? (from too much thinking of the Sun).

14. With C to see some models and it was hot and they would have been more beautiful nude and the Count at luncheon and he is seventy-five years old and we had a raven pie and we went to Auteuil where I lost a thousand francs betting on Sunset and I bought a book on gamebirds and one on monsters and one on witchcraft and at Sunset walked around the Tuileries alone thinking of and gazing into the Sun.

20. To the Odilon Redon exhibition—the carnal flowers and the dark lithographs and the strange red-golds of the paintings and then to the Circus, trapezists, crocodiles, acrobats, the three Fratellini and Fortunio the lion tamer. Lions of the Sun.

28. Bought a whippet and we name him Narcisse Noir. Why not Black Sun? And in the evening a ball-bouncing competition with the children and I bounced the rubber-ball three thousand three hundred and thirty three times! (each time pronouncing the word Sun to myself).

> "As when we dwell upon a word we know
> Repeating, till the word we know so well
> Becomes a wonder and we know not why"

April 4. Easter and to Notre-Dame and to Saint-Julien-le-Pauvre and to Saint-Séverin and our Narcisse Noir was beaten by a "rien" in the Prix Beau-Soleil.

Shadows of the Sun

April 11. Forgot to say that Narcisse won the Prix Coram and to-day we borrowed and I telegraphed to England for an Oscar Wilde letter and I bought de luxe editions of Rimbaud and Pélléas and Mélisande and Le Jardin des Caresses and I bought a Renaissance key (the better to open your heart my dear) and I bought a boat model which I shall call Jacqueline and afterwards Narcisse ran in two races and won the second (from scratch) and now he is the best whippet in France, and he defeated Luynes and Castellane, a neck and neck finish, and on the way home we stopped to see the Count (who was hurt in a taxi accident after he left us on his birthday) and we sat in his old-fashioned den and drank chartreuse and I smoked my pipe.

17. Bought a stuffed sea-gull for B and bought for myself at the Nain Bleu a small model of the Sydney Lasry, a freighter that we saw in the port of Marseilles on our way home from Africa, and sent Saint-Mark's School a silver cup to be offered for cross-country.

"à Walter Berry, grand explorateur des paysages littéraires," this in a book dedicated to him by Edmond Jaloux and a bonjour to the Degas Nude in the dining room and I looked at the first edition of Leaves of Grass with the Whitman Letters in it (I never read Whitman). And Cousin Walter told us the story of the five men who went elephant hunting in Africa, each of whom wrote a book on his return. The Englishman called his book "The Elephant, his Life and Habits;" the Frenchman "Etude sur l'Elephant et ses Amours;" the American "In favor of Bigger and Better Elephants;" the German: "The Metaphysics and World-Weariness of the Elephant;" the Pole "The Elephant and the Polish Question." And I suppose I should have entitled mine "Elephants of the Sun."

Gave away my brown suit and from this day to the day of my death (rose within gold) shall wear only dark blue suits and from this day a black knitted neck-tie ('asserted' by my pearl pin) and from this day in my buttonhole a black (artificial) gardenia. And always bareheaded.

20. C's birthday and I give her the sapphire ring and we take an "ultra-violet" sunbath and M.T. (dull as ditch-water) comes to tea and stays all of two hours.

W.V.R.B. appeared later on and found me sitting on the floor arranging books and told me the story of the New England school-mistress who put all the male authors on one shelf, all the female on the other!

Bought and read Paul Valéry La Soirée avec Monsieur Teste: ("Je m'immole intérieurement à ce que je voudrais être.")

27. Saw at the Hotel d'Alsace Rue des Beaux-Arts, the room in which Wilde died and the table at which he wrote and the little garden he looked out upon. Shall arrange to have a marble tablet put upon the house in his honor.

Bought a Chinese boat model in an antique shop and gave it to the Musée de la Marine.

My Library is a Stronghold (Stronghold of the Sun).

1926

April 30. Paris to Loches and at Luynes (the Duc de Luynes who ran against us in the whippet races) Narcisse attacked and killed a chicken. The old market place. The old sixteenth century house (à vendre) and on to Langeais with glimpses of cave-dwellers on the way and tea in the little house where Rabelais used to live and so over the Loire and on to Azay-le-Rideau and water overflowing the fields and flowing between the trees and the long sloping-down avenue and the interior and the great kitchen and the kitchen utensils. In the park Narcisse ran and there were two gigantic trees with entangled branches and there were school-children who scrambled for pennies. Then Loches (passed by a family (Troglodytes) on the way that lived in a great cave near Montbazon in which blazed a wood fire, the smoke coming through above) and nine years since I was here last.

May 1. The same custodian as in 1907 (Girardin). Vous allez voir, vous allez voir, and we saw the cell inhabited by Ludovico Sforza and the sundial he carved in the rock and the words carved in the wall near the window "dixisse me aliquando penituit, tacuisse nunquam (I have sometimes repented of having spoken, never of keeping silent)" and how in 1510, on hearing that he was to be set free, he died for joy. But the cage designed and inhabited by the Cardinal Balue has been removed to Paris. To Chenonceaux and the Hotel du Bon Laboureur and to the Château which was cold and dismal (it reminded me of the House of Usher). And there was the old woman guardian "attention au courant d'air" and the sound of the gurgling waters and the signature of Diane de Poitiers and the gardens and the park (where Narcisse had his tail bitten by a big police dog) and through the woods, and it was a soft gray afternoon and there was quietness and a good potage for supper

2. The gold of the Sun and as we lay in bed I wrote

CHENONCEAUX

> Red torches and rich fêtes at Chenonceaux
> And lights that wove strange patterns out of gold
> Over the river and the gardens old
> While silver music's soft adagio
> Slowstreaming into Ronsard and Tasso
> Outpoured in golden poesies they told
> To royal guests assembled to behold
> How Diane posed for Primaticcio.
> Bright pageantries, but now mere emptiness,
> The château sleeping in its riverbed,
> The waters like the gurgling of the dead,
> The forest overarching overhead,
> While I sun-dreaming at your feet, Caresse,
> Unqueen the past for present loveliness.

On foot from Chenonceaux to Amboise through the forest of Amboise and there was the tomb of Leonardo da Vinci with the stained glass window and the fireplace at his head and then Chaumont and the staircase in the tree and the view of the Loire and the well with its extraordinary multiplication of echoes (three chimpanzees for a coin to strike bottom) and I called into the well Sun Sun Sun Sun and there were sonorous overtones and there was the Chapel and gules and goldness to Sun and there was Catherine de Medici and Diane de Poitiers in the Château (no stronger than the Castle of my Soul) and we raced Narcisse in the Wood.

May 4. The House of all Nations and saw the Persian and the Russian and the Turkish and the Japanese and the Spanish room and the room which King Edward used to use and the bathroom with mirrored walls and mirrored ceilings and a glimpse of the thirty odd harlots waiting in the salon and there was the flogging post where men come to flagellate young girls and where others (masochists) come to be flagellated. Asked the Madame many questions. How many men a day? Average one hundred and fifty. What prices? Fifty francs for ten minutes, one hundred for an hour, three hundred for all night. Does flagellation really exist? Yes.

5. With C to the Bois to gallop Narcisse Noir plus vite que le vent, plus noir que le soir and afterwards to see A and S in their little apartment overlooking the Tuileries.

7. With W.V.R.B. to the Manet sale at the Hotel Drouot and it was as thrilling as a horse-race and he bought the lithograph "Un Corbeau" to go with his book of Poe's poems translated by Mallarmé which has the frontispiece (Un Corbeau) by Manet. And there was a girl Sur la Plage that was bid up too high and there was the sanguine Homme au Chapeau Haut de Forme that went for twenty-five thousand and there was a little drawing of a Leaf I wish I had bought for it has suggested a sonnet and it went for almost nothing. The pièce de résistance, however, came with "Polichinelle." The initial bid was two hundred thousand, then in four moves to three hundred thousand, then a long long pause until everyone thought that it would go at that price when someone in the back of the room shouted four hundred and twenty thousand! (at which price it was bought.) With the taxes, almost half a million!

8. In Rambouillet a Dutch scene at a humble café where we drank steaming bowls of coffee at a rough wooden table and there was a Rubens woman (see the Baroness Blank at Vienna) ponderous, strong, loud-laughing giving suck from an enormous mammal to a sturdy, delighted child (who at the same time was watering the floor) and her heavy husband was watching her and at his feet a big dog lay asleep (not so Narcisse and Zulu) and in a corner by the door two soldiers with blank expressions were drinking beer and staring at G and C and there was darkness in the room and rain outside and the desire to paint what I saw: the woman primitive, naïve, proud of her tremendous breasts (and rightly so) the child sucking in ecstasy, his legs widespread and no drawers.

Chartres at six and grayness (about-to-rain grayness) and the grayness of the Cathedral and the slow shuffle of feet over the stone floor and the cierges gold-twinkling in the gloom and the incense and the stained glass windows. Burnt a cierge and prayed through a stained glass window our dark colors into the invisible Sun.

In a little hamlet in a little café we spent the night all in one room and it was cold out of doors and a glorious sunset over the fields (at first a chipped blaze of gold, then silver-purple all soft and filmy) and my thoughts (C) arrowed in Oneness towards the Sunset Loveliness (for an instant of ecstasy my soul left the dark dungeon of the body and entered the Beauty of the Sun). And there was a dog race to the great excitement of the villagers and Narcisse won and there was an onion omelette and dubonnets and much laughter at a jeu de billard and much more laughter when we went to bed, Narcisse on ours, Zulu on theirs.

May 9. Hayricks meadows cows chickens barking dogs peasants in sabots strong Sun virgin air mild breezes farmyards dungheaps little hamlets little churches and late in the evening Le Haras-au-Pin where we galloped the dogs through the forest and there was a chocolate soufflé for supper and a bottle of Burgundy and forest quietness.

10. Saw Irismond (the horse I bet on in the Grand Prix two years ago) faire la cour in the Sun to Violette de Parme (neither seemed to be enjoying it very much) and we had luncheon at Sai with an old man who had been there forty years and we saw country scenes and then mile after mile towards Paris (in particular I recollect a roadmender in a ditch on a lonely road, death and the country in his eyes, all of the fields and woods, autumns and winters summed up in the face of a man).

Then Verneuil and the Tour Grise (an old Twelfth Century Tower built by Henry the Second of England). We pounded upon the door. No answer. We pounded again. No answer. We pounded a third time and there was a creaking of rusty locks and a sinister woman motioned us in. At first so dark we couldn't see, then gradually we made out huge wooden statues, giant statues twice lifesize, that towered up from an undescribable heap of débris, broken bottles, half-eaten food, pots and pans, old newspapers, ordures, empty tins. On one side an enormous fireplace yawned into blackness. From an obscure corner came the muffled sound of a groan. Il a la grippe, il a la grippe, the old woman kept repeating as she leered at us through the gloom. Vous habitez ici? Oui. An odor of dead rats, of vermin, of evil things. Poe or Dickens or Goya—but especially Poe could have described the scene, the evilness of the place, the uncanny imprisoned feeling of a madhouse, the misery and darkness, the cruelty and torture of sunless things. Old clothes, old iron, a leaning table and somewhere in the wall in a dark frame a darker portrait (Henri II she said) As we turned to go a black cat scurried out into the light. A monstrous, diseased, malevolent chamber of horrors and always the low moaning of the man and the unholy gibbering of the woman, of the gargoyle woman. Black-hearted wickedness and a strange sense of the unreal which persisted long after we had driven away.

Afterwards the Bois Joly and while the girls were washing, Croucher and I played at bowls in the garden and I felt strong and jumped over tables and we ate a prodigious supper in the tiny fourneau cottage "ami le verre en main, buvez, jusqu'à demain." And there were black sausages (boudins) and galette with raspberries and thick cream and a bottle of Clos Vougeot and to sleep with the nightingales singing in the Wood.

May 11. Nursery wall-paper, eaves, soft beds, old prints, polished pots and pans, things rustic, sunshine, quaintness and the smell of breakfast. And before leaving to sit alone in the little cottage where we had had supper, to realize I was there and alive and to pray in sun-circles, innocent prayers and joyous, while a rouge bird that flew in through the door fluttered among the sunny curtains of a sky-light like my soul trying to escape earthly trammels in order to soar into the Sun.

14. When S.V.R.C. is sixty I shall be thirty. Sent him a set of Napoleon. And a cable. Tea at T's and met a critic called Firmin Roz who spoke for Anderson and Lewis, I for T.S. Eliot. There was a pretty, sleepy, picture-hat countess there who lives in Limoges and who has a husband and a grayhound and a deceased grandfather who gave the city a museum. The rest of the tea was bourgeoisly dull. And after supper wrote a poem inspired by the little Manet Leaf I should have bought.

LAMENTATION

A little leaf is dancing on a tree
And checkered sunlight weaves the forest glade
The summer sleeps in silence in the shade
And flowers yield their sweetness to the bee.

But winter comes with hollow savagery
And from the sheath of night unsheathes the blade
Of ice-envenomed winds, and thus arrayed
Dismantles nature, suppliant at his knee.

And so it was with us, who for a day,
Bedecked with faëry flounce and furbelow,
Made merry in the house of innocence;

Until old age turned gold to hodden gray
And love, unfriended as a leaf on snow,
Defiled itself with blank indifference.

18. Cold water from the conch-shell and the sound of the sea (Etretat and Nubile) and its flesh-colored beauty (C)

Read Ethan Frome. Wonder how much W.V.R.B. had to do with it?

Met T on the staircase—the pretty doll-like girl was the Comtesse de Moncabrier.

1926

With S on foot through the quarter and we stopped for a Claquesin (tar and hair tonic) in a tiny bistro on the corner of the rue l'Echaudé and then into a tiny brothel (Aux Paniers des Fleurs) on the same street and a timid knocking on the door and a "Qu'est-ce que c'est ici, Madame," and her brilliant reply "C'est le contraire d'une église, Monsieur."

Tea at Croucher's and his cousin on the floor in front of the fire and I felt like laying my head in her lap. (The Virgin and the Unicorn).

May 21. Morning at the Bois-Joly; among orange-pink pretties, sun-gold softnesses and the soft cries of love's delight. Mirrors everywhere.

Paris and tea with A and he divulges as usual, how he has had a cable from B how he and Lady C sleep in the same bed but never make love, how D tells girls that he is a pederast in order to get rid of them, how the other D has slept with four different women in the last four nights and how he (A) has had to pay for them.

24. The Cimetière de l'Abbaye de Longchamp. Chequered sunlight and prayers and I read the Rubaiyat sitting against a tree trunk and there were twin trees upgrowing in oneness from a humble grave and their branches were interlaced and there were the lichened walls and the dense foliage and the moss-covered tombstones leaning awry (like love-thoughts leaning in the brain) and there were prayers into the Sun (my soul a fountain playing into the Sun, gushing sunthoughts into the Sun).

25. Narcisse won a first prize in the dog show (tenue en laisse par des dames) and there was a ribbon and a medal and a cup (promised) and I won a competition for quick drinking at the Ritz (a glass of champagne in two and a half chimpanzees) and I bought a jereboam of champagne for the Ks— an enormous bottle as heavy as a baby and ten times more important and afterwards to hear Geneviève Vix in Salomé at the Opéra and she was terrific in the lascivious dance with Iokanaan's head and it was marvelous and macabre and I began a poem (and weaves her maggot fingers through his hair) and it is a great and very French mistake to give afterwards L'Heure Espagnole, for Ravel after Salomé is nothing at all.

June 7. Finished.

SALOMÉ

Proud panoply of fans and frankincense
Gold blare of trumpets, flowered robes of state,
Unnumbered symbols of magnificence,
To lead Salome through the palace gate,
Where loud the prophet of the Lord blasphemes
The red abominations of her race
And chides her for her flesh-entangled dreams
And turns his back upon her painted face.
Thus do we turn from some red-shadowed lust
That through the broken forests of the brain

Weaves silently with tentacles out-thrust
Groping in darkness, but for one in vain,
For like a sliding sun the soul has fled
Leaving a princess and a vultured head.

June 8. My soul a flame of autumn gold encitadelled by C's flame (lyric gold) and by Jacqueline's (dark gold). The gorgeous flame of poetry is the moat and beyond, the monstruous (and menstruous) world, the world that must be continually beaten back, the world that is always laying siege to the castle of the soul. (I wonder if you will always be able to keep this modern life at bay?) Yes (Because of the Sun).

9. A introduced us to Koussevitsky and he is to conduct a symphony of A's this Autumn. Chez Shakespeare saw an exhibition of Walt Whitman manuscripts and talked to Sylvia Beach about Joyce. And to the tennis at the Racing and there was Lacoste and Helen Wills who has lovely breasts and Narcisse surprised a herd of deer (yet not as beautiful as the sundeer in my soul) and after supper, I finished reading Grimm's Fairy Tales (Arthur Rackham) to the Wretch, and wrote

APOLLO

Dryad
Of this gnarled oak
What color are your eyes
Tell me for I stray in search of
Daphne

and before going to bed studied Joyce words in Ulysses: ungirdled, smokeplume, upwardcurving, sandflats, chalkscrawled, harping, crunching, trekking, winedark, redbaked, miscreant, firedrake, orifice, lesbic, cartload, turfbarge.

10. Untermeyer says: Of Robert Frost "for twenty years Frost continued to write his highly characteristic work in spite of the discouraging apathy, and for twenty years the poet remained unknown." Of Maxwell Bodenheim: "he wrote steadily for four years without having a single poem accepted." Of Amy Lowell: "for eight years she served a rigorous and solitary apprenticeship, reading the classics of all schools and countries, studying the technique of verse, exercising her verbal gifts—but never attempting to publish a single line" But never attempting to publish a single line—that is good advice.

"You boys don't know how many times men fail
Perforce o' the little to succeed i' the large,
Husband their strength, let slip the petty prey,
Collect the whole power for the final pounce!"

Only this time it was a woman.
And the first edition of the Rubaiyat was unsaleable and it might never

have been sold at all and have been already forgotten if Rossetti and Swinburne had not stumbled upon a copy in a two-penny box.

June 11. With C to the Rue des Beaux-Arts to see the marble tablet we have placed on the Hotel d'Alsace in honor of Oscar Wilde.

OSCAR WILDE

Poète et dramaturge

Né à Dublin

Le 15 octobre 1854

Est mort dans cette Maison

Le 30 novembre 1900

and we drank a toast to him in absinthe (he loved absinthe) from my silver flask and then went home to read Dorian Gray only we didn't read Dorian Gray for people came to tea.

13. This is how Baudelaire symbolizes the sonnet: "Avez-vous observé qu'un morceau du ciel aperçu par un soupirail, ou entre deux cheminées, deux rochers ou par une arcade, donnait une idée plus profonde de l'infini que le grand panorama vu du haut d'une montagne?"

17. Tea at W.V.R.B.'s and we met Edith Wharton and everyone sat in the dining-room (where she wrote Ethan Frome, poor Ethan as she called him)—and there was Paul Morand of Ouvert and Fermé la Nuit and he was heavy and oriental with a pale opium face and there were the young Count and Countess (not the Countess) de Noailles, and a pretty Comtesse de Ganay and a Mrs. Hyde and last but not least a delightful Abbé Meugnier who said he wished that someone would invent another sin, he was so tired of always having to listen to the same ones, and who remarked when he saw Narcisse: "Mon coeur, c'est tout un jardin d'acclimatation."

18. Preparations for the Quatz Arts and the students are building an enormous serpent in the Rue Allent, and tickets are being distributed "Femme donne ton Soleil en adoration aux Incas" and costumes are being prepared and C tries on hers and she is passionate with bare legs, bare breasts, and a wig of turquoise hair.

Many people undressing and painting for the ball. Ellen B in her garters, C in her chemise, Raymonde in a peignoir while Lord Lymington (Gerard) and Vicomte du Vignaux (Gérard) and Croucher and a Foreign Legion Man and two or three students and Mortimer and myself all naked rubbing red ochre all over ourselves. (my costume a frail red loin-cloth and a necklace of three dead pigeons).

At eight in the Library eighty students with their girls, and supper and a tremendous punch (forty bottles of champagne, five whiskey, five gin, five cointreau). And mad yells of Venez Boire and then pandemonium and more drinking and more and more and C and Raymonde were the most beautiful and C won the prize (twenty-five bottles of champagne) for the Atelier by riding (almost nude) around the ballroom in the jaws of the serpent while myriad students roared approval. I was ossified and was rescued by Raymonde who found me sprawled against a pillar and who was afraid of the mad antics and asked me to take her home or I her and there was a red blanket and the reek of dead pigeons and then complete oblivion.

June 19. A hot bath to scrub the paint off, then a cold one in an effort to revive, and a reading aloud from Beardsley's Venus and Tannhauser of the Ecstasy of Adolphe and the Remarkable Manifestation Thereof (Adolphe was the Unicorn—and what an ecstatic time he had!) and later on baccardi cocktails ("and lapped her little apéritif") and they give one a faraway (my thousand francs on Faraway) forest breath.

Luncheon at W.V.R.B.'s and the Ned Holmes are there and they have been scouring Italy for paintings for the Boston Art Museum and W.V.R.B. argued that the Museum should also buy modern paintings and I was lost with the Degas Girl and there have been times that I have lived with her in some experience of the mind. Suns within Suns.

To the Antheil Ballet Mécanique at the Théâtre des Champs-Elysées (C and G in the orchestre, Croucher and I in the balcony) and below us in a box Brancousi, Koussevitsky, and James Joyce, a black band over one eye, the greatest of them all. (Looked a little like the 1881 portrait C showed me of her father and the same sensitive features). And I would rather have seen Joyce than any man alive. Did not like the Ballet Mécanique but liked Antheil and the verve with which he played. It was exciting and there was hooting and whistling and cat calls and wild applause and cries of silence Taisez-vous, Taisez-vous, and always the mad music.

20. After Rouen and Croisset (Musée Flaubert a disappointment) and Caudebec, at last the quietness of a Normandy farm to curl up in a grenier on the straw and fall asleep while Zulu and Narcisse stood guard under the Moon.

21. Gray morning and Normandy farms. (My soul is like a farm in Normandy). Thatched roofs and chaumières, and silver streams and red poppies in green meadows and cows and sheep and old wrinkled peasant women with white lace caps and the smell of loam and byres and the song of birds. Fécamp where they make the Bénédictine and then Saint Claire and the Manoir and to Etretat where we all bathed naked in the sea (the beautiful C and the Beautiful G—bare breast and knee) and it was invigorating and I thought of last summer and of Nubile and of the cliffs and the sea and the big round pebbles of the beach (her eyes round as pebbles) and three cormorants and then away towards Paris and at midnight in the moonlight we halted at Magny (Le Rideau Cramoisy) and to-day is the longest day of the year.

23. To the Jeu de Paume to see the Sert mural decorations for the Cathedral at Vich the "Marché dans une Ville de la Méditerranée peinte sur quarante feuilles de paravent" (silver-strong) and W.V.R.B. was there and he introduced us to Sert and we met Dezarrois who governs the Jeu de Paume and we saw Foujita and we talked with the Godepskis.

1926

June 25. Raymonde at the Prix de Drags and she was dressed in lavender and she was frail and fragile as a moonbeam and tea at the Pré Catelan and she has no intelligence but she is beautiful and is only nineteen and lives with a Roumanian tenor and she has pale blue eyes and we drank champagne and danced and there was the sadness of jazz and so Paris and goodbye. "Je suis parti sans baiser ses lèvres parce que je ne les aurais plus désirées." Is that true. Lèvres de la Lune. And where are the lips of the Sun?

29. Two arrows strike the shield of my heart—strike but do not enter—strike like arrows on a marble floor and to the Cimetière after supper and we ran Narcisse—a black arrow through the long grass and at ten o'clock "Madame la Comtesse dort." (Il y a un Monsieur qui dort).

30. Departure for America and enormously depressed. Read again Le Jardin des Caresses. "Es-tu donc le Soleil pour vouloir que je me tourne vers Toi?" (Jacqueline).

July 2. Symons writes of Gérard de Nerval "It was during one of his holidays that he saw, for the first and last time, the young girl whom he calls Adrienne and whom, under many names, he loved to the end of his life. To Gérard it seemed that already he remembered her, and certainly he was never to forget her." (Jacqueline).

And a marvelous short essay on Baudelaire—"Baudelaire desired perfection—Of the men of letters of our age he was the most scrupulous. He spent his whole life in writing one book of verse (out of which all French poetry has come since his time), one book of prose in which prose becomes a fine art, some criticism which is the sanest, the subtlest, and surest which his generation produced and a translation which is better than a marvelous original."

3. More of Symons—the essay on Villiers de l'Isle-Adam. "Become the flower of Thyself. Thou art but what thou thinkest: therefore think thyself eternal," And "Thou art the God that thou art able to become." (Thou art the Sun that thou art able to become).

4. More of Symons—Léon Cladel who (like E. E. Cummings) employs "oddities of printing, of punctuation, of the very shape of his accents!" and "l'âme de Léon Cladel était dans un constant et flamboyant automne." This is me and my Cimetière de l'Abbaye de Longchamp and my red-gold Sun.

And before going to sleep the essay on Mallarmé—"Symbolist, Decadent, Mystic"—"that chimerical search after the virginity of language"—and most, most important Mallarmé's "to name is to destroy, to suggest is to create."

5. "But to Verlaine happily, experience taught nothing; or rather it taught him only to cling the more closely to those moods in whose succession lies the more intimate part of our spiritual life. It is no doubt well for society that man should learn by experience; for the artist the benefit is doubtful. The artist it cannot be too clearly understood, has no more part in society than a

111

monk in domestic life; he cannot be judged by its rules, he can neither be praised nor blamed for his acceptance or rejection of its conventions. Social rules are made by normal people for normal people, and the man of genius is fundamentally abnormal."

The next two chapters (on Huysmans) are magnificent and I am anxious to begin A Rebours and La Cathédrale. "And the whole soul of Huysmans characterises itself in the turn of a single phrase 'that art is the only clean thing on earth except holiness.' "

July 6. Fog and the Nantucket Lightship and for the last time naked into the pool and there were cocktails and Ambrose Lightship and cocktails and Fire Lightship and then land and passports and pourboires and then New York looming gray ahead and as we docked Mrs. W. and I were holding forth on the Symbolistes (why are all the most important talks of life held on the running board of a car or in the middle of a horse-race or during a good-bye or among the whirlpool of the crowd?) Then three dreadful hours in the customs and I had to wear my fur coat the entire time (hotter than hell) and C lost her suitcase and it was found again (damn lucky) for it contained all her new manuscripts and there was a mother-in-law and a brother-in-law and the wife of the brother-in-law and eventually midnight and so, naked, to bed.

7. Watched the building of a skyscraper and it suggested a poem and how one builds the city of the soul with dreams (the city of the body with hard experience or with copulation I suppose).

Spent two hours in the Grand Central, city in itself,—but prices! Two orange juices the equivalent of two bottles of champagne in Paris. Jesus Christ.

At tea-time gin-ginger ale. (mélange adultère).

8. With C to Uncle Jack's[30] Library and the Original Manuscripts, in particular Pope, Shelley, Browning, Lafcadio Hearn (Hearn's writing was like a butterfly). My favorites are Endymion and Dorian (dead heat) (Uncle Jack has never read Dorian) then the Christmas Carol and Ivanhoe. An emotion to read aloud from Keats' own hand

> "A thing of beauty is a joy forever
> Its loveliness increases, it will never
> Pass into nothingness but will furnish
> A bower for us full of sweet sleep and health and quiet breathing."

A glass of straight gin, a hair cut and a manicure, and another glass of straight gin, all this at the Ritz, and the girl of the white polo coat took me to a cavern underground. Absinthe cocktails and vintage champagne (hands and thoughts entangled) and I smoked a cigarette for the first time since the gray dawn last September. En face du miroir and at four to the Grand Central and with C on the Merchants to Boston. Sat on the observation car, clickety-click, clickety-clack (like coming back from New York five years ago after the Dempsey-Carpentier fight) clickety-click, clickety-clack at a mile a minute and the same dust and cinders and the same sunset loveliness on water—a path of gold running into the Sun, clickety-click, clickety-clack, and New London, and iced coffee and club sandwiches and the drone of electric fans and the rattle of the train going over switches clickety-click, clickety-clack, click-click, clack-clack and Baudelaire.

> "Ce Soir, la Lune rêve avec plus de paresse:
> Ainsi qu'une beauté, sur de nombreux coussins,
> Qui, d'une main distraite et légère, caresse
> Avant de s'endormir le contour de ses seins."

And at ten Boston (scene of my former woes) and a wave of depression and H.M.C. is there and Narcisse is rescued from the baggage car (1 baby-carriage, 1 bicycle, 1 coffin, 1 dog—I am glad ours was the dog) and off we went by automobile for Manchester, and there were nauseating drug-stores and gasolene smells all the way as far as Beverly and then the real Shore (first time in four years) and then the Apple Trees.

July 10. No chance to read, no chance to write, a sleepy place but altogether unintellectual and there is bathing on the beach but I like best the grayness of Essex Links and there have been baccardi cocktails with brown sugar in them and the Vulture in my old Bugatti, and many others, many too many others.

11. Sunday at six in the morning with the Vulture in the Bugatti to the Beach and there was a silver-soft calm and a bathe without bathing suits and a naked run on the beach, and I recovered the shoe I hurled at the electric lamp last night and there was a spider in it (good omen) and I made a wish and it was for the Sun. The Beach again at noon and I was bored and C was terribly bored and I thought of the Cimetière and also of Goldenhair's lovely breasts (she sat in the sand beside me, the way she used to ten years ago).

12. C to Nantucket to see her mother and I do not like to have her away and it makes me nervous.

Discovered in my room a letter signed by Theodore Roosevelt, the one he wrote about Monks and me being admitted to the division he was going to raise and to take to France but which he never was allowed to take to France. "Not Allowed" this is the American slogan.

Uncle J here and I gave him my Longfellow letter a gift from my Library to his.

To bed to sleep upon the piazza, Narcisse curled at the foot of the bed, C curled in my thoughts.

14. Cocktails with Ted[31] and his attractive Frederika: the rose-gray orange of the cocktails (and there were plenty of them) the charm of the old house, the conversation on T. S. Eliot and Paris and the French Symbolistes.

S.V.R.C. is back and is being very nice and didn't even say anything when he knew that my account was overdrawn at the State Street (as it invariably is nowadays; for I cannot seem to and I do not want to stop being extravagant.

July 15. Luncheon at L's and R was there and a musician called Charles, or was it Childs, and there was sherry and whiskey and a four-year old daughter who had painted the trunk of a tree and L's gray, gray-blue eyes and the chambre aux miroirs and an extraordinarily fine Delacroix (a centaur with a young child with a bow and arrow on its back) and there was a fascinating copy of Picasso (blue period) and some Degas bronzes (of horses) and a Mary Cassatt (which formerly belonged to Degas) and a Carrière and a Constantin Guys and a Carpeau bust and a nice library and best of all (exception made for the Delacroix) the White Blackbird (which is a portrait of L by L) and it was strange and very much like a Goya. And Charles or Childs played at the piano and R sang and L sketched while I curled into the corner of the great sofa and thought of C (and of the girl in the white polo coat) and why has R such a nice singing voice and such a horrid speaking voice?

16. Boston and Ninety-Five and The Library, The Salon (my portrait: hair of gold, in a white smock, white socks, red slippers holding a great red India-rubber ball) and best of all the Chinese Room where I should like to smoke opium. Great credit to H.M.C. Tore up things and gave away old clothes and shook hands with poor old Mrs. Crowley the oldest of the family retainers and her deaf-as-a-post daughter Mary and at noon I met K and he presented me with a magnificent Paul Revere pitcher (archaicly simple) in solid silver and I had luncheon down town (clam chowder and strawberry short-cake) and it began to rain and afterwards I bought a pair of white silk pyjamas for ten dollars (four hundred francs). Boston a dreary place (dreary, drearier, dreariest) and entirely sunless. Aphelion.

To the Art Museum and there was a Monet with cliffs and a beach like Etretat which is the feminine half of my soul (golden-gray-green) and there was a Turner, the masculine half of my soul (red-gold). And there was the statuette in ivory and gold sixteenth century b.c. (gift from Aunt Henrietta) of the Cretan Snake Goddess. Why not a Parisian Sun-Goddess?

17. To-day remarked (à propos of I forget what) that Beatrice X had beautiful breasts, this in front of a group of men. One and all they looked embarrassed. What if I had said clitoris? This is a queer country.

18. A walk through the woods with Ted [32] and we considered editing some de luxe edition of Amy Lowell or of Poe or of some French Poet and he recommended Concerts and Humbert Wolfe (as did Mrs. W.) and I recommended E. E. Cummings and Paris.

This morning did not go to the beach fearing to find too many people.

Went alone to the beach in the afternoon and lay in the sand and bathed and ran along the shore to the rocks and back.

A sudden and tremendous thunderstorm with thunder and lightning around the house. Tonnerre de la guerre.

1926

Vers Toi (C) Je Cours.

July 19. Played a game of croquet by myself. But there was no Queen to shout "Get to your places" no hedgehogs for balls, no live flamingos for mallets, no soldiers to stand upon their hands and feet to make the arches. Nevertheless it was a game and Sun triumphed over Moon.

20. A fishing smack with an engine and among a heap of fish-nets and there was a sunstar and the harbor slipped back, sterile and empty, slipped back out of sight, and there was an evening breeze and the slow Sun was about to begin to set and the boat was a berceuse, and there was spray and frail wisps of smoke from the exhaust, and the land slipped past to the rear, the vague shoreline and deserted beaches, and sea-gulls circled in silence and there was quietness (only the chug chugging of the engine) and the orange Sun was a Sun-Goddess going down step by step into the sea, step by step wrapped in her golden veil of clouds, majestically step by step into the arms of the sea and prayers into her beauty-color prayers into the beauty (now disappearing, now disappeared of the Sun) and the color of the Sun seen through a glass of crystal gin and the color of eyes C. J. P. and the color of the eyes of poetry and the color of my own eyes. One Color into the Vanished Color of the Sun.

Health and the tang of salt-sea air and the Moon-Goddess rose step by step and waves rippled against the side of the boat (and always the chug-chugging of the engine) Cool sea-breezes and the Moon (O Beauty Thou Art God) and black weirs and gray destroyers and a flock of moored hydroplanes gently rocking, rocking gently like birds asleep and all the world was lullaby. Wave thoughts and inner rhythm and the two men up ahead straining their eyes into the evening mists

> "Or an old battered lantern hung aloft
> To light poor travellers to their distress."

Twin-gazing out to sea and the sadness of the soul and then around a point into the river and the approaching shore-line, black trees, black houses silhouetted against the golden meshes of the moon and gold eyes twinkle from dark farms and there is the neverending swish of waves and the weariness and hopelessness of life ("on est si peu de chose devant l'immensité du monde") Where have we come from? Where are we going to? Why are we always alone? The black hull of a ship, the sleepy sound of a far-off train, the absinthe color of the water, calm with a gentle swell like the rise and fall of a breast, color of absinthe, color of a woman's breast (Beatrice) and like Venice the faint odor of stagnant water and the smell of wharves and the pier-stakes (Nocturne) and

> "Around us fear, descending
> Darkness of fear above"

and the name of the boat was the Aeolus.

Shadows of the Sun

July 21. and the tintinnabulation of the bells

"Of the bells, bells, bells, bells, bells, bells, bells—
Of the singing and the tinkling of the bells."

22. E gave me a bottle of absinthe. (multiplication of the cocktail)
My costume here: a white tennis shirt (no necktie) white cotton trousers
(no socks) a black belt and red leather bed slippers.
Sun words from C.
(My soul is a Sun which is C.)
L's dinner party and Charles played Ravel and Debussy (Feu d'Artifice and
l'Après-Midi d'un Faune) ("ces nymphes, je les veux perpétuer") and Harry
Sleeper was there and there were gold lamps (like suns) and R and L and I sat
on a sofa on the balcony and I asked her the color of her soul: "Noir."

25. Red drug-stores, filling stations, comfort stations, go-to-the-right
signs, lurid billboards and automobiles swarming everywhere like vermin
over a charogne. A clean emptiness, an atmosphere of frustration, disillusion
and a great many unimportant things and unimportant people. How I hate
this community spirit with its civic federations and its boyscout clubs and its
educational toys and its Y.M.C.A. and its congregational baptist churches
and all this smug self-satisfaction. Horribly bleak, horribly depressing.

"We leave you to the dull assemblies
Charades, cantatas and lectures;
The civic meetings where you lie and act
And work up business;
The teas of forced conversation,
And receptions of how-de-does,
And stereotyped smiles;
The church sociables;
And the calls of your young men of clammy hands
And fetid breath
Pay to anaemic virgins—"

Well this is modern America and I would rather "live in Pekin and ride a
camel any day!"

"taste of ancient wine,
And put flowers in golden vases,
And open precious books of song,
And look upon dreaming Buddhas."

I hate the multitude, je suis royaliste and to hell with democracy where the
gross comforts of the majority are obtained by the sacrifice of a cultured
minority. And the telephone rings all day "coiled like a serpent ready to
strike" and I have been criticized for refusing to answer it. And all the life
here is like this, broken up into ridiculous little ten minute scenes, wherein is
no contemplation, no melancholy, no imaginativeness. Golf, bridge, tennis,

teas ("the teas of forced conversation") and nearly always the same commonplace, bourgeois, uninteresting people.

> "Le poète est semblable au prince des nuées
> Qui hante la tempête et se rit de l'archer;
> Exilé sur le sol au milieu des huées,
> Ses ailes de géant l'empêchent de marcher."

July 26. Little hope of doing any writing: newspapers and magazines flood the house, the telephone tinkles at all hours ("the winds that will be howling at all hours") it tinkled nine times after supper and the buzz of motors on the main road is unceasing. Not to mention the dreary voice of the singing kitchen maid (no one dares to tell her to keep quiet). Little hope of doing any reading and it is time we were returning to France.

27. Mrs. Gardner's Palace which is a credit to Boston; the red soul-lantern light in a vague blue-black darkness (Whistler) and the Rape of Europa (Titian) and the next best Raphael I ever saw (very small as is the best Raphael (The Three Graces at Chantilly.)) But there were too many unimportant bric à brac. Thought in colors: the purple of a plate, the sun-green light in the courtyard, the gold yellow of the big Sargent, the inner red of the vague Whistler, the rust-gold of a Japanese screen, the pastoral greens and blues and reds of the remarkable and erotic ceiling, the shower of red-gold in Cushing's painting of Ethel and the dull reds and greens and golds of the book-bindings.

28. Green and Gold and Alligator Pears and Where are the lions? Where are the lions?

29. Rain and orchidaceousness and gin-ginger ale (from a silver flask) and through the fog to the Shore. The Enormous Fog. Yet always the Invisible Sun. Seek ye out of the Book of the Sun and read.

30. To Nantucket with Narcisse. Two chocolate milk-shakes and a fat chicken sandwich (typical U.S.A. hurry-lunch). A dreary trip. Wood's Hole a horrid place. Horrid boat. Sat out on deck on a coil of rope and read a chapter on Japanese Female Names (Lafcadio Hearn) Saw a man called Graves (used to play with him fifteen years ago when we were children.) We drank all the bottle of gin I was bringing down to my mother-in-law. Nantucket and down the gangplank holding a leash and empty collar unaware that Narcisse had slipped out of it and disappeared into the crowd! C in her pink sweater and where is Narcisse? Across the bleak island to Siasconset. Thanked the Sun for and thought of Aeolus and Green and Gold. (And the Alligator Pears)

31. Siasconset of all places the most dreary. Bourgeois. Mediocre to a degree. Frightening. Shrill voices of children, unsympatheticness, the horrid manners of Helen the cook. No opportunity for reading. Decided to leave with C Tuesday instead of Friday as planned. The day after to-morrow.

Shadows of the Sun

After supper C and I and the mother-in-law to the Cinema and it was disgusting, especially the audience, and there was rowdyism among the children (they hissed a picture of the parade of the French Mutilées) for whom this damn country seems to be run and how the place smelt, stank rather, of bananas and cococola and ice-cream. Resolved to become a Persian. Thank Christ (if the Sun-God is willing) a month from to-night we should be back in Nineteen Rue de Lille.

Before supper to-night holding an orange-blossom cocktail towards the red sun, the red-gold knowledge of the color of my burning shone into the remoteness of my soul. Thank You O Sun and Prayers and Aeolus and Green and Gold and the Cimetière de l'Abbaye de Longchamp.

August 1. "And I saw that the light which was mine shifted tint with each changing of thought. Ruby it sometimes shone, and sometimes sapphire: now it was flame of topaz; again, it was fire of emerald ("carved of one emerald centered in the Sun") And the meaning of the changes I could not fully know. But thoughts of the earthly life seemed to make the light burn red; while thoughts of supernal beings—of ghostly beauty and of ghostly bliss,—seemed to kindle ineffable rhythms of azure and of violet. But of white lights there were none in all the Visible. And I marvelled"—(and here is the most important thing Lafcadio Hearn has said, for me terribly important)—"Even as the color of thy burning, so is the worth of thee." But what of you and I who are Noir? Black Suns.

Liked very much his chapter on Old Japanese songs:

> Kano yuku wa
> Kari Ka? Kugui Ka?
> Kari haraba,
> That which yonder flies,
> Wild goose is it, Swan is it?
> Wild goose if it be;

And this other one in particular

> Bindatara wo
> Ayugaséba koso
> Ayugaséba koso
> Aikyo Zuitaré!
>   Yaréko toto
>   Yaréko toto!
> With loosened hair,
> Only because of having tossed it
> Only because of having shaken it
>   Oh, sweet she is!
>   Yaréko toto!
>   Yaréko toto!

and thought to myself "What shall be the first word I shall speak in August." Narcisse. Heard discussions about the children's washing, about time-tables, about Helen and how she must have two hours to spend on the beach, about food, about the neighbors, about uninteresting plans. Et toutes les hideurs de la domesticité.

Thought of Aeolus and Gold and Green. The mauve frailness of her hair. The roundness of her knees and of "how it was worth while being born just to read Baudelaire."

August 2. A bathe before breakfast with C and the Sun is a path of gold towards France. Cocktail before luncheon. The color of the cocktail: pale orange-gold. Color is Beauty. My thoughts are like the colors of the sun. A walk on the sand through the fog. The summer half-way mark. A sea-gull lost in the fog. O lost sea-bird. The fog creeping in over the sea. As I grow older, more every day, I draw into my own stronghold, with thoughts of J and C in circles around my soul with poetry for outer wall.

3. Boston and the Chinese Room. Perfume and pearls and the prolongation of pleasure. Narcisse Noir upon the soft black carpet, the red flamingo in the black picture frame, the black lacquer bed, the strange exotic flowers of the wall-paper.

5. In the afternoon on the roof naked and alone and after supper champagne on the roof and stars (children of the Sun) overhead.

6. To the glass collection and liked best a branch of dark autumn leaves and a pale flesh-rose stamen (most physical.) How Madame Godepski would have loved this collection. Then across the river to the Museum and the Monet (feminine side of the soul the sun soft pale green gold). Then Turner's Slave Ship. The red-gold strength of my soul. A blaze. Oneness. With all the slave-sins, the chains and shackles, the sharks and sword-fish rereward going into the abyss of the sea. The soul red-gold in the Sun. Fog creeping in over the Shore and the dull far-off booming of the fog-horn. Interior feeling. And to-day I have repeated to myself a hundred times the word "Cramoisy." (Adieu Rose).

7. I awake and look at my watch. It is seven minutes of seven and this is the seventh day of the month. Miraculous. But too bad it isn't July. My superstitions legion. Always put on right sock before left, right shoe before left shoe. Believe that right foot is masculine, the left feminine. Cross myself before every drink and think of J.C. (not Jesus Christ). Believe that 7, 1, 4, 8 are the best numbers, that T, O, H, C, X, are the best letters. Knocking on wood. And mirrormania in relation to Prayer. But they can all be explained.

The beach and the heavy surf and C in a fascinating new black-silk bathing suit. And a run on the sands. Alice Gould here and we talk about poetry on the piazza in the thunderstorm.

8. Sunnygolden. So glad we didn't go to the dance last night. To the Unitarian Church in Manchester. All the family for the dedication of the stained glass window. The colours of the painted glass and the Sun filtering through, gold filtering through red. Simplicity. But afterwards the regular service. Dreary. Weak hymns and a sermon I disagreed with. A wooden church is like a house built on sand; no strength, no mystery. The unsecurity of bric à brac. Religion should be strange, mysterious, with dark colours. Here one is too much in the open. Afterwards to the beach. Gigantic surf and many people.

August 12. The new modern trees are the green and red and orange gasolene tanks that sprout like iron weeds along the roads. And the myriad dull telegraph poles. But no real trees. A quiet dinner quietly served. And afterwards upon the terrace Aunt E in gray read to us from Nehemiah Grew, my supposedly great, great great (not more) grandfather. I quote from one of his books: "The Womb of a Woman, blown up and dried. Together with the Spermatick Vessels annexed; and the arteries in the bottom of the Uterus, undulated like the Claspers of a Vine; all filled up with foft wax. Alfo the Membranous and Round Ligaments of the Womb, the Ureters, Bladder, Clitoris, Nymphal, Hymen, Fallopian Tube and the Ovarys, commonly called the Tefticles; all made moft curiously vifibly, and given by Dr. Swammerdam."

13. Picnic on Coffins Beach. Soft orange-gray sun on gray-gold water. Memories of Goldenhair. Built a bonfire. Ted and I went in bathing and ran up the beach, Narcisse at our heels. Soup with sherry in it. Chicken salad. Alligator Pears (Green and Gold). And soda biscuits and beer. The redgold of the flames against the blackness of the night. Home at one o'clock and disapproved of and lectured for staying out so late. Will they ever give up treating us like children?

16. The red bookbindings in the colonial room, the dark lacquer on the ceiling of the bedroom, the jars of cookies and the crude furniture in the old New England dining room. (Gin and 405). A house where one would not mind being prisoner: so sombre, so rustic and yet so luxurious, so vague and yet so absolute. (Pouring rain on the way home).

20. Saw L very quiet in a murasaki (purple dress). What letter of the alphabet do you like best. "I" of course. Is particularly interested in repetition and showed me some reproductions of Giotto. Liked best a little drawing of hers in the shape of a fan representing a nude like Maja Desnuda while above seven shoulders of seven girls. "Not possibly to put over a door." Gave me three books to take back to Levitsky. Left her standing in the sun. No time for luncheon as I did not want to be late for golf. Played for a book and I won. Three threes. Play ended at my favourite hole and I prayed through the rocks of the cavern, dark-gold to the Sun. Then back to the clubhouse. The almost-autumn sun and the crisp tang in the air. Told her (not L) she was like marble. Chiselled and chaste like a poem of H.D.'s. Eyes que je ne peux pas dire and I have never seen anyone so pure. (Orangeades and buttered toast with cinnamon). Chasteness of sea-girls.

21. Tom Barbour an authority on reptiles. Has written a book called Reptiles and Amphibians. Told us the extraordinary story of how a twelve-foot python he was bringing back in a canvas box escaped at four in the morning in a Pullman car and how the porter was terrified and shot at it and killed it. Pythons he said can go for three months without eating and they live so long that no one has as yet been able to determine their length of life. Afterwards discussed fighting-fish in Siam. How fish-fighting was a real sport in Siam, how they fought in a large bottle, how they fought with their fins and to the death, how they were very small, and how they changed colours when they were angry. Knew about this what with my studies in the Encyclopedia on Siam and the description by the man from Siam at Etretat. Barbour gave me the address of a man in New York who has pythons for sale. Goodbye to Goldenhair. Like a naiad and her lips were cool and tasted of the sea. Late for luncheon and the lecture in consequence. Too bad on the last day and all because I took the long road home through Cathedral Woods.

August 22. Boston and the Back Bay and the Knickerboker to New York clickety-click clickety-clack mile after mile clickety-clack clickety-click away away away from Boston, clickety-click clickety-clack and sat in the observation car and read the walls of advertisements along the way Colonial Ethyl (the revolutionary gas) Old Gold (the dawn of a better cigarette) Ning Young Chop Suey the Checker Cab Company (every driver an escort) M.C.A. cigars, cigarettes and chewing gum Keep Cool Electrically The League of Zionest Revisionests sanitary rooms for furniture storage educational toys glove-fitting corsets hot and cold rolled strip steel polished plate wire glass Unguentine Dr Caldwell's Syrup Pepsin (the family laxative, millions of children love it) Zemo for skin irritation 35 cents and $1 all druggists relieves rashes chafing and eczema clears the complexion fine after shaving The latest in Dress Shields Kleinert's Brassierette slip-over garment shield You said a pipeful 10 cent tin union Leader smoking tobacco Musterole rub it on better than a mustard plaster for coughs colds neuralgia headache rheumatism and congestion Hathaway's Bread famous for fifty years Menthol Cough Drops make breathing easier Unmatched (camel cigarettes) four out of five of them will get pyorrhea brush your teeth with Forhan's for the gums more than a tooth paste it checks pyorrhea Ventilated Refrigerator etcetera ad nauseam. One gradually gets so that it is impossible not to look at them they are everywhere in horrid blues and reds and oranges, everywhere waiting to attack one's brain like beasts of prey. Industrialism is triumphant and ugliness, sordid ugliness is everywhere destroying beauty, which has fled to the museums (dead) or into the dark forests of the soul (alive). (Beauty is in my inmost me facing a circle outwards to shield my soul from sordidness).

(And the Madonna of the Pearls).

28. *At Sea.* Letter T: turquoise, tusk, tankard, tapestry, Tartar, tea-chest, teak, temperamental, tempestuous, tenderness, tetrarch, thousand, threnody, throng, thrust, tiara, timber, tintinnabulation, toadstool, typhoon,

topaz, tortoise, traceried, trackless, trample, triumphant, troglodyte, trumpet, tufted, tuneless, turbulent, turmoil, tigress.

August 30. Xebec, xanthic, xylograph, xystus. Yak, yammer, yashmak, yellow-blossomed, yew, yoni, yielding, yoke, yen. Zenith, zebra, zephyr, zigzag, zoo, zither, zodiac, zythum. And now I have finished the English dictionary and have read them from aardvark to zythum.

The gold beam from a light house. France. Prayers.

31. Paris. And all other lands and cities dwindle to Nothingness. Paris the City of the Sun.

September 8. "Fuis-la, tu entends. Ou sinon, tu es perdu! Tu passeras ta vie à courir après un fantôme que tu ne rejoindras jamais! Car on ne les rejoins jamais. Ce sont des ombres. Il faut les laisser se promener entre elles dans leur royaume d'ombres! Ne pas s'en approcher. Elles sont dangereuses—

"Elles ne sont pas pour nous—

"Seul devant l'alliance secrète de deux êtres qui s'entendent, qui se devinent parce qu'ils sont pareils, parce qu'ils sont du même sexe, d'une autre planète que lui, l'étranger, l'ennemi—

"Et souviens-toi que tu auras beau faire elle n'est pas pour toi. Elles ne sont pas pour nous, jamais".

16. The Louvre and the Primitifs, the Piéta (Ecole d'Avignon) and the Fouquets and the Clouets. After supper read a preface to Villon and then the Petit Testament.

> "En ce temps que j'ay dit devant
> Sur le Noël, morte saison,
> Lorsque les loups vivent de vent
> Et qu'on se tient en sa maison."

And in stanza twenty-five:

> "Derechief, je laisse en pitié,
> A troys petis enfans tous nuds,
> Nommez en ce présent traictié,
> Paouvres orphelins impourveuz,
> Et desnuez comme le ver;
> J'ordonne qu'ils seront pourveuz,
> Au moins pour passer cest yver."

19. After supper drank green mints with C. Frosted green. More chaste than the green and gold of the alligator pears and C philosophizes and arrives at a conclusion—She says: "To create is instinctive not logical. The female is more instinctive than the male. Therefore the Creator is Female." To substantiate this she goes on to say "Before one can create something logically one has to create the will to create, which is in itself instinctive." Sun God or Sun-Goddess?

1926

September 21. At last a gray day. And the interior feeling. J - H - C - Poetry for Eternity in Sun. Studied in the Encyclopedia. I wonder how many Children of the Ritz know who the Acoemeti were or what an Acrolith is or the meaning of the word Albedo?

By myself to the Cluny. Gray day outside, moyen age within. A dagger with skulls on the handle, Leda and the swan (wood panel) the two chastity belts, the superb collection of old keys, the illuminated manuscripts, the stained glass windows, the dame à la licorne, the old book bindings, and the old sixteenth-century bed. I walk in the grayness of the garden. Then home along the quays stopping on the way to buy a La Rochefoucauld and two ponderous tomes on Amphibians and Reptiles which I shall send to Barbour.

Wilde says "Books, I fancy, may be conveniently divided into three classes:

1. Books to read, such as Cicero's Letters, Suetonius, Vasari's Lives of the Painters, the Autobiography of Benvenuto Cellini, Sir John Mandeville, Marco Polo, Saint Simon's Memoirs, Momsen, and (till we get a better one) Grote's History of Greece.

2. Books to re-read, such as Plato and Keats: in the sphere of poetry, the masters not the minstrels; in the sphere of philosophy, the seers not the savants.

3. Books not to read at all, such as Thomson's Seasons, Roger's Italy, Paley's Evidences, all the Fathers except Saint Augustine, all John Stuart Mill except the essay on Liberty, all Voltaire's plays without any exception, Butler's Analogy, Grant's Aristotle, Hume's England, Lowe's History of Philosophy; all argumentative books and all books that try to prove anything."

24. Pelléas and Mélisande and Mary Garden sang and we sat in the second balcony (the nine and the seven in the first row) and A sat below us in the first balcony and I dropped coins on his head. During an entr'acte saw Bill Burgess. He has been in India and is now starting off for the Belgian Congo to hunt Gorillas (to Basle to paint Locomotives).

25. Rue de Lappe. This time to the Bal des 3 Colonnes, men dancing with men, accordion music, the cobblestones and the gendarmes and the girls in the street. Afterwards through little side streets, the Rue des Lions, the Rue Charlemagne, past low dives and hoarse laughter, past isoloires and réverbères, past a drunkard asleep on a bench, past lovers embracing, past the only timbered house in Paris, past an empty lot, over the Seine, the quai d'Anjou and the Rue des Deux Ponts and over a bridge again with Notre Dame to our right and through the Rue Zacharie and up the Montagne Sainte Geneviève and the Rue de l'Epée de Bois and the Rue d'Ulm and the Rue Pot de Fer, and then the Luxembourg and then to Les Vikings for sandwiches and champagne. And always above us the unbarricaded Moon.

28. Virginia Woolf: "Should you wish to make sure that your birthday will be celebrated three hundred years hence, your best course is undoubtedly

to keep a diary. Only first be certain that you have the courage to lock your genius in a private book and the humour to gloat over a fame that will be yours only in the grave. For the good diarist writes either for himself alone or for a posterity so distant that it can safely bear every secret and justly weigh every motive. For such an audience there is need neither of affectation nor of restraint. Sincerity is what they ask, detail, volume; skill with the pen comes in conveniently, but brilliance is not necessary; genius is a hindrance even; and should you know your business and do it manfully, posterity will let you off mixing with great men, reporting famous affairs, or having lain with the first ladies in the land." Or having lain with the first ladies of the land.

October 1. Finished the chapter on Aristotle in the philosophy book: "That the soul in infancy is scarcely distinguishable from the soul of animals, that everything in the world is moved by an inner urge to become something greater than it is, that the aim of art is to represent not the outward appearance of things, but their inward significance. That above all, the function of art is catharsis, purification—"

5. In my thoughts (mêlée de couleurs de toutes sortes) is an arc-en-ciel and I believe that the soul is a fire of colours, burning year in year out into the perfect colour that is the Sun. I believe that love is like a stained glass window. I believe that the only relation of the body to the soul is that of the colour of the body to the colour of the soul. I believe that the Sun is the perfect combination of all colours, *the perfect* Colour. I believe that my soul is a rainbow, a Queen to whom the mind which is male brings all the treasures (colours) that it can offer. The queen selects what is most beautiful and stores it away within her colour, colours within a colour, Suns within a Sun.

6. Douglas Burden, and he has returned from a successful expedition to the Dutch West Indies in quest of a new and heretofore undiscovered species of lizard. He shot fourteen of them and captured and sent back to the New York Zoo two of them alive. He said that lizards had wonderful eyesight, a wonderful sense of smell (they would travel for miles for bait) and that they could devour a boar in ten chimpanzees, also that they had a tendency to vomit at the slightest provocation and that even as they ran they would sometimes vomit. Their age no one can tell. He brought back a little bear which he keeps in the garden of their hotel (Princess) (Not the Bear).

7. C cramoisy, J grey, I gold, three in one into the red-gold of the Sun. The dying day. Darkness and a Star "et la met dans mon coeur loin des yeux du soleil" and from the Wretch's Catechism I read aloud over and over again the Lord's Prayer in Latin:

Pater noster, qui es in coelis, sanctificetur nomen Tuum; adveniat regnum Tuum; fiat voluntas Tua, sicut in coelo et in terra.

Panem nostrum quotidianum da nobis hodie; et dimitte nobis debita nostra, sicut et nos dimittimus debitoribus nostris; et ne nos inducas in tentationem; sed libera nos a malo.

Amen.

and to Boris again (La Chanson du Fou).

October 8. Pelléas and Mary Garden sang and Bourdin is a wonderful Pelléas. "L'âme humaine a, enfin, trouvé son langage furtif et suppliant." (parmi des dentelles).

9. Plato, Aristotle, Bacon and Spinoza in the book of philosophy. And now Voltaire.

> "Dors-tu content, Voltaire, et ton hideux sourire
> Voltige-t-il encore sur tes os décharnés?
> Ton siècle était, dit-on, trop jeune pour te lire,
> Le notre doit te plaire, et tes hommes sont nés."

But before leaving Spinoza I must note how he writes that "pleasure and pain are the satisfaction or the hindrance of an instinct; they are not the causes of our desires, but their results; we do not desire things because they give us pleasure; but they give us pleasure because we desire them, and we desire them because we must," and how he defines happiness as "the presence of pleasure and the absence of pain." And most important "in so far as the mind sees things in their eternal aspect it participates in Eternity (thus my soul because it sees sun color in its eternal aspect participates in Sun Eternity).

And in the garden touching the tree I pray for a cramoisy-grey shadow within my gold shadow into the invisible Sun.

11. "that unflagging intellectual conscience which enslaves a man to make a genius," and in defense of suicide he (Voltaire) writes "for is there anything more absurd than to wish to carry continually a burden which one can always throw down?" (Sun-Death)

12. Sherry and Schopenhauer. I like him best of the philosophers (and sherry best of the light wines.)

(1) What was it that led the cynics to repudiate pleasure in any form, if it was not the fact that pain is, in a greater or less degree, always bound up with pleasure.

(2) We are unhappy married and unmarried we are unhappy—

(3) We can survive certain experiences or fears only by forgetting them.

(4) The final refuge is suicide. Here at last, strange to say, thought and imagination conquer instinct. Diogenes is said to have put an end to himself by refusing to breathe—what a victory over the will to live!

(5) A life devoted to the acquisition of wealth is useless until we know how to turn it into joy, and this is an art that requires culture and wisdom. A succession of sensual pursuits never satisfies for long; one must understand the ends of life as well as the true art of acquiring means. Men are a thousand times more intent on becoming rich than on acquiring culture, though it is

quite certain that what a man is contributes more to his happiness than what he has.

(6) In the end everyone stands alone.

October 14. More Sherry and more Schopenhauer. "By seeing so far he (the genius) does not see what is near; he is imprudent and 'queer'; and while his vision is hitched to a star he falls into a well. Hence, partly, the unsociability of the genius; he is thinking of the fundamental, the universal, the eternal; the others are thinking of the temporary, the specific, the immediate; his mind and theirs have no common ground, and never meet. As a rule a man is sociable just in the degree in which he is intellectually poor and generally vulgar. The man of genius has his compensations, and does not need company so much as people who live in perpetual dependence on what is outside them. (The Children of the Ritz) The pleasure which he receives from all beauty, the consolation which art affords, the enthusiasm of the artist, enable him to forget the cares of life, and repay him for all the suffering that increases in proportion to the clearness of consciousness, and for his desert loneliness among a different race of men. The result, however, is that genius is forced into isolation, and sometimes into madness; the extreme sensitiveness which brings him pain along with imagination and intuition, combines with solitude and maladaptation to break the bonds that hold the mind to reality." Aristotle was right again: Men distinguished in philosophy, politics, poetry or art appear to be all of a melancholy temperament. The direct connection of madness and genius is established by the biographies of great men, such as Rousseau, Byron, Poe, etc., etc. "Yet in these semi-madmen, these geniuses, lies the true aristocracy of mankind" (applause of Suns crashing against Suns) and "The Hindus were deeper than the thinkers of Europe, because their interpretation of the world was internal and intuitive, not external and intellectual"—

15. Finished the Story of Philosophy.

> "Myself when young did eagerly frequent
> Doctor and Saint, and heard great argument
> About it and about: but evermore
> Came out by the same door where in I went."

Yet I must write my philosophy. Sun and the Prayers to the Sun, Sun and the Sun-Death.

16. Last night in the bordel ("dans ce bordel où tenons nostre état") they wanted us to pay a thousand francs to see a girl tied to a post and flagellated. Would I have the courage to flagellate a girl, for in a queer way it would take courage. Yet is it any crueler than the sharp sarcastic lashes of the tongue? And to-day I feel the need of rain. And I read to the Madonna of the Pearls from T. S. Eliot in the taxicab. And there was the smoke of a brushwood fire and red embers.

1926

October 17. "I must go to bed now—you see I am thinking of you just before I go to bed as you asked me to—and I shall probably be thinking of you before I go to sleep tonight, wondering where you are and why you don't write." (cri de coeur from the dark).

Darkness and the quiet sound of the rain. And the relaxing from tension. And I finished the Knight's Tale by Chaucer ("so that I have my lady in my arms") and J is dark grey and C dark cramoisy.

18. Cocktails at the Crillon. The black trees against the dying day. And a dark red sun (darkness and silver fire). And a large silver moon.—And if I had a daughter I should name her Mélisande. Or Beatrice? Or Aurora?

19. Burden to tea and he talks on the Cambodian jungle and the ruined temples and Khmer art, and of red and black centipedes and scorpions and cobras, and of strange fish that can climb trees. Read aloud to him what Schopenhauer said about the bulldog scorpion of Australia—how if it is cut in two, a battle begins between the head and the tail, how the head seizes the tail with its teeth, and the tail defends itself bravely by stinging the head, and of how the battle may last for half an hour, until they die or are dragged away by other ants. B had never heard of this but had seen lizards who on being pursued sloughed off their tails which whirled round by themselves and attracted the pursuer while the lizard escaped. As queer as my sonnet

> Within the strange menagerie of my brain
> Fantastic figures fornicate and fuse
> Into deciduous monsters that abuse
> The girl gold visions over whom I reign.

21. It is raining. Yellow and red is the color of my Magyar, yellow and red in my heart, yellow and red in my soul and read Aucassin et Nicolette. "C'est en enfer que je veux aller!— Et là vont les belles dames courtoises, qui ont deux amis ou trois outre leurs mari; et là vont l'or et l'argent et les fourrures, le vair et le gris; et là vont harpeurs et jongleurs et ceux qui sont les rois de ce monde: avec ceux-là je veux aller, pourvu que j'aie Nicolette, ma très douce amie, avec moi!" (pourvu que j'aie Caresse, ma très douce amie, avec moi!)

23. Cold and gray. We took Narcisse for a long walk through the Bois. Dead leaves and dead water on the ponds. Pale swans drifting. Shadow-shapes drifting through trees. Sadness and grayness and at half past four darkness. I love I love gray days.

Read Montaigne on suicide or sortie raisonnable as the Stoiciens called it —(Sun Death I call it)—"car il y a en la vie plusieurs choses pires à souffrir que la mort mesme; tesmoing cet enfant lacedemonien pris par Antigonus et vendu pour serf, lequel pressé par son maistre à s'employer à quelque service abject: Tu verras, dit-il, qui tu as acheté; ce me serait honte de servir, ayant la liberté si à main, et, ce disant, se précipita du haut de la maison"—"C'est ce qu'on dit que le sage vit tant qu'il doit, non pas tant qu'il peut; et que le présent que la nature nous ait fait le plus favorable et qui nous oste tout

moyen de nous pleindre de nostre condition, c'est de nous avoir laissé la clef
des champs. Elle n'a ordonné qu'une entrée à la vie, et cent mille yssües"—"à
mourir il ne reste que le vouloir. Et ce n'est pas la recepte à une seule
maladie, la mort est la recepte à tous maux: c'est un port très assuré, qui n'est
jamais à craindre et souvent à rechercher. Tout reviens à un, que l'homme se
donne sa fin où qu'il la souffre, qu'il coure au devant de son jour ou qu'il
l'attende; d'où qu'il vienne, c'est toujours le sien, en quelque lieu que le filet
se rompe, il y est tout, c'est le bout de la fusée. La plus volontaire mort, c'est
la plus belle. La vie dépend de la volonté d'autrui; la mort, de la nostre."

October 28. To Perugia for my shoes. At last they are ready. They are
black and I have a new pair of pearl-gray spats. I leave my old pair of shoes,
faithful friends since I came back from the war in 1919. Seven years. How
many hundreds of thousands of steps, how many million steps have I walked
in them, how many countries have they seen, how many streets have they
crossed how many stairs have they mounted, ("the secret place of the stairs")
how many bars have they known, how many rendez-vous have they led me
to, how many storms have they passed through! Farewell faithful shoes
Farewell. Adios. October darkness and the sadness of dead leaves and an
Orchid to C (One because we are One).

> "I should have been a pair of ragged claws
> Scuttling across the floors of silent seas."

30. Darker and darker. (I drink sherry.) And at five o'clock on foot
through the rain to the Place Vendôme, the sky an inverted bowl of purple-
gold, the wet bronze column like a gold-black phallus yearning for the night.
Down Pretty Alley past Boué dresses and Mercator ships and Tristesse to the
Mauretania. (The Ritz bar and a bacardi cocktail). And a book-shop just off
the Rue Royale in a sort of a corner between The Trois Quartiers and Cooks.
There I found the first edition of Bilitis on handmade paper in the most
luxurious of bindings, the copy that Pierre Louys gave to Heredia, with a
dédicace and the poet's signature. Price seven thousand five hundred. "Il
m'étreint si fort qu'il me brisera, pauvre petite fille que je suis; mais dès qu'il
est en moi je ne sais plus rien du monde, et on me couperait les quatre
membres sans me réveiller de ma joie." (Etretat)

To Le Grand Guignol. What with reading Monsieur de Phocas all
afternoon ("le passé est une charogne qui empoisonne tout votre moi") and
seeing l'Etrangleuse and the Spectre Ensanglanté in the evening I am ready to
bid adieu to the macabre and seek beauty through strength and simplicity
(The Sun.) Still raining as we drove off in the Hispano to somewhere on the
Avenue du Bois, where a queer-looking pale-faced Chauve-Souris in a
brown robe-de-chambre and leather bed-slippers opened the door.

31. It is midnight and a Sunday and as we lie among the cushions I can
hear the rain pouring down upon the street ("il pleut dans mon coeur comme
il pleut dans la ville"). Z is busily preparing a pipe, deftly twisting the treacly
substance over a little lamp while Y paler than I have ever seen her reaches

out white hands like a child asking for its toy. The Chauve-Souris is crouched in a corner a monocle stuck in one eye reading aloud from La Légende des Sexes. Opposite us a coal fire burns in the grate. The lamplight is dim and the smell of opium is sweet and heavy. Far off I hear the lonely tooting of a taxi horn. Inside warmth and drowsiness. Dolce Farniente.

C smoked five pipes and I seven. A dizziness when the light went on and we rose unsteadily to our feet. So through the rain to 19 Rue de Lille and after letting Narcisse out and touching the tree and praying prayers I crawled into our warm bed (C already asleep) and after half an hour of nervousness, windows were banging everywhere and curtains flapping in the wind and Grand Guignol scenes in hordes, I fell asleep. It must have been three or four in the morning. And between the folded sheets of the heart the purple petal of an orchid.

November 2. Walk in the Bois through the rain. On returning home we find Burden and we discuss the theory of evolution. So many nowadays who believe there is no after-life. And science has so many seemingly conclusive proofs. But for me there is the soul absolutely without one doubt whether it be a shadow or a tree or a fountain or a sun and I believe this soul is as eternal as eternity, as eternal as the Sun.

6. H.D. very crisp, very chiseled. Amy Lowell says "H.D.'s life is that of a true artist. It is one of internal mental and emotional experiences not of external events." And so my life is an internal life, from the security of the inside, towards the unsecurity of the outside.

Burden for luncheon and we went through the Catacombs. Pilfered three skulls and two huge bones which I concealed in a scarlet bag under my raincoat, and afterwards to the Bois to exercise Narcisse and the Bear.

Read l'Eloge de la Paresse. "La paresse est aussi la poésie. Ovide nomme les poèmes otia, c'est-à-dire les fruits de la paresse. Dis-moi: que serait un poète sans la rêverie? Un poète que ne connaît pas cet état d'attente, de disponibilité, de solitude, le seul où les ombres consentent à venir, ses propres ombres, témoins de sa vie et d'autres, plus incertaines et toutefois lancinantes, qui dictent d'une voix inconnue. Paresse de Baudelaire, Paresse de Musset, Paresse de Villon."

10. Wrote

SUN GHOST

The sun that leaves the body
Is naked as the pool
Through whose forgotten beauty
It passes, sorrowful,
Among the frightened naiads
Who tremble in their cave
To sea a phantom weeping
Like eyes within a grave.

Shadows of the Sun

Armistice Day. (eight years now) And the students carried flowers to the graves of their friends and then came here for champagne. And we opened a jereboam for them and in ten minutes there was not a drop left and C and I with the Crouchers to watch the parade on the Champs-Elysées and there were tattered battleflags and cavalry and infantry and the cannon over by the Invalides firing salutes. And a glass of brandy to Oliver Ames Junior and a glass of brandy to Aaron Davis Weld.

November 12. Baigneuse (ce titre a été donné par Redon), Eau-forte (ours).

"En un paysage irréel, émerge au milieu de floraisons fantastiques une femme nue debout dont la tête inclinée laisse retomber devant elle sa longue chevelure pendante.

"Redon grava ce cuivre avant 1914. Il ne le considérait point comme achevé et pensait y ajouter un paon." Peacocks of the Sun.

13. To the Cimetière de l'Abbaye de Longchamp and the Roux presented us with a "canard" (nourished on corpses?) and it was wonderful to see the pleasure they got from giving us this gift and there were Prayers and the Lady of the Gold Horse with the Diamond Eyes came to supper and we three sat on the cramoisy cushions and drank green mints and then went through the rain to visit the Chauve-Souris.

14. Last night for the first time really experienced the kief, and saw strange but clear visions, not vague as in a dream, but chaste with colors of pure gold and sun shining through green water and a fountain under the sea spouting jets of silver fish and an autumn-gold forest with a path leading into infinity (I have never seen such a depth of perspective) and white bodies of fauns and nymphs appearing and disappearing, copulating and uncopulating.

17. In Montaigne I read: "Nous ne pouvons dignement concevoir la grandeur de ces hautes et divines promesses, si nous les pouvons concevoir: pour dignement les imaginer, il les faut imaginer inimaginables, indicibles et incompréhensibles" (Invisible Sun) and C finished her sonnet-sequence and a search for a title for her new book of poems (not Painted Shores) Painted Lanterns, Occupants of the Heart, Evening Faces, A Goddess Asks, Red Leafage. And it is hard to decide. Occupants of the Heart? And is Raymonde an Occupant of the Heart?

19. Within a wall of silver ice a wall of emerald; within a wall of emerald a wall of purple; within a wall of purple a gold wall; within the gold wall a castle of cramoisy and grey (C and J).

22. Raymonde chez Philippe. You are very beautiful Raymonde. Fire-golden. Baron Z all the way from Italy to dine with C.

24. Raymonde chez Philippe. You are very beautiful Raymonde. Fire-golden. Lord L. all the way from England to dine with C.

[handwritten margin note: CRIMSON Cloth]

1926

December 7. Jumped over the bench in the Tuileries à rebours, feat that took me a year to make up my mind to do and counted the Books (almost a thousand) and made by dipping the tail of Narcisse into ink his signature (reproduction impossible).

12. Ninon de Lenclos in a letter to the Marquis de Villarceaux writes: "Je vous ai dit cent fois que je ne voulais vous enchaîner que par les plaisirs. C'est un amant que j'aime et non pas un esclave—Vous allez me trouver bien indulgente. C'est toujours notre faute si l'on nous est infidèle, sûrement nous avons oublié d'ajouter quelques fleurs à la chaîne qu'il fallait embellir de tout le prestige de l'amour, pour la rendre éternelle." And in another: J'ai soupé hier avec des personnes qui vous connaissent beaucoup; elles voulaient me persuader que vous étiez léger, même infidèle, les méchantes gens! J'ai bien vite rompu la conversation peut-être auraient-ils détruit ma tranquillité— L'aveuglement vaut mieux qu'un jour qui blesse." No. No.

22. C'est fou comme j'ai froid
C'est fou comme j'ai chaud
C'est fou comme j'ai soif
C'est fou comme j'ai sommeil

and "if two lie together then they have heat, but how can one be warm alone?"

Christmas and the Silver Christmas Tree. (It is the Sun. The Sun above us governs our conditions) and One as the Sunray with the Sun (and I give to you my soul and I give to you my body—in a silver stream of fire). And a black gardenia on the grave of the Danseuse du Roi. And H within C within J into the red-gold of the Sun (For Eternity). And no supper and I caught the Orient Express. And this is the second Christmas in succession that I have not heard or spoken a word of English. And the train was cold and so was I and I curled under my fur coat and fell asleep.

28. Across the snow with C and the blinding sunshine and the myriad gold suns on the snow and she skis and I watch her swoop down the hill and I carry her skis for her uphill and Narcisse is a black arrow flying across the snow. And with M and H to a hof bar where we drink the new wine. H the realist and M the dreamer. And there was potato salad. And they both know Joyce and go to his readings. And they said he spent 1000 hours on the last chapter of Ulysses. And I asked them what they thought of Cummings and they both liked The Enormous Room best and I haven't read it. And they both think Cocteau is an ass and so do I and all three of us despise the English. And M said to read Anabase (Perse) and H said he wrote the story about the Wind Blows (the best story in the book) in half an hour. And M is quieter but they both have charm—rare in anyone, especially in men— nowadays. And M said he read very little. And H had been to the cock-fighting in Seville. And we drank. And H could drink us under the table. And everyone wanted to pay for the wine. And M won (that is he paid). And out into the cold and a hard walk uphill.

The last day of the year and Paris in the rain and I love Paris "jusques à ses verrues et à ses taches." and there was Raymonde at the Ritz and a Soleil Chinois and a bottle of Napoleon brandy for the Count and two Persian lions carved in wood for W.V.R.B. and a Persian Print for the "charmeuse d'âmes" and Prayers: cramoisy within gold within grey into the red-gold Sun (for Eternity). Forever and Ever mêlée de couleurs de toutes sortes and

If I die C dies
If C dies I die

A SUN-DEATH INTO SUN.

sthhe fous on ssu eod
ethueeu touud on ssu eod
htetouetdu tds foett
fhtdeueeue on ssu eod

ioes ehtnotee ihue sthe

oduduee noh usuhdtse
tdso ssu husioes
on Eod [33]

C
A
HARRY
E
S
S
E

1 Caresse, according to her own annotated copy.

2 In the margin Caresse has pencilled "To fetch C."

3 Caresse was Harry's companion in each of these entries from May 1 to July 22. She has indicated this in pencil in her copy. She had been living in London with her aunt and uncle, but came to Paris with Harry and rented a room there near the apartment he shared with another boy, Lou Norrie.

4 Harry's family belonged to the Myopia Hunt Club in Boston. Caresse's notation identifies the Vicomte and Vicomtesse Myopia as "H C & C C."

5 In the margin Caresse has written "C C returns to U.S." and against the second paragraph of the next entry, "C C in U.S."

6 Caresse's notation identifies herself as the woman.

7 "Marries C C"—Caresse's note.

8 "Back in Paris. Hotel de l'Université"—Caresse's note.

9 Harry's club at Harvard.

10 Caresse's note says simply "imaginary." Apparently this lady lived only in Harry's mind. He refers to her often in *Shadows of the Sun,* had her name tattooed across his chest, left her $5000 in his will. In 1929, Harry purchased the etching "Valkulla" by the Swedish artist Anders Zorn and said it was she. From this we know she looked like him. Caresse, jealous of her, called Jacqueline "the girl of infinite mystery. . . . the everlasting shadow."

11 "C C"—Caresse's note.

12 Morgan, Harjes & Co.

13 "from Rue des Belles Feuilles"—Caresse's note.

14 Perhaps this entry refers to the story Caresse tells in *The Passionate Years* (pp. 113-115). Her painting teacher, after two days of class, suggested private lessons. At his "Vaugirard atelier" he had Caresse sit beside him on one of the couches. His model had been unable to come this afternoon, he explained, and so he could not work on his painting. Recognizing the game, Caresse suggested that she pose nude for him. When she had undressed and "sat down, very firmly," he began arranging her scarf; just then the doorbell rang ("Harry was never late.")
   "That must be my husband," she cried joyfully, "I told him to come at four."
   "The Devil! Put on your clothes," he shouted.
   When the Master returned ("very slowly") with Harry, Caresse was fully dressed. "I knew I had taught him a well-deserved lesson," she concludes.
   Harry's entry here may record the Master's ingenious efforts to delay his entry into the studio.

15 The Apple Trees was Harry's family's summer home at Manchester, Massachusetts.

16 "Jacqueline imaginary"—Caresse's note.

17 "to bank"—Caresse's note.

18 "Marthe Bibesco"—Caresse's note.

Notes

[19] "C C C"—Caresse's note.

[20] "C C C"—Caresse's note.

[21] "Polly"—Caresse's note: her daughter.

[22] In the margin Caresse has written "father?" The quotations are from a letter Harry received from S V R C.

[23] "Hashish his first introduction to dope?"—Caresse's note.

[24] "from W V R B"—Caresse's note.

[25] "Polly"—Caresse's note.

[26] "dog"—Caresse's note.

[27] This will be the Crosbys' Paris address for the rest of Harry's life.

[28] Billy Peabody, Caresse's son, attended various boarding schools in England and Europe.

[29] "Raymonde"—Caresse's note.

[30] "Morgan"—Caresse's note: J. P. Morgan.

[31] "Weeks"—Caresse's note.

[32] "Weeks"—Caresse's note.

[33] In the 1928 edition the code and the acrostic occupied separate pages. The code can be broken by a substitution of letters:

> sthhe fous on ssu eod
> harry poet of the sun
>
> ethueeu touud on ssu eod
> caresse queen of the sun
>
> htetouetdu tds foett
> jacqueline and polia
>
> fhtdeueeue on ssu eod
> princesses of the sun
>
> ioes ehtnotee ihue sthe
> gold cramoisy grey dark
>
> oduduee noh usuhdtse
> oneness for eternity
>
> tdso ssu husioes
> into the redgold
>
> on Eod
> of Sun

Shadows of the Sun

Note that several letters of the code may each have several answers: *s* may be decoded by *d*, *h*, or *t*; *e* by *c*, *k*, *l* or *s*. This is because the key to the code is also a code. If the code's key is spread alphabetically, it reads as follows:

a b c d e f g h i j k l m n o p q r s t u v w x y z
t _ e s u n i s t h e e n d o f t h e s o _ _ _ e _

Harry Crosby didn't happen to require *b*, *v*, *w*, *x* or *z* in his message, but it is clear that *b* must encode as *h* because no other letter makes sense. For the final letters there are several options so long as one considers them part of two or more words, but none that seem particularly relevant. However, if the letters form one word, there is only one feasible possibility, *soldier*. The key then becomes "the sun is the end of the soldier."

TWO : 1927/1928

Sol ministrat umbram (the Sun provides the shadow)

"and a sixth sect worshipped an image of the Sun formed in the mind. Members of this last sect spent all their time in meditating on the Sun, and were in the habit of branding circular representations of his disk on their foreheads, arms, and breasts."

Frazer. The Worship of the Sun.

for
Caresse
Queen of the Sun
"si ma dame mourroit je mourrois avec elle"

1927

VI

January 17. Read in Montaigne. "si le monde se plaint dequoy je parle trop de moy, je me plains de quoy il ne pense seulement à soy."

Read in Sterne "for when my views are direct, Eugenius, I care not if all the world saw me feel it."

This is the way I feel about Shadows of the Sun.

18. Smoked for the first time this year: my pipe (and in the grey car through the dark and the rain to Versailles) and at Versailles red port and silver gin and back to Paris through the ruin and the dark (four hands are four flowers interlaced) and a cigarette at 19 Rue de Lille and opium (suns within suns and cataracts of gold) with C at the Chauve-Souris' and to-day read Anabase by St. J. Perse (Saint Léger Léger) the best French Poem since Bateau Ivre.

22. Snow is falling in slow enormous flakes softly falling as I walk through the woods to the Tree and prayers into the Invisible Sun and orchids and it is night (rain and snow) and she is pale ("rose neigeuse couleur de la neige et des plumes de cygne") and her lips are touching the orchids. Orchidaceous.

February 15. On the train to Saint Paul and while finishing l'Immoraliste ("je ne prétends à rien qu'au naturel et, pour chaque action, le plaisir que j'y prends m'est signe que je devais le faire") did not see that the train had gone past Antibes and was already coming into Nice where I got out and took a taxi back to Antibes and so to Saint Paul a little fortified town built on a small hill about ten miles from the sea. Narrow cobblestoned streets and houses in ruin and black cats and dung heaps and a lavoir. And here A has a studio looking out over the battlements towards the sea (I look out over the battlements of my soul towards the Sun).

March 4. Out of Angers and off the highroad along country lanes stopping here and there for Benedictines and then away on our search for the Château des Pins which at last we discovered hidden away in a great forest and they were out walking so the maid began to ring a tocsin and we wandered into the parlor where Zulu knocked a china teapot off the table (a terrific crash and a long silence) and Mrs. G appeared and there were apologies and strained feelings and then Mr. G appeared and there were more apologies and more strained feelings and no luncheon offered but we were invited to taste wine (stored in huge barrels) and we began with the white Anjou, first from the ordinary barrel then from the less ordinary until at last we were drinking the very best wine from his little fourteenth century vineyard—one of the famousest (still tight) vineyards in all of France. And Croucher and I had a dozen large glasses of white wine then a half hour intermission (during which I smoked my pipe) followed by a dozen more glasses this time of red Anjou, all this on an empty stomach. And there was eau-de-vie and a windmill where I climbed to the very top and came down again plastered with flour and it was pouring rain and we sat before the miller's fire and drank and there were three old ladies with starched caps and the disc of the sun began to revolve and whirl in my head and how was it I found myself in the nursery surrounded by children and I asked them what they wanted me to send them from Paris and Tom wanted soldiers Beatrice a camel Kay une poupée qui se déshabille Elise a rubber doll Reginald an autocar—then a gigantic effort to get down to supper and supper was a failure from my point of view (didn't dare eat or talk) but Bed afterwards was Paradise the Harbor after the Storm.

March 5. Cold bath and a run through the woods before breakfast and toast and coffee (the first food for twenty-four hours) and then we departed (speed the departing guest) and we had come to stay twenty minutes and we had stayed twenty hours and a long ride stopping for food at a wayside farm (potage and cider and there was an old peasant to whom I gave my waist-coat) and on and on and in the late afternoon we came to Dol (une poupée qui se déshabille) where we made inquiries and were directed to the Menhir which stands in a field like a giant phallus about a mile outside the town and I said phallic prayers a gold firebrand thrusting into the red-gold of the Sun and I ate a raw turnip and talked to an old peasant woman who lives alone in a small house at the corner of the field (there was a Brittany bed built into the wall) and she had no relations left (her husband and sons had been killed in the war) and I gave her a piece of gold (I always carry gold) and so towards Saint-Malo to the town through cabbage-fields and there was the stench of rotting cabbages and ugly factory houses and mud and rubbish and a cold fog ghosting in from the sea (we could hear the waves pounding against the ramparts) and so past the inner docks (the Terre Neuviens a forest of masts and the ships all painted green) and it was dark when we drove into the Garage de la Demi-Lune (entrez doucement) (the Garage of the Sun—crash in with an explosion) and there were oysters and sea-food in a little bistro and afterwards to Number Twelve a bordel where we drank brandy and talked to the three harlots and to the old Madame who had been there nineteen years and there was a dreary music-box and the stale aroma of beer and underarms and cheap perfume and towards midnight down a narrow street to the hotel and so to bed and if the sound of the waves pounding against the ramparts was depressing the sound of the waves of the sun pounding gold upon gold against the ramparts of my soul was exhilarating.

6. The beauty of a copper-colored sail is the beauty of the copper-colored sun and we are on our way to the Mont Saint-Michel and we are at the Mont Saint-Michel and there is a huge omelette and glasses of cider in the Fourteenth Century Tavern and there was a poor little idiot girl (we gave her a rag doll) and we bought boat models and walked up and down steps and I sent a postcard to the Girl of the White Polo Coat and then a long run in the car through Avranches and Argenten towards Le Haras Au Pin throwing coppers and candy to the children along the road (it was Sunday and there were many children along the road) and there was a dark forest and a new moon silver among dark clouds (a virgin among eunuchs) and I am glad to be inland from the sea and there was a hot potage and pâté de fois gras with truffles and many glasses of dark Burgundy (a glass of Burgundy is a prayer) and afterwards an enormous chocolate soufflé and then the quiet feeling of perfect health mind body and soul and in came the young officers we saw here last year and then brandy and then bed all four of us in the same room Zulu at the foot of their bed Narcisse at the foot of ours.

March 8. Grey day out of doors red-gold in the soul and if you don't want to be a pigeon you must be a shark (but if you don't want to be a shark must you be a pigeon?) and in the restaurant I asked the violinist for the Prelude from Tristan (exquisite columns of gold emerge and disappear in the river of soul like the gold columns at night upon the Seine) and to-night when I got home a cable from S V R C thanking me for sending him the cable this morning. Shades of Columbus!

19. At last at last after not having won a bet on the horse races for over a year I play a thousand francs to win on Sun-God and he wins the Grand Prix de Nice (very Nice) and for the first time since the summer at Etretat (little Barbara-Jane to carry up the staircase in the rain) I launch the Caresse and paddle against the strong current and the strong wind up the Seine to the Barge (when I got there I was drenched and the boat half full of water) and Frans lent me a pair of trousers and May lent me her bed-slippers (she was wearing the red dress) and we drank brandy and talked of books and etchings and we drank brandy and C arrived and we drank brandy and then C and I went off to the Théâtre des Champs-Élysées where we saw some extraordinary Chinese Acrobats who wore gorgeous costumes and who spun plates on the end of a stick and who did tumbling and who hung by their pigtails on a wire (as my soul hangs by its pigtail to the Sun) and when they disappeared a rifleman appeared who played Weber's Clair de Lune by the *simple* process of shooting rapid fire at a nickel organ hitting the right notes with never a mistake and not content with this performance he shot blindfolded at a target perched on his wife's head which I am sure was unpleasant for everyone. But the real fun was looking at the Bourdelle Frescoes. And back to the Barge again and here we met Jean de Gourmont the brother of Rémy de Gourmont (small dark Spanish with a cruel discontented face) and we met T'Serstevens the Belgian writer and Frans was reading aloud from Maldoror ("on doit laisser pousser ses ongles pendant quinze jours") and I must have my nails manicured to-morrow (rouge on my ongles) and I looked out the window and the river was liquid black a black ribbon powdered with rose and gold flowers (the street lamps) and the stars overhead were like notes of music.

April 10 and 11. To the Chauve-Souris' to smoke opium and a perfect "ambiance"—a long façade of houses (each house a day) shortening and lengthening like an accordeon with never a chasm or an abyss (thus do the days of the year lengthen and shorten) and there was a red exotic flower dressed like a girl stepping step by step through the dark forest of my soul step by step step by step and I could *feel* the silence of each step and I could *hear* silence but I could not see her face and when she had gone (step by step) there were red funnels vomiting sharp smokeplumes gold and cramoisy and grey and emerald into four high round suns which converged nearer and nearer until at last they collided into One Great Sun.

And the bubbling sound of another pipe and another and another and the round contour of a breast and the touch of delicate fingers delicately gently snow upon snow and the metamorphose into oblivion beyond the beyond until the dreary awareness of a cold grey dawn and home to find a letter to say that in spring it would be wholesome to dive down into the depths of the black earth where all the flowers are aflaming still unsmitten and unbegun and all day across my soul red icebergs have been drifting like tombs across the Sun.

April 23. And recklessly for my account is overdrawn at the Bank I telephone the bookmaker to play a thousand francs for me on Man In The Moon and a thousand francs on Black Hawk and at five o'clock I walk down the Rue de Lille to the little bar at the corner of the Rue du Bac to read on the ticker

       I. Black Hawk

and Man in the Moon took a second and I have won three thousand francs and I drank a glass of port color of red velvet and after supper on the way home from dinner we went to say goodnight to the de Geeteres but the Barge was black and though we hurled stones at it no one answered and having no calling cards C took off one of her silk stockings I one of my silk socks and these we left hanging (two flowers rose and black) upon the knob of the lavoir door.

May 5. To the Barge to undress and to bask in the Sun and I begin a poem

> Xairo (I rejoice)
> naked in the Sun
> under the sun-clouds formed like skulls
> and a bateau-mouche
> thrusting under the arch of a bridge
> is a silver thread
> > drawn by invisible fingers
> through a gold needle
> (or a silver soul
> > threading a gold body)
> and the train of barges
> (gold leviathans)
> under the bridge of jade
> under the bridge of rose-colored marble

and beyond—down down beyond
under the bridge of sunstone
and beyond—

were it not for the Abyss
there would be no need for bridges
no need
for the sun-triumphant
arches of the soul
no need
for sunsets seen at dawn
(the sun's reflection in the water
is a tree of gold
and the arches of the bridges
are windows to the sea
and at sunset
windows to the Sun)

a last faint touch of gold
the blackness of the river
swallows gold

and supper with Frans and May then with them to the Gare du Nord to meet C and she comes running down the platform carrying two ponderous volumes of Aubrey Beardsley and two bottles of Absinthe.

May 8. "Thou shalt not let thy cattle gender with a diverse kind; Thou shalt not sow thy field with mingled seed" (Thou shalt not let Thy Thoughts gender with a diverse kind; Thou shalt not sow thy soul with mingled seed but sow it with the seed of the Sun) and to the Barge and Frans covered from head to foot with tar for he had been tarring the deck and he showed me the secret hiding place (the wall opens inward back of the bathroom) where he hid in order to cross the Dutch frontier and it is a magnificent arrangement and if I am ever pursued I shall hide there and Frans looked like a débardeur strong virile black woolen shirt open at the neck hair in disorder blackened hands eyes smouldering and in the evening to the Conservatoire (Ada MacLeish Concert) and Joyce was there and afterwards C and I went behind the scenes and we saw Hemingway who introduced us to Joyce and afterwards to Footits for a gin fizz and from a Paris Sport lying on the floor I read the huge headlines announcing "Nungesser et Coli sont partis pour New-York!"

11. To the Montparnasse Cemetery to get our gravestone and in a taxi I took it out to the Cimetière de l'Abbaye de Longchamp and A for luncheon and he was dressed in a symphony of gray—gray suit gray fedora hat gray silk handkerchief gray socks gray gloves and he carried a cane that had a gray knob (how different from Frans the other morning) and he has won the Prix de Rome (damn good) and he is going to Rome in October. And to the

Barge and in the "Caresse" for a spin on the Seine, hard paddling under the Pont Neuf against the current to where the old morgue used to be then around the corner and a fast run back down the narrow canal "sous les yeux horribles des pontons" and then the Barge again and a long bask in the Sun and I drank beer and fell asleep and when I awoke it was after sunset and so home along the quays waving goodnight to May.

May 21. Along the Seine to Saint Denis and Le Bourget to wait for Lindbergh who is reported two hundred miles off the Coast of Ireland and it is eight o'clock and cold as we park the car and pass through the gate onto the field (thanks to Croucher who is a member of the Aviation Club) and we are among the first to arrive and an hour later there is an enormous crowd and a mad French flyer acrobating overhead and then he comes down and his plane is wheeled into the hanger (it was dark sunset almost night) and a large plane is seen emerging from the clouds and in a minute it lands (it is the London Express) (and now quite dark) and like a phantom the plane from Strasburg alights and now at short intervals red and gold and green rockets shoot into the air and there are acetylene searchlights searching everywhere but the most mammoth is the giant searchlight on the Mont Valérien at Saint-Cloud and it is ten o'clock and the crowd is impatient and there is a half-hearted attempt at a song and always the hiss of the rockets and always the searching searchlights and I wish I had brought a coat and there is no gin left in my flask and C and I huddle together for warmth and I smoke my pie and S V R C wanders off nervously and Croucher crouches and Gretchen whistles and it is cold and suddenly unmistakeably the sound of a aeroplane (dead silence) and then to our left a white flash against the black night (blackness) and another flash (like a shark darting through water). Then nothing. No sound. Suspense. And again a sound, this time somewhere off towards the right. And is it some belated plane or is it Lindbergh? Then sharp swift in the gold glare of the searchlights a small white hawk of a plane swoops hawk-like down and across the field—C'est lui Lindberg, LIND-BERG! and there is pandemonium wild animals let loose and a stampede towards the plane and C and I hanging on to each other running people ahead running people all round us running and the crowd behind stampeding like buffalo and a pushing and a shoving and where is he where is he Lindberg where is he and the extraordinary impression I had of hands thousands of hands weaving like maggots over the silver wings of the Spirit of Saint-Louis and it seems as if all the hands in the world are touching or trying to touch the new Christ and that the new Cross is the Plane and knives slash at the fuselage hands multiply hands everywhere scratching tearing and it is almost midnight when we begin the slow journey back to Paris (traffic like the traffic in the war) and it takes us three hours to cover eight miles and it is freezing cold but what an event! Ce n'est pas un homme, c'est un Oiseau!

26. S V R C has given me since he has arrived black silk socks white silk pyjamas a dark suit a dark overcoat black shoes six hundred black cigarettes an entire wine cellar a Chinese robe three Siamese pictures a Zebra skin a

Polar Bear rug (he bargained the man down from twenty to ten) gold not to mention gold for C and three dresses for C and a coat for C and I went with C to Notre-Dame to hear the Berlioz Requiem (the trumpets of the Last Judgment resounded from the Four Points of the Compass) and from the white light and noise of the street through a thick door into the tremendous-ness of the Cathedral (incense and candlelight and stained glass windows and blare of trumpets) and it was dark and cold as stone and gold as candlelight and sombre as the stained glass windows and it was grey in the afternoon at Longchamp and I smoked my pipe and said prayers into the smoke and the Dark Princess was there frail as a flower and she was dressed in black and a horse called Blackness won and a stupid dinner at the Piebald Horse (not an intelligent remark for two hours) and R's whole idea of Paris is "I have to think of what they think back there" (there meaning the City of Dreadful Night—Boston) and what an *enormous* wall between the older and the younger generation.

June 4. Twenty-Nine to-day and a mad morning and S annoyed because we neither of us care for Benson etchings because I wear a black gardenia in my buttonhole (knight-errants wore black plumes) because I put red varnish on my nails because I never wear a hat (Caesar Hannibal and Company) but I don't care a damn and to-day a red-gold fire in the hearth (a red-gold fire in the heart) and to-day Tea (read Cocktails) at the Ritz with G W and she upholds Humbert Wolfe and quotes to me

> "As you could take the music in your hand
> And drop it, note by note, between your fingers"

And I uphold T. S. Eliot and quote to her

> "I should have been a pair of ragged claws
> Scuttling across the floors of silent seas"

And to-day I wrote a preface for Comtesse Tolstoy's Memoirs and to-day I put a thousand francs to win (always play to win) on La Grande Mademoiselle and after four false starts and after being almost blocked at the beginning she came up in the straightaway to win as she pleased (comme elle voulait) and she paid 7 to 1 but I shall probably lose to-morrow on Queen Iseult and what is that wonderful thing I read to-day about the combat between candlelight and the last rays of the departing sun.

10. I buy ten live snakes on the Quays and take them home in a sack (this a preparation for the 4 Arts) and the house is in disorder (the Library stripped of its paintings and its Chinese porcelaines and all the bookcases turned to the wall) and the caterer man (harbinger of the fête) arrives and Narcisse sniffs the air (rats know before a shipwreck) and the Crouchers arrive and May appears and we go out for fard and perfume and I buy seven dead pigeons to wear as a necklace and then a hot bath May and I and C and afterwards with Lord L to put on green paint and it does not seem a year ago that we were doing exactly the same thing and at Eight the Students begin to appear—more and more and more and more (many more people than last year) and the Punch Bowl is filled and the Party has begun and soon everyone is Gay and Noisy Noisier and Noisiest toward Ten O'Clock and seventy empty bottles of champagne rattle upon the floor and now straight gin Gin Gin Gin like the Russian refugees clamoring for bread and everyone clamored and the fire roared in the hearth (roared with the wine in my heart) and the room was hot and reeked with cigarette and cigar smoke with fard and sweat and smell of underarms and we were all in Khmer Costume and there was Renée in yellow with her nombril showing and there was Raymonde in red and there was the Dark Princess and at Eleven we formed in line in the courtyard (I with the sack full of snakes) and marched away on foot ("perpetual girls marching to love" signed E. E. Cummings) and away on foot across the Concorde up the Champs Elysées to the Rond Point (stragglers disappeared into Footits Bar) down the Victor Emmanuel past the Piebald Horse ("when all white horses are in bed" signed E. E. Cummings) past the Piebald Horse and thank Christ I dont have to think of what they think back there and to the left and up the Faubourg Saint-Honoré and at last exhausted into the salle Wagram (snarling of tigers at the gate snarling of tigers inside) and up the ladder to the loge and up another ladder to an attic and up an imaginary ladder to and into the Sun and here I undid the sack and turned it upside down and all the snakes dropped down among the dancers and there were shrieks and cat-calls and there was a riot and I remember two strong young men stark naked wrestling on the floor for the honor of dancing with a young girl (silver paint conquered purple paint) and I remember a mad student drinking champagne out of a skull which he had pilfered from my Library as I had pilfered it a year ago from the Catacombs (O happy skull to be filled full of sparkling gold) and in a corner I watched two savages making love (stark naked wrestling on the floor) and beside me sitting on the floor a plump woman with bare breasts absorbed in the passion of giving milk to one of the snakes! Then the prize for warrior costumes and all the miraculous headgear and the black and white night and day of Zebra Skins and there was a man in a Leopard Skin and then the Prix de Beauté and the naked models ("fashioned very curiously of roses and of ivory" signed E.E.C.) ivory white against the blackness of the velvet curtain up and down the steps like girls of the Ziegfeld Chorus up and down the steps to the dais. And cheers and howls and searchlights and clangor of jazz. And gold of champagne. And a staggering out into the rain and it was cold and raining hard when we got home.

June 22. To the Gare Saint-Lazare with S V R C (stopping on the way at Bodegas for a glass of port) and we got to the station *exactly* one hour before the train was scheduled to start and a farewell drink of straight gin (silver from the silver flask) and the shriek of the locomotive (partings are always so depressing) and back to the hairdressers where I had Germaine put red varnish on my nails ("on doit laisser pousser ses ongles pendant quinze jours") and so back along the Quays and I basked in the Sun on the Quays lying flat on my back on the cobblestones and I went to sleep and the rays of the Sun entered into my body and when I awoke it was late afternoon and I wandered home along the Quays half asleep and full of Sun and I met C on

Harry Crosby wrote on the back of this photograph, "With my brancardier friend Grigene at the Front. He's the best scout I've met over here in the French army."

Top: Harry Crosby took this photograph as a sudden wind levelled his tent at the Front. On the back he wrote, "Fox with Spud in background peering up from the wreckage of our tent. This picture is a wonder." *Center:* Ambulance Corps. "At the relay point." *Bottom:* Taken by Harry Crosby during the First World War. "Bringing them in."

Facing page, top: First World War. Harry at the bath. *Bottom:* Harry Crosby's comrades in the war. They called themselves "The Hounds." From left to right: Way Spaulding, Philip Shepley, Harry Crosby, Richmond Fearing, Stuart Kaiser. Each wears the *Croix de Guerre.*

Mr. and Mrs. Henry Grew Crosby. On the back of this photo Caresse has written "Wedding Day, 1922."

Harry and Caresse Crosby, Etretat, Summer, 1925. On the back of the photograph Harry has written, "This is the best picture that was ever taken of us."

Top: Harry and Caresse Crosby.
Bottom: Harry Crosby at Le Pavil-
lon, 1924.

Top: One of Harry Crosby's crosses, about three inches tall and threaded at the bottom. Another cross, made before he met Caresse, has a sun engraved on one side. *Bottom:* A tombstone ordered by Harry Crosby for himself and Caresse.

An untitled photograph by Harry Crosby.

A photograph by Harry Crosby titled *Voices*.

Top: Harry and Car[...] Crosby with their dog N[...]cisse Noir. *Left*: Ha[...] Crosby in his library a[...] rue de Lille, 1928. (Note [...] skeleton, rear right.) *Rig[...]* Harry Crosby and his fa[...] SVRC (Stephen Van R[...]selaer Crosby).

p: Walter Berry (stand-
), Caresse Crosby (seat-
). The woman standing to
left of Walter Berry may
Edith Wharton. *Bottom:*
e Master Printer of the
ack Sun Press, Roger Les-
ret.

Top left: Hart Crane and Caresse Crosby at Chantilly, 1929. *Top right:* D. H. Lawrence and Frieda sunning at Le Moulin, 1928. *Bottom left:* Harry Crosby, D. H. Lawrence and Frieda at Le Moulin, 1928. *Bottom right:* Harry and Caresse Crosby at Le Moulin, 1928.

Top left: Harry Crosby on phallic tower at Le Moulin, 1928. *Top right:* D. H. Lawrence and Caresse Crosby on a donkey cart. In the background is the Forest of Ermenville near Le Moulin. *Bottom left:* Kay Boyle and Harry Crosby at Le Moulin, Winter, 1929. *Bottom right:* Hart Crane at Le Moulin.

Top: Hart Crane at Le Moulin. *Bottom:* Laurence Vail and Kay Boyle.

Harry Crosby, 1929.

Eugene Jolas at Le Moulin.

Harry Crosby kept a photo of a girl in a silver frame on his desk. A cousin once asked him if the girl was his sister, so much did she resemble Harry. The "Lady of the Golden Horse" asked the same question. The photograph was of Josephine Rotch and it was in Harry's wallet when he died.

Caresse Crosby, New York City, 1929. Taken the day Harry Crosby died.

"It is difficult to describe Harry completely, for he seemed to be more expression and mood than man—and yet he was the most vivid personality that I have ever known, electric with rebellion."

—Caresse Crosby

the Rue de Lille and we turned round and walked over to the Louvre where we took a bateau-mouche up the Seine (the setting sun and the curtseying trees and the strong oaken barges) to Charenton where we surprised Frans and May in their Barge kneeling face to face in a tin tub scrubbing themselves and with them for a wretched meal in a wretched café and there was the smell of manure that had been sprinkled over the boxhedge and there was flour and water for soup and wretched fish (that I am sure had been living on sewerage) and weak beer (see Ulysses Page 145). And the omelette had garlic in it. But all the time I thought of red icebergs drifting like young dryads across the Sun.

June 26. Dark morning with rain and I went to the Faubourg Saint-Honoré and stood in front of the portrait by Nanteuil of Madame de Sévigné and thought of Ninon de Lenclos (why have I not thought of her for so long?) and of how she had had for lovers the husband and the son and the grandson of Madame de Sévigné and I went home and there were many people for luncheon (among them the Dark Princess wearing a white gardenia) and afterwards to Longchamp in the rain (my sixth successive Grand Prix—Kefalin Filibert de Savoie Transvaal Reine Lumière Take my Tip and this year Fiterari and the Count was there and I smoked my pipe during the big race and prayed into the smoke and so home through the rain and a mad hot bath with who shall we call her and people came in and poured a bottle of champagne over us and I am alone for supper and I curl into myself (a hot water bottle at my feet) and inside are orchids gardenias dark violets yellow roses but outside and all around weeds weeds weeds.

29. Prayers to the Sun and at noon goats in the Rue de Lille and we drank hot goat's milk and watched the shepherd drive the herd away and in the afternoon we bought red raincoats and to-day read in Schopenhauer that the centre of gravity (for me the Sun) should fall entirely and absolutely within oneself.

July 2. and it is raining and I pack Rimbaud Eliot Cummings Hemingway and MacLeish and clothes (mostly silk pyjamas) and she leans from the window red lips and red wrapper to wave goodbye and to the bank for gold and to the dressmakers to send her the gold coat (gold into gold) and then away with Mortimer down the wet black road to Orléans and soup and brandy at Orléans and on through Blois past Chaumont (Diane de Poitiers Catherine de Médicis) past Amboise and on through Tours and Poitiers (Diane de Poitiers) and on at seventy miles an hour along the road to Angoulême (the last hour we averaged a mile a minute) and a dreary merry-go-round hurdy-gurdy (like the hurdy-gurdy in Maya) till late at night in the square and before going to bed two bottles of red wine ("the Nightingale cries to the Rose that sallow cheek of hers to Incarnadine") and fishing in my bag for my pyjamas I discovered curled like the frailest of flowers her loveliest set of black dentelleries.

July 4. Strong Sun and hot even at sunset and supper in our bathing suits on the beach and the warm sand and cocktails and the cool sand and champagne and the cold sand and midnight a hundred yards off shore and the bewildering lights from the Casino dancing dancing on the water and the cold blackness below and the small dark hand on my shoulder as we swam back to the beach and to Biarritz and the Bar Basque and the strongest hot grog (cold from the swim and tired by the sun and dizzy from the rum) and coming back in the car fell asleep my head in her lap like the unicorn in the tapestry at the Cluny.

7. We charter a boat the Queen Iseult a fishing boat with two masts and two cabins and an engine and it is painted green and we are anchored a hundred yards off the beach (if my soul were a boat how many hundred yards am I anchored off the Sun) and it is rough weather with a storm threatening and the storm explodes with dark fury and it is dark and the Queen Iseult quivers and plunges like a mare in heat.

8. Two in the morning and the lights on shore have gone out and the sea is angry and black and the Queen Iseult plunges and plunges and the tiller is loose and banging and I am afraid she will break loose from her moorings and I go on deck in the rain in my pyjamas to see what is happening ("the wind that will be howling at all hours") and I make fast the tiller with the belt from my wrapper but it is soon loose again and there is a cracking and a pounding and a plunging and a sickening swish of water and more rain and more tempest and then grey dawn and a going on shore in the cockelshell dory precarious proceeding for the waves were angry and high and on foot to the little tavern the Pigeons Blancs and there are two little pigeons painted on the big beam over the door (frail little pigeons white little pigeons poor little pigeons) and inside a low ceiling with strong blackened beams and two long low wooden tables and long low wooden benches and there were bottles of red and white wine and barrels of red and white wine and funnels for decanting red and white wine and a kitten fast asleep under a newspaper and a sick cat and a dog and a canary bird in a wooden cage—it was all like a scene from Maya the low room all packed with fishermen all talking Basque gutteral menacing and there was the savage slapping of cards and there was a zinc bar and an old sea-clock and pictures of boats on the wall (pictures of sun in my brain) and two whores and the patronne in a heavy green sweater and the patron in bed-slippers and a son that looked like the husband of the girl of the White Polo Coat and there was a daughter that was deaf and dumb (from time to time she uttered cries like a parrot) and there was an idiot man who came in and insulted people (he fed crumbs to the canary) and there was a man with a wooden leg who drank and pounded with his wooden leg on the stone floor and there was roaring and singing and there were little children (poor little pigeons frail little pigeons) who came with empty bottles to have them filled from the great tonneau in the corner and I sat with the Dark Princess near the wall in the corner and I smoked my pipe and we drank red wine and always the storm out of doors and always the

sound of the waves and she went away and I drank rum and out of doors it began to rain even harder and I went out in quest of a letter and there wasnt any and somehow I fought my way out to the boat and it began to rain even harder and harder and it was dark and I fell asleep my red raincoat over my head.

July 10. To Biarritz in the Green Renault and a bottle of champagne at the Casino and I won a thousand francs at Boule and we went to the Bar Basque and we drank Martinis (très sec s'il vous plaît) and there was a graphaphone playing a tango and an old woman who sold us a newspaper (Queen Iseult won again) and who blessed us upon the receipt of ten francs and it was time to go and when we got back there were Martinis at the Villa and we sat on the stone steps (only there were others) and I was asked to dinner and I refused and I said goodbye and went down through the garden to the wharf where I saw M and we ate a potage at the Pigeons Blancs and with Antonio and the Mechanic and the Pirate and two bottles of champagne we started off on the Queen Iseult and cruised from the inner harbor to the beach and here we anchored and before going to sleep I read Rimbaud and I believe with Rickword that all the great visionary poets have been more than human in their moral strength and their demoniac fury of self-belief.

11. Dawn and before breakfast a plunge into the sea naked and alone (body) and before breakfast a plunge into the Sun naked and alone (soul) and breakfast at the Pigeons Blancs and then away along the road to Spain and champagne at the frontier and it began to rain and so along a ravine and there were little walled-in meadows green in the rain and a little white village by a little river then the road wound up up up and up and more and more rain and thick fog and many miles in the rain into Pamplona and there were crowds standing under the arcades in the square and there were crowds in the cafés and the bull-fight was postponed because of the rain and there was the Hotel La Perla and absinthe one absinthe two absinthes three absinthes and I said goodnight and wandered the streets (wet and dark) and someone indicated Number 30 (Number 12 at Saint-Malo) and there were six women selling for five pesetas each and thirty men clamoring and I did not stay and so out alone along black streets and somehow I found the big square and the hotel and somehow I undressed and went to bed.

12. Wandered out into the Sun and saw a miraculous toy horse grey with a pink saddle and a wooden toy automobile (Reginald an autocar) and a wooden rake and a wooden shovel and a wooden hay-fork and a red flag on an iron rod and a coarse rope belt and green sea-rubbers and a ding-dong bell for the boat and all these I threw into an enormous sack and a breakfast of eggs and beer cold beer in tall glasses (later on cold absinthe in tall glasses) and Hemingway of the Sun Also Rises drove past in a carriage and shouted at us and Waldo Pierce was with him looking like Walt Whitman and everyone began rushing off for the Bullfight (one last round of absinthe) and there was a young bootblack kneeling at someone's feet shining and singing

and everyone forgot about the absinthe and the bullfight and he sang weird half-Spanish half-African songs with a sort of a whine and he might have been seventeen almost in rags with a mouth like a jockey's a queer thin slit for a mouth and he had a cap on his hand and a hard and cruel face (almost a syphilitic face) and he had dirty teeth and he was bronzed and we took him with us to the Bullfight and his song was the Sun and there were the colors flashing in the Sun the purple and the gold and the green and the rose-colored scarves that the banderillos waved as they danced and side-stepped like colored spiders and there were lean horses tossed on cruel horns (is it true they cut their vocal cords before they are blindfolded and led into the ring) and there was the dark dark line of red along the shoulders of the black bull and always the dancing banderillos and there was the roar of the crowd and a fluttering of white handkerchiefs (papilonaceous) and at last the last bull who frisked and bellowed and galloped and plunged until he too was dragged out in the dust and the Boy sang to us all the way back to the square and in front of the hotel people gathered and were lost in his voice (moths lost in the Sun) and the little girl of the perfume shop was lost and the ragamuffins of the street were lost and the waiter who brought the absinthe was lost and we were all lost and the Boy himself was lost and we were all part of Eternity Sun-Eternity and we gave him all the gold we had (gold for gold) and we said Adios (all life is Adios) and we sped out of Pamplona swift as a gold arrow along the road to France and the Sun set and it was dark and there was a sharp corner and a tire blew out and we stopped by a stream and there was a white house with a gold light (like a painting by Cachoud) and a quiet peasant who stood and stared and a dog who barked and there was the sound of water pouring among stones and on again through the dark (four hands are four flowers interlaced) and we were tired and there was the frontier and sleepy questions and sleepier replies and Adios Spain and it was France and soon we were crossing the bridge (it seemed years since we crossed it two days ago) into Saint-Jean de Luz and there was the new Auberge and the bubbling of gold champagne ("millions of bubbles like us and will pour") and a jazz orchestra playing Bye Bye Blackbird and the going away up the hill to the darkness of the Villa and another Adios and so down to the beach to row out to the Queen Iseult

July 25. Had the goat skin gourd I bought yesterday in Spain filled with red wine at the Pigeons Blancs and here we drank glasses of red wine and here we painted a flag for the boat—a red heart on a black background with the letter M.O. written in red (three guesses) and a morning of lying on the hot deck of the Queen Iseult (would it had been on the hot body of Queen Iseult) and all afternoon with C on the beach between Biarritz and Bayonne watching the waves thunder upon the shore ("the surge and thunder of the Odyssey") and there was a tramp steamer putting out to sea (a fisherman's son putting out into the world) and there was gambling at Biarritz (lost a thousand francs in ten minutes) and there was the Bar Basque and whiskey sours and in M's car four of us to Itakssoun to eat in a tree only we ate in the kitchen (it was cold out of doors and there were enormous beetles) and back to the Villa (a voice walking through a dark house) and at last the green beach and the lush seaweed under bare feet and our cockleshell dory and the rowing out in the dark to the Queen Iseult C and Narcisse in the bow M in the centre I in the stern and it was cold and we drank hot rum before going to sleep.

August 1. Morale very low for this is a morning of remorse why was I so drunk last night and why should she be standing in a white dress upon the stairs ("in the secret places of the stairs") so very white so very frail (poor little pigeons frail little pigeons) and why should the tempest rage as we struggle out in the cockleshell to the Queen Iseult and why does Narcisse howl at the wind and the rain and why do the waves curl angrily (they are so very black) and what are those flashes of lightening in the dark beyond the breakwater?

6. Paris and crystal gin and the dark gold of a kiss and then the listening for the closing of the door. On est si peu de chose devant l'immensité du monde.

11. "Whose fan is in his hand, and he will thoroughly purge his floor, and gather his wheat into the garner; but he will burn up the chaff with unquenchable fire" and this is what I am doing to my soul. And Robbie appears and quotes Napoleon "Behind me lies Paris and her bedchamber hung with mirrors. That is Happiness. It is mine. Over there across the mountains in a hostile land is fame. That is the goal of my desire." And Robbie disappears and Merveilleux appears and he was in a cynical frame of mind (no wonder with the Red Jew against him) and he quoted en amour il y aura toujours un des deux qui aime plus que l'autre, c'est celui là qui souffre, mais c'est l'autre qui s'ennuie. And Merveilleux disappears and a Letter from the Count appears. Chacune de vos nouvelles est toujours la bienvenue et fait cesser la monotonie des choses et cet isolement moral dans lequel nous vivons tous. Terrific la monotonie des choses et cet isolement moral dans lequel nous vivons tous especially the latter cet isolement moral dans lequel nous vivons tous. And at Footits (we go there every day) Narcisse is referred to as an "araignée à quatres pattes" and whiskey sours bring sullen hours and life is a hurting and a being hurt.

18. we desire to die together
   we desire to be cremated together
   we desire that our ashes be mingled and taken up in an aeroplane at sunrise and scattered to the four winds
   let a cannon be fired as a symbol of our explosion into Sun

22. A whiskey sour a stinger a 00 sherry and away to Brest with my two enormous sailor bags a little book on Cryptography which I bought in the station and a bottle of beer and this is the first day I have not shaved for over six hundred days.

Shadows of the Sun

August 23. Morlaix and "the old man's face at Morlaix lifted to the birds" signed MacLeish and not long after Breast (the "a" makes it more physical) and it is more than eight years now since I saw the sea (Thalassa! Thalassa!) that sunnygolden morning on my way home from the war. And more than eight years since they marched us in close formation down that winding hill road to the docks. And here on the docks I find C and the Crouchers drinking brandy in the Bar de la Tempête and here I am presented to Madame Suzanne bar-lady (the last comer always feels so uninitiated) but I liked the sawdust floor and the smell of beer and the outlook over the docks and there were good colored postcards a provocative girl with bed-room eyes in a pink chemise (no drawers) sitting upon a sailor's knee (prelude to M.O.) and soon we shall be starting out across the Bay of Biscay for the Death Coast of Spain on the good ship Emily and eventually we may reach Marseilles and I have never seen so many bars along the docks Bar à l'Arrêt du Tram, Bar du Retour du Conquet, Bar du Grand Rade, Bar de l'Inscription Maritime, Bar de l'Océan, Bar du Carénage, Bar des Navigateurs, Bar du Champ de Bataille, Bar du Jet d'Eau, Bar Nautique, Bar de la Salle des Fêtes and last but not least our own Bar de la Tempête (why isn't there a Bar du Soleil—a sun-cocktail please) and there is from where I sit a forest of masts and dray wagons creaking over cobblestones and enormous barrels of wine and while the others are at work in the boat I begin to read the little book on Cryptography and I work over a secret code of my own and I must study the Code Diary of Samuel Pepys and Poe's Essay on Cryptography.

25. To my castle of Philosophy I add two towers two solid towers the first from C "to never have any regrets" (that is the strongest tower of her philosophy) the second the erecting of strong inner walls so that it makes no difference (from the point of view of happiness) what exterior place one is in Brest or Boston, Teheran or Reykijvik, Heliopolis or Fez and to-day we moved our sailor bags on board and to-day we bought a sack of marine biscuits and to-day we drank Benedictines (innumerable) and to-day C read in Valéry something that certainly applies to me "aisé à impressionner impossible à convaincre" and to-day somehow I felt homesick for America and somehow I longed for Essex Woods and the sound of the Fog Horn booming through the Fog.

30. We are in Paris again. At the last moment we decided not to go. Each day there was something new required for the boat (the sail was ripped in the trial up the harbor) the bilge-pump would not work, there was a leak in the gasoline tank (as for the water-tanks they looked like red coffins and one was under C's bunk and the other under mine I think it was these that really decided us) and we were devoured by sea-fleas (having slept two nights on the boat) and there was a row with the "mousse" and his father and they both had to be kicked out and there was a storm threatening at sea so the fisherman said and we had waited a week already (all ready) and now Autumn is here and Paris for the thousandth time is not to be resisted. And the Crouchers were very nice (how understanding people are over here compared to people in America, everyone over here realizes that everyone must lead their own lives and not interfere with other people's lives) and they came down to the station in the rain and we all shouted goodbye (Zulu and Narcisse barking goodbye). And we are very glad to-day. We are like des Esseintes when he started out for London and it was raining in Paris and he stopped at Bodegas and drank a bottle of English stout and then went to an English restaurant where he saw English people and ate roast beef and plum pudding until at the last moment he decided he had really been to England (it was raining in Paris) right in Paris, so why take a long journey for a second experience. So he quietly went home. And in our eight days at the Bar de la Tempête we have had enough of wharves and enough of the sea and it will be a month before the Emily reaches Marseilles and we are glad we are home very glad.

September 5. Imaginary (had we sailed on the Emily). Third day at sea and we are out of sight of land and we are becalmed. Croucher tried to start the engine but it wouldn't work. Saw porpoises close by the boat. If we had had a harpoon we could have had porpoise meat for supper. Instead ate bully beef. We are all infested with sea-fleas. Even the sailors are scratching ("on doit laisser pousser ses ongles pendant quinze jours"). Wish we had gone back to Paris.

Actual. Saw a young girl crossing the Rue de Rivoli, the wind blowing her skirts up around her neck. Followed her across the Tuileries (a lean hungry greyhound walking after a heifer—see the Portrait of the Artist as a Young Man) and over the bridge (there was a metallic aeroplane overhead flashing in the sun) and then I lost her and found her again in the Rue de Poitiers (Diane de Poitiers) and we had tea together in the Bois and oysters Chez Prunier and cocktails at the Piebald Horse and her name is Adrienne Wishwater and she is the first girl I ever met who has eyes like mine and every time I see a new girl I think of S V R C and how he once said that there were plenty of fish in the sea plenty of birds in the sky (stirring of birds in my arms) and when I got home I looked at my eyes in the mirror (green and gold tiger eyes). Yet my totem is the Eagle.

6. Imaginary. Still becalmed. Still devoured by sea-fleas. Still depressed by the red coffins under our bunks. Shot at a sea-gull without hitting him and went in swimming over the side. Found a book someone had lent Croucher The Formation of Vegetable Mould Through the Action of Worms (The Formation of Heart and Body Gold through the Action of Sun) and ate a large quantity of coarse sea-biscuit (round and hard) and drank a glass of brandy. C tried to fish. Caught nothing. Croucher tried to fish. Caught nothing. Gretchen tried to fish. Caught nothing. How long will this go on? No engine. No wind.

"As idle as a painted ship
 Upon a painted ocean."

Actual. Began an essay on the Punishments of China and read Poe's

Eureka not to mention his Essay on Cryptography and I adopt for secret code "le plaisir de l'amour est d'aimer." This from La Rochefoucauld whom I read after supper (strange coincidence that God should become Sol) And read the Love Poems of John Donne (centric immedicable menstrous hydroptic burdenous endammaged.) and weeded out a hundred books from my Library and gave them away. And it is almost midnight and to-day has been a Reading Day.

September 7. Imaginary. Signs of a wind and Narcisse of the sea-sick eyes perks up an ear. Our conversation hinges on when we shall first sight the Death Coast of Spain. Croucher cooks up some baked beans. Sea-Gulls and Porpoises. Which would I rather be? Sea-Gull for it can soar into the Sun. There is a wind and we are making about four knots. Took the tiller for an hour at sunset.

Actual. Finished my essay on the Punishments of China thought of Adrienne and stayed in bed all day with a fever. And after supper (chicken broth and apple sauce) read in a book on Egypt "and a shapeless block of stone was left for the head to await the client whose likeness it was to receive." This is important.

8. Imaginary. Thick fog last night and towards seven in the morning we heard a fog horn out ahead like a lost soul. And soon we could hear the throbbing of engines. A tramp steamer? And wind again this morning and at noon we saw three fishing smack one with a light blue sail two with orange sails. We must be approaching the Death Coast. There is a heavy swell but the Emily is sturdy. I like our great brown sail that catches the wind as my soul catches sunlight.

Actual. Ran across the word "esculent" (must look it up) and fever all day (I wonder what the matter is) and Burgess to supper. He is just back from the Congo where he shot a gorilla for the British Museum. Five days without water. No fun. Is getting a divorce. Never knew he was married. He has that far-away look one sees among the people of the desert and he has that lean quality I like. Confirmed the fact that Paul Rainey was murdered by someone in the pay of the Hindu (See Shadow 17-9-23).

10. Imaginary. To our left is the Death Coast of Spain and it is getting warmer and to-morrow we may reach Lisbon. The worst is over. Many fishing smack and C caught a fish and we opened two bottles of champagne and the graphaphone played "Il ma vue nue" and there was a gorgeous sunset a great crumbling of red and black clouds with explosions of color and the Sun a gold point in the centre.

Actual. A high fever. I have the jaundice lurida praeterea fiunt quaecunque tuantur arquati (everything appears yellow to those who have the jaundice).

11. Imaginary. At sundown Lisbon and the cruise for C and I at least is over and to-morrow we shall start back by train for Paris. We have had enough of adventure.

Actual. Fever not so high as yesterday and Adrienne appeared all in black with a gold necklace and a wide gold bracelet and her eyes are tigress eyes and she is young and pretty and she sat on the edge of my bed and I told her how pretty she was and when she left I looked up the word "esculent" thinking it might apply to her and in a way I suppose it does. Fit or good for food Edible. A thing suitable for food. And to-day I read Gérard de Nerval's Le Rêve et la Vie (disappointed) and Fragments from Katherine Mansfield's Journal (disappointed). But I was not disappointed in the Love Books of Ovid.

September 29. Chez Philippe for luncheon (Adrienne's tigress eyes) and to Le Tremblay for the races (Red Sun lost) and to a mad rendez-vous (censored) and to-day I saw Joyce three times—near the Goya near Mouna Katorza near Ames'—he was walking slowly (felt hat overcoat hands in pockets) lost in thought (Work in Progress) entirely unaware of his surroundings. Sonambulist. And in me the same emotion as when Lindbergh arrived. But what is the Atlantic to the Oceans Joyce has crossed?

October 9. The pounding of the building (ravalement) is unceasing like the pounding of thoughts upon the brain and think how much older the brain is than the oldest house and after luncheon (there was Indian pudding) I read Sebastian Van Storck "his mother thought him like one disembarrassing himself carefully to make shift with as little as possible, in preparation for a long journey" (I too, one two) for the long journey to the Sun and to the Bank (account overdrawn as usual) and coming home over the Pont Royal there was a Moon, Frail Queen drawn in her chariot by the rushing rivers (horses) of the world with moonbeams for reins and leaving in her wake a dust of stars and where is she rushing to—to the Sun of course.

12. "Un jeune homme ne doit jamais acheter de valeurs sûres" so I decided not to get a car at the automobile show but to wait and buy a racehorse and to the races with C She cramoisy I gold and the Lady of the Gold Horse was there and we were too late to bet on Sun-Myth (he lost) and coming back to Paris in the yellow Hispano there was a Red Sun round like the Sun on the Japanese Flag and when we got back to Paris we found that Cousin Walter died this morning (and they never let us know). Néant or Sun? And shall we ever know?

14. That my body be cremated and that my so-called ashes be not taken to America for burial but shall be chucked out anywhere (so like Cousin Walter) and Jules the valet appears with the undertaker and from the pantry comes the sound of a blow torch (there is a period of waiting) and then a man enters with the blow torch and approaches the mahogany coffin (there is a light from the chandeiler directly above) and now the lid of the coffin is lifted from a corner and placed on the coffin and the smell of violets into the smell of the blow torch into the smell of burning gas and the undertaker in his lugubrious dress suit is like a prestidigitateur and I notice the bare floor and the empty brass bed pushed into a corner and the blow torch absorbs the air of the room and the minutes drag until at last the coffin screws (thirteen) are screwed in and the blow torch is extinguished and the presti-digitateur produces from nowhere an American flag which he drapes over the coffin and there are violets and chrysanthemums and orchids and there is a silence and we tiptoe out (Goodnight Cousin Walter) and as I am going out the front door (I was the last to leave) Jules undoes a piece of paper and gives me two of the blackest (onyx) cuff links (je les ai pris sur Monsieur avant qu'on est venu l'enfermer). And it is always afterwards, almost never at first (and this applies equally to separation when one is in love) that one begins to feel the Loss.

October 17. And the funeral and black black black and the taking down the coffin and there was General Weygand and Pershing and Walter Gay and Barthou the Minister of Justice and at last everyone was put in the proper order back of the hearse and there were crowds in front of the house and the procession (not "procession of perpetual girls marching to love" EEC) began and we moved off along the Rue de Varenne and so down the Rue de Bellechasse and slowly over the Concorde Bridge and across the Place de la Concorde (the obelisk weeping its granite tears—O.W.) and up the Champs Elysées (he did not believe in an after-life I am glad of the Sun I am strong in the Sun) and then through the Rue Pierre-Charron (past the Gallia—why didn't I ever sleep with little M?) and then the Avenue of George the Fifth and the Church (pro-cathedral they call it) and there were people and people looking on from the curbstone and the coffin was taken out of the hearse and we were inside the Church and there was an autumn smell thanks to N's chrysanthemums and then the voice of the hypocrite minister (thank Christ I am not a Christian) and there were Hymns and various Prayers (I said Sun-Prayers) and then the standing in line for the interminable defile and a shaking and a shaking of hands—moist hands strong hands exquisite hands coarse hands hands gloved and ungloved left hands (parmi les mutilés) duchess' hands, general's hands, the Count's hand, Veuve Biron's hand, white hands, dark hands, limp hands, bony hands, plump hands, young hands, old hands, hands, hands, hands, shaking, shaking, shaking but cold and motionless are the hands of the dead. Then suddenly Mrs. H. her face streaming with tears and she was the last of the long line.

Then in a car to follow the hearse across Paris to the Père Lachaise (it was hard work keeping up through the traffic) and we drove up an avenue to the Crematorium and here the corpse was uncoffined and I removed the Legion of Honor from his neck (this for his sister) and a last look (goodbye farewell adieu Adios) and he was placed in a slender white pine coffin (brought up from below on an elevator) and the coffin was placed on a little track and the master of ceremonies (he looked like a sommelier with chains round his neck) asked my assent and I nodded assent Yes to him and the door of the oven opened and the coffin slid in and the door of the oven closed with a sharp metallic click and the master of ceremonies went away and all the men went away downstairs to eat and I was alone listening to the crackling of wood and there was the pale light of the Autumn Sun slanting down through the tall narrow windows and there was a strange indescribable smell a charnel-house smell and there were sinister-looking instruments propped up in a corner like instruments of the Inquisition and there was no one around only the empty coffin in the next room (I could see half of it from where I sat) and the hoarse laughter of the coffin-carpenters eating their luncheon in the cellar underneath. And I unscrewed the stopper from my flask and drank a silent toast (Dieu it must be hot inside) and an inspector appeared and opened the door of the oven (there was a roar of fire) and the coffin had been burnt through had crumbled away but there was still a crackling and a crackling and it was all red-gold, chaste and red-gold, and cremation is clean no worms no white bloated rats (see Ulysses page 110) and there is nothing terrifying nothing unhealthily gloomy as at the Church and I read aloud to myself from the prayer book I had taken from the Church. And to every seed his own body. There is one glory of the sun (Sun) and another (lesser) glory of the moon and another (also lesser) glory of the stars for one star differeth from another in glory. So also is the resurrection of the dead. It is sown in corruption it is raised in incorruption it is sown in dishonor it is raised in glory it is sown in weakness it is raised in power it is sown a natural body it is raised a spiritual (I remember the way the Girl of the White Polo Coat used to pronounce the word "spiritual") body. There is a natural body and a spiritual body (an earth-body and a sun-body)—And now the cremation was almost over (Red Skeletons) and workmen emerged from below and my flask was emptied and the door of the oven was opened and the rack was drawn out all smouldering, red and white ashes, hot white ashes and the master of ceremonies scooped for me the ashes of the heart and I poured them into a little gold box and all the rest of the ashes were poured into a white cement box and we carried it out to the car and I sent the master of ceremonies with the extra wreaths to lay them on the grave of Oscar Wilde (it was his birthday two days ago) and N appeared wandering among graves (impression) and I went to meet C at the Grande Porte d'Entrée and it began to rain and rain and rain.

October 18. Salle Pleyel much too enormous and no bar and too long a programme but we did hear Ravel conduct his Valse and we did hear Stravinsky conduct his Oiseau de Feu (C liked the Waltz I the Fire) and when we got home I wrote

Q.E.D.

I am a tree whose roots are
    tangled in the sun
All men and women are trees
    whose roots are tangled in the sun
Therefore humanity is the forest of the sun.

October 26. To Chartres C and I and Alastair and the Black Wave as he calls Narcisse and there was the cold disappearing of the sun and it was cold and there was the sudden huge emerging of the Cathedral (within the great cathedral of the soul) and we went up the steps and pushed open a door and went inside (the uneven floor the shuffle of feet incense the low intoning of a litany the gold light of candles) and I prayed into the gold sun of a cierge (the sun of the cierge becomes a vierge (sun-virgin) inside of me) and there is blackness and darkness of stained glass windows and cold incense of stone. In America one never becomes part of a church at Chartres one becomes part of the Cathedral.

27. Notre Dame and a Cramoisy window through which my soul an arrow of gold wings into the Sun and if Chartres = Evening: Notre Dame = Morning (Sunset and Sunrise) and to an exhibition of etchings by Ensor and Narcisse upset a pitcher in cut glass and we bought (because of this) the most expensive etching and the best and I met Raymonde in the Tuileries and we watched the Red Sun go down back of the Gare d'Orsay and then dinner (C and I and the Lady of the Gold Horse and M) and I behaved badly and got up and left (I dont know why) to go and see Maya (stopping at Footits on the way for a whiskey sour) and this is the third time I have seen Maya.

> Comment t'appelles-tu?
> Comme tu voudras
> Qui es-tu donc?
> Celle que tu voudras.

30. Morning Sun looking out over Reims and the Cathedral and at noon by train with C to Paris (N in a red velvet jacket to say goodbye) and so to Longchamp and I lose on Aurora but I win on Soun who wins the Gladiateur (our sixth in a row) and we must win it some day—(I like endurance races better than sprints) and we must find a horse that will win it some day and to-day was the last day of Longchamp and at home in the bathroom after supper it took me twenty minutes to attack and kill a huge horsefly who buzzed and buzzed and who showed great courage (or was it anger) and I love the sound of the rain on the roof and I read in a hot bath before going to bed that the cube of the sun's distance equals the cube of the moon's distance, multiplied by the square of the number of sidereal months in a year, and by the ratio between the masses of the sun and earth and why should I enjoy this more than a novel or a play but why dont I enjoy it as much as the sound of the rain on the roof?—I guess it is time for me to go to bed.

November 7. To the Salon Nautique and we almost bought a boat (sun-boat) and there was an aquarium (the eels waving like eel grass the carp motionless and ugly) and there were engines (luisant) and slender fragile sculls (not skulls) and there was a red speed boat and a giant revolving phare (the Sun is a lighthouse on a Sea of Clouds) and then with C to see Polia Chentoff a Russian painter (we smoked black cigarettes) and then to the Rue

Duroc where we saw the largest Picasso in existence (quantity is not always quality) and were we met Ortiz the Spanish painter (he is a great friend of Picasso's) and where we met the Lady of the Music Shop (Lady A) and she is strange and she wears strange hats from Reboux and I liked her and to-night not to the Blue Room to dance (to know one's limitations is the beginning of old age) and to-night I wonder what made me write in my notebook that life is a ladder of disillusion the higher one climbs the greater the disillusion. But beyond all ladders thunders the Sun.

November 11. Armistice Day day that for me is the most significant day of the year more significant than Anniversaries Easters Fourths of July Labor Days Christmases (unless Christmas be looked upon as the Birthday of the Sun) and at Eleven the Minute of Silence (the Somme Verdun the Argonne Saint-Mihiel-Soissons) and then the Students arrived and we drank two jeroboams of champagne (they don't make nebuchadnezzars any more) and we all sat in a circle on the floor clockwise and drank from an enormous loving cup and there was the crackle of talk and the crackle of the fire and the Count arrived (old magnificence among the young) and we went to the races at Saint-Cloud and I did not play on Sac à Papier and I did not play on Maltese Kitten and they both lost and it was very cold and we drank hot grogs and before going to bed I smoked my pipe and drank two glasses of brandy

> to Oliver Ames Junior
> (killed in action)
> to Aaron Davis Weld
> (killed in action)

17. I gather Sun-Titles for Chariot of the Sun: Déjeuner de Soleil, Arctic Sun, Flame Analysis, Jeu de Reflets, Cemetery Sun, Concerning the Eyes of the Sun, Experiments with the Pendulum, Ladders to the Sun, Solar Tumult, Egyptian Eclipse, The Lick Observatory, Separation of the Sunbeams, The Littlest Sun, Oriflamme, To an Inhabitant of the Sun, Il est dangereux de se pencher en dehors, Abbadon, Zèbre du Soleil, Horologiographia, Splendor Solis.

19. Polia is here (she has a madonna face) to paint C and there is a queer snow-sunset (my idea of what Moscow must be like) and we went to the Circus with the Count and there were two remarkable acrobats (genre harlequin de Picasso) in black and white silk tights (Ryan and Burke—their names deserve to go down to posterity) and this was Art (A majuscule) and then at the end (after the entr'acte pour le montage de la cage) (I was afraid of "iron bars do not a prison make") twelve lions prowled swiftly out from a long cage tunnel and the Lion-Tamer (Peterson—his name deserves to go down to posterity) dressed immaculately in evening clothes (Hart Schaffner and Marx) ruled them whip in hand and they growled and roared and there was the sharp crack of the whip and the crouching fear of beasts and the strong glare of the arc-lamp up above and man may be the conqueror over beast but as I looked at the ignoble faces in the crowd I thought how much better it would be to be a lion a great roaring lion of the Sun and who was it (D. H. Lawrence I think) who said that a man can only be happy following his own inmost need, and my inmost need is the Sun.

November 22. Ten years ago to-day the hills of Verdun and the red sun setting back of the hills and the charred skeletons of trees and the river Meuse and the black shells spouting up in columns along the road to Bras and the thunder of the barrage and the wounded and the ride through red explosions and the violent metamorphose from boy into man.

24. I send to London for books: Arms and Armour, Bygone Punishments, Flagellation, Tortures, Finger Rings, Moon Lore, Cyphers and Monograms, Phallic Worship, Snakes, Sun-Dials—and to-day I wrote

SUN-RHAPSODY

The Sun! The Sun!
a fish in the aquarium of sky
or golden net to snare the butterfly
of soul
        or else the hole
through which the stars have disappeared

it is a forest without trees
it is a lion in a cage of breeze
it is the roundness of her knees
great Hercules
and all the seas
and our soliloquies

winter-cold anchorite
summer-hot sybarite
to-day a lady wrapped in clouds
to-morrow hunted by the hungry clouds
it is a monster that our thoughts have speared
The Queen we chanticleered

a monster's womb
a child's balloon
red burning tomb

and to-day Lord L arrived from London with the manuscript of his poems (Git-le-Coeur) which C and I are going to edit at our Black Sun Press.

27. Walk in the Bois and Prayers at the Tree (the need for a spring board —of a point de départ—in this instance the Tree) and the Arrow into Sun for Eternity and to-day there was a chimney-fire in my Library and the firemen arrived and I gave them a bottle of champagne and little Anne-Marie says that a fire in the house brings good luck (but what does the Sun say) and to-day I read that the attraction between the sun and the earth is equal to the breaking strain of a steel rod three thousand miles in diameter but what is this compared to the *unbreakable* chain of fire between the Sun and the Soul.

December 1. With C to the Circus to interview the Lion-Tamer and we sat at a table in the Bar and drank Benedictines and before training lions he began at the age of eighteen to train chimpanzees (he taught himself) and now he has been training lions twenty-five years and he has been wounded four times (he showed us scars on his arms and wrists). Yet he says they like him and he likes them (is it true what N says?). And where do they make love? In a huge cage in Denmark. And do they ever see the Sun? Almost never. And what are they worth? About two thousand dollars untrained. And how old are they? The youngest in the ring is a year and a half the oldest twelve. And are they intelligent? They are intelligent and they have moods like people so that sometimes they are easy to manage at other times almost unmanageable. And he said that they had never escaped (do solid sun-thoughts ever escape?). And the lions do not belong to him (always that way editors-writers, jewelers-pearl divers). And of the lions here Hercules is the oldest but his favorite is Rasso five years old four hundred pounds whom he carries round on his shoulders. And the others are Negus, Pasha, Mamelick, Chaplin, Prince, Elsa, Raia, Hexe, Lux, Fatma. And it appears that the lionesses are more difficult to handle more feline more treacherous than the lions who are more like dogs. And sometimes when he is sick his wife replaces him in the cage. And her name is Pola (not Polia) and she is German and she appears and more Benedictine and she has gold teeth. And he said they would not attack me if I went into the cage with him (ils ne dévorent pas). And here in Paris he said it was hard to work because of the concentrated light (trou de lumière concentrée). And I asked him if he had any children? Rasso is my son and again is it true what N says and he had a friend who tamed lions who was torn limb from limb and devoured in a lion-cage in Spain ("and Ralph the lion was engaged in biting") and apparently there was no attempt made to save him and here in Paris for precaution there is a fire-hose (he also carries a loaded revolver) and when I asked him if he were insured he laughed—no insurance they won't take lion-tamers too dangerous—and the lions eat ten kilos of raw horse meat a day and drink milk twice a week and he says he is never nervous (I don't believe it) and that all that is necessary is to employ concentration to concentrate his efforts once he is in the cage and that the only danger is if he falls down Must Never Fall Down or they would pounce. Yet he says: "les lions ça sont des gosses" and he has given performances in Moscow Leningrad Kief Berlin London Copenhagen Milan Rome Turin and now Paris. But never in America. And he speaks five languages. And he said a lion lives to be twenty-five. And I gave him an Inca dagger. And he said he would name the two cubs Harry and Caresse.

2. Read in the morning Newspaper that a lion-tamer named Pohl (not Pola not Polia) at Etoile (Soleil) Somme went into the cage where he had been in the habit of training his "pets" but that the lions became enraged ("nay do not blame them") and leaped on him inflicting about forty wounds (the serious nature of the injuries imperils the life of the trainer) and again to the Circus this time with MacLeish and Hemingway and we drank beer with the Spanish Clowns (H talked to them in Spanish) and then Peterson took us back to see the lions (they were yawning and stretching) then more beer (M believes there is no after life "there in the sudden blackness the black pall of nothing, nothing, nothing—nothing at all") and I am glad for my Sun and then more beer and then we went to our seats to watch Peterson and the Lions (he bowed to us from the ring) and there was a great growling and he cracked his whip and handled them to perfection and there was a storm of applause (white birds flying in a storm) and then we went back to the rue Férou where we met Mrs. H. and drank whiskey and so to the Escargot Rue de la Gaieté for oysters and white wine and when I got home I realized I was quite tight. How?

(I) because I wanted to throw things (I threw a bottle of Enos Fruit Salts out the window)

(II) because my hands were dirty (they always seem to get dirty when I drink)

(III) because my cigarette case was empty (I almost never smoke).

December 9. Posed for Polia.

(I) one must be born and die in the same picture.

(II) you will always come back to being like the way I saw you the first time.

(III) il faut se développer.

(IV) il faut toujours porter plus loin les frontières

and at noon across the Tuileries through greyness and coming down the Rue Cambon ran into MacLeish I going like an express train he controlled and collected (like a jockey holding his horse in) and a short talk on Léon Paul Fargue (river of red taxicabs eyes of windows girl selling violets) and away again like an express train towards the Station of the Ritz Bar and here four glasses of sherry (I forgot to eat luncheon) and at four C and I and Polia in the car through the traffic out the gates through the darkness to Meaux (three brandies) and on through the darkness to Château-Thierry (three brandies) in a bar where we all used to get drunk during the war and on through the darkness to Reims (three brandies) and supper and a quickly-to-bed-all-of-us-tired.

12. Back to Paris in the car and a drink of port in Château-Thierry in the big bar by the bridge (the first drink in the morning is always so good) and at Meaux we stopped for luncheon at a little place I had once taken luncheon at during the war and we drank a bottle of Burgundy a dark dark red and it was dark and cold out of doors and dark and warm inside (she too is a Dark Princess) and then over the river (the water-mills and the twin brothels) and the road to Paris and brushwood fires smoking into the winter sun and great wagons of hay and stark trees black and wintry and the sun disappeared dark red like my glass of Burgundy then Paris and the lighting of the lights and it began to drizzle as we crossed the bridge over the Seine.

1927

December 13. Lioness springs at her Trainer. London, Wednesday. An audience at the Holborn Empire had an unexpected thrill in the Kelso brother's act, in which two lions figure. Captain James O'Connor, the trainer, was trying out a new trick, in which he lies full-length in the cage, with a piece of meat across his throat for one of the lions to take. He had discarded his whip and lay on the floor when the lioness sprang at him. The attendants held the door ajar and Captain O'Connor leapt to his feet, dodged the animal's rush and got out just as the door was slammed in the beast's face. The curtain was rung down.

16. Fidèle Koenig accompanied by a man he introduced as Mr. New or Gnu? And I was in a hot bath when they arrived and suddenly all the lights went out and Célestin knocked over cocktails and C and Ganay left to go to the Claridge and I had to get dressed to go out to dinner and Koenig who has been working in Madrid (Telephone and Telegraph) wanted to start a new bookshop of old books and all the time Mr. Gnu never said a word (I guess he was too busy drinking cocktails) and then they left and I finished dressing and Frans appeared and more cocktails and he talked about Van Gogh (il était fou de soleil il est mort de ça) and as I was rushing out exactly three quarters of an hour late Ortiz appeared and C had not yet come back and I remember vaguely the Clos des Lilas (cocktails) Larue (oysters and champagne) Chang (a holding of hands) and at midnight The Blue Room.

17. A cold bath and a mad rush (fur coat over pyjamas) to the Bank just in time to overdraw my account and when I got back I found a great many people here: Frans and May, Ganay, the Scotts and a man they had with them and there was a drinking of cocktails and a looking at erotica and a mad luncheon with C Chez Philippe (four dozen oysters caille and cocktails) and we went out to the Bois and there were people skating along the stream by Jacqueline Island and we walked on the ice all the way up to the Tree (gold-cramoisy-grey into the Sun) and the Sun shone grey on the ice and Narcisse was afraid of the ice and later on I bought a pocket Sun-Dial on the Rue des Saints-Pères and there were horrid people to tea and I was very bored (a rare occurrence particularly in our own house).

18. C and I Frans and May to Melun and on a little way to a small house where we smoked opium with a man who was a captain on a French submarine during the war. Ambiance and Visions. Infinitesimal grains of sand on a sliding beach and suddenly each grain of sand turned into a Lady Clothed with Sun and each Lady was the same Lady and each Lady was clothed in exactly the same Sun. Then the whole beach slid away into the Sea and there were no more Ladies clothed with Sun but only a gigantic red umbrella opening and shutting against a windy sky at night (the stars had all been blown away). Then a long long girder bridge across a river without end and across this bridge a dark column of marching men (not "perpetual girls marching to love") (I could hear the sound of their feet). Then suddenly a Tower of the Future towering into the Sun (below a sea of revolving metal discs) and on Top of the Tower (I had to climb this Tower step by step) I found again a Lady Clothed with Sun and all the way back to Paris in the car I looked into the strange dark eyes of this Lady clothed with Sun.

December 25. Chrismas for the Christians but for Sun-Worshippers the Birthday of the Sun and I walked out to the Cimetière de l'Abbaye de Longchamp and there were skulls lying in a heap (they are rearranging things) and I moved our gravestone from the chicken yard to a place of security under a fir tree and I gave the Roux a hundred francs and we drank together Benedictine from my flask and I fed an apple to the goat ("a woman for necessity a boy for pleasure a goat for delight") and then I ran back as far as the Cascades and jumped into a taxi and went home and took a hot bath and went to bed to read a new book on the Sun.

Last Day of the Year and to the Bois with C and to the Tree and again the Arrow (cramoisy-grey within gold) into the red-gold of Sun and an orchid for the ashes of W V R B (in the Library) and three orchids for C (in our Bedroom) and at one minute before midnight in a glass of red champagne we drink a prayer cramoisy-grey within gold an Arrow for Eternity into the Red-Gold of it (it is midnight now)

SUN

1928

Harry Crosby's holograph notebook for 1928 survives. Phrases that were originally struck from the holograph are here enclosed in brackets.

VII

First Day of the Year. Sun (the last word said in 1927) the first word said in 1928 Sun-Warrior Queen of the Sun Princesses of the Sun and an I-drink-to-you in a glass of red champagne [and prayers in color into the Sun] and out to the Cimetière de l'Abbaye de Longchamp where we found the frightening queer old Madame Roux wandering among the graves like someone walking in her sleep (c'est-il vrai Monsieur) and Narcisse went sniffing about among the leaves and it was cold and winter-grey and I prayed into the Invisible Sun and there were strange goings on—graves being rearranged and six tombstones have disappeared and we went away and walked through the fog all the way back past the Tree to the Porte Dauphine and it was dark and all the street-lamps were lighted (fog flowers) and we took a taxi and went to see N who was sitting in a chaise-longue having her feet pedicured and afterwards to Gît-le-Coeur to dine with Lord L and there was a chimney-fire and showers of sparks and Croucher appeared and then we all went down to the barge to smoke opium.

January 19. [The littlest room (forteresse) on the very top floor and to Phillipe's for oysters and caille and Château Yquen and then] To Chantilly (very gold and very cold) and the carp had all hidden away and the peacocks had disappeared and the château was closed and we went to a little bar and drank hot grogs and then swift as an arrow (the wind and the sound of the tires making symphony) back to Paris and the street lamps were like gold eyes (partout des prunelles flamboient) and the river was like a broken bottle of dark wine and her hands were live white jewels in the dark.

26. Departure [Paris to Egypt] and only in departure is there freedom but I am waiting for the real departure the last departure into Sun then there will be no more departures and hence no more freedom but who wants freedom once he is clothed in Fire.

27. Milan and Il Redentore (a copy of a Leonardo) two Guardis (Il Canal Grande di Venezia) and two Breughels not to mention the famous Mantegna of the dead Christ with its unbeautiful foreshortening and on and on and a plate of minestrone in the dark station of Bologna and on and on through darkness and winter rain: Parma Olio Lodi Imola Ancona.

28. Brindisi Brindisium and the pilfering of the Rabindranath Tagore signature and a red fire in our dark room and a reading of André Breton's Manifeste du Surréalisme "dictée de la pensée en l'absence de tout contrôle exercé par la raison en dehors de toute préocupation esthétique ou morale".

[**29.** Red halo of sunfire over my head on the wood of the head of the bed and up quickly so as not to break the charm and at noon we board the

Shadows of the Sun

Vienna freshly arrived from Trieste & we leave Brindisium for Alexandria.]

January 30. The Mediterranean is a high mountain the Mediterranean is a precipice the Mediterranean is a chasm a high mountain a precipice a chasm a high mountain a precipice a chasm and we are hurled up to the heights to poise before rattling down into the depths this from early dawn to late at night rolling and creaking and pitching nor did a glass of champagne help very much nor did the baked potato bring any relief but Gide's Nourritures Terrestres saved the day "and if our soul has been worth anything it is because it has burned more fiercely than other souls" which reminds me of Lafcadio Hearn "as is the color of thy burning so is the worth of thee."[1]*

[31. At last at the very end of the day we see Land and there are American destroyers and fishing smack and tugboats and barges and a lighthouse and the old Adriatic battered by the seas and then the lights of Alexandria and the wharfs and so by train to Cairo and to the Semiramis on the Nile and above the Nile was a Moon the wife of the Sun.]

February 1. To the Pyramids at Gizeh. Disappointed. Throngs of Cook's Tourists Ford Cars and Italians who had turned out to see the Prince. Not to mention a horrid English Colonial atmosphere that hung like a pall over the Mena House ("un peuple pratique sans idéal"). The Tomb of the Blonde Queen. This is what I have done for my daughter. This is what you have done for her daughter. Caught a glimpse of the back of the head of the Sphinx and of the Prince standing on top of a pyramid. Depressed and thought of the North ("if there are roads towards the North; sleighs (rose et bleu) scattering up the snow; frozen lakes . . .") and to-day I began The Plumed Serpent (D H Lawrence) "There are only two great diseases in the world to-day—Bolshevism and Americanism; and Americanism is the worst of the two because Bolshevism only smashes your house or your business or your skull but Americanism smashes your soul." Only he forgets the third disease the English disease of stagnation. Better to smash than to stagnate.

3. C and I in a boat (felûka) on the Nile opposite the Semiramis and it was dark except for a lantern and the stars overhead (the princesses of the sun) and I knelt on a red mat while a Hindu tattooed a Sun on my back ("and a sixth sect worshipped an image of the Sun formed in the mind. Members of this last sect spent all their time in meditating on the Sun and were in the habit of branding circular representations of his disk on their foreheads arms and breasts").

4. The Museum and the Treasures *stolen* from the Tomb of Tutankamen: the coffin of thick plates of gold (a work of unparalleled splendor and sumptuousness) the five bird-collars cut out of sheet gold, the solid gold mask which covered the head of Tutankamen's mummy (the eyebrows and eyelids are inlaid with lapis lazuli), the solar boat in gold, the three plain

---

*Notes for Volume Two begin on p. 223.

rings of solid gold, the scarab rings, the gold bracelets, the gold daggers with gold sheathes, the royal diadem of gold found on the actual head of Tutankamen, the perfume box of gold, the gold sandals found on the feet of the mummy, the ten gold finger-stalls which protect the hands of the mummy and the ten golden toe-stalls which protect the feet of the mummy, the two gold belts, the girdle knots of gold, gold gold gold but can it compare to the Gold of the Sun.

February 5. Horse races at Heliopolis the great seat of Sun-Worship in the time of the ancient kingdom which the Egyptians called An, the Hebrews On, and the Greeks Heliopolis, that is the City of the Sun. But the modern Heliopolis is horrible, the only redeeming feature being that C won forty dollars on a horse called Parasol.

6. To Sakkara and by donkey along the edge of the desert after touching the great Step Pyramid (five thousand years old) towards the Great Pyramids of Gizeh (the Sun the way it was at the Bar de la Tempête at Breast last August) and we came to the Sphinx (how long O Sphinx before I go to the Sun?) and so to the Mena House for eleven pieces of hot buttered toast during the eating of which I read Aknaton's Hymn to the Sun

> "When Thou settest in the Western Horizon of heaven
> The world is in darkness like the dead,
> They sleep in their chambers,
> Their heads are wrapt up,
> Their nostrils stopped, and none seeth the other
> Stolen are all their things,
> That are under their heads,
> While they know it not,
> Every lion cometh forth from his den
> All serpents they sting
> Darkness reigns
> The world is in silence
> He that made them has gone to rest
> In his horizon."

7. Luxor chaste and sunnygolden in contrast to commonplace Cairo and there are felûkas and dahabeeyahs and yellow bulbuls and the Cook's Steamboats and the Song of the Nile Sailors and a Real Sun (The House of Ra) and at sunset a walk alone through the native quarter along dark and narrow streets past little stone rooms from which rose the aroma of cooking past lanterns stuck on iron prongs past the rabble in the coffee house and I ate the piece of hashish (about the size of a small caramel) which Champagne Charley had given me in the morning and went back to the Hotel past black female figures their skirts dragging in the dust their hands balancing colored jars on their heads and it was time for supper and suddenly towards the end of supper I began to feel queer but instead of going to bed I went out to the Temple of Karnak lying like a stone forest under the silver disk of the moon

every moment a horrible struggle to keep from fainting (a clinging close to C
to keep from falling) and I experienced all the sensations of dying an agony
of parting when the soul bids farewell to the body and voices sounded far off
and the vast columns of stone became pistoning trees up and down up and
down upsidedown We were lost in a dark and giant forest of dead silence
where Champagne Charley was the evil genii and C the faery queene. A
gagging in my throat an intense feeling of cold and a violent attack of dizziness which was accentuated by the stone pillars thrusting upwards erect and
phallic in their desire for the Moon. But to the last I remained I with the Sun
churning inside.

> ["Thou liftest up to him every
>   tree that is in thee.
> Thou liftest up to him every
>   tree that is about to be in thee"]

February 8. Feel like hell and my eyes look queer. Last night the first time
I had eaten hashish and eating it gives one ten times the effect that smoking it
does ("I was parched, my throat burned and I said 'This is the taste of
death' "). And even Champagne Charley opened lizard eyes in astonishment
[when I told him I had eaten the piece he had given me. Never again.] But in
spite of feeling like nothing human there was a programme to be followed
(how I hate things being arranged for me) and we crossed the Nile on a
felûka with a red sail and so on donkeyback to the Tombs of the Kings the
road winding white and dusty along a rock-ravine and there was a strong
white Sun beating down on us from a blank blue sky and how I cursed
myself for having taken the hashish. We came to the Tomb of Tutankamen
dismounted and groped our way down wood-steps and down rock-steps like
going down into a dugout during the war and the same smell of underarms
and the same lack of air and I thought of all Tutankamen's Treasures
displayed in the Museum at Cairo and of what Aknaton wrote

> "Stolen are all their things
> That are under their heads
> While they know it not"

and we came to the Tomb of Seti where his mummy uncoffined lay under an
arc light so that people could come and crane their necks and stare and make
stupid observations. For shame! And we turned and climbed steep stairs and
came out into the hard light of noon blinding after the darkness of the tombs
and we rode down to the Ramesium where the flies swarmed and where we
ate hard boiled eggs (I hate hard boiled eggs) and where I bought from a
young beggar three mummified hands—blackened hands stiff each with a
blue ring on the forefinger. But there are other hands her hands (ïdeiha)
hidden forever in the dark fires of my soul.

9. Wandered [with C] through streets barefooted children at our heels
screaming *Bakshish* and a flinging of copper coins and along a long alley to a

courtyard where twenty or thirty hooded men crouched in silence along a dark wall staring staring into a little red fire near the door to the mosque. We went down a side street which curved into the street of ill repute where lanterns shone like the eyes of cats. From behind one of these emerged a girl in a white dress. She beckoned and we followed her passing under the lantern into a dark house and up a ladder into her room. Her name was Alia and we made signs [that we did not want to sleep with her but] that we wanted her to dance for us whereupon a friend (Hasema) appeared bearing a tom-tom and four bottles of beer and we began to drink the beer and the tom-tom began and Alia began to dance with all her clothes on very prim and proper and then we all drank more beer and the tom-tom began again this time with more rhythm and intensity and she undressed and danced naked a stomach dance her head darting backwards and forwards like a serpent and she was young and physical (she reminded me of Zora) and we drank more beer and the bed invited but we gave her a gold coin and walked back to the hotel the blood throbbing in our veins.

February 10. With Moussa the snake-charmer to watch him draw scorpions from the walls and cobras from the fields but perhaps he held them up his sleeve (the way the magician gilly gilly gilly hid the chicklets up his sleeve). But whether Moussa was genuine or not the chant he chanted to charm the scorpions and the snakes was more wonderful than Alia and her danse de ventre for his song was the soul and her dance only the body and afterwards to the donkey races (let the Sun be the song of the soul *and* the body) (we each of us lost about ten lengths at the start) and there were camel races the camels "such as I never saw in all the land of Egypt for badness" and then to the Temple of Luxor (there is the word 'Rimbaud' cut in bold letters on one of the stone columns) to watch the Sun go down—"behind the fierce sun the dark eyes of a deeper sun were watching" and The Plumed Serpent is the most inspiring novel I have read since The Enormous Room.

11. Dawn and down the street on a donky towards the station (down the street of the sky towards the Sun) and a cup of coffee with Champagne Charley (he invariably turns up no matter where the place or what the time) and soon C and HMC drive past in the hotel wagon [both annoyed at me for not riding down with them] and the train is an hour late and I sat on my suitcase on the platform in the sun and read from The Plumed Serpent (difficult, for the dragomen were thicker than flies) "I without the Sun that is back of the sun am nothing" and something about the arrows of the soul, mindless shooting to the mark and about the prayer reaching its goal (for me the Sun) and about breaking the cords of the world in order to be free in the other strength (the sunstrength). At this juncture the train arrived a white train like the white train from Touggourt to Biskra and we left Luxor and ran southward between the Desert and the Nile—a long procession of scenes— stately lebbakah trees, ancient fragments of temples, the graves of crocodiles, the ancient Aphroditespolis, then Esneh with her slender minarets like blue ribbons 2 in the distance then little villages of low houses of sun-baked bricks usually girdled by a wall all desert-colored blending into the rocks—then a red hill with the ruins and tombs of Hierakopolis or City of Falcons then Kom Ombo then Assuân and a game of roulette on the platform with my roulette watch—forty of us, mostly natives—and there was a native policeman who stood behind me with a gun he (looked like a painting by Kipling if Kipling could paint) and someone won ten pieces of silver and a whistle blew and we took the train to Shellal where we boarded the government boat [and C and I have cabin 4 my favorite number because of a sun-warrior a queen and grey princess and a star]. And we went on up the Nile—in the distance the back of the great Assuan Dam—then the Island of Philae and the three-fourths submerged Temple of Philae referred to as the Pearl of Egypt but only the upper parts of the columns were visible and we are now in Lower Nubia which stretches from Assuan to Halfa and we lay on the deck in the sun and looked out at the flesh-coloured sands of the desert and at the low rock hills and at the stray palm trees standing like the columns of Philae half submerged like queens in wading and there were little sun-baked villages at the edge of the river (like unimportant thoughts at the edge of the mind) and there were little felûkas with queer red crescents on their sails and this evening we crossed the Tropic of Cancer.

February 12. "Wake! For the Sun, who scattered into flight
    The Stars before him from the Field of Night
    Drives Night along with them from Heaven and strikes
    The Sultan's Turret with a Shaft of Light" the Sultan's Turret being the Temple of the Lions standing some three hundred yards back of the little village on the riverbank and there was a short avenue of sphinxes and three sun-boats painted on the wall and on my way back I met H M C rushing towards the Temple (I had expected to steal a march on her [but she never misses a trick]) and I went down to the riverbank and took off my pyjamas and plunged naked into the Nile (fortunately there were no timsâhs—crocodiles) and then a naked plunge (soul) into the Sun (fortunately there were no clouds—crocodiles) and then back again still in pyjamas to the Temple and all the English soldiers who are on our boat about fifty of them were there and I offered a prize of a gold coin to the man who could get back to the boat first and C started the race by dropping her red handkerchief. And it was damn hard going over the sand! Finished fourth and drank a cup of coffee with the village patriarch a camel at our side and at half past ten we passed Korosko "in the valley behind the town is a British cemetery with the graves of British soldiers" and at Noon I put postcards in bottles and threw them overboard arrows towards the target of Paris. And all afternoon the sound of creaking water-wheels (sâkiyeh) of crude construction worked by oxen or camels and we passed the Little Sun Temple of Amada (card in a bottle) and the ruined Castle of Karanog (card in a bottle) and the Remains of Pyramid and Brick Tombs (card in a bottle) and we watched the Sun set for the fourth evening in succession (a breast suddenly tucked away behind the gold bodice of the hills) and towards eight o'clock we came to Abu Simbel and we went

on shore and scrambled up a precipitous bank to follow the sand path (we were escorted by [the blackest] Nubian soldiers who held oil lamps to show the way) to the great Temple of Abu Simbel and in the dark we craned upwards to see the giant colossi of Rameses Second each figure over sixty five feet high and we went into the Temple and there were figures of the king thirty feet high and the ceiling was adorned with flying vultures and stars and there were sun-boats painted on the wall and it was very difficult to see by the small oil lamp and the lack of length of the erect black arm that held it and then the siren blew and we rushed back to the boat and as we cast off we bombarded a pack of dogs with chunks of dry bread (Where are you Narcisse?) and to-day I began for the second time the Bible "and the Sun-God formed man of the dust of the ground and breathed into his nostrils the breath of life and man became a living soul."

February 13. Halfa at dawn and in a Ford at top speed across the Desert bound for Semna—the real Waste Land—black boulders, lava-colored rubble, a rock-strewn road, an abandoned fortress of sun-dried bricks on a steep rock close to the Nile (we are above the Second Cataract) more ugly black rocks with here and there the whiteness of bleached bones. No vegetation. Not a flower. Not a tree. Only the White Sun striking its hot white fist on the empty face of the Desert. And once a heavy black buzzard, bird of ill omen, perched on a pile of black granite. Once too a long weary caravan the camels heavily laden with enormous sacks of grain. We were bumping and rattling along an abandoned railroad the twisted rails uprooted and dragged to one side. Far to our right and across the river shone the Lybian Desert with its lion-colored dunes in striking contrast to the ugly Nubian Waste Land which we were crossing like a black beetle crawling across eternity. The Abomination of Desolation—At last at noon we came to Semna—low mudhouses Sudanese women in black with large earthenware jars on their heads a naked child running in fear from the Monster (our car) and a long grey dune behind which we discovered a stone hut and here we were greeted by two men who were excavating under Reisner and we were shown the excavations and we each ate a sandwich and drank a glass of water and said goodbye and this is the furthest South I shall ever go and I said a prayer into the Whitest Sun and then a waving goodbye and we rounded the curve of the grey dune ("am I the blue curve of day around thine uncurved night") and a last look at the grey dune as we headed back (thank Christ) towards Paris and the North! And a hard rough ride across the Waste Land the road hard to find and already the wind in many places had obliterated our morning tracks and we saw three gazelles frail shy hesitant their big ears pointed forward—three shy thoughts on the barren brain of the desert, and we came to a ridge of jagged black rock and passed beyond it and found again the abandoned railroad line the railroad that Kitchener had built when he was too late to save Gordon and the Ford rattled and rattled and the radiator boiled over and the Sun beat down and all the land was sterile and parched. It never rains here. And across the Nile the "very gold of very gold" of the Lybian Desert dunes of beaten gold undulating into infinity. And we overtook the caravan we had seen in the morning and rattled on and on across the arid land (the road to Bras during the war could not have been more desolate) with sometimes an occasional mud-hut or an occasional group of graves with a red bowl for water at the head or an occasional herd of goats who would scramble off the road as we lurched past. At last towards sunset the black boulders disappeared and we could see five miles away the white minaret of Halfa. And much drinking of coffee in a café whose walls were decorated with red camels and yellow pyramids and a crude likeness of a Nile Steamboat and C did sketches of the colored wall and of a shy Sudanese soldier and I bought six spears and gave a silver coin to a Tofla (little shepherdess) and the siren blew and we went on board the boat and it was ten o'clock when we left Halfa-in-Nubia Halfa of the Two Suns and now we are an arrow fleeting towards Paris and the Winter Sun.

February 14. Awoke at Abu-Simbel and again the great Temple and the gigantic Colossi and the king in his chariot and I touched the disk of the chariot wheel (the Sun) and I touched the figure of Amon-Ra in erection to give me strength and vitality and I touched the two sunboats on the walls to the south and to the north of the Altar (where on the longest day of the year a ray of sun strikes in the exact centre) (where on the most amorous day of the year a ray of sun strikes in the exact centre of the womb) and I smoked my pipe and walked out into the Sun and the siren sounded and we rushed downhill and went on board and slowly the Temple disappeared from outward vision to reappear in inward vision another block of shadow and stone to strengthen the walls of my Sun Fort. And so down the river down past the groaning water-wheels down past the ruined fort (not Sun-Fort) of Kasr Ibrim down past the ruined castle of Karanog down past the rock temple of Derr (the Temple of Rameses in the House of Ra) down past the ruins of the little Sun-Temple of Amada (a red jewel set in the gold chain of the Libyan Desert) down down until an hour after sunset we passed "The Lions" but it was too dark to see the temple and near here we recrossed the Tropic of Cancer.

15. The flash of a white sail in the Sun is the symbol of the soul in the Sun and after breakfast I watched a Sudanese sitting crosslegged on the deck brushing his teeth with a piece of wood about the size of a pencil. [3] Apparently with the Sudanese this ceremony of the brushing of the teeth is a religious ceremony for they brush their teeth not for a minute or two minutes as we do but for an hour or even longer using no tooth paste of any sort no Colgates no Forham for the gums no Kolynos nothing but Nile water. I offered my tooth brush in exchange for his. He refused. I offered him my toothbrush and a tin of tobacco. He refused. I offered him my toothbrush a tin of tobacco and four silver coins but he refused and continued to brush his teeth. Finally persuaded a sailor to sell me his as I wanted to take one back to my dentist who appreciated it when I brought him the teeth of the skeleton I took from the sarcophagus at Syracuse. And now we are approaching

Philae. Now Shellal. Now Assuan which is a dry dusty Necropolis and we drive up to the Cataract Hotel ("be at home away from home") which stands directly opposite the ancient City of Elephantine and to-day I rode in a donkey race (run the straight race into the Sun's Gold Palace).

February 16. To the Bazaars stuffed with Sudanese and Abyssinian weapons and I bought four cruel daggers and a sword in a red sheath and a necklace of green amber (tested with tissue paper) and a bronze cobra and an apron of leather fringe adorned with amber and silver which is the costume of the women of the Sudan and we rode over to see the Bisharin village a dry carcase under a white sun and there were queer faces peering from white huts and filthy children flies stuck in their eyes shrieking *Bakshish Bakshish* and we shrieking Harra Burra to our donkeys and the donkey boys running behind. And at sunset with C and a Nubian Nimrod on donkeyback through the necropolis to a pile of rocks beyond the slaughter house where we concealed ourselves and waited—and waited—and waited—and perhaps we saw the shadow of a jackal—at any rate I was asleep at the switch and it was gone and there were mosquitoes innumerable and vultures hovering overhead and from the direction of the river the dreary creaking of sakiyehs and it is four years now since that jackal hunt at Biskra. Thank Christ I never live in the past.

17. To Kom-Ombo after a sail in the morning to the Dam in a felukâh (will the bottles ever drift by?) and Kom-Ombo was hot and full of flies and we went in a toy tram-car drawn by a blind-in-one-eye donkey across the sugar plantations to the Temple on the bank of the river dedicated to the worship of the falcon and the crocodile and for once we had a silent guide and we could wander as we pleased and there were two great wingèd suns and there were mummies of sacred crocodiles (like trunks of trees) and there was a deep well into which we dropped stones (the Sun is a deep well into which I drop the gold coins of my soul) and C and I had a walking race along a long stone corridor and it seemed strange to see in the distance the black smokeplumes pouring from the tall smokestacks of the sugar factories and after supper I read things about Ancient Egypt a nation where nothing impermanent was esteemed just as I am forging my soul to be a soul where nothing impermanent shall be esteemed.

18. Iced grapefruit for breakfast sitting out on the piazza in the sun and on to Edfu I riding on a flat car and there was dust and dirt and cinders and Edfu was swarming with flies and filth and we crossed the Nile on a felukâh and rode by donkey to the Temple (Baedeker double-starred Harry double-damned) and here we met Moi Je Fais Le Kodak only they wouldn't let him take pictures and here the stupid Christians have destroyed the pagan faces not to mention the phallus of Amon-Ra—the damn busybodies why couldn't they let beauty alone (I refer to the phalluses as well as to the faces) and we went back to Edfu and took the train to Luxor and in the train I read in the Plumed Serpent this which is important "Living I want to depart to where I am." The Sun.

Shadows of the Sun

February 19. Basked naked on the roof of the hotel in the scorching sun what is it Valéry says "Midi le Juste" (parce qu'il laisse tomber d'aplomb ses rayons) and I liked listening to the barbarian refrain of the Nile sailors and I liked looking across the river or down into the garden and if the gazelles in the garden like the gazelles we saw in the Waste Land are thoughts frail and shy what are the vultures circling and circling overhead are they thoughts ugly and obscene or merely unimportant thoughts circling and circling and are these vultures to the shadows they cast what my thoughts are to my thoughts in the mind of another or is all this conjecturing merely the result of the strong cocktail I took off the waiter's tray (it was destined for someone else) on my way up to the roof? And to-day at sunset a walk along the riverbank watching the native women come down to the Nile to fill their jars —black figures barelegged wading out stooping down to fill their jars ("I should have lost a gesture and a pose") and the river was gold and then purple and then grey and I learn in my little red dictionary that Es-Sems means The Sun Burns Me. It certainly did this morning.

22. First day of Ramadan the month of the Fast and it is also the birthday of Schopenhauer and a dreary luncheon "he withdrew his consciousness away from them as they all three sat at table leaving the two women as it were seated outside a closed door with nothing more happening." Egyptian Exterior and the Gold of the Desert Paris Interior and the Snow of the North The Nile The Valley of the Queens The Tombs of the Queens The Valley of the Queens The Nile.

24. C won the Visitors donkey race on Sweet Chocolate I third on Whiskey and we played tennis and ping-pong and built a coal fire in the room (damn cold it is) and today I finished The Plumed Serpent "and beware when you break the pomegranate—it is sunset you take in your hands. Say I am coming come Thou".

28. Observed Ramadan and did not eat or drink until after sunset when I went into the bar and drank champagne cocktails with Champagne Charley and he came down to the station with us we were both very tight and waved his long yellow handkerchief at us as the train pulled out of the station towards Cairo and the North.

29. The Sun-Ring!

March 1. Extraordinary that we should have found the Sun-Ring on a day that comes only once every four years (one chance in fourteen hundred and sixty) and because of this I am strong and happy the tree of the past is chopped down with an axe of gold no branches no roots dragging me back and I am unchained to arrow into the Sun and in the Museum we saw the giant Aknaton columns from Karnak (C says I look like him) and the famous fragment of Aknaton adoring the Sun and a gold drinking cup of beaten gold and the gold rings of Tutankamen (I would not trade my gold sun-ring for all his rings put together nor for all the rings in the world) and we saw wonderful serpent bracelets and the mummies of kings and queens in coffins under glass ("stolen are all their things that are under their heads while they know it not") and we saw the papyrus from the Book of the Dead and we went to the bazaars and bought three gold necklaces the third for Narcisse and we bought twenty brass camels (ah! les chameaux) and when we got back to the hotel (Shepherds) there was a letter for me from Zurich to say that I could have Polia's Jeune Fille de Province (a good counterattack after a retreat but I should have bought it in the first place at the Autumn Salon) and after supper (Miss R at the next table in a blue dress) with H M C to hear Salomé. "Tuez cette femme."

March 2. Three dry martinis on the sun-piazza of Shepherd's with C before luncheon that is we each had three and after luncheon talked to Miss R (no introduction) and she was pretty as a picture by Laurencin and again mental adultery and we drank brandy together and then she went off to the Zoo—and we left for Jerusalem and crossed the Suez Canal from West Kantara to East Kantara and I took on going to bed in the train an opium pill and now we are in Asia and "I give a road to my feet northwards."

3. Jerusalem and the Dung Gate and the Damascus Gate and the Jaffa Gate and the Golden Gate and the Gate of the Prophet and the house of the poor man Lazarus and the house of the rich man Dives and the tradesman with a graphaphone on his head (Paris c'est une Blonde) and the policeman with a cap of black fur on his head (c'est une Négresse) and the pastry man with a plate of sun-cakes on his head and the beggar man with scrofula on his head and Mount Zion and the Ecco Homo Arch and the Tomb of David and The Upper Room of the Last Supper and the Sisters of Zion and the Via Dolorosa and the Mosque of Omar and the Jewish Wailing Wall ("for the palace that lies desolate we sit in solitude and mourn for the temple that is destroyed we sit in solitude and mourn for the walls that are overthrown we sit in solitude and mourn") and the Old Jerusalem Wine and the Old Jerusalem Bazaars and David Street and the Camel Market and the strange Moon which balanced on a white cloud like a polar bear on a cake of ice.

4. To the Dead Sea and there are many names for the Dead Sea the Salt Sea or the Sea of the Cadmonites the Sea of Asphalt Bahr Lût or the Lake of Lot and it is fifty miles long and ten miles wide and thirteen hundred feet below sealevel and there was a flock of Bedouin tents on the shore like a flock of black sheep with a small one-story hotel for shepherd and there was a graphaphone playing Paris c'est une Blonde and I undressed and went into the Sea and it was heavy with salt so that it was impossible to sink and as much as my body was naked in the Dead Sea so was my soul naked in the Gold Sun and there was rotten brandy to drink while I was getting dressed (Jesus Christ I have never tasted such [awful] stuff) and as we were preparing to go I filled an Elisabeth Arden eye-wash bottle which I had brought with me full of water from the Dead Sea for baptisms if I ever have any children and so back to Jerusalem by way of Jericho looking back at the polar [bear] moon climbing over the Dead Sea and there was some very old Jerusalem wine for supper and I wrote to Paris for a book called Une Croisière Autour de la Mer Morte—Mar Muerto Mare Morto La Mere Morte The Dead Sea.

March 5. Bokhara the Temple-Boy and I fall in love with him (to hell with women) and we were photographed sitting together in the Sun on the steps of the Temple and afterwards I explored through the enormous substruction called Solomon's Stables a harmony of arches with sunlight pouring through then up and along the ramparts and across a garden with three beggars like the picture by Breughel following us until we arrived at the Pool of Bethsaida into which I threw a coin instead of giving it to the beggars. This took strength but a prayer is more important than an act of charity and in the afternoon to Bethlehem ("has existed without change for thousands of years" —like the minds of the majority of Bostonians) and the place was swarming with automobiles and Cook's Tourists like so many maggots but these were forgotten among the stone-cold Coptic singing of the Greek and Russian Copts. When we got back to Jerusalem the British Regiment Band was playing or rather trying to play (how the hell can the British with their temperament expect to play jazz) Paris c'est une Blonde from behind the great wall opposite our balcony and C and I drank brandy in the Sun from my silver flask and we dropped walnuts on the passers by below (I concentrating on Cook's Tourists) and at sunset I wandered off through queer streets and had my hair cut by a young jew in a dark niche under an arch and I searched everywhere for my Temple-Boy but could not find him and I heard the cannon to break the fast and watched the fasters run for their hot bread and beans and I watched the moon rise and peered into low dives (does the moon peer into the low dives of our brain) and got lost and drank beer in a dark bar with orange walls where there was a game of cards going on (The Queen of Hearts) and a red bird in a cage (The King of Hearts) and why shouldn't a playing card make love to a red bird?

6. Little Bokhara the Temple Boy and we dropped inkbombs from the balcony and made paper darts and ate breakfast together and said goodbye in the Sun and away out the Jaffa Gate (C waving goodbye to her policeman friend I never turning around) and out the Damascus Gate and beyond the hill through a driving hailstorm towards Tiberias and the North [and I like my new Bokhara-Color] and we passed Jacob's Well and we passed Joseph's Tomb and this is the first rain since January and I am glad. Food and a Bottle of Medoc at Nazareth and afterwards we came to the Hill of Ahab where Salome danced before Herod (tuez cette femme) and then we came to the Hill where Saul ran upon his sword (the same hill where Judas hung himself—I prefer the hills of your breasts) and now down and down with Mount Tabor on our right and down below into the Town of Tiberias and Tiberias it appears is notorious throughout Syria for its fleas and they say the king of fleas has his court here and it appears that there are two queer kinds of fish in the Sea of Galilee; the Chromis Simonis the male of which carries the eggs and the young about in its mouth (as I carry the eggs of the Sun about in my heart) and the Clarias Macracanthus which emits a sound. We ate one of each of these fish for supper not worth a damn compared to the fish of André Masson and went out to watch the full moon over the Sea of Galilee the Bokhara Moon over the Sea of my Heart.

March 7. Breakfast in the Sun and the Sun over the Sea of Galilee (the Bokhara Sun over the Sea of my Heart) and we left Tiberias and came to Magdala the birthplace of Mary Magdalene and we passed a cavern once the haunt of robbers and we went to Capernaum (near here Christ walked on the waters as Bokhara walks on the waters of my heart) and over on the other side of the Sea we saw a precipitous mountain and I read aloud from my Bible "behold the whole herd of swine ran violently down a steep place into the sea and perished in the waters" and we went past an abandoned caravanserai and saw the traces of the old caravan road from Jerusalem to Damascus and we went down a hill and over the Jordan over the Bridge of the Daughters of Jacob (over the Bridge of the Daughters of the Sun) and Palestine is behind us and we are in Syria and what joy to see the French flag instead of the British! Rock-barren land and at noon bread and wine by the side of the road and we watched the flocks of sheep go bleating by and we watched a lonely caravan go by and then we drove on and on until at sunset in a hurricane of dust we entered Damascus.

8. Damascus and the Mosque, Damascus and the Museum (a grain of wheat on which is written a poem of sixty words), Damascus and the Palace, Damascus and the Bazaars where C and I bought a Hindu Love Book with little handpainted miniatures to illustrate the various positions of love and where H M C bought a Byzantine Gold Cup of the Third Century "very gold of very gold" and it was found near Antioch and it is of old beaten gold and it has four figures supporting the shallow cup and it is frail to feel and fire for the eyes and it has a soul and when C and I die I should like to drink the poison from this cup. It is the Cup of the Sun.

And after supper we met the Argentine who was with the pretty girl at Luxor and he showed me a necklace he had bought (for the pretty girl at Luxor?) a ponderous gold necklace incrusted with uncut emeralds that some Moroccan Prince once gave to a Courtisane in Damascus and he was with his nephew and they took us out on a party to a native cabaret where we saw Druses who are the wildest fighters in the world and who believe that when they die their soul goes on living in the soul of another, and there was dancing by a fat brothel-woman and we smoked nargilehs and drank Turkish coffee and afterwards champagne and what with all this and all we had seen and done during the day my head began to whirl with camel markets and saddle markets and pastry shops and barbers and hawkers and water-carriers and fig dealers and silk vendors and refreshment vendors (lemonade and other beverages are cooled with snow from Lebanon—only I felt too hot-headed to cool) and I could hear the Muezzins in the Minarets calling to Prayer "A Muezzin from the Tower of Darkness cries Fools your reward is neither here nor there" and it was almost midnight when we drove back to the hotel down the street called Straight and straight into bed was no word for it!

March 9. Up the snowcovered road over the Anti-Lebanon range (hard sledding all the way) and on the way down we passed a long caravan thirty camels long (thirty freight cars long) going back empty through the snow towards the East and so down to level ground and off towards the right towards Baalbek which was in more ancient times (and perhaps shall be in more future times) the centre of the worship of Baal whom the Greeks identified with the Sun-God Helios. The Ruins of the Temple are magnificent great broken blocks of stone in gargantuan disorder, the fallen columns lying like leviathans among patches of snow, the shattered fragments of reliefs in stone, the six immaculate columns color of red and orange standing erect in the centre, the broken arches, the enormous paving-stones, the fortress walls, the subterranean passageways and a real wild ass that "stamps o'er his (Baalbek's) head but cannot break his sleep." So that I seemed to be wandering through a giant soul (as we all wander in a certain sense through our Belovèd's Soul) among great broken blocks of thought cast here and there in disorder by the hand of Time the fallen columns symbolic of fallen ideals, the shattered fragments of reliefs in stone being the shattered fragments of the past the six immaculate columns color of red and orange standing erect in the centre being the six most perfect nights of love, the broken arches being the broken ambitions, the paving-stones the stones of a philosophy now overgrown with weeds the fortress walls the walls that we all of us have to erect against the outside world the subterranean passageways representing the mysterious undercurrents that flow through the soul as blood flows through our arteries and the wild ass is posterity. Let him stamp he will not break our sleep.

10. Still dark when I woke up fog and the smell of damp earth then grey light and it was a grey-and-gold morning and I went to the Temple and buried a gold coin as an offering to the Sun and I threw snowballs at the Sun four—for gold grey cramoisy dark and a little one for Bokhara. Then out the big gate past one little Temple of Bacchus and the little Temple of Venus to the little Bar for Soldiers (bar autorisé aux troupes) and here I ate a plate of rice and drank four glasses of dubonnet and looked out the door at the ruins of the Temple which looked as if they had been made by modern artillery and on the road there were little ungay children playing about a puddle and a roadmender cracking stone and winter trees and peasants and four soldiers in blue coming towards the bar so that I was reminded of a village at the front during the war only it was difficult to account for a camel tied to a tree. Anachronism. [And H M C appeared with some Phonecian glass a queenly pitcher for C and a tall and slender phial for me a Curic vase honest and good for herself and I ate another plate of rice. . . .] Ate another plate of rice and then we left Baalbek and went by train (I sat in the baggage car and drank red wine) up over the Lebanon Mountains (there was a snow-ball fight at a mountain station) and down the long incline into Beyrout and there was

a superb view of the Mediterranean Sea (Thalassa Thalassa) and an iron sign marked Dames Seules which I unhooked from the first class car to take back to the Students for their collection of curious signs and in Beyrout I bought an emigrants trunk for three dollars made out of wood and tin in a shop next La Rose Noire a Russian Bar where we drank gin cocktails until we moved to Le Chat Noir which is a German Bar next door to drink champagne. [Here we met a young Armenian who had studied in England who had been out to Persia who talked eight languages so he said who was an archaeologist whose uncles owned an antique shop and a concession for excavating in Tyre and Sidos and he invited us to go out on the town. C was tired and went to bed. We went to Cabaret One. Whiskey and there was a pretty French girl. To Cabaret Two. A second whiskey and a Syrian Girl dark and voluptuous. To Cabaret Three. A third whiskey and a Viennese Girl sixteen years old who danced naked before a house crammed full of men. To Cabaret Four. A fourth whiskey and a Russian girl gracious and affectionate. By this time it was about three o'clock I was ossified so was the Armenian but he wanted to go on so I left him and drove back to the hotel in a red hack and H M C was worried and waiting for me just as she used to in my wild drinking days and she used the same word 'wicked.'] "It was *wicked* of you to stay out so late" but C was asleep so I undressed in the dark and went to bed. Beyrout is a mad city!

March 11. Breakfast [in the Sun] on the terrace and there was a Gypsy Girl dressed in yellow and red dancing in the street she was very young and pretty and brutal (Beyrout seems to be a great place for girls) and we left by car to motor to Tripoli along the Phoenician Coast ("The coast of Syria is a long cemetery of ancient shipwrecked cities") and we went over the Dog River and got out and climbed a precipitous hill to look at some dreary rock inscriptions—everyone doing their stuff H M C trudging bravely upward interested in everything good or bad C gay and papilonaceous flitting from one rock inscription to another I angry and in revolt and Fat-Head the Guide talking with no one paying not the slightest attention and spitting into his handkerchief. At Sunset (a magnificent fire-colored Phoenician Sunset) we came to Tripoli where there are soapfactories and medieval streets and a forest of orchards (inside a forest of orchids) and a castle and a monastery of dancing dervishes and we drank black wine in a cold hotel and ate a wretched supper and said goodbye to Fat-Head and drove by carriage to the station where we went to bed on the train which does not leave until six in the morning. This is the furthest point out of the Orient Express as the Sun is the furthest point out of the Sun-Express.

12. Tripoli Hadidi Geuzlahir Hourbetine and at noon the train stopped at Homs and it was here that Heliogabalus was high-priest at the temple of Baal and there was a citadel and I climbed up on the roof of the freight car to bask in the sun and was just drowsing away when I heard shrieks and whistles and saw that the train was moving out of the station and that the freight car which I had thought was attached to the Express had remained stationary. I

dropped down the ladder sprinted fifty yards down the tracks and swung on to the last car just as the train began to gather speed very lucky for I had no money and there was no train for three days. From Homs (our Sun-Cup was unearthed near Homs) past a village with white cubical houses without windows each house with a lofty conical roof—so that the village looked like a square of beehives and near here we saw a mirage with a hayrick floating in the middle of it (I wish it had been Bokhara) then Hama where there were huge waterwheels and minarets and after Hama more beehive villages and we sat all afternoon in the Sun on the floor of the baggage car until at sunset we came to Aleppo smothered in dust and we got out and drove to the great citadel on a hill in the centre of the city (the importance of a citadel in the centre of the soul) and all around were prisons and hospitals and filth and we were glad to get back to the station for Aleppo is bar none the filthiest city I have ever been in and on towards the North and at midnight we crossed the Turkish Frontier and the custom's man was very disagreeable about my Sudanese Spears and my Brass Camels.

March 13. At Eregli we pass the down-going Express and now we are half way between Tripoli and Constantinople and on all afternoon until we came to Konia the ancient City of Iconium ("they shook off the dust of their feet against them and came into Iconium") and here we got off the train and bought beer and peanuts and held a mad walking race back of the station and then it grew cold and we boarded the train and rattled on through the night towards Constantinople.

14. Constantinople.

15. Wild party last night after listening to the prayers at Saint Sophia and Voronoff was on the party at the beginning and we remembered each other from that day last spring out at the hospital at Neuilly and the two Argentines we had met in Damascus were there and they had a young Turkish guide with them and we went to a place called the Turquoise and afterwards to a bordel to admire two people making love I dont see how they did it the room was so damn cold and they stark naked and for me at least it was a chaste spectacle like two strong flowers curling and uncurling and to-day we ate at the Embassy only Cousin Joe was sick in bed and we went through the Bazaars and afterwards to visit the Blue Mosque a rhapsody in blue and afterwards to read Gide in a hot bath "know that at each instant of the day you can possess God (for me the Sun) in his totality."

16. More Gide "let every emotion become for you an intoxication—if what you eat does not intoxicate you it is because you are not hungry enough" and we ate dozens of oysters and went for a mad motorboat ride in the Bosphorous the spray pricking like gold needles and this was certainly intoxicating and we went to see Cousin Joe and he is the ideal type for an Ambassador—a gentleman in the fullest sense of that distorted word, good-looking, intelligent, artistic (he loves poetry and music and plays the piano) energetic gracious and we saw Anita and Elsie, Anita or Elsie?

March 17. Gide again (I like him much better than Constantinople) He says good things "I have carried everything of mine inside of me just as the women of the East carry with them their entire fortune. At each little moment of my life I have been able to feel in myself the totality of my possessions I have constantly held all my possessions in my power" which for me means fires of gold fires of cramoisy grey fires dark fires Bokhara fires exploding madly inside a Sun.

18. Mad party C and I and a man from the Embassy and it was his birthday and we began with hashish and we ended with hashish and in between we drank chianti and went out outside the walls of the city to look at the Kurd shepherds dancing and stamping their feet in an enormous tent (like the Mexican dancing in the Plumed Serpent) and we took opium pills and went somewhere to drink champagne and dance and Christ only knows how we got back to the hotel.

19. Seriously frightened and there were colors exploding suns within suns and cataracts of gold and I felt cold and trembled as if I had had the ague and had a terrible time getting dressed my brain in a maelstrom and a fear of falling forwards. Afraid but not panic stricken. Remembered the little dictionary and looked up antidotes for poison (stimulants coffee artificial respiration keep patient awake) and I drank four cups of black coffee and there was a roaring of lions in my ears and columns of color pistoning through my head and the telephone rang (the ringing of the bell sounded like a barrage at Verdun) to say that the Embassy Man was very sick (he had had at least twice the amount I had had) and it was time to go and there were bells ringing and flags crackling and banging in the wind (glorious spectacle) and I told his valet to administer hot stimulants and to keep him awake and we went to the Embassy to say goodbye to the Grews and so to the station in Cousin Joe's car the Stars and Stripes crackling in the wind from the left front mud guard (a delicate attention in our honor) and there was a bewildering saying of goodbyes and colors dressing and undressing tops whirling—then a long locomotive wail and the train crashed out of the station with fire clouds crashing against the windowpanes and the Sea was a Sea of Fire and the Sun tattooed on my back whirled like a top with sparks flying in every direction (I could feel the Sun boring deeper and deeper into my back) and everything was violent—a flock of birds became a flock of comets the telegraph poles were women burning at the stake the clickety click of the train going over the rails was the bursting of firecrackers. Suddenly a sharp severing of a cord "the flash of what a tongue could never tell" the sudden touching of a match and my head cracked open and I exploded into Sun.

20. Belgrade and it was hard and cold a real New England cold and we sent a telegramme to the Man in the Embassy (I am still worried about him—what if he should die) and I was angry I dont know at what and went off by myself and looked at a stuffed boar in a saddle store and ate cold caviare in a cold store and looked into the winter sun and ran down the hill just in time to catch the train.

March 21. Budapest and the Red Sun rising over the train-yards and we drove along immaculate streets to the Ritz where I found a telegramme from the Man in the Embassy. Thank Christ. Have I ever worried so much about a man? And we ate caviare and drank cocktails and went to see the Goyas and the Dutch Interiors in the Museum and we walked up to the Fishermens Bastions to look down over the city (I should like to put it in my pocket to give as a toy to Bokhara) and we found a bar next the hotel called the Mignon Bar and here we drank brandy and watched the cocottes in action and at dinner time in the Ritz there was Tzigane Music but it isn't worth a damn compared to good Jazz.

22. Stuffed birds like certain stuffed souls I know pretty but unalive and snakes in bottles like dead phalluses this at the Museum of Natural History and then we went to the Zoo and bought a box of fishes and hurled them at the seals and we fed peanuts to the bears and to the monkeys who are onanists and there were peacocks (pava) a gnu and two peasant girls raking leaves and a gazelle exquisite and frail with the most gentle eyes that I should have liked to have made love to and when we got back to the Ritz there was a fashion show going on in the front hall girls in fur coats and underwear and the lure of the black and gold triangulairs and the lure of perfume and of fur and it began to rain as we drove off for the train and next to Paris and New-York I like Budapest best.

23. Budapest is behind us and now Vienna is behind us and C wins the series of word games (Constantinople Aphroditespolis Jerusalem Horticulturalist Interpolation Sun-Worshipper) and in the afternoon we came to the little castles and little white churches of the Tyrol and at sunset to Innsbruck scene of that awful row four years ago and it must have been about midnight when we came to Zurich where I descended in pyjamas upon the platform to receive from the hands of the art dealer the picture by Polia and now the Jeune Fille de Province is mine and I am glad. But I would rather have a Jeune Fille of the Sun.

24. Paris and all other lands and cities dwindle into nothingness Paris City of the Sun and our long journey is over (the Sun-Ring won with Bokhara second and the Sun-Cup third with Baalbek and Aknaton close behind) and S V R C was shrieking on the platform and Narcisse was wagging his tail (dry chunks of bread to the dogs at Abu-Simbel) and in the afternoon I went to the races and tried to buy Red Sun but his owner would not sell him. Damn.

29. Packed five pieces of gold (twenty dollar gold pieces) into a small hollow book and took it to the Gare du Nord and asked a man who was looking out at the rain from the door of a blue pullman car marked Firenzi if he would be willing to mail my package in Italy (gold is not allowed to cross the frontier) and he said yes and he turned out to be the Duke of Argyll (Ian's cousin) and there was a piercing whistle and the blue car with the duke and the five pieces of gold backed away and disappeared into the fog and I went home to dine and to go to the de Falla Operas and there was wonderful Spanish dancing by Argentina (we never saw anything like this in Spain) and she was feline and defiant and infuriate and there was a little Mademoiselle Joselito who danced like the Gipsy Girl at Beyrout tock tock gold and defiant stamping her foot tock tock a brutal little girl defiant barbaric tock tock whom I should like to take in my arms and violate.

April 1. A thousand on Aurora but she was nowhere and to the Surrealist Exhibition at the Sacre du Printemps where we bought a Malkine painting of a steel wheel churning sparks off into space (Death churning souls off into space) and to-day the Sun setting behind the Gare d'Orsay was like the pulsating heart of Mathô that the high-priest offered upon a spoon to Salammbô.

4. "Who when he had found one Sun-Cup of great price went and sold all that he had and bought it" and the Sun-Cup is here for two days and we poured into it champagne and drank in it to the Sun and it was as if we were drinking Fire.

6. In a bookshop opposite the shop where we bought the Zebra skins I saw a Skeleton which I bought for six hundred francs and which I wrapped in my yellow raincoat and took home in a taxicab her feet dangling on the steps and I hung her to a bookcase in the corner of my Library and to-day I read in Black Armour

> "One of these men will find my skeleton
> To one it will be delicate and slim,
> With stars for eyes, and portent of a sun
> Rising between the ribs to frighten him;
> Yet, being bold, he might embrace it soon
> With quick insensate passion in the night,
> And by the holy taper of the moon
> Encouraged, and because its bones were light
> As filigree of pearl, he might depart
> Bearing my jangled heart-strings on his heart"

and who was this woman, princess or harlot actress or nun young or old pretty and passionate or ugly and dumb?

8. Easter and to Chartres to drink gin and to burn a cierge in the Cathedral and we went to the Bois Joly to play at bowls and to run with Narcisse [(the difference in speed between an aeroplane and a steam roller)] and to eat black sausages and drink red burgundy in the little thatched cottage and I am glad Easter is over. It is the time of year I like least. Too Christian too lily-white too much the opposite of Dutch interiors.

Shadows of the Sun

April 9. Baudelaire's birthday and I send him imaginary black irises and we went to the Mont Saint Michel and watched the tide surge up over the sand as the sunset surged up over the sands of my soul and some day I should like to cross over to Tombelaine and after supper with C to drink Calvados in the Fourteenth Century Tavern and here we read aloud the magnificent cursings in Deuteronomy Twenty-Eight.

13. Friday the Thirteenth and if last Friday was Good Friday it follows that this Friday must be Bad Friday and sure enough M would not take luncheon with me because I had bitten her on the neck. Absurd. Lunched instead on a ham sandwich at the Six Day Bicycle race thereby saving four hundred francs (I had intended taking her to Philippe's) Offered a 'prime' in honor of Mademoiselle Jacqueline Soleil but was told at this hour no sprints could take place so I went home to drink a bottle of red wine in front of the fire (I don't see why people dont spend more time looking into the fire instead of looking at pictures in the Louvre). Then back again to the Bicycle Races and wild sprints and great excitement and a standing on tables and the roar of the crowd was like the roaring of lions.

15. The shadow of a disaster C believing that woman is independent and the equal of man I believing that woman is dependent and the slave of man. Here is our Impasse. Let us imagine it is a giant tree then let us together chop down this tree.

17. I go to see Saint Léger Léger. He inspires—Self-Control Equilibrium Mysticism Allure Race Timelessness Seriousness Simplicity Innocence Mépris Plaisir these he said are the qualities necessary to a great poet—"et ce qui est plus important d'avoir rencontré un homme."

20. Lausanne and sharp knives and red hot irons down my throat and I installed myself at the little hotel on the banks of the lake where Byron wrote his Prisoner of Chillon. I certainly hope I can do better.

24. Letter from Lawrence to say that he is going to write an introduction for my Chariot of the Sun and the Herald from Paris to say that Aurora won at seventeen to one and as I had a thousand francs on her to win I won seventeen thousand francs and this is the most I have ever won on a bet and this is the first day this year that neither of us have touched a drop of alcohol —not even red wine unless it be the red wine of sunset (we saw swans mating in the sunset).

29. Sunday in Paris and to the races to lose a thousand francs on Sun-Goddess so home and to bed to begin The Anatomy of Melancholy "And as that great captain Zisca would have a drum made of his skin when he was dead, because he thought the very noise of it would put his enemies to flight, I doubt not but that these following lines when they shall be recited, or hereafter read, will drive away melancholy (though I be gone) as much as Zisca's drum could terrifie his foes."

1928

May 1. Walked with Narcisse from Versailles to Paris this in preparation for the Versailles to Paris walking race. And a grand distribution of clothes from the W V R B collection. What a scramble! Shoes and shirts and trousers and tailcoats and overcoats and neckties and socks and dressing-gowns and sweaters and gloves heaped to the ceiling on the guest room bed. But by tonight not a smitch remains not a trouser button not a sock!

4. Books Books Books Books eight thousand of them crate after crate crate after crate borne upon the shoulders of solid men came cascading all morning and all afternoon into the house and my library is a pyramid of books and C's atelier is stacked high with books (I hope the ceiling won't fall through) and the staircase is blocked with books and the guest room is blocked with books and the front hall is blocked with books—books books books and what books!—a leaf from the Gutenberg Bible two chained manuscripts from a monastery an illuminated Koran illuminated Psalm books an enormous Book of the Dead (the largest book I have ever seen) the first edition of de Quincey's Opium Eater bound by Zaehnsdorf the rare first edition of Les Liaisons Dangereuses a microscopic volume of old French songs (the smallest book I have ever seen) the Sacred Books of the East in fifty volumes an Histoire Naturelle in one hundred and twenty seven volumes a magnificent set of Casanova with erotic plates superb sets of Bacon of the Decameron of Beaumont and Fletcher of Audubon of Henry James [(with sixteen letters to Cousin Walter)] of Maupassant of the Arabian Nights of Orlando Furioso books from the Aldine Press from the Elzevir Press from the Plantin Press books of Ancient Travel (Marco Polo Hakluyt Tavernier and the more modern Arabia Deserta) books containing priceless maps books on art (enough to constitute a library in itself) books with the bindings and arms of the Kings of France books with the arms of Mazarin of Richelieu of Napoleon of Madame de Pompadour of Le Roi Soleil and the signatures of Le Roi Soleil and of Henry Fourth and of Voltaire and of Alexander Pope Italian Books French Books English Books Spanish Books Books in Latin Books in Greek every kind of Book imaginable from the oldest Incunabula down to the most recent number of Transition for which treasures I offer thanks to Cousin Walter on the Book of the Dead [and in the name of the Sun].

5. At cocktail hour Mortimer appears with a Lady from Dalmatia known as Ginetta by Gin out of Miss Etta and there was a drinking of absinthe and gin and we all went to the Bal Nègre and Frans and May were there (how May could dance with those negresses!) and afterwards a mad party (censored) on the Barge.

6. Lost a thousand on Le Soleil and a thousand on Sundown and went for a long walk through the Bois and afterwards to Cartier to sell the pearl pin (collection W V R B) for a thousand dollars this to pay for the taxes I have to pay on the books and I went to bed at teatime for to-morrow is that damn race (course pédestre not pédéraste) and I was sitting up in bed with my gold necklace on when some stinkstone cousins appeared and I was bored by them and C was bored by them and the Wretch said Nausea and then Ginetta appeared and she sat on the edge of the bed and talked about her breasts.

May 7. Joan of Arc Day and I go out with Frans to Versailles and put on my old sweater and a pair of running drawers and there are over a thousand starters and to my astonishment everyone began to run and when after the first hundred yards everyone was still running I realised that Course Pédestre meant a foot race and not a pedestrian or walking race as I had imagined. All in after the first mile (I had not run in a race for five years) and there were no taxicabs in sight (we were already going into the forest) and Frans came up to my shoulder and said he intended to stick it out to the finish so that there was only one thing to do and that was to go up hill and down hill through woods and along a macadam road and a terrible hill to the park of Saint-Cloud (how I regretted that mad party on the boat) and downhill again my heart going a mile a minute and down across a bridge and along a long straight stretch over the cobblestones (about a mile and a half—it seemed ten) then down a narrow lane walled in by the crowd, and into the Parc des Princes. Finished 737 Frans 918 but what a struggle—fourteen kilometers in all and I went home and took a hot bath and went straight to bed. I am getting too old for foot races.

14. S V R C is sixty to-day twice my age and I drank a toast to him bottoms up in a glass of red wine and I went to the baths where I was massaged by a girl called Marguerite, (I feel stiff and completely all in from the race) and C and I are going to edit the Proust Letters to W V R B (I never realized that Proust dedicated to him his Pastiches et Mélanges) and a letter to-day from Lawrence to say we could edit his story called Sun in a de luxe edition and that he would draw a sun to use as frontispiece and X and Y came to tea and there was much scandal how Mr. A had signed a false cheque how Mrs. B although married ten years and mother of four children had never as yet felt any ecstasy how Mr C had slept with a gondolier.

15. The Black Sun Press announces a rare and interesting edition minutely reproduced from an ancient erotic illuminated manuscript found in Damascus representing in twenty-two colored miniatures the various positions of love. This edition is strictly limited to twenty numbered copies on handmade paper price per copy forty dollars or one thousand francs and to-day I went to the Mexican Exhibition in the Louvre where I saw the head of the eagle man that Bourdelle once showed us and I went to the Salon des Tuileries in the Palais du Bois to see the superb Brancousi the famous Oiseau dans l'Espace and for me there is no modern sculpture that can compare to it. No bric à brac here and as a critic remarked you get a glimpse of the Sun.

19. Mad party at the Bal Nègre: Jolas Kay Boyle Ganay Little Rock Face Armand de la Rochefoucauld the Crouchers the Crosbys and Frans and May were there and

May 20. Imagine my surprise on waking up to find myself on the floor of the boat fully dressed a zebra skin pulled over my head (I must have been terribly tight) and breakfast with Frans (May was in bed asleep) and so with C who had come to get me to Longchamp to lose a thousand francs on Le Soleil and to-day I found an Emerson letter and a Ruskin letter and a Valéry letter and a Foch letter among the books but I couldn't find anywhere the Baudelaire letter I once gave to Cousin Walter.

21. Saw the dark princess for the tenth part of a moment in her dark-blue painting smock her jade necklace her red lips her black hair her dark and madonna eyes and went to the Crouchers where Croucher took pictures of C and then of me and then of C and me and a riot with C on the subject of O (not MO) and there was much weeping and gnashing of teeth and Sundown lost at Saint-Cloud and it has begun to rain and all is desolation were it not for the red-gold nombril of the Invisible Sun.

27. Won seven thousand francs on Sundown (casaque blanche toque blanche—rhymes with avalanche) and went home to go to bed to finish Gulliver's Travels—"That which gave me most uneasiness among these maids of honour (when my nurse carried me to visit them) was to see them use me without any manner of ceremony, like a creature who had no sort of consequence: for they would strip themselves to the skin, and put on their smocks in my presence, while I was placed on their toilet, directly before their naked bodies, which, I am sure, to me, was very far from being a tempting sight, or from giving me any other emotions than those of horror and disgust. Their skins appeared so coarse and uneven, so variously colored, when I saw them near, with a mole here and there, as broad as a trencher, and hairs hanging from it thicker than pack threads, to say nothing farther concerning the rest of their persons. Neither did they at all scruple, while I was by, to discharge what they had drank, to the quantity of at least two hogsheads, in a vessel that held above three tuns. The handsomest among these maids of honor, a pleasant frolicsome girl of sixteen, would sometimes set me astride upon one of her nipples, with many other tricks, wherein the reader will excuse me for not being over particular. But I was so much displeased, that I entreated Glumdalclitch to contrive some excuse for not seeing that young lady any more."

31. To Versailles [with C and Narcisse] to see Alastair and Thoma of the Four Leaf Clover was there and A showed us his drawings for the Birthday of the Infanta and he told us when we asked him that he had destroyed both pictures that he had drawn of us (he must have been very annoyed and now I am annoyed) and we drank apricot punch in a red bowl and it began to rain a rain of stars and on the way home we stopped at the Cimetière de l'Abbaye de Longchamp to get our gravestone and to say goodbye to the Roux (too disgusting of the park commissioners to destroy the walls and to put all the skulls and skeletons in one common grave—I am furious with them especially as I had offered to pay for the preservation of the walls) and when

we got home I went to bed and read Valéry. "To find is nothing. The difficulty is to add to oneself what one finds." [4]

June 1. Thunderstorm with mad lightning and there were people all day— Frans before breakfast to take C to the flower-market (they brought me back a red orchid) Ortiz after luncheon with René Crevel (he reminded me of Antheil) Lescaret to go over proof sheets Barreto at teatime to invite me to see his collection of erotica, Croucher to say hello (he spent most of his time looking at pictures in the Casenova) and for dinner Armand de la Roche-foucauld Ganay (Little Rock Face left behind) and Ginetta smothered in orchids and while they were out dancing I went to bed and began and finished the Sentimental Journey "so that when I stretched out my hand, I caught hold of the fille de chambre's."

2. The thunderstorm yesterday infinitesimal compared with the Black Storm to-day. Dark words and C went off with the Crouchers to the country and now the sun is gone from the dial and the cramoisy color disappears and it is dark dark but in the centre I am undaunted with the Grey Princess (who corresponds to Gérard de Nerval's Adrienne) in the centre of me and I pray a grey and gold prayer into the centre of the Red Sun.

3. To Chantilly with Mortimer and the Lady of the Gold Horse and we drank silver gin fizzes in the Manor House Bar and then the races began and no C and a great searching of hats and faces and legs and derrières but no C and I saw the Count and the first race and the Lady of the Gold Horse and the second race and the Lady of the Blue Pyjamas (the first time since the blue pyjamas four years ago) and the third race (Sun-Goddess lost) and more searching of hats and faces and then at last when black disaster seemed imminent C appeared all frail and delicate and there were dark words and tears and then the Sun and a great restatement after contrast cramoisy and gold and the Sun returns to the dial and the last hours in the twenties and I smoked my pipe and said a cramoisy and gold prayer and C's eyes are my towers of strength and now we have advanced another rung up the Ladder of the Sun.

4. C and the Invisible Sun and it is a grey morning (grey-cramoisy-gold) and our oneness is the color of a glass of red wine and there is a gardenia and the frailest silks (my Lady's favor) and I am thirty and I make laws:

to read four chapters of the Bible every day
to read a book every week
to continue rites but to abolish superstitions
to be taciturn not talkative
to be ascetic not hedonistic
to be lean not fat
to shave and exercise and take a cold bath every morning
to never take more than four drinks a day
to be inextravagant in everything except as regards books and gifts for C
to be bright and delicate and gentle and chaste

to worship the Sun with a chaste heart and a chaste soul and a chaste body
and to-day gold won the horsegame with cramoisy second and grey third
and this is as it should be and today the Lady of the Gold Horse appeared
and to-day there was a reading of the Bible and to-day there was caviare and
champagne with C and to-day there were fire prayers into the red fire of the
Sun.

June 7. Sold two thousand dollars worth of books (they were weighing
me down) and went with C to eat caviare and drink champagne in the Forest
of Chantilly and we went to the races and I bet on Le Soleil in spite of there
being a thunderstorm and he ran through the thunderstorm and won and the
Sun came out as he passed the winning post and the Count was there and the
Lady of the Gold Horse and we drank gin fizzes at the Manor House (how
often one does the same things over and over and over again—I wish they
were all as pleasant as this) and then C and I motored to Ermenonville to see
the Rochefoucaulds and everyone went for a walk but I was depressed and
went into a cold library to read again The Green Hat (how did it ever get
here) and when they had all come back from walking I was very disagreeable
and made C drive back with me to Chantilly and it was getting late and the
Manor House was cold and we were depressed and we telephoned to
Ermenonville to say that we wanted to come back (this took courage) and we
strengthened ourselves with hot rum grogs and I bought five revolvers in a
bicycle shop so that they could shoot me for my disagreeableness and so
back to Ermenonville and the Château and they were all at table and Ginetta
sang and Erik Doll talked of heraldry and Evelyn told about the circumcision
her friend had seen in Morocco and Barreto did his ventriloquism and there
was a great open fire and much brandy and an enormous double-bed with
monogrammes on the pillow-cases as large as birds.

8. I look out the window and there is Henri fishing in the moat and behold
a silver carp on the end of the line and out in the meadows Ginetta is picking
white daisies and beyond Narcisse is putting to rout a flock of sheep and so
to bed again and to sleep until a butler knocks discreetly at the door and
there is a gin cocktail and a hurried dressing and after luncheon C and I
discovered a Tower and a grenier enclosed by a wall (it used to be an old
mill) and with our usual enthusiasm we offered A a hundred thousand francs
for it and he said he would think it over and we all drank brandy then C and
I left for Pierrefonds where we ate an enormous chocolate soufflé and went
to bed in the Hotel de l'Enfer how much more romantic a name than those
frightful Grand Hotels or Continentals.

9. A glass of brandy a prayer with the tower of the castle as springboard
(to dive off into the sea of Sun) and so through the forest to Compiègne and
on to Filerval and here we drank red wine and went for a long walk and they
are burning charcoal in the forest a burnt sacrifice to Apollo and on the way
back Narcisse chased rabbits and put to rout a flock of sheep and when we
got back there were twenty guests arrived from Paris—a Mr and Mrs

Shadows of the Sun

Bullwinkle a Mr Hank (call me just Hank) a little Mrs Hatmaker, etcetera, etcetera, what names what names and there was a man who had just bought a Flaubert Letter (I would have been more interested had it been a Rimbaud Letter) and there were cocktails (as I had only one drink left according to my rules and regulations I had to drink a cocktail in a tall whiskey and soda glass with the result I was as tight as a mink) and there was champagne only I couldn't take any and there was the noise of the Savoy Orchestra in London heard over the radio (the noise of the Sun exploding through space heard in the listening centre of my soul) and after supper while the others were playing bridge I read some more of The Green Hat "they call it, she said, the desire-for-I-know-not-what. They will find it one day when we are dead and all things that live now are dead. They will find it when everything is dead but the dreams we have no word for" and before going to bed I went out past the bridge-players and their colored cards to stare up at the stars.

June 10. The color of the sun on the waters of the moat is the color of the sun on the waters of my soul and there was a stand-up luncheon and a fast run over to Chantilly and there was a tremendous thunderstorm and everyone went about holding chairs inverted over their heads and everyone was drenched and Kantar was beaten by a neck a superb race the horses their necks elongated kantaring kantaring [5] up the green rise with the Château in the background and we drove back to Paris and I left for Lausanne on the Orient Express (my throat hurts me again) and in my compartment was a characteristic American who took off his coat and rolled up his sleeves and talked in a hoarse voice of sailing and hockey (he had broken his nose playing hockey) and who weighed (so he confided to me) a hundred and ninety pounds and he drank a large bottle of beer (one hundred and ninety one) and he had sold taximeters in Philadelphia and he believed that one should work for the sake of working (see Baudelaire—"Il faut travailler, sinon par goût, au moins par désespoir puisque, tout bien vérifié, travailler est moins ennuyeux que s'amuser") and he was going to Lausanne to build a boat and he sat up until late at night reading aloud excerpts from the Cosmopolitan.

11. My compatriot up at five in the morning fresh and frisky (the advantage of strength corporeal) then Lausanne and a reading of Esther in the garden of the hotel ("let there be fair young virgins sought for the king") and a breakfast in the sun then the sharp knives and the red hot irons then drugged sleep (I had been given cocaine) and at teatime two glasses of champagne with a woman in red whom I saw in the bar of the hotel. But where are the young virgins brought for the king? [6]

12. Farewell to the sharp knives and the red hot irons and I went and procured in a bookshop a bottle of very old absinthe (it was a choice between this or an erotic book with pictures of girls making love) and the man in the book-shop recommended Ramuz La Guérison des Maladies but as I already had the Guérison to all Maladies i.e. the absinthe I did not buy

the book but went instead to an apothecary's where I bought two empty bottles marked hair tonic into which I decanted the absinthe one bottle on each hip and down the hill to the station where I sat in the sun and drank beer and read Endymion until the train for Paris arrived and a rattling away towards Vallorbe and a rattling through the long tunnel in to France (the rattling of the soul through the long tunnel into Sun) and it began to rain and we went through Dôle and Dijon and there was brandy on the platform at La Roche and I finished the Green Hat and fell asleep and when I woke up it was Paris and there were red and white roses and the clashing of arms and armour as in the days of the wars of the roses.

June 16. A strong consolidating of finances at the bank (why in hell wont they transact business with gold coins instead of with those filthy germ-ridden paper bills) and on the strength of this consolidation I go to the Rue Richelieu to buy for a hundred dollars a magnificent copy of the first edition of Ulysses signed by Joyce and bound in a magnificent blue binding and when I got home I found a letter from X to say he had lost his virginity (N.Y.7.20) "c'est fait my twenty-nine year drought is ended" and it is about time and I cabled him congratulations and I began George Moore's Memoirs of my Dead Life and I was disgusted with it so damn unclean and I threw it into the scrap-basket and continued with the Anatomy of Melancholy, Here is a real book—"Beroaldus will have drunkards, afternoon-men, and such as more than ordinarily delight in drink, to be mad. The first pot quencheth thirst, the second makes merry, the third for pleasure the forth makes them mad. If this be true, what a catalogue of mad men shall we have! what shall they be that drink four times four? They are more than mad, much worse than mad." And what of him who delights all day to drink the Sun?

17. My soul to-day is a young phallus thrusting up-wards to possess the young goddess of the Sun.

18. Alastair for luncheon and he arrived bearing the most marriageable looking lilies and our Black Sun Press is going to edit The Birthday of the Infanta with nine of his drawings and hardly an hour after he left a bookseller from New-York whom we had never heard of before appeared and bought from us the entire edition of the Birthday of the Infanta but is this any more of a coincidence than the coincidence before luncheon when I went up to the library to get my copy of Chariot of the Sun and found the long gold finger of the Sun touching the very center of the Sun engraved on the book which was lying on the table near the window?

20. Worked on the books weeding out and rearranging (dirty hands and dust in the throat) and it is extraordinary that among such an enormous number of books ("of the making of books there is no end") there should be so extraordinarily few great writers three or four in a generation (Saint Léger Léger Joyce T. S. Eliot—and perhaps Cummings and perhaps Kay Boyle and perhaps Hart Crane and perhaps MacLeish) and to-day at Cocktail Hour Gold from Ophir (read Boston) brought over the seas by a young painter called Sykes who hid the aforesaid gold in the toes of his riding boots—twenty pieces of gold twenty twenty dollar gold pieces stamped with the Eagle and the Sun and we all went to a cocktail party at the Harper's (Little Mrs. Hatmaker was there) and I got tight drinking *one* enormous cocktail served in a flower-vase and afterwards in company with the Crouchers to the Barge so home and to bed to read a book by Jan Gordon on Modern French Painters—"a color can be green by Knowledge and blue by vision." A Sun can be a Sun by knowledge and a Sun-Goddess by vision.

June 23. With C to undress and bask on the barge in the Sun and then to Longchamp to buy Red Sun but sixty thousand was too much so we went to the Rothschild sale where we bought for thirty thousand Gin Cocktail a good name but I wanted Red Sun and a riotous tea-party in the library at which eight magnums of champagne were drunk down and to-night I finished Job "I made a covenant with mine eyes; why then should I think upon a maid?"

24. Grand Prix (my seventh in a row) and Cri de Guerre won with Flamingo the favorite nowhere and there was a great drinking of gin and there was a girl serious, impassible, her chin held high, laying her arm across his shoulders in token of affection. Embryonic.

29. Bal des 4 Arts (Hun costumes this year) and the usual smearing on of red ochre and the usual gathering of crowds in the street and the usual riotous dinner with a magnificent brandy punch manufactured by Mortimer in the most enormous bowl and there were ladies and models and tarts and a stampeding up and down stairs ("in the secret places of the stairs") and Lord L was there and Raymonde (the first time I have seen her this year) and Little Mrs. Hatmaker and Mme la Marquise and Merveilleux and Erik Doll and Barreto and the Rochefoucaulds and Ginetta and the Crouchers and at ten o'clock we rushed off on foot and in taxicabs (I sat with Raymonde on the roof of a taxicab) to the Salle Wagram and the costumes were magnificent this year and there was the usual pounding and stampeding and a climbing up and down ladders and queer scenes in the corners (one plump girl lying naked on the floor while three men color of red ochre made love to her et comment—a regular concours à la mort) and so home and to bed (many people in the house many people in bed but the best fun was painting girls' breasts (breasts by Crosby and Croucher) before the party.

30. Awoke to find six of us (not counting Narcisse) in our bed and there was a strange man in a pale blue undershirt on the chaise longue who was playing the graphaphone the same tune again and again Paris c'est une Blonde and there was a knocking on the door and the Goof appeared with two coffees (vous pouvez descendre chercher encore cinq cafés) and afterwards hot baths à deux (my partner was little forget-me-not) and we had a hell of a time scrubbing off the paint and by luncheon time the bathroom

looked like a pig-pen and the Goof and her sister appeared and announced they were leaving and I went on foot across the Tuileries and had luncheon (caviare and grapefruit and sherry cobblers) with the dark princess and came home and sat in the sun in the courtyard (while X was making love to Y up in the salon) and later a mad throwing of things mostly books into a suitcase and with C to the train (Ginetta and Erik Doll to see us off) and so a gentle rocking to sleep on the Orient Express clickety-click clickety-click clickety-clack clickety-click clickety-clack clickety-click clickety-click clickety-clack clickety-click clickety-clack clickety-clack clickety-click down the long rails towards Venice while I disappeared up invisible rails towards the Sun.

July 1. Sun pouring gold through the windows of the train and cold red cherries on cold silver ice ("and every man that offered offered an offering of gold unto the Sun") and there was the intensity of the heat at noon and there was the fire of the red dragon and the chasteness of the rose florescent and there was Verona (I saw only one of the gentlemen on the platform) and there was Padua but no wild duchess and then the train ran across the lagoon into Venice and we went by gondola past the Casa Petrarca (memories of the Viscount and Viscountess Myopia) to the Hotel de l'Europe where we took a room with a terrace overlooking the roofs and the bay and although the sun was setting it was still hot so we took a cold bath and drank orangeades as cold as the cold bath and as orange-colored as the setting sun.

2. Breakfast on the sun-terrace and out to the Lido to scorch in the sun (they insist that Narcisse wear a muzzle—I am surprised they dont ask the Sun to wear a muzzle) and a plunge into the sea and a run up and down the beach and a bagno di sole and a reading [at sunset] about Van Gogh and the delirium of his vision—"Cézanne represents the foundations while Van Gogh is the banner waving from the topmost pinnacle." Van Gogh the example of triumphant individuality Van Gogh the painter of suns the painter of that Sun which consumed him and which was responsible for his final madness and suicide. A Sun-Death into Sun!

3. A sun-bath and a sea-bath and a sun-bath and a sea-bath and a sun-bath and this evening sitting out on our sunset terrace I built with my imagination a bridge over the enormous river of sky that runs between the sun and the moon (the clouds are fishing boats and the stars are fish) a bridge as frail as a spider's web and as interwoven as honey and the honeycomb and over this bridge I projected the gold monster of my soul (half princess and half prince) and the princess lay in the arms of the Man in the Moon (sword into sheath) and the prince lay in the arms of the Sun-Goddess (sword into sheath) and afterwards there was minestrone soup and cut up oranges and a white falling asleep under the white mosquito net—our eyes are ever towards the Sun for he shall pluck our feet out of the net.

4. "Because our men are the fire and the daytime and our women are the spaces between the stars at night" and again a strong scorching in the Sun and the men here go naked to the nombril and there are pretty women in

frail pyjamas ("Will you not join the Living Bronzes? Would you not see the Lido Sun and stroll on the Plage des Pyjamas?") and I can feel myself slowly turning into gold turning into fire turning into Sunfire turning into the breast and the womb of the Sun turning into Sun.

July 5. Learned things about the Sun: that the ancients believed that the sun and earth were connected by a chain (ombilical?); that the ancient Egyptians called the Sun the Cat because the pupil of the cat's eye grows larger with the advance of the day (the Egyptians imagined that a great cat stood behind the Sun which was the pupil of the cat's eye); that Egyptian Sun-Worship included a worship of the actual disk of the Sun; that every wheel has throughout the ages symbolized the Sun; that every morning the Brahmans may be seen facing the east, standing on one foot and stretching out their hands to the Sun; that in Lucien's time the Greeks kissed their hands as an act of worship to the rising Sun; that the emblem of the Japanese Sun-Goddess was the mirror; that in Peru a certain relationship was thought to exist between the substance of gold and that of the Sun ("in the nuggets dislodged from the mountain sides they thought they saw the Sun's tears"); that human sacrifices to the Sun were common in Peru; that the Iroquois regarded the Sun as a god and offered him tobacco which they termed "smoking the Sun"; that in the course of their service of Sun-Worship the Apalachees released the sacred Sun-Birds through a crevice in the roof of the cavetemple and that these as they winged their way upward were thought to convey their expressions of adoration to the Sun; that of all the Indian customs and forms of worship of solar significance the great ceremonial of the Sun-Dance best exemplified the worship of the Sun; that to make the Sun go faster the Australians throw into the air and blow with their mouths towards the Sun (the Indians used to pull out their eyelashes and blow them towards the Sun); that Christmas is nothing but an old heathen celebration of the winter solstice; that Sun-Masks were a prominent feature in the solar ceremonials of many of the Indian Tribes; that the red colors at sunset are caused by the blood flowing from the Sun-God when he hastens to his suicide (31-10-42);[7] that the Sun was regarded by the Greeks as the symbol of perfect beauty and that they formerly painted the Sun's Disk on the cheeks of the bride; that it seems to have been an almost universal belief among primitive people that the Sun and Moon were the abodes of departed souls; that the appearance of three suns denotes war and that these three suns appeared just before Napoleon's disastrous campaign in Russia; that Mexicans have a belief that blondes cannot see the Sun; that to dream the Sun shines means success to the lovers; that the stones at Stonehenge were so arranged that at sunrise at the summer solstice the shadow of the stone fell exactly on the stone in the centre of the circle indicating to the priest that the new year had begun; that in the Book of the Dead the Sun is often represented as an eye provided with wings and feet; that the Hawk was dedicated to the Sun and that the Lion was a symbol of the Sun; that the cross symbol of the Christian faith is a symbol that antedated the birth of

Christ and one that found its origin in solar worship; that in solar symbolism there are rules which connect the Sun with gold, with heliotrope, with the cock which heralds day, with magnanimous animals such as the lion and the bull, that 92,930,000 miles is the Sun's distance from the Earth; that no fewer than one half a million of full moons shining all at once would be required to make up a mass of light equal to that of the Sun; that the rate of speed maintained by the Sun is estimated at from ten to twelve miles a second.

July 6. Met the Lady of the Blue Pyjamas going over the bridge of a little canal (so damn hot it was I dont see why she wasn't wearing them) and in a glass factory I bought a huge drinking glass that will hold two quarts and to-night in Nietzche I read a significant passage: "Die at the right time." Die at the right time, so teacheth Zarethustra and again the direct 31-10-42. Clickety-click clickety-click the express train into Sun. [8]

7. "The voluntary death which cometh unto me because I want it" and to the Royal Academy with C and I hate Museums (I like things that are Alive) and we walked back over the iron bridge and over little stone bridges to the Church of Saint Marks where we were not allowed in in accordance with the law "le donne devono entrare in chiesa convenientemente vestite, con abiti accolati e con le maniche lunghe" (all the women must be modestly dressed to enter the church with the neck covered and long sleeves!) and to-day I finished Proverbs "as a bird that wandereth from her nest so is a man that wandereth from his place" (for me the Sun) and all day to-day a being scorched by the Sun.

8. I like the word 'barbaric' I like the word 'conch' I like the word 'prophetic' I like the idea of a sun-death (like Lowenstein) from an aeroplane for when the body strikes the ground Bang, Twang flies the Arrow of Soul to and into the Sun For Eternity.

9. Enter the Youngest Princess of the Sun! [9]

13. Wrote an

> Invocation to the Sun-Goddess
> I would you were the hollow ship
> fashioned to bear the cargo of my love
> the unrelenting glove
> hurled in defiance at our blackest world
> or that great banner mad unfurled
> the poet plants upon the hill of time
> or else amphora for the gold of life
> liquid and naked as a virgin wife
> Yourself the prize
> I gird with fire
> the great white ruin
> of my desire

> I burn to gold
> fierce and unerring as a conquering sword
> I burn to gold
> fierce and undaunted as a lion lord
> seeking your Bed
> and leave to them the
> burning of the dead

July 14. "Or ever the silver cord be loosed or the golden bowl be broken" and I like Ecclesiastes best of all the books of the Bible with Job next and then Esther and then Proverbs and then the Song of Solomon then Isaiah then Revelation (I like knowing always what I like best statistics sharp and clear no blurrings) and this morning before breakfast we went in swimming and I swam underwater into the Sun "truly the light is sweet and a pleasant thing it is for the eyes to behold the Sun" (and I wonder if the fish enjoy their underwater Sun or have they eyes that see not) and the water was cool and invigorating and we were alone and then we got weighed 111 and 127 and there were cold cut-up peaches for breakfast.

> "do I dare to eat a peach?
> I shall wear white flannel trousers,
> and walk upon the beach"

and at noon another run on the beach and in the afternoon a long swim from the Limite Inesperti past the Limite Sorvegliana out and around the Red Buoy and back again and a goodbye [to the Youngest Princess] adios "simple and faithless as a smile or shake of the hand" and a supper aboard an illuminated barge and we drank two bottles of Lanson and danced until two in the morning (it was the fête of Il Redentore) and there were fireworks over the Giudecca (14-7-22) and gondolas with Japanese lanterns swarming everywhere and there was a fiery jazz orchestra and when we got back to the hotel we took off our clothes on the beach and disappeared into the cool black water.

15. "There are threescore queens and fourscore concubines and virgins without number" as I read in the Song of Solomon and this is true at the Lido only I don't believe there are many virgins and we lay all day in the Sun recuperating from the party and I lost the Eversharp pencil I have had for over a year and now I am ready for the North and the Dark Woods and the Burning of Charcoal and the Autumn Rains and to-day we met the Baron and Baroness Napoleon Gourgol and they own that wonderful Van Gogh I saw last spring on the Rue Royale.

17. Champagne with the Tigress and Madame Cavalieri who is in love with her dog Toddles and whose one desire is to go mad the way her grandfather did because when he went mad he imagined he was a dog and used to eat and sleep with his dogs and then a fast motorboat ride from the Lido to the Grand Canale and all the way up the Grand Canale past the

Santa Maria della Salute past the Casa Petrarca under the Rialto until we reached the station. Departure from Venice and I am glad and chianti and I am glad and all night on the train towards the North.

July 18. Paris and all other lands and cities dwindle to Nothingness Paris City of the Sun.

19. "But the same wave shall bring them new playthings and spread before them new speckled shells" read new pencils and they are gold this time solid gold one for H and one for C and marked with the sign of the Sun and today I imagined a spark invisible without glasses. Visible with them. And I imagined a spark still further off invisible with my glasses but visible through a telescope. And lastly a last spark invisible through a telescope but visible through the imagination and this Last Spark is the Sun-Goddess.

20. A [Van Gogh] Sunset sharp orange-red round as the moon no rays and double because of the reflection in the windshield and a giving of myself always without ever taking anything else into account even to the extent of dying all this into the sharp-as-fire sun on the way to Fontainbleau and we found the de Geetere barge and there was supper and a graphaphone and dancing the men bronzed stripped to the waist and there was the great bed and four arms were four chains of fire and there were twin suns crashing in my head and the stamp of feet on the deck above and afterwards we went in swimming without any clothes on and coming back to Paris in the car there were two heads with sleepy eyes and as everything we wish for very much comes. [10]

21. Gin Fizzes at the Ritz and always the Twin Suns are crashing in my head.

22. Paris to Fontainbleau to the Boat the Boat to Fontainbleau to Paris (Twin Suns Explode) Paris to Fontainbleau to the Boat the Boat to Fontainbleau to Paris.

23. Kicked out Henri the chauffeur because he did not appear last night and I had to take a taxi to the boat and back last night (four hundred francs) and this morning engaged a new man called Auguste whom we chose because he was the meekest of ten applicants (I hate fighting with servants) and this afternoon gin and a green tea-gown to coin the utmost gold of passionate memory.

24-25. Sunfire and a strength of gold within the heart Sunfire and the sound of a burning fire within the heart.

28. C and I buy a little mill at Ermenonville from the Rochefoucaulds for two hundred twenty dollar gold pieces and we decide to call it the Moulin du Soleil and it has a suntower and now we own Land but always there are the words of Diogenes that a man's wealth should be judged by the things he can do without and to-day I wrote a tirade called the Sun-Death.

Shadows of the Sun

July 30. The procession of days are crossing a Desert the width of which is unknown but Inside there is a predominance of fire with the twin suns still clashing and there are important Explosions into Sun.

31. Saw a Van Gogh (La Moisson) at Bernheim Jeune for four hundred twenty dollar gold pieces and it was a furious mad painting of the Sun and I would rather have owned it than the Moulin du Soleil and Gin Cocktail combined but I would rather have the Fire-Letter than either picture or mill or horse and to-day I am mad with desire mad with Fire.

August 1. The attraction between the sun and the earth is equal to the breaking strain of a steel rod three thousand miles in diameter but this is infinitesimal when compared to the attraction between the Twin Suns (still clashing) which attraction is beyond all breaking strain and now I am being influenced by Van Gogh who burned with desire to see the Sun-God face to face to absorb himself forever in his implacable flame.

10. Paris to Deauville in the car and we stopped for a wretched luncheon at a wretched restaurant by the river somewhere near Mantes and there was a dead white rabbit that floated past in the current and the fear that in the future this meal would reduce itself in the memory to one dead white rabbit afloat on the river but why not an interior sword to thrust it through and toss it away into oblivion? And Deauville was mad and overcrowded and there were no rooms to be had anywhere but at last after much bribery we were allowed a small room at the Normandy for the modest sum of a thousand francs a night. Merde alors! Especially as we only had five hundred francs. But we forgot all about finances as we basked on the beach and the gold of the Sun was reassuring and the Sun began to set and turned into a chariot of fire to carry a strong firethought across the sea. Back to the hotel to dress for dinner but Auguste had forgotten to take the bags out of the car and it took an hour before I ferreted out the car in a garage by the docks and then the car was locked and I had to find Auguste who was in a bar and a giving him hell and so back to the hotel and a late dinner at Ciro's which reduced our finances to the extent that we had to retire to bed instead of going to the Casino. I must win on the races to-morrow.

11. Grey Sunday morning and a cold run down the beach (cold in spite of the four [mermaid beautiful] girls) and it began to rain and the sea was cold and there was a strong undertow and a rushing back to get dressed for the races (no money for luncheon) and I found my bookmaker and bet a thousand francs on Le Soleil who was beaten and then a thousand on Xander who won at six to one and now we have gold again and we went for cocktails and caviare to S's, C and I and E, and La Karoly was there and there was a man specially imported from America to play jazz.

13. S has invited us to stay. More cocktails. More caviare. And to-day I read somewhere in a book that a cause of impotency is the allowing the parts of generation to remain too long in a state of inaction. Strong argument for much making love!

August 14. A bathe a run on the beach more caviare more cocktails and won forty dollars at baccara and for once in my life had the sense to stop and walked home the Twin Suns crashing in my head and I am glad because A[rmand] wants us to rent and not buy the Moulin because their mother was all upset about their selling it so we agree to tear up their receipt for the cheque and to rent it instead. I am glad. I hate being weighed down and if we had continued to own the Moulin we would in a way be anchored to this land and I only care to be anchored to the Sun.

15. Last bathe of the year (the first was the bathe in the Dead Sea) and a run on the beach and then to the races to lose on Ivanhoe and we went to the sale and bought a yearling (terribly cunning and young and fiery) and his name is Sunstroke and his sire's name is Sunfire and among his ancestors are Suicide and Red Queen and so back to Paris and this afternoon summer ended for me (the best summer so far) and Autumn began and from now until the shortest day of the year Autumn and I am glad and I pray into the Mad Red Sun and when we got home we found that the stupid maid at S's hadn't even taken the trouble to put stoppers in the bottles of perfume and honey-and-almond cream with the result that C has two dresses absolutely ruined and I my wrapper not to mention the wetting of the leaves of my Bible and Christ how I hate servants.

16. That young brides were required to seat themselves upon the monstrous and obscene member of Priapus; that the foreskins still extant of Jesus Christ are reckoned to be twelve in number; that a rule of paramount importance in making love is the retention of semen for the prolongation of pleasure; that Montaigne says that married people, having the year before them, ought never to compel, or so much as offer at the feat, if they do not find themselves very ready; that female elephants after eating the leaves of the mandragora are seized with so irresistible desire for copulation as to run eagerly in every direction in quest of the male; all this information in the Book of Aphrodisiacs by Davenport.

18. To the Bois Joly in Barreto's Rolls-Royce (B C and I and E) one hundred and ten kilometers an hour and overhead the red crescent of the moon like a wound in the dark breast of the night and much drinking of burgundy and after we had gone to bed we could hear B doing his ventriloquism so that the desperate voice of a wounded man called from the dark wood and people went to look with lanterns and there was the crunching of boots on the gravel outside our door.

19. Hot Sun and a bath in the Sun C pouring a huge watering pot over me and afterwards another bath in the stream down in the valley and so back to Paris and a letter from Lawrence "Savage rumours that Lady Chatterly is to be supressed in London and that it is stopped from entering America. Liebes Ding! Better read it—it's a direct phallic book i.e. the direct *nocturnal* connection of a man with the sun—the path of the dark sun" and there is a

good line in it about "fucking little jazz girls with small boy buttocks." The day of the voluptuous harem-woman is over.

August 20. What is it that Cocteau says about poets singular, poets plural, Rimbaud singular, Victor Hugo plural. C'est de naissance. A good definition. O Sun-Goddess make me singular.

21. Decided to call my new book of poems Transit of Venus Venus being the Youngest Princess of the Sun. But occasionally at her inferior conjunction Venus passes directly across the disk of the Sun the phenomenon being known as a Transit.

22. Saw a pretty American girl looking into a store window on the Rue Castiglione (she was looking at a pair of lace drawers) and asked her if she would take tea with me next door at Sherry's "I don't see how I can I'm with my family" and sure enough there they were and how in hell could their union (uglification) have created such beauty? So back across the Tuileries jumping over the stone benches and wondering what smells I like best— smell of tar or smell of aviation oil smell of opium or smell of a gardenia smell of tabac blond or smell of new-mown hay smell of fur or smell of tobacco smell of moist earth smell of love. And if the Sun has a smell?

23. Read about Anwari the Persian Poet and of how when the sultan was besieging the fortress of Hararasp a fierce poetical conflict was maintained between Anwari and his rival Bashidi who was in the beleaguered castle by means of verses fastened to arrows and in a way the giant ocean liners plying between Paris and New York are arrows winging back and forth and if they do not carry verses they at least carry pretty American girls (I am becoming more and more pro-American pro New York) and in a way sunbeams down from the Sun and sun-prayers up into the Sun tell the same story.

24. Saw a man jumping over a chair on the Avenue du Bois de Boulogne in the morning sun and the understanding I had of his mood (it could never have been a Frenchman—never) and all afternoon I sat in front of the fire looking in the Secchi book at pictures of the Sun.

25. Read a chapter on the extravagances of Heliogabalus (they are magnificent what of it if he did have megalomania it is better to exalt oneself into Sun than to whimper in the dust) that even as a boy of fourteen he refused to stir without a procession of forty chariots; that he gave feasts where in ungirdled tunics the guests lay on silver beds fanned by boys whose curly heads they used as napkins; that even his dogs were fed on foie-gras, his horses on grapes, his lions on pheasants and parroquets; that among the spectacles he gave in the amphitheâtre were naval displays on lakes of wine, the death of whole menageries of Egyptian beasts, and chariot races in which not only horses, but also stags, lions, tigers, dogs, and even women figured; that he himself had teams of naked women to draw him from place to place; that in driving he had splendid nerve as we learn from the record of his chariot races with camels and elephants even over the Vatican and its

Tombs; that even in the relief of his natural functions he was magnificent using only vases of gold and onyx.

August 27. When I was a child I remember they flew flags on the beach red to show the water was warm green to show it was medium blue to show it was cold and if I were to fly flags for these shadows (red to show good white to show ordinary blue to show bad) I would begin to-day with a double-red flag to show the shadow is miraculous for to-day a Letter full of Fire.

30. Read Montaigne: that health is a precious thing; that it is better to forge one's soul than to furnish it; that one must be master of one's self at all costs; that the first requisite in making love is to know how to take one's time that the second is the same and the third also; it is a point which can make everything possible, and to-night we went to the Jungle and Polia was there (she has just finished the illustrations for the Sentimental Journey which we are editing) and we drank champagne and to-day I flew the green flag.

31. Finished the Old Testament which I had begun on the Nile February Twelfth and to-day in a footnote to Montaigne I read that Strato lodged the soul between the two eyebrows (entre les deux sourcils) and this is where I lodge mine but I think there are a great many people especially women who lodge it between their two legs.

September 1. Began the Sacred Books of the East there are fifty volumes and read in the preface by Max Muller that meditation on the syllable Om consisted in a long continued repetition of that syllable with a view to drawing the thoughts away from all other subjects, and thus concentrating them on some higher object of thought (for me the Sun) of which that syllable was made to be the symbol and that the highest aim of all thought and study with the Brahman of the Upanishads was to recognise his own self as a mere limited reflection of the Highest Self, to know his self in the Highest Self and through that knowledge to return to it, and regain his identity with it. This is exactly the way I feel vis-à-vis of the Sun. [11]

2. [With C to the Moulin de Soleil and a luncheon in the Sun on the grass in the courtyard then] To Chantilly to bet on Sun-Goddess and it was one of the best perhaps *the best* horserace I ever saw and at the very last after they had galloped past the Ecuries and down around the turn with the Château in the background and up the long rise towards the winning post, at the very last the Casaque Cramoisi Toque Noir flashed past the post and Sun-Goddess had won by the shortest of short heads with a dead heat for the second place. Terribly exciting and good odds eleven to one and I made over four hundred dollars (twenty twenty dollar gold pieces) and now I am a thousand dollars ahead for the year with Aurora Sun-Goddess and Sundown as the big winners and I am glad I bet on Sun Names.

4. In the footnotes to Montaigne read about the Synapothanomenos or band of those who wanted to die together formed by Antony and Cleopatra after the battle of Actium and I should like to have influence strong enough to lead a band of followers into the Sun-Death.

September 7. At last I have finished Montaigne's Essays (Shakespeare The Bible Browning Montaigne) and I am glad for I began them way back in 1926. And of all the things he says I like most his "j'ayme mieux forger mon âme que la meubler" but he has his failings in his unidealistic attitude towards women, his lack of inner centrality, his lack of vision beyond death. But he is human he is strong and he loves the poets.

8. Always the strong desire for Fire (close your arms like a girdle of fire around my body) and to-day in the Sacred Books of the East I read that in our Self there we always can possess those whom we love. The Sun-Goddess, the Queen of the Sun and the Two Princesses of the Sun.

9. Six Years Six Orchids Six Kisses Six [Gold] Suns.

10. Felt like going down to the Quays to buy birds and rabbits in order to let them loose. Instead went to the Tuileries and sat on a chair and read about Eudoxus who prayed to the gods that he might see the Sun right near that he might understand his shape his grandeur his beauty even though he should be suddenly burned as Phaëton was. And Van Gogh. At this point an old woman with a moustache dressed in black interrupted me. Wanted me to pay for my chair. Twenty five centimes or one cent. She went away and I looked into the Sun which was beginning to turn from gold to red back of the Gare d'Orsay and my soul became a Sun-Hawk soaring into Sun a mystic union of flesh with Fire. For this sudden knowledge of the Truth I am willing to sacrifice all other knowledge that has gone before.

13. Read in the New Testament what Christ said about his life "no man taketh it from me, but I lay it down of myself" proof enough of his "mort volontaire" and to-day we discovered hidden away in an old paste-board box letters from Henry James to Walter Berry which we shall edit at our Black Sun Press and to-day we had a gold sun put on our gravestone which we shall take out to the Moulin du Soleil and to-day a letter from N "their white bodies and their purple faces" (referring to the orchids) and to-day to see at Olivares' the painting he is giving to C (Le Silence et la Rose—cool and geometric and chaste—a marvelous painting) and to-day I killed my fear of 13 and to-night for the first time in many moons the merde wagons appeared in the Rue de Lille.

14. Thoma of the four leaf clover appeared and he is writing a book on the Marquis de Sade and I lent him the little book by Ball called La Folie Erotique which states the principal theory of the Sadists that in making love the pleasure of one is measured by the suffering of the other and to-night in the Sacred Books of the East I read that he who had had connection with a Guru's wife shall cut off his organ together with the testicles take them into his joined hands and walk towards the south without stopping until he falls down dead—or he may die embracing the heated metal of a woman.

1928

September 19. Finished the Bible.

20. Read about Pythagoras and his belief in rites and abstinences to purify the soul and about his doctrines of the ideas of number (mathematical and astronomical) and about his identification of the Odd and Even with the Limited and the Unlimited and of how the universe was in a sense the realized union of these opposites (as for instance the number 5 signifying marriage because it is the union of the first masculine number (3) with the first feminine number (2) and I read all about his discovery of the famous doctrine of the harmony of the spheres—that the velocities of the bodies depend upon their distance from the centre the slower and nearer bodies giving out a deep note and the swifter a high note, the concert of the whole yielding the cosmic octave and the reason why we do not hear this music is that we are like men in a smith's forge ("I like better to forge my soul than to furnish it") who cease to be aware of a sound which they constantly hear and were never in a position to contrast with silence. And if Pythagoras identifies one with reason because it is unchangeable I for the same reason (because it is unchangeable) identify One with the Sun.

27. Wrote a poem of revolt called Assassin taking as a point de départ our hashish-party at Constantinople and influenced by Rimbaud's "voici le temps des assassins" and by Kay Boyle who wrote me to become stronger and harder in my writing and to-day Transit of Venus has been completed (forty-four copies) at the Black Sun Press and to-day Mad Queen was beaten and I lost a thousand francs but I do not care because Mad Queen is the Sun-Goddess.

28. La Karoly to tea and a mad talk on politics. She is a Socialist I am an Anarchist believing as I do in the rule of the individual but we both agreed that rebellion is life and the only way to progress—what does Blake say about the tigers of wrath being wiser than the horses of instruction—and then Kay Boyle appeared "How shall I come to you, with soft steps saying hush in the leaves or with anger, to say that a wind dies down in an old country, that a storm makes rain grow like white wheat on the sand" and let them talk of their Amy Lowells and their H.D.'s and their Edna Saint Vincents and their Sara Teasdales (O Christ) or of that poem of putrefaction on John Brown's Body which has sold seventy-five thousand copies (no wonder I am an Anarchist) and how I hate unfairness why is it that the public is so stupid not to appreciate the beautiful. Answer Because the public is unbeautiful sordid ugly therefore they cannot appreciate the beautiful.

29. Mad party C and I and the South Americans and Nada and Evelyn and Esmé—to the Jungle the Grand Ecart and Florence and I would rather hear good jazz than all your Bachs Beethovens and Brahms in the world. Why the hell not?

30. Longchamp on a grey afternoon and I lost Esmé in the crowd (my own damn fault for running to bet on Elsa de Brabant) and Elsa de Brabant lost and I lost my black flower (it must have dropped out of my buttonhole as I was running up the stairs) and Mortimer lost and Sykes lost and Tolstoy was out there and she lost but to-day has not been a lost day for after supper I read some good omens in the Reports of the Magicians and Astrologers of Nineveh and Babylon "When the Sun enters the Moon all lands will speak the Truth, Welfare of all the world."

October 4. Party at the Moulin du Soleil stopping on the way out at Chantilly to see Sunstroke and Gin Cocktail and to drink gin cocktails at the Manor House and at the mill there was champagne and caviare in the Sun and we all climbed to the top of the Sun-Tower and we went for a walk in the woods and then drove over to Gargantua a tavern in Senlis where we drank the best and strongest hot rum grogs and so back to Paris a mile a minute everyone feeling very gay and the wind stinging our faces and it was dark when we got to Pruniers for a great eating of oysters.

[5.   "Iffe I cude have a sonne I
                  wude want his mother to
          Be a beautiful happye ladye
                  andde she to shayke her hed atte me
          Lyke a marygolde"
                              (Ernest Walsh)]

6. Much sniffing and taking of aspirin tablets and to Longchamp with Esmé (she also sniffing) and we drank hot rum grogs and it was grey and dark and little Fléchoise was beaten by a neck and we drank hot rum grogs at the Cascades and then (very dark by now) we rushed to the sale chez Chéri where Mortimer and Sykes were waiting for us and we all four decided to buy Mad Queen and I told the trainer to buy her and we were all pleased when she went for nine thousand francs. But what a surprise when that stupid man came up to us looking very "lugubre" and it appeared that he bought the wrong horse and I was madder than any Mad Queen and it is almost impossible to believe he could have made such a stupid mistake (of course he had to keep the stupid horse he bought) but really the stupidity of the French is beyond imagination and we were disappointed and went away into the rain and drank brandy from my flask on the way to Prunier for oysters and so home and to bed and to-morrow Gin Cocktail races at Long-champ.

7. Lion-Hearted wins the first race and I win four pieces of gold but in the next race I lose two pieces of gold on our Gin Cocktail (casaque rose, disque et toque noirs) but Kantar won the big race and I finished with seven gold coins to the good—so home and to bed to read in a book of astronomy that Venus has no light of its own but shines only as it is illuminated by the Sun.

8. At the Automobile show saw an Isotta car—lemon-colored and low and strong as a locomotive and to hell with all the old coaches in the Cluny

and to hell with museums and libraries—I want a long straight road into the Sun and a car with the cut out wide open speeding a mile a minute into the Sun with a princess by my side and to-day in America someone in a plane broke the world's speed record—three hundred miles an hour almost as fast as the speed of the Sun.

October 10. Dreamt last night for the first time that I was gazing into the Eye of the Sun. Is this prophetic?

14. A great drinking of cocktails in our bathroom—it was too cold in the other rooms—and there were eleven of us all drinking and shrieking and we went to eat oysters and then to the Jungle where there was a great drinking of whiskey and mad music and life is exciting nowadays with all the pederasts and the lesbians—no one knows who is flirting with who and someone had the Paris-Sport which said that neither Aurora nor Sundown had won.

17. Opium with the submarine captain in his little house outside Melun and we motored out through the rain May and I and her girl-friend and I had eleven pipes which produced images—a procession of scenes slender chains of fire suns made of ice to break into fragments, naked fire-girls with peacocks under their arms, panthers smothered in red, and so out into the cold dampness of night and back to Paris through the rain with flocks of birds of fire flying through my brain to perch on the tree of soul and there were long long flights of stone stairs leading to a red door and there were intervals of silence and then the panthers again and then a great sun of sealing-wax red whirling like a great hoop into the centre of my soul.

18. I finish rereading my Mad Queen and now I have read a thousand books and I feel very queer to-day "like a lace handkerchief in a slaughter house" to quote Kay Boyle but to-morrow I shall go out and shriek at the Sun.

21-22. Heliotaure!

24. The Enormous Room with Rain outside and Fire within and I write in my Last Will and testament that I should like my bequests to be paid in twenty dollar gold pieces.

25. To the Baron Gourgol's to see the paintings Picasso and Braque at their best—a superb Douanier Rousseau of his first wife (there was a kitten playing with a ball of worsted in the corner) the Van Gogh I saw in the Rue Royale last spring, a remarkable Derain, two fine Corots not to mention Matisses and Marie Laurencins and Renoirs and Degas and Manets and a Delacroix and some Fernand Légers and a Brancousi brass so that our heads were whirling like tops when we came out.

26. Took the Wretch to Longchamp and she bet on Badabent by Badajoz and Bent (who won at fifty to one) so that with ten francs she made five hundred and there were people to tea La Karoly, etcetera and everyone

drank absinthe cocktails and before going to sleep I read again that miraculous last paragraph in Anna Livia Plurabelle.

October 28. Last day at Longchamp in the pouring rain (four gold coins) and the Lady of the Gold Horse was there and Buddha won the Gladiateur by a courte tête (the ground was sodden) and we drank brandy out of my silver flask and Croucher was there and the old Count and all the leaves were falling off the trees and it was dark and Le Soleil lost and so dark for the last race that I could hardly see that Sir Lancelot was beaten and so home through the rain strong fire burning inside. I love Late Autumn.

Last Day of October. And fourteen years from to-day is our Sun-Death and to-day out to the races to bet a thousand to win on Amon-Ra and he won (I don't think my heart ever beat so fast) and he paid twelve to one and now I am twelve hundred dollars ahead for the year and it was dark coming into Paris and I love October and Late Autumn (this has been the best October) and I love Amon-Ra and the Star of the East and I love the Mad Queen who is the Sun.

November 1. There is a Moon for Target. There is the Sun for Bull's Eye. There is a Star, symbolic of the barb of an arrow, sticking into the Bull's Eye.

4. Auteuil and the Sun reflected in her eyes and Lady Helion fell at the open ditch and I walked an hour through the woods in pursuit of prey (the red-gold birdileaves and the goldabbits of the setting sun) and after supper I read how wizards acquired the mantic powers of certain birds such as ravens and hawks by swallowing their hearts—and if I were to swallow the heart of the Sun?

6. Electricity for my eyes and many people here for cocktails and N and I sat on the zebra rug in front of the fire in the bathroom and after supper before going to sleep I read about Augurs and of their methods of interpreting the signs (auspices) in the sky or from birds and animals. I never read novels any more unless one considers the Joyce "Work in Progress" as a novel for they so seldom offer one either beauty or knowledge in a *concentrated* form as does the Encyclopedia for instance or certain parts of the Bible or Rimbaud. "Et j'ai vu quelquefois ce que l'homme a cru voir" or Blake

> "In futurity
> I prophetic see"

7. C sails for New York and it is a grey day and rain is about to fall and it gets dark very early and I drink a rose-gold Baccardi cocktail (always the desire to pray when drinking cocktails) and so to the tiled house owned by Lu Yung Ting himself North of the Race Course on the North side of the big road and if in China a man is a very very great man because he has Star Thoughts perhaps in my soul I shall become great because I have Sun-Thoughts and this Autumn I am very happy. It is very rare to be so very happy.

1928

November 9. Two great grilled gates and aluminum wheels which whirl [these at the Autumn Salon] and I see the submarine captain who renews my supply of black idol and I see May who gives me a water-color she has done of a girl of a young deep rose ("o fleur de la pucelle neuve") and with Sykes to buy a Marie Laurencin head of a girl for H M C and coming back over the bridge there was a sharp orange sun disappearing between the sharp tower-legs of two buildings (I am there already where I wish to be) and I have never seen such a sharp angle of sunset (hard as orange-colored diamond) and we went to see Kay Boyle who showed us a damn good criticism she has written against that stupid John Brown's Body poem and then to see La Karoly (I think there was a detective outside) and she vehemently denied the report that S had been fired out of France for giving money to the Communists and then home and a great throwing of things into my trunk and a waiting in front of an orange-colored diamond fire and out into the cold night but indoors the rose-gold color of twin baccardis and the white gold of Château Yquem and the black idol and the clear gold of her eyes.

10. And the coming out into the cold under the diamond stars and a gold flower and a star-voice saying goodbye and a sitting up alone in my bed waiting for dawn while silver spearpoints prick the rose-gold hearts of panthers being born and suddenly the dawn and Sykes appears and a rush for the boat-train and a drinking of champagne on the platform and the intentional breaking of the glass against the tracks and a goodbye and the train starts and as I look back at Paris the Sun rises over the roofs and all day the roofpeaks of dream then Cherbourg and the sea and the tugboat in the dark and the Berengaria and the first vibration and the dwindling points and commas and exclamation marks of the shore lights and the vibrations increase as we tunnel through the long black trough of the sea.

11. Ten years ago to-day A.D.W. and O.A. and I drink to them in straight gin (diamond-colored) from my silver flask (I want to buy a gold flask) and all day and all night the Berengaria rolls and lurches like a drunken turtleox and the wind sh sh shrieks and the breakers explode to the crashing of glass.

13. The slowest run for eight years and we are buffeted by the storm and there are strong head winds and I hate the stench of the boat and I hate the creaking all day and night and I hate the English Jesus how I hate the English so damn bourgeois and banal (how in hell did Blake emerge) and the dreary steward (poor devil going back and forth that way) asking Aren't you going to Church (no I never go to church) or Aren't you going to dress for Dinner (no I never dress for dinner) and I walk around and around the deck so rough that it was like walking up and down stairs and the wind hurricaneing driving the black storm clouds back to France driving the black waves against the ship and I climbed up to the radio room and sent radios to cut their way through the black clouds into New York and I went to bed at six to read Tristan Corbière

Shadows of the Sun

Voyez à l'horizon se soulever la houle;
On dirait le ventre amoureux
D'une fille de joie en rut, à moitié soûle

November 14. Almost a day late already Christ how depressing and I feel like hell and I drink ale with an African black as a panther whose name is Amoah and he is chief of thirty thousand people on the Gold Coast of Africa and he told me the word for Sun "Awear" and then I went down into the engine rooms where in one place the temperature was a hundred and twenty and I love the churning propeller shafts (so clean and phallic) and the giant boilers and the great turbines (O Columbus could you but see and hear this symphony) but what a hell for those poor devils those slaves of the machine only somehow I would rather tender a flock of boilers (for there is something dynamic in this) than be a steward tendering a flock of Jew tourists (ignoble and inglorious occupation) and to-day I met a man who was in the jewelry business who talked of black diamonds and star sapphires and to-day I read again the poem by Corbière

"L'âme d'un matelot
Au lieu de suinter dans vos pommes de terre
Respire à chaque flot"

and why shouldn't I be a sailor hurricaneing through oceans of clouds on the Ship of the Sun.

17. New York gold city of the Arabian Nights towering into the gold of the Sun and a drink of gin to the Sun from the silver flask and I smoke a black cigarette into the Sun (I believe in rites) and the tugboats are leeches sucking at the black and white carcass of the Berengaria and the battered tramp steamer sliding out to sea is the Past (how quickly it is forgotten) and there are fat ferry-boats busily pushing snub noses towards the shore and there are coal barges strung out in line behind a red tug and the steerage passengers are emerging from the depths of the hold (there is a girl with a rose-colored scarf) and the donkey-engines are at work and up from the hold come the green and the red and the black and the yellow trunks like colored thoughts from the hold of the soul and there comes across the harbor the noise of the City yawning and stretching itself in the morning Sun ("et, à l'aurore, armé d'une ardente patience, nous entrerons aux splendides villes") and sirens and factory whistles are blowing and there is a roar of trains and a clock is striking and there are the fog horns of ships crying and answering each other like leviathans in distress and there are engine bells and the sharp hiss of escaping steam. A quarter mile away tall factory chimneys point like fingers into the Sun. Directly below broken crates refuse orange and banana peels empty bottles drift past. Our huge propellers are churning the water. Black smokeplumes pour from the tugs. A fast motor-boat crosses our bow. Red and white buoys are the red and white roses of the harbor. The gold sea-gulls are the gold coins scattered by the Sun. There is the feeling that there are no people that everything is automatic. I can feel the shaft of the Sun thrusting like a sword into my heart. There is a four-master the Lloyd H Dazel a black hulk against the Sun. There is the Haymarket bound for Marseilles. There are barges with red and yellow freight cars on them. The Sun is higher now pouring its gold into the upreaching arms of the skyscrapers. The horns increase and the echoes reverberate and vanish into Sun. We are approaching the New Babylon. Calm water with splotches of oil contrast to the precipices and chasms of the sea. There is a smell of iron and rust and coal. There is a gold restlessness. And now the tugs are drawing us past Pier 13 (the Lackawanna Railroad) past the Fall River Line past the Pennsylvania Railroad Pier past the Clyde Line past the Mallory Line past the New London Line past the North German Lloyd and there is the hum and stir of activity and there is a dredger—chug chug—chug chug chug (why aren't their dredgers for the mud of the soul—the Sun is a dredger for the gold of the soul) and now the tugs are edging us into the Cunard Pier and people with faces like pieces of paper are staring up at us and there is a frantic woman shaking a red handkerchief and there is the Majestic alongside her smoke up ready to sail and now huge coils of rope are thrown and caught gangplanks are thrown down and there is a great pushing and crowding and stepping on people's feet and there is a great sign No Smoking Allowed and I shout at C and I go through the customs my pockets stuffed with opium pills flasks of absinthe and the little Hindu Love Books and at five o'clock we take the Merchant's Express for Boston (Narcisse in the baggage car—1 dog 1 baby—1 carriage 1 corpse) and we sit outside on the observation car and listen to the clikety-click clickety-clack clikety-click clickety-clack and the rattling over the switches clikety-click click click click clack (Symphony of the Rails—there is no other Symphony) and we watch the red and green signal lights and the great electrical signs (Nujol for Constipation) and the gold windows of the buildings and the blaze of light from the streets below—then out into the country and darkness and into the dining-car (last call for the dining-car) for iced coffee and clam broth and cornbread and pumpkin pie then Providence then Boston and the Back Bay O City of Dreadful Night then the Pink Room and so to bed Cramoisy in the arms of Gold.

[November 18. A Fire-Voice heard over the telephone and so to the Apple Trees and the feeling that it all means nothing anymore. I am Free and sandwiches in the cold greenhouse and so to Burrages to see his collection of miraculous orchids—carnivorous and passionate-colored.]

20. Yes it is certainly the City of Dreadful Night and it appears I cannot go to the dinner-party for the Infanta unless I promise not to wear my black flower and of course I refuse not to wear it (would a knight cast aside his plume) and everyone is angry and C and I decide to go back to New York to-morrow.

21. On the train saw Ned Holmes and attacked him on the subject of buying a Van Gogh for the Boston Museum and I drank an enormous glass of gin as we got to New York. The syllable Sun is the Door.

November 22. Eleven years ago to-day on the hills of Verdun and here to-day Four Roses Or and Rimbaud

"I dreamed of crusades I believed in all the enchantments I saw gold"

24. One hour for us to get to the Grand Central the traffic here blocks everything (there is so little traffic on the road to the Sun)[12] and a bolting down poached eggs on hash and we just caught the last special to New Haven and we read the billboards all the way what is it that Stendhal says about ugliness "je ne me sens pas encore assez savant pour aimer le laid" and there were signs to proclaim Forty Fathom Fish Fresh from the Sea and signs to proclaim Pluto Water (if nature won't Pluto will) and signs to proclaim Peggy Hopkins Joyce in the Lady of the Orchids (why not James Joyce in Ulysses) and signs to proclaim The Office of the Gate of Heaven Cemetery and signs to proclaim Henry F Bultitude Lighting Fixtures and signs to proclaim the Sun Chemical Company of New York Etcetera Etcetera Etcetera—one can read all the way and it was cold when we got out at New Haven cold and grey and we walked all the way out to the Bowl and because of C in her grey squirrel coat all the signs and horrors faded away ("tous les souvenirs immondes s'effacent") and we were late for the game but there was a squirrel who scurried out bewildered upon the field with a drunken student in pursuit and there was the Sun strong and gold going down opposite us behind the black cheering sections and there was a sharp glimpse of Fire and there were red torches after the game as we hurried off to the station C to New York I to the City of Dreadful Night (I rode up in an empty day coach in preference to the crowded Club Car) and I got out at Back Bay and ate a poached egg on hash at a little hole in the wall called the Alps Luncheon and walked home through empty streets. This country more than any other country drives one into oneself and this at least is a good thing.

26. A run in the snow along the river and a bright gold cramoisy gold luncheon at the Ritz and a mud massage at the Ritz barber-shop "barbers who are afflicted with tuberculosis venereal parasitical or other communicable diseases must not practice the barber trade" and then the dinner-party for the Infanta of Spain and I wore my black flower and there were cocktails and champagne and a pretty but stupid woman who had thrown C's book of poems into the fire because one of the poems had shocked her and there was a Mono Lisa woman in a red dress and there was an old Marquis Etcetera Etcetera but the best part of the evening was the voice of fire over the wire.

27. To see Argentina and her Fire-Dance and I should like to learn the Dance of the Sun with its cruelty of roses and its simplicity of explosions (like the exciting simplicity of love) well why the hell don't you and we sat in the second balcony and drank gin from my flask and when it was over we walked home through the cold to the Pink Room. Tesol. Tolse. Tesol.

28. The Crouchers arrive from New-York and we walk out of the house (apparently there is no room for us) and we stand on the sidewalk ("the persons dropping paper glass or refuse on the sidewalk will be prosecuted")

(Jesus what a country) and we hail a passing wagon marked Fresh Fish (Forty Fathom Fish Fresh from the Sea) a red wagon drawn by a stallion and in this we drive past the Ritz to encamp at the Statler—a radio in every room. So to the Ritz (there was a red shred of winter sun) to eat alligator pears at a dollar a piece and then a mud massage "mugs brushes razors scissors clippers tweezers combs rubber disks and parts of vibrators and all other utensils and appliances that come in contact with the head or face must be immersed in boiling water and rendered aseptic after each patron". Then a manicure I reading aloud from the Bible to the manicure lady (from Norway). The rest of the afternoon tried to get Paris on the telephone during which time Croucher and I sat in the lobby with our feet on the imitation fire. Cocktails at teatime in the pantry (there were children and callers all over the rest of the house—there is no privacy in America—even in the pantry the telephone kept ringing until I poured a cocktail down it) and afterwards to a cabaret-restaurant called Lido-Venice about as much like the Lido-Venice as an electric bulb is to the Sun and so to the Statler to bed to lie between the sheets listening to barbaric jazz over the radio [(the Crouchers doing the same thing—or at least I think so—in their room)] and so to the sound of jazz we fell asleep.

November 29. Thanksgiving Day and I give thanks to the Sun for my Strength in the Sun for the two Queens of the Sun for the two Princesses of the Sun and the radio this morning sounded like a Philistine drowning gurgle gurgle gurgle drown you bastard and there was a shaft of sunlight pointing to the Ritz and there was caviare and cocktails and orchids give me o you whose arms are soft and slender and a large family dinner in the country where someone suggested that it must be awfully nice to write what you wanted to write O Christ O Christ and in the evening to a stupid place called the Karnak Club so sordid so dismal and it cost thirty dollars for eight bottles of White Rock (water) and the music was wretched and we left and went to the South Station full of cinders and fog and cold as a refrigerator box and I only just got off the train as it was moving out beyond the platform (I had stopped to unhook a sign) and so back to the house in a cold taxi and so to bed in the Pink Room and the last thing I remembered were the orchids lying like stars in her lap in the morning Sun.

30. No concentration here, no stimulus, no inner centrality, no exploding into the Beyond, no Sun. It is the City of Dreadful Night, a Target for Disgust. And I went to the Museum ("visitors are requested not to touch objects placed on exhibition") to see the Grey Princess (Valkulla by Zorn) and there was a good Bellows and the little Minoan Snake Goddess from Crete and a good Turner but O Sun preserve me from the Stagnation of Museums. Three quarters of the stuff here is rubbish and should be [unceremoniously] dumped out and a few fiery Suns by Van Gogh inserted in their stead. Otherwise how can the Museum develop? But do Bostonians want anything to develop? I doubt it. So to the Ritz through the falling snow and I like the green searchlight on top of the Ritz to guide wandering aeroplanes through the storm (as the Sun guides wandering souls through the storm of life) and now November is over and the pistol bangs to announce the last lap come and sit in my lap.

December 1. That life is to be lived not made a slave to words and if this is the creed of the surrealists it is also my creed and I went and bought tickets to New-York not to mention a pair of nail scissors "bring beauty to your finger tips: tweezers scissors nippers"—you cannot beat this country for advertisements, and I cut my toe nails (Christ only knows they needed it) and put rouge on my toe nails and ate luncheon with my mother and sister (the former was interrupted twice the latter three times by the telephone) and afterwards to Blackbirds a magnificent negro review and I would rather hear this sort of barbaric jazz than all the violin recitals in the world and what sting and fire this show had compared with the dreary musical shows in Europe. Walked back across the Common with the green light of the Ritz staring like a star and many people for tea in the house and many cocktails in the pantry and the telephone rang and I ran to pour gin down it only I heard the Fire Voice and there was a dashing out the front door and a sitting on the sidewalk and the sudden dark shadow of a car and there was the black road back of the river and the long row of silver ash cans glinting in the headlights —And a last supper with the family they have tried so hard to be nice and I remember concentrating on the red pomegranate on the fruit dish in front of me and I went out and crossed the Commons to the Boston Herald and here I saw iron hands opening and closing setting type and iron pistons thrusting and thrusting and the lavender light shed a color of nausea [on the men as they worked] and we went through a room where they kept files and into another where they were developing photographs of this afternoon's football game (why not of this afternoon's Sun?) then down a flight of stairs to kick open a door. To a huge basement where there was a roar of machinery (it reminded me of an engine room on a ship) and there were stokers feeding giant rolls of blank paper to the presses—in went the paper into the jaws of the dragon and when it was vomited forth it was all blackened with printed petertracks to turn our living eyes to stone.[13]

2. Last listening to the radio "a Lady from Cincinnati has asked us if Bananas are indigestible no Bananas are not indigestible if they are eaten when ripe Bananas are indigestible only when they are not ripe" and to the Kreisler Concert so civilized after the barbaric rhythms of Blackbirds (how can a violin compete with a tom-tom) and I said goodbye and went with Jack Watson to the South Station drinking gin from my flask all the way and there were cinders and there was fog and it was cold. Goodbye Jack Goodbye Harry (just as we had said goodbye two years ago—how quickly the leaves of goodbye fall from the tree of life) and the Merchants Limited became our escape from Boston a tempestuous escape ending in the Grand Central Fortress of New York.

3. Fire burning in the heart [14] and The City of Dreadful Night no longer menaces (I have forgotten it already all except what that man said about the

Lady of the Gold Horse that the only way for her to save her soul was for her to live within her income O Christ O Christ O Christ O Christ) and rode round in a taxi most of the day (please do not ask me to violate this pledge by fast driving or taking unnecessary chances) and with C to see about our Black Sun Books at Marx's at the Gotham Book Mart, at Random House. S and G and a hot shower-bath and to the Show Boat the most characteristically American and hence depressing musical review weak and sentimental devoid of humor fireless and bourgeois to a degree the exact antithesis to the sting and fury of Blackbirds and I felt like a fox in a trap and anywheres else I would have gotten up and left but for once I was unselfish and by concentrating on the fire in the heart [15] managed to stave off complete boredom. The final curtain a crowding out into the cold night the little naked fires in the streets where they are tearing up things and a great tirade with C as we were undressing (there is nothing more fun than a tirade à deux against a common pestilence and if there ever was a pestilence it is the Show Boat—I wonder which one of us hated it the most?)

December 4. Modern French Paintings and I liked the Van Goghs best (he makes me want to paint Suns that would scorch up the dirty souls and dirtier bodies of the Philistines) and I gave a tirade for the Surrealists and I went to look at a magnificent Picasso (great art gives great confidence) and I went and bought a picture called Stove-Pipes by Diego Rivera and a gold coin for a luncheon à quatre not worth it and I love New-York—a madhouse full of explosions with fog horns screaming out on the river and policemen with shrill whistles to regulate traffic and the iron thunder of the elevated and the green searchlight stabbing the night.

6. H M C appears from Pittsburg where she has been lecturing on Wild Flowers (is a sunflower a wild flower) and with her to Marx's where we found C standing among a heap of Suns (D. H. Lawrence [and Birthdays of the Infanta products of the Black Sun Press]) (Sun had been held up at the Customs because of the use of the word "womb" but had been released by our bribing with two gold coins—the low-down bastards) and there was a wild man in the bookshop who had been drinking whiskey in the back room who begged us (he had never seen us before) to give him the great pleasure of presenting us with a small Shelley association item whereupon he presented us with Sir Walter Scott's Minstrelsy of the Scottish Border in three volumes the set which Shelley had presented to his wife Mary Shelley (Shelley has written "Mary" on each of the three title pages). Not content with this Mr Wildman after having disappeared into the back room reappears and addressing H M C begs her indulgence in allowing him in honor of Montana (Mr Wildman was born in Montana and Grandpa C was governor of Montana) to present her with a trifling Jane Austen item whereupon he presents her with a magnificent illustrated Pride and Prejudice exquisitely bound in "full light green levant with extra inlaid and gold tooled peacock design of varicolored leather on front cover with a genuine ruby chip for the eye" all this enclosed in a red cloth case lined with swansdown. But the real

excitement came at the Intimate Gallery I did not care for the Marin water-colors but just as we were leaving someone came in the door and the draft blew a photograph off the table on the floor and I picked it up. It was a photograph of a painting representing the Sun above a skyscraper and I asked where the painting was and the next thing I knew we were looking at the most miraculous paintings ever painted by an American not even Bellows excepted—these paintings by Georgie O'Keefe an Irish woman from Texas—comparatively unknown but Christ what paintings passionately chaste and cool explosions into things cool and white (almost hospital white) and there were great vagina flowers color of orchids and young roses, flowers young and strong and magnificently physical and rich in color and as simple as silence, the body flower unfolding in the soul. A painter singular as opposed to plural singular as the great poets are singular a painter with all the trivialities swept magnificently aside a painter with inner centrality painting from within out with the coolness of cool sheets with the cool flamboyance of flowers. No petty schools no littlenesses but cool and white as a mind of diamonds. How Odilon Redon would have bowed before these flowers. But any description I might give would be overshadowed by the simple critism of Steiglitz "a woman gives herself" [and here is the truth about Georgie O'Keefe].

To the Grand Central and dark violets for Mamma and another leaf falls from the tree of goodbye how many more I wonder and she disappears through the gates on her way to the City of Dreadful Night while I storm out into the Madhouse of New-York paying on the way out one dollar for the Evening Sun. This for reasons of my own. While she ate her supper on a card table [((the Queen of Hearts)]. While I drank up all the hot soup. While the electrically-lighted city mocked the stars.

December 7. There were two hundred businessmen but we found him [16] huddled up in the corner of a sofa his coat turned up about the ears his hat pulled down over his eyes. So does a poet stand apart from the flock a hawk among pigeons. So does a mad street lead to a speakeasy. So does a green douche bag give birth to a bottle of Red Heart Rum. Good drinking and it was four o'clock and grey and growing dark when we emerged into Washington Square. The taxi: The flask. The hotel—there we found the books we had left in the taxi this morning (American efficiency) and there we found Carlos Williams and his wife [((to whom Kay Boyle had given us a letter of introduction)] and we all went across the street and stumbled upstairs (the elevator wouldn't work) to Tom's studio and there was champagne and Christ knows what and I knocked over by mistake one of Tom's statues Leda with Swan and it broke into pieces and I insulted his mother over the telephone (stinking tight by this time) and the next thing I remember I was banging on the wall inside a closet at a cocktail party wondering why it wouldn't go up or down (I thought it was an elevator) until someone pulled me out to introduce me to the hostess. Cummings had disappeared. Revolving faces reek of perfume and cigarette smoke and roar of talk turmoil and pandemonium comets exploding and a running out into the street no hat no coat. Blank. A waking up on the bed a dishevelled head reflected in the mirror. Suit crumpled. Condition disorganized. Drank eight glasses of water took a cold showerbath gargled listerine and pulled myself into the semblance of a human being. C appears, We go to the Studio to pack my trunk. Everything in mad disorder With C in a taxi to the docks—and the sound of donkey-engines and the long black hull of the boat and the smell of wharves and people coming and going and all the stir of departure [and the indecision whether to sail or not to sail] and there was caviare and cocktails (CC) and the Crouchers appeared (CCC) and with them Coates (CCCC) and others invited and uninvited—a woman called Weaver (there was a young girl from Geneva) [17] and there was hot soup and then that terrorizing blast of the bugle to say it was time for visitors to go on shore and another leaf (pure gold) from the tree of goodbye and a stumbling down the gang-plank and that desperate goodbye feeling and there was a great bonfire burning as I came out into the street and it was beginning to snow and to bed à trois on the twenty-second story of the Victoria and as I fell asleep I could hear the fog horn of the Majestic crying like a lost ghost as she moved out to sea through the snow. I love only you.

December 8. Cold as a frozen heart with tears of snow against the windowpane and I am horribly depressed (O Christ why didn't I sail) and I can still hear the fog-horn calling to me and a long depressing day wandering the streets looking into shop windows (too cold for any girl to wear those pink dentelleries) watching the derricks and dredgers at work on new buildings, praying into the fires in the streets observing the traffic jams (why not feed them all Nujol) staring into ugly Drug Store windows or else shivering at the crossstreets. But the day ended in fire in front of the roaring fire a boy and a girl [18] [asleep on the sofa] in front of the fire while the empty bottles rattled together on the floor Moan O wind outside window and door Burn fire into the very core of sleep.

9. When hushed awakenings are dear and the fire has gone out and the streets are covered with snow and it is bitter cold because it is Sunday all the barber shops are closed and I buy the New-York Times (it would take a week to read it all) and in a new car to the country (four on the front seat) and there was a quaint farmhouse and people and we all went walking slipping about on the ice of the main road while a procession of cars spattered us with ice or skidded perilously near and it was bitter cold and very grey and I had to take off my shoes and walk in my socks so as not to fall going downhill and I was glad when we got back to whiskey and fire.

And at night the green searchlight and firelight and the light from two eyes. [19]

[10. "Please let Mr Crosby use 9M at any time" and I install myself at the Hotel des Artistes I go out to find Goops First time I had seen him for six years and we went to La Cantina where he drank six whiskeys straight And at night the green searchlight. And a studio party downstairs cocktails lobster salad dancing and to Blackbirds and back to cocktails and lobster salad and at last upstairs again to fall asleep under my polo coat on the sofa. Sleep is a metamorphose into Sun]

December 11. Blackbirds again I can't give you anything but love dearest and a drinking champagne from the bottle (milk from the breast)—a taxi with the top thrown back and the empty bottle thrown overboard and the breaking glass on the street and a red fire in the studio and a girl stood before him gazing into the fire.

12. New York is a Madhouse stark staring mad full of explosions and madnesses hard and violent and I like it I like the dredgers snouting up whole streets like so many wild boars I like the great derrick swinging iron girders into place I like the naked fires for the workmen I like the noise of trip hammers the whistle of the foreman directing the work the great trucks lumbering off with their load of rubble the onlookers their hands in their pockets staring at the work with the Red Sun like a danger flag in the sky. And always the Twin Suns crashing in my heart. [20]

13. Absinthe cocktails in a teacup and to Black Star and Frost to see the six hundred and eighty-five thousand dollar pearl necklace supposed to be the finest pearl necklace in the world and they didn't want to show it to me so I became infuriate and they disappeared and reappeared with a superb metallic dark color of metal necklace and each pearl *perfect*. If I were rich I should like to buy them and offer them to the Sun and this afternoon the Sun between two buildings was like a garment hung out to dry and to-night we hung the magical sign

QUIET
is requested for the benefit of those who have retired

14. The clank *clank* of the turnstile and the long roar and rush underground read Hart Crane's The Tunnel and there was a negress opposite and advertisements for everything from Bible Classes to Kotex and then the subway soared into the elevated and of all the sordid scenery I have ever seen this was the most sordid; a field scattered with broken down bodies of cars (Automobile Cemetery) lurid signboards proclaiming the Latest Laxatives or what to do about Halitosis (even your best friend won't tell you) then a street all dug up lined with tumbledown shacks drab houses and telegraph poles I see an empty tram car is there anything more depressing I see children playing about a puddle a dog wearily lifting its leg a red drug store at a cross-street four factory stacks vomiting poison and a long row of tenement houses with drawers and shirts and sheets and Christ knows what hung out to dry. Bedding hangs from a window. A man in shirtsleeves stands in a door. The train stops it is one hundred and eighty something street and out the turnstile clank *clank* and down iron stairs "it is a violation of municipal ordinances to place garbage or other refuse in this or any public passage" and so into the Bronx buffalo and bears and grey wolves and condors and vultures and asps and anacondas and adders and rattlesnakes and cobras and a mongoose (Riki-tiki-tavi) and pythons and primates and pelicans and panthers and pumas and the lions and tigers roared and were fed and there was a great hippopotamus and a great Sudan elephant but there were no giraffes to nibble gold off the plate of Sun and no unicorn to provide cocktails for Venus (see Venus and Tannhauser page seventy-one) and no petrodactyl to carry us into our Castle in the Sun.

And all night the green searchlight sweeping over the roofs.

December 15. Oysters sherry and clam broth. La Cantina is an Oasis as Roxy is the Temple of the Motion Pictures and a sound movie is a senile politician cackling stupidities and a woman with a bosom like a bed-pillow is an opera singer and the End of Saint Petersbourg [is the beginning of Love] is a sheet of flame and a D.B. may mean any number of things and there was a red fire and champagne (gold fire) and the combination a red-gold Fire.

16. Whiskey sours. Twin Suns crashing, the feeling of just before snow, the winter lawns, the Red Heart Rum, the little ears the fingers and toes the underclothes the ivory and the rose the winter snows, the green searchlight like a finger touching the breast of the night.

17. "I like my body when it is with your body It is so quite new a thing" and the first edition of Tulips and Chimneys and a magnificent Perfumed Garden for ten gold coins the exciting illustrations and it was raining and there was a red and gold fire hydrant and whiskey sours and oysters and Rosenfeld who said if you mean by explosions explosions into the Beyond and on to the bank for a new supply of gold coins and there was Red Heart Rum and a ride to the docks past La Cantina past Roxy past the Victoria past hard blue and red electric signs and there was a locomotive in the street (locomotives and roses) and the covered shed of pier 57 and a fog horn blowing ("rien de plus effrayant") and champagne and a gong and four eyes are One Fire in the Sun Sunfire.

18. Empty Bed Blues.

[19. The same]

[20. The same]

21. Shortest day of the year. The sun is flat and grey as slate. A pale winter Sun. Arctic. I understand this sea. I understand this Sun. And like a girl "lasciviously frail"

22. I read in my notebook that an Acrolith is a statue half of wood half of marble (New York is a city half of steel half of gold)); that an Anaconda combines an arboreal with an aquatic life (a Lover combines a bedroom with a prophet's life); that Aphelion in astronomy is that point of the orbit of a planet at which it is most distant from the Sun (the City of Dreadful Night); that the most simple Sun-Death is from an aeroplane over a forest (31-10-42) down down down down Bang! the body is dead—up up up up Bang!!!! the Soul explodes into the Bed of Sun (pull over us the gold sheets Dear); that the wolf the hawk the snake and the griffin are attributes of Apollo; that among the astronomers of antiquity Ptolomy stood out with unchallenged pre-eminence (Ptolomy had no successors he found only commentators); that among the writers of modernity Joyce stands out with unchallenged pre-eminence (Joyce has no successors he finds only commentators); that I like a girl "lasciviously frail"

December 23. Something inside me is strong and steady. It is the Sun. It is the Sun pouring through the porthole into my soul there is a first sea-gull gold as a cannonball in the Sun there is a second sea-gull a third a fourth a flock of sea-gulls then the black smokeplume of a boat the black and silver hull against the horizon then the white unicorn of a lighthouse (But where o where is the green searchlight sweeping over the roof of love) then Land and another journey is over a part of the Great Journey into Sun another Landmark has been past and I am climbing like an aeroplane into the Sun.

24. Cold winter dawn cold and red with great cranes and derricks dragging apart with iron arms the red curtains of the dawn and Paris is dead after the madness of New York and we drove out in the dark to the Moulin where I stared and stared into the red-gold of the Fire—"Must we who once would not allow even the thickness of a garment to part us be now far from each other for whole night on end?"

25. The Birthday of the Sun and a walk with C in the woods to the Pôteau de Perthe and a prayer into Sun from the top of the suntower and to Paris to see the Lady of the and black idol and a taxiing out late at night drugged with the drug and the moon and a constant losing of the way and the final arrival at the gates of the Moulin and I shout and shout and C appears in a frail lovegown but the gate is locked and the key is lost so I climb over the high white-in-moonlight fence and in the Moulin there is a snoring (a drunken man from the Embassy) and a squeaking (Kay Boyle's child) and a lying awake in the dark while gold coins fell sharply one by one on the marble courtyard of my mind. O Invisible Hand take away the grey dawn and let me sleep with the Sun.

26. The words I like best: Sun Fire Sunfire Arrow Strong Chaste Queen Princess Gold Barbaric Catapult Explosion Hurricane Eagle Madness Attack. [21]

27. Red Black Red Black Red Red Black Black Black Red Black Red Red Black Red Red Red Red Black Red Black Red in other words we are experimenting with a system at roulette with my little roulette watch and it was already growing dark when I got up and got dressed and walked through the dark woods with C and it was drizzling and very dark (la forès estoit hisdouse et faée the forest was grisly and enchanted) and we were glad to be back by the red-gold fire roulette watch and pencil in hand Red Black

Red Red Black Black Black Black Black Black Red Red Black Red Red Red Black Red Red Black Red Red and after losing theoretically a hundred thousand francs we went downstairs and undressed and went to bed.

Last Day of the Year.
        "Of days spread like peacock tails
        Of days worn savagely like parrot-feathers"
to quote Kay Boyle and I ran out to the Pôteau and back and played polo on the donkeys and I ran out again to the Pôteau de Perthe and back (it was dark and pouring with rain) and I climbed to the top of the sun-tower and looked off through the rain towards the Invisible Sun (I should like to be a necromancer I should like to be a prophet of the Sun I *am* a Prophet of the Sun) and when I came down (a fragment of my soul had arrowed into the Invisible Sun) a fire-cable arrived for me and it was from America and I read fire-words in front of the Fire and was glad and there was a Fire Princess in the red-gold fire and a merry supper oysters and champagne and for me red wine and it was ten minutes before midnight when we began to drink the last toast to 1928 (for me the Year Magnificent) and then it was five minutes of twelve four minutes of twelve (I had my stop watch) three minutes of twelve two minutes of twelve one minute of twelve I lit my pipe drank a glass of red wine and looked and prayed into the red-gold of the fire shy birds of Sun stirring in my soul Oneness (mid) for Eternity into the Red-Gold (night) of the Sun

                                                          SUNFIRE

rinnu nirln na orn xyz
minnttn itnni na orn xyz
wntngroin mnitoiimn wimitnloin
gnoimnttnt na orn xyz
anfrini onygln anu na orn xyz

aonn mniynotu rnla toin rnnu ynni

ninintt ann nonnioou
oion orn nna-rnla aonn na Xyz [22]

C
A
HARRY
E
S
E

[1] Harry's holograph notebook extends this entry with more quotations from Gide. He crossed these out, but inserted most of them into his entries for March 16 and 17, 1928.

[2] The holograph notebook entry is "needles."

[3] The holograph entry is "the size of a phallus (in erection)."

[4] The reference to Valéry does not appear in the holograph notebook. Instead, this entry ends: ". . . when we got home I went to bed and corrected proof sheets for the first series of these Shadows of the Sun."

[5] In the holograph notebook: "galloping galloping."

[6] This sentence does not appear in the holograph notebook. Instead, Harry wrote "then a manicure and a return to bed where I read the Cenci."

[7] The date Harry and Caresse planned to die together. On this date earth reaches its perihelion.

[8] This sentence is not in the holograph notebook.

[9] Josephine Rotch.

[10] The holograph notebook reads: "two heads on my shoulder fast asleep."

[11] This sentence does not appear in the holograph notebook.

[12] In the holograph notebook: "(I hope there will be no traffic on the road to the Sun)."

[13] In the holograph notebook the passage ends: "it was all blackened with printed peter-tracks so back through the Public Garden to look goodnight at the green light on the roof of the Ritz."

[14] In the holograph notebook this entry begins "Where hushed awakenings are dear."

[15] "fire in the heart" does not occur in the holograph notebook. Instead, the phrase reads "hushed awakenings."

[16] E. E. Cummings.

[17] In the holograph notebook the phrase in parentheses is "and we all shouted Beaver."

[18] Harry is with Josephine here and in subsequent entries until December 17, when he sails for France.

[19] This sentence is not in the holograph notebook.

[20] This sentence is not in the holograph notebook.

[21] The entry for December 26 is not in the holograph notebook.

[22] In the 1929 edition the code and the acrostic occupied separate pages. This code is similar to that at the end of the "First Series," page 133, but the key code differs significantly. Spread alphabetically, it reads:

Shadows of the Sun

a b c d e f g h i j k l m n o p q r s t u v w x y z
i a m a n a r r o w f l y i n g i n t o t _ _ s u n

Clearly, *v* and *w* encode into *h* and *e*, respectively; the key is "I am an arrow flying into the Sun." Note that the coding of "sun" is inverted—the code works "backwards" for this one word. Here is the decoded message:

rinnu nirln na orn xyz
harry eagle of the sun

minnttn itnni na orn xyz
caresse queen of the sun

wntngroin mnitoiimn wimitnloin
josephine constance jacqueline

gnoimnttnt na orn xyz
princesses of the sun

anfrini onygln anu na orn xyz
bokhara temple boy of the sun

aonn mniynotu rnla toin rnnu ynni
fire cramoisy gold star grey moon

ninintt ann nonnioou
oneness for eternity

oion orn nna-rnla aonn na Xyz
into the red-gold fire of Sun

THREE : 1929

Harry Crosby's diary for 1929 was edited posthumously by Caresse Crosby. Harry's original manuscript survives, written in pencil in a looseleaf notebook. So does a typescript made from that manuscript, paginated for entries through November 11 in Harry's hand. This varies slightly from the holograph and shows additional editing, some of which was certainly done by Harry before he sailed to New York on November 16. Caresse edited it further, although it is sometimes difficult to distinguish her marks from Harry's.

Phrases that originally were struck from the looseleaf holograph are here enclosed in brackets. Phrases originally struck from the typescript are here italicized within brackets. Passages that appear solely in the Black Sun Press edition of 1930, obvious additions made by Caresse, are identified in footnotes. Since the entries for 1929 do not evidence the same care in preparation as those edited and published during Harry's lifetime, I have silently corrected spelling.

Harry Crosby's diary after November 11 poses an additional problem. There are two sets of entries. One appears to be the raw material for the other, even though it occurs in the middle of Harry's notebook. He may simply have opened his notebook to pages that happened to be blank, or Caresse may have rearranged the material when she edited it. In either case, there can be little doubt that Harry wrote these out-of-sequence entries during the last days of his life. A few are dated; internal references identify others. Some contain phrases identical with those in Harry's sequential entries.

Caresse included certain of the out-of-sequence entries in her posthumous edition, but she ignored others—including the last words that Harry wrote. The present edition restores most of these entries, enclosed in brackets to show that they come from the holograph, and identified in footnotes as belonging to the out-of-sequence section. The entries are inserted at their appropriate dates, whenever possible. A few that cannot be dated with precision are grouped in a footnote and in an addendum.

VIII

January First 1929
Sunfire

Oneness for Eternity Red-Gold of Sun and I looked into the red-gold of the fire and drank a first toast to 1929 (let this year be the Sunfire Year) and we all kissed each other CC and HC HC and CCC (one minute past twelve) H and J H and J Etcetera Etcetera and I smoked my pipe and we all drank and there was much laughter and toward one o'clock a wandering off to bed after gin and champagne silver and gold and a pipe of opium and so the New Year has begun (auspiciously—I have never enjoyed the crossing over the bridge more—I hope the crossing over the sun-death bridge into the Sun will be as sincere and strong) and so an undressing and a blowing out of candles and so to sleep.

Morning and I look out the window straight into the gold of the Sun and a huge stork coming from the West flies over the courtyard (is this an omen) and I walk to the Poteau de Perth and when I got back I climbed to the top of the Sun-Tower and exploded into the Sun

| | (gold | cramoisy | grey | fire | star) |
| | H | C | J | J | C |

and in the afternoon polo on the donkeys and fire into flower and Lord L came out for the night.

7. Monday and into Paris in the car and when I got there I found a Fire-Letter from the Youngest Princess and I ran around buying books (The Wild Party) [*a marvelous poem by a man or is it a woman called March*] and black neckties and black flowers and caviare and Christ knows what and then into a hot bath (it was raining and I had no coat) and then into bed and then (after the caviare) into a sound sound sleep.

8. A pair of lovelies for C (the dernier cri all lace with a silk heart little muff and derrière) and a luncheon together chez Philippe (one cocktail the first of the year and a prayer) and afterwards to see Picasso but he was out then with C to see Kay Boyle she was in a chaise longue at the Princess of Sarawak's and here we met a man called Laurence Vail and then I went to the Black Sun Press to talk to Lescaret about my Mad Queen and then out to the Moulin in the dark and it was very cold but I did not want to miss my daily prayer on the Sun-Tower (almost a Star-Tower at night) nor my daily walk to the Poteau de Perth and I took my rifle and a flashlight and started out but the flashlight was very dim and it was very dark and I kept bumping into trees and there were queer sounds in the underbrush and the cracking of branches deer or wild boar and there was the hooting of owls and pitter-patter of feet rabbits or squirrels running over dry leaves and I walked and walked until I suddenly realized I was lost and I hunted and hunted for the right path and walked and walked and Narcisse had disappeared and at last I came out almost where I had started having made a complete circle so I had

to begin all over again and after a quarter of an hour I could see the white post looking like a white ghost against the black trees and all the way home queer sounds in the woods and it was very cold and the stars were like silver birds in the black tree-tops and always that queer feeling as if someone were walking behind me following me step by step and I was glad for the Sun tattooed on my back (to ward off evil spirits) and I was glad I did not turn to look behind (Lot's Wife and the Pillar of Salt) and I was glad for the Fire-Letter strong and secure in the pocket of my leather coat and when I got back I found Narcisse shivering in front of the front door (I wonder how he found his way back) and when I had let him in I went into the kitchen and took the lantern and climbed to the top of the Tower and said my prayers (looking out towards the West) and then down the stairs and back to the kitchen to get lumps of sugar for the donkeys and at last to the Grenier (time ten o'clock) (I had been out in the woods two hours) for a potage and a côtelette and a fromage not to mention a bottle of red wine—then work on the Bible and a Letter to the Youngest Princess (the candles had all gone out so I had to write by the light of the fire) and it must have been nearing midnight when I got to bed.

January 10. [gold cramoisy grey fire star
17-10-1-29
(on my Sun Tower)
(H C J J C)]

Letter

you were in me with me all around me
you were me
I was very happy and for the first
time worshipped gold and fire
as part of you and the Sun
because you are part of it.
[*The Fire Letter*]

11. Wrote S V R C to sell four thousand dollars of stock to make up for certain past extravagances in New York (visions of gold pieces the eagle and the sun) to use for taxes over here to pay for B's operation to pay for the Wretch's operation (appendicitis) to put into the Black Sun Press (in particular towards The Sentimental Journey and the Liaisons Dangereuses) and told him I hoped that our racehorses would win some good prizes this year but that I never counted on a horse until I saw him cross the finish line anymore than I count on a girl until she is undressed and in bed with me after which I continued my work on the Bible

What is sweeter than honey (Caresse)
What is stronger than a lion (Harry)

and to-day I drank a bottle of red wine and to-day with the help of the New York Telephone Directory and the New York Times I began a poem on New York, I shall call it Madhouse.

January 12. Simplicity—Strength 8 AM a prayer into the Sun, a shave, exercises, a bath, breakfast, work until luncheon (on Madhouse) a fast walk (seventeen minutes) to the Poteau and back, polo-practice on the donkeys and a climb to say prayers from the Sun-Tower more work (the Bible) supper and more work (Madhouse) and so to bed 10 PM.

13. It is early morning I look out my window and see a red wolf shouldering his way through the black trees It is the Sun but when I return from my bath the red wolf has turned into a great gold bird a fire-bird perched on the topmost branches of the tallest tree. At noon when I have climbed to the top of my Sun-Tower to pray the Sun is a great chariot-wheel wheeling across the desert of the sky but in the afternoon when I come back from my walk to the Poteau de Perthe the chariot-wheel has disappeared leaving a red letter-box into which I drop an imaginary letter for New York. Then suddenly it is dark and the Star of the East appears and there is a crying of a loon.

14. Much drinking of red wine and a walk to the Poteau de Perthe and Narcisse chases sheep in the park (he chased them all through the woods and out all over the ice on the pond) and the Star of the East disappeared (in a yellow Hispano) and the Cramoisy Queen appeared (in a cramoisy Coach) and to-day I have repeated a thousand times the word sunfire.

[gold-cramoisy-grey-fire-star]

15. It is snowing. I walk out to the Poteau de Perthe with C and again alone in the afternoon (C had had to go in town again to see Proust about the Proust Letters to see Polia Chentoff about the Sentimental Journey to see Hélène Perdriat about the Liaisons Dangereuses to see the Wretch who has had appendicitis to see K[ay] B[oyle] who has had an abortion) and afterwards to the top of the Sun-Tower to say prayers and to draw our cross

```
        C
        A
   H A R R Y
        E
        S
        S
        E
```

and pictures of the Sun in the snow (I began a poem in the snow but there was not enough space to finish it) and then a mad session of polo practice first on Sunset then on Aurora (much having to beat them but many lumps of sugar afterwards) then a love letter to the Cramoisy Queen then a correcting of the proof sheets of Mad Queen then red wine then a looking into the fire. When I went to bed it was still snowing.

Shadows of the Sun

Love-Letter

Our Moulin du Soleil

Caresse, it is snowing and I want you here with me (do you realize we have never been here alone) and I "desire" you again in all the sweet ways imaginable. I want to lock the door at the foot of the stairs and come running back to kiss and be kissed and to be loving again. I do love you terribly. I feel strong and young and amourous and it is so nice here in front of our fire and I want to belong to you. Anything I said last night is absolutely untrue. It may not always seem so but in the real me, in my inmost sun-centre you will always find yourself my Cramoisy Queen all clothed in Sunfire. No fun being apart only we can never really be apart for you are here curled inside of me. Inseparate (See Sonnets for Caresse).

I walked out again to the Poteau de Perthe. It was snowing and growing very dark. I thought of you all the way, how you looked this morning in your brown skirt (very young) and how you looked up at me when we kissed on going around the post (even younger) and when I got back (nineteen minutes and nineteen seconds) I climbed to the top of our Sun-Tower and drew our cross in the snow

<pre>
            C
            A
      H A R R Y
            E
            S
            S
            E
</pre>

with suns of all sizes to protect us and I wrote "I love you Caresse" in the snow along the ledge all this will be covered by to-morrow but the Prayer I said (very intimate) will be still another acorn of gold waiting for us up there in the Sun.

I want to surprise you, I want to be very gentle, very shy and delicate with you (Knight-Errant and Lady Poet and Queen) with never never a cross word and always my arm around your shoulders to protect you.

Being together one sometimes loses the true sense of values but the moment we are apart my compass needle points strong and steady penetrating straight into your heart (true is the dial to the Sun). There have been magnetic storms but Always the needle has returned seeking its target in your centre.

We must love to-morrow night. (To-night when you read this) no matter whether you are supposed to be taking a rest cure or not. I want to touch you, I want to be strong inside you, belonging to you, making you happy.

Then everything else, every one else will finish and we shall be Alone and One.

I like my body when it is with your body to quote E E C.

You must never again be afraid Beloved because you see you are curled in

my heart all quiet and secure with a wall of the loveliest sun to protect you
and you must never be afraid because you are my Caresse as I am

Your

Harry

January 16. Twice to the Poteau de Perthe AM 18.35.3 PM 17.8.1. and
polo practice on the donkeys during which a great banging on the front gate.
Enter a chauffeur with a superb green Voisin car and it is for sale and I look
at it and buy it for thirty-five thousand francs and then more polo practice
on the donkeys and much work on Mad Queen and then C arrives from
Paris with a bitch-dog that someone wants us to buy but a Voisin is enough
for one day and then C and I climbed to the tower-top and the cross and the
suns I drew yesterday were not obliterated but frozen hard and we kissed
under the Stars and went down and went up and had supper in front of the
fire and at last (it has taken two weeks) I have trained myself to write the
letter O not countersunwise as I used to do but sunwise turning in the
direction the sun turns and to-day in the Bible I came to David and Goliath
"and David put his hand in his bag and took thence a stone and slang it and
smote the Philistine in his forehead that the stone sunk into his forehead and
he fell upon his face to the earth".

17. Fire in the Centre and this is of the utmost importance a tremendous
advance in the development of my soul so that the colors are now grey
cramoisy Fire gold star Fire being the Centre and Alive and forming with the
Sun.

Sunfire

[**18.** I exchange eyes with the Mad Queen
the mirror crashes against my face
and bursts into a thousand suns
all over the city flags crackle and bang
fog horns scream in the harbor. Fire
wind hurricanes through the window
I roar with joy
black-footed ferrets disappear into holes
naked colors explode into red disaster
I crash out the window
naked widespread upon a Heliosaurus
I uproot an obelisk and plunge it
into the ink-pot of the Black Sea
I write the word SUN
across the dreary palimpsest of the world
I pour the contents of the Red Sea
down my throat
I erect catapults and lay siege to
the cities of the world
I scatter violent disorder

throughout the Kingdoms of the world
I stride over mountains
I pick up oceans and spin them
like thin cards into oblivion
I kick down walled cities
I hurl giant firebrands against governments
I thrust torches through the eyes of the law
I annihilate museums
I demolish libraries
I oblivionize skyscrapers
I become strong as battle
hard as adamant
indurated in solid fire
rigid with hatred
I bring back the wizards and the sorcerers
the necromancers
the magicians
I practice witchcraft
I set up idols—
with a sharp-edged sword
I cut through the crowded streets

comets follow me in my wake
stars make obeisance to me
the moon uncovers her nakedness
to me

I am the harbinger of a
    New Sun World
I bring the Seed of a New Copulation
I proclaim the Mad Queen

I stamp out vast empires
I crush palaces in my rigid hands
I harden my heart against churches

I blot out cemeteries
I feed the people with stinging nettles
I resurrect madness
I thrust my naked sword
    between the ribs of the world
I murder the world!]

January 19. [I like dictionaries better than novels—I have an English
Dictionary a Larousse French Dictionary an English-French Dictionary a
Russian-French Dictionary a Dictionary of English Literature Hughes' Dictionary of Islam Collin de Tlaney's Dictionaire Infernal a Chinese Biograph-
ical Dictionary a Dictionary of Phrase and Fable a Rhyming Dictionary a

Slang Dictionary a Dictionary of Archaic and Provincial Words a Magyar Dictionary a Little Green Dictionary a Dictionary of Synonyms and Antonyms a Classical Dictionary of Foreign Quotations a Concordance to Shakespeare a Concordance to the Old and New Testaments and the Apocrypha The Young Folks' Cyclopedia of Common Things The Browning Cyclopedia Bartlett's Familiar Quotations Roget's Thesaurus of English Words and Phrases a book of Synonyms Discriminated a book of Ten Thousand Wonderful Things a book of the Laws of Language and the Encyclopedia Britannica in thirty-five volumes.]

To see CCC she was out and the valet couldn't find any note paper for me all I could see was a piece of blotting-paper and he didn't know where the whiskey was and just then the bell rang and CCC appears and we found the whiskey and afterwards to see the Wretch and C was there and we went to the bar in the Rue de la Chaise for a CC (champagne cocktail) so home and there were people for cocktails Jolas, Allanah Harper, Crouchers, I forget who else, then CC left for London and I went with Jolas to the Deux Maggots where we found Hart Crane and all three of us to Prunier for oysters and anjou then to see CCC and when I got home I read Hart Crane's White Buildings

> ["let thy waves roar
> more savage than the death of kings
> some splintered garland for the seer"]

and to-day is the first day this year I have not walked to the Poteau de Perthe or climbed to the top of my Suntower.

January 20. A Sunday in the city and in the beginning depression but encouraged by reading about Explosives and Fireworks in the Encyclopedia and in the afternoon to see the Wretch (the depression returns) and in the evening CCC appears (the depression vanishes) and we go to Prunier (oysters and Anjou) and afterwards to take pills (black idol) and the most exquisite ambiance "Perfection" a Catherine Wheel beginning with a point of chaste green (the heart of a rose) and developing around and around in larger and larger circles (always green until a revolving Sun burned and revolved in the inmost depths of me) then suddenly the point again then it vanished and I saw a queer Mexican blackened white adder eye staring at me from a distance of a quarter of an inch then the sands of a beach which might have been the Lido (I have never taken opium without being aware of sand) each particle of sand a unity in itself sharp grain of gold millions of millions until one can feel one's brain grow tired then a blank then the sea dark and very calm and to the left a tall tall lighthouse with no gold light dark dark very tall and ghostly and dark always to the left and always the feeling the "sure certainty" that around the corner loomed death a dark and calm Death then a vanishing away and the curtains lifting and parting in the wind and the faint red of the embers in the fireplace and the sound of the shifting of a log and warmth and the knowledge of perfect ambiance and Sleep.

January 21. In a daze [most of the] all day I managed to get up for luncheon (soup with sherry in it in front of the fire) and I bought C at Cartier a diamond guard ring and at tea time Jolas and a man called Noll who seemed to be very depressed (Jolas always dynamic and inspiring) and we talked about Hart Crane and Cummings and in the evening dinner with CCC and to the theatre (Départs) and after the first act to the Cheval Pie to drink beer.

22. Up at six in the morning (still dark) and out in the Voisin in the car (much fog) arriving with half a minute to spare there were many hay wagons coming in from the country which blocked the way only to find that because of the fog the aeroplane would not go therefore a cup of coffee and a telegram (urgent) to C and a returning to Paris and a luncheon with Jolas and Mrs Jolas at a place on the Rue Saint-Dominique and they told me a lot about Joyce how he always made changes and changes at the last moment so that Transition was never on time how his eyes were so bad that he had to use an enormous magnifying glass how he had endless note-books through which he roamed how he was always learning a new language how his mind is like a great vampire reaching out and sucking in all that he desires and transforming it into Work in Progress and to-morrow they are going to Saint Dizier to finish the Winter Number (I hope my Aeronautics and my Sun will look well) and afterwards I walked down the Rue Saint-Dominique and bought a hammer for twelve francs (a marvelous thing with which to kill someone) and so to the hospital to see the Wretch and so to the Galerie Zak to see the Kandinsky Exhibition (some of the things damn good Dynamiques Tendres in particular) then to the Black Sun Press to collect proof sheets for Mad Queen then supper and the forest in the fog and gold champagne and black idol and all the sensations of Alice in Wonderland when she drank from the bottle marked, "Drink me" and grew taller and taller and bigger and bigger so that her head hit the ceiling and her arms went out the window and there was no room in the room and I grew and I grew (Harry Grew Crosby head and shoulders arms and legs torso and phallus) until I was more than frightened and at last a driving together off through the Fog.

23. Hart Crane for luncheon and he says he will let us edit his long poem on the Brooklyn Bridge fragments of which have appeared in the Criterion the Dial and Transition but it is not yet finished (he is thinking of going to Villefranche to finish it) and then he showed me a MSS of poems Blue Juniata by Malcolm Cowley and then the frotteurs came to frotter the floors and they made a great noise and broke a huge glass and I kicked them all out and CCC appeared and we talked in front of the fire and went to look at pictures on the Rue de Seine and at six o'clock I took a hot bath and went to bed and corrected proof sheets for Mad Queen which I have dedicated to

T.N.T.

never so mad a ladye.

January 24. Up at six in the morning—it was still very dark—and in the Voisin out to Le Bourget and this time no fog and at eight o'clock exactly on the dot the chocks were pulled away from the wheels and we took off the twin exhausts spouting their feathers of red flame Altitude 1000 feet Air Speed 90 miles an hour and soon we were over Beaumont and then over the Cathedral of Beauvais then Poix then Abbeville and there are windmills and weathervanes and two men crouching by a hayrick warming their hands over a fire and there is a river reaching a silver arm around a hill (a lover reaching his arm around his lady-love and the trees on the hill are her hair) and there are fields like brown canvases on which I draw pictures in red with the finger of my imagination and we are flying over a cemetery the tombstones like lumps of sugar or else like cigarette butts tossed aside by the twin fingers of the steeples and there is a peasant ploughing a narrow field (a man ploughing a woman) who stops and turns and looks up at us his face the size of a white pinpoint and below us a silver pond in the form of a horseshoe (water in a giant hoof print) and to the right there is a train a long puff puff powder—puff of white smoke dancing dancing like ballet-girls and now we are approaching the Channel we are over Le Touquet and the empty race course and there is a little black fishing smack chug chugging up the river and we are over the shore line "to throw a thin faint line upon the shore" and I understand the bravery of a lighthouse facing the cold wintry sea and we pass through a tempest of sleet and over a freighter directly below (it must be fun to drop bombs) then the dim outline of chalk cliffs and in another moment we are flying over England while back of us a smoky fulminating Sun crashes through the angry clouds and now we are over Dungeness speeding speeding over rivulets zigzaging like flashes of silver lightning over fine ponds of silver fire over toy trains over crows swarming like black rats over the churches and houses of Lympne over a green dray wagon creaking along like a slow thought over a red car speeding like a swift thought along the Main Road over stationary cows over a red barn over railroad tracks stretching like the black threads of a fishermen's net (and the houses of the country side are the captured fish and the Sun the fisherman drawing them up into his ship of gold) then Croyden and a sudden sharp bank and a sharp descent and the first faint shock to resume connection with the earth and this is England and the coffee is wretched but soon C appears in a Rolls-Royce accompanied by a little whippet-bitch (Clytoris) for Narcisse and we open a bottle of champagne I had brought over, twenty minutes later the Silver Wings took off for Paris (13 on board including the two pilots and the barman) (fourteen if we count Clytoris—her English name is Abbingdon Faithful [*but Clytoris is so much more intimate!*]) and we pass over Lympne and through a flurry of snow and soon the barman (after pouring us a drink of straight gin diamond-coloured as the silver wings diamond colored as the diamond ring I give to C) is scrawling in chalk on the piece of black wood Now Over Dungeness and the Sun pours gold on the Silver Wings and the exhausts pour twin flames of fire and back of us I see a red hawk of an aeroplane hurtling through space in pursuit now a red hawk now hidden by a sheet of cloud now visible again nearer and nearer and we are over the Channel (the white caps are like white mice) and the speedometer needle finger is scratching 101 and we are drawing away from the red hawk. We are the Bird in Space! Then France below us the fields like a pack of cards flung at random on the table of land with hayricks and barns and bonfires and ponds for markings and the dunes are left behind as camels are left behind by the eagle and even the express train whose gold plume thrusts through the heart of the dark forest is left behind and even the red hawk is nowhere in sight and we are hurtling through space Now Over Abbeville on the black-board and out again over square fields over oblong fields over fields in triangles and rhomboids and parellelograms the Sun to our West and our shadow pursuing us like a giant bird and the curves of the road below us is like the curves of a person's handwriting and there is an orange-colored farmhouse and a red bonfire in a black wood (coeur de négresse) and it is two o'clock and we are a thousand feet high and we are flying o a hundred miles an hour. Then the Aérodrome of Le Bourget directly below and down we come to alight as gracefully as a Stork and we taxi up to the shed and step out and Clytoris is extricated from the cockpit and we pass through the customs (100 francs duty on Clytoris) and we drive back in the Voisin to Paris my ears ringing with the noise of engines.

January 25. Hart Crane for luncheon and a long talk on poets and sailors he is of the Sea as I am of the Sun and to-day I put the finishing touches to Mad Queen and to-day I read in my book of Etymology "la forès estoit hisdouse et faée" "the forest was grisly and enchanted". What Forest? The Forest of the Sun.

26. At six to the Black Sun Press to sign the bon à tirer for Mad Queen [a book of explosions if there ever was one] and then out through the snowstorm C and I and the Crouchers Narcisse and Clytoris to the Moulin and hard going all the way and it was bitter cold I sat out in front and I thought of the Silver Wings as we past Le Bourget a red signal light flashing and flashing and red lights along the edges of the field and I thought of that night Lindberg arrived (ce n'est pas un homme c'est un oiseau) and then on and on our gold headlights devouring the long flakes of snow the trees black black along the side of the road but in my soul red fire mad and fiery as I thought of "I would like to die giving you a child suffering for you" and then we came to the lights of Senlis and took the road to the right and at last the Woods all silver and chaste and the Moulin and the gold of fire and after supper to the Poteau de Perthe a silver moon almost as white as day and then branches all crusted with snow crisp and faery-like and the Poteau as white as a virgin thought and when we got back we climbed to the tower top and I rubbed snow on my face and prayed through the moon into the Invisible Sun and so to bed after drinking a bottle of red wine.

27. A day of clean fresh air and walking through the woods and climbing to the tower top and riding on the donkeys [(*C and I raced all the way back* *on them from the Pôteau I won by employing the hammer as whip but even so much slower than walking)]* and eating raisins and drinking red wine and looking into the red gold of the fire Sunfire.

January 28. The Crouchers rushed off and missed their first train. The Crouchers rushed off and missed their second train. The Crouchers rushed off.

C and I and Narcisse and Clytoris to the Poteau de Perthe (twice) and the Sun-Tower (a firing off of the cannon) and writing and drawing in front of the fire and a toasting of marshmallows.

29. Read again that wonderful last paragraph from Anna Livia Plurabelle "Can't hear with the waters of the chittering waters of, Flittering bats, fieldmice bawk talk" and threw snowballs from the tower at the donkeys down below in the courtyard and scored two direct hits (Sunset and Sunrise) and drew mad pictures of the Sun on the frosted window-panes and fired the noon-salute with the cannon and walked twice to the Poteau de Perthe with C and drank red wine and wrote to the youngest Princess and looked for a long long time into the red-gold of the Fire drawing the strength of the fire the cruelty the color the aliveness into the center of my soul Sunfire.

February 1. Wrote Infuriate annihilate assassinate infuriate yourself against the herd prognosticate the Bird of Sun take cardiac and aphrodisiac be maniac demoniac run towards the Maddest Queen precipitate yourself through Stars to find your Dream.

2. Le Moulin Hart Crane here and much drinking of red wine and he reads aloud from Tamburlaine and he is at work on his long poem The Bridge and CCC arrives with a goose and I made fire-oblations by throwing glasses of red wine into the fire and there was a goddess in the flame and her name was Trinitrotoluol.

3. Mob for luncheon—poets and painters and pederasts and lesbians and divorcées and Christ knows who and there was a great signing of names on the wall at the foot of the stairs and a firing off of the cannon and bottle after bottle of red wine and Kay Boyle made fun of Hart Crane and he was angry and flung the American Caravan into the fire because it contained a story of Kay Boyle's (he forgot it had a poem of his in it) and there was a tempest of drinking and polo harra burra on the donkeys and an uproar and confusion so that it was difficult to do my work on the Bible.

4. To Paris C and I LV KB ED and rum grogs on the way I stuck to my red wine resolution and we drove up the road exhaust wide open scarfs crackling in the wind and we ran into a ditch so that it took four percherons to drag us out and then we went off in the wrong direction so that we didn't get to Paris until four—six hours to do what ordinarily takes an hour and a half the hare and the tortoise and the Cutty Sark whisky has arrived from Berry Brothers "we know how good the whisky is and we have no doubt whatever that it will meet with your entire satisfaction" and there was a bill for designing the sun on our tombstone (I thought I had paid it) and there were fire-words from the Fire-Princess.

February 6. Heavy fog over Paris and there was an explosion in the electric plant so there were no electric lights and everyone rushed out to buy candles there was immediately a shortage and I went to see Sylvia Beach to ask her if Joyce would be willing to let us edit a fragment of his Work in Progress and coming home I bought candles of all sorts and sizes in the candleshop on the Rue Saint-Sulpice and I came home through the Rue Princesse (I wish we lived on the Rue Princesse or that the Rue de Lille was called the Rue Princesse) and I went to a picture show but it was too dark to see any of the pictures and I went and bought a Rimbaud signature and a Rimbaud letter and it made me want to reduce my Library to one hundred books I have about twenty seven hundred now and Hart Crane came to tea and he gave us the MSS of his O Carib Isle (one of the five best poems of our generation) and so into a hot bath into a hot bed (we had three hot water-bottles) and a reading of Blake's Marriage of Heaven and Hell "no bird soars too high if he soars with his own wings".

9. Le Moulin—spent the afternoon with C shooting at a wretched oil painting done of us long ago (C won with a direct hit in the brain in the nose in the eye I scoring a direct hit in her heart)—after which donkey races around the house with much shrieking of harra burra and much flogging with whips and sticks harraburra harraburra.

10. Snowstorm—Hart Crane and the Jolases arrive Croucher arrives and there was a great drinking of red wine and the Empty Bed Blues on the graphaphone and a magnificent snowball fight and we rode donkeys and we pulled the old stagecoach out into the centre of the courtyard and a mob for supper and I take a lantern and walked out through the storm to the Pôteau de Perthe and on the way back I stumbled on a tree that had fallen across the path since I had passed by and the gold eye of my lantern threw giant shadows against the trees my legs like great pistons forward forward with precision and when I got back the wild mob had left [there were bottles upset graphaphone tuner and glasses all smashed to bits candles guttering in the sockets].

11. Paris and a thorough weeding out of books—a library must be weeded every so often like a flower-garden and to-day I weeded out seven hundred weed-books so that now the library is reduced to two thousand books which is still a thousand too many. But to think that last spring there were ten thousand—now at last one can breathe.

12. Intense cold—the coldest I have ever known it in France and all the pipes are frozen and bed is the only nice place in the world—nevertheless we got up and went with Croucher and the Jolases to see Gertrude Stein and she was terribly nice (reminded me a little of what Amy Lowell must have been like) and I have never seen such Picassos the one of the nude girl holding up a basket of fruit, the one of Gertrude Stein (someone once reproached Picasso that the portrait didn't look like her—"it will" he said) and there was a Juan Gris and a remarkable Cézanne (portrait of his wife) and we met a young painter called Kristan Tonny (he had an exhibition in Paris when he was eight years old) and Croucher showed his pictures of New York and then we went to Kay Boyle's and Laurence Vail's and he gave C a marvelous picture called Explosion.

February 14. No food to-day only milk and we went to Evelyn's there were too many people there and I was cold so I went in and took a hot bath and drank a bottle of red wine in the hot bath so home and to bed and I forgot to say that to-day we bought a painting by Tonny at an exhibition on the Rue de Berri and a sun-dial at Mercator and to-day a Valentine for us from KB and LV [—*LV did the painting KB did the poetry*].

18. I was reading Joyce aloud when I heard the gurgle of the bath running out—at last the pipes are unfrozen at last we can take a fresh bath (we have been bathing in the same water for six days) and at last at last spring is here La Primavera.

26. Party on the Boat—Kay Boyle Laurence Vail Evelyn Nada Carlos Hart Crane a Dolly Sister Croucher H and C Etcetera Etcetera and Hart Crane tattooed his face with encre de chine and little Masie Mousie little Mousie Masie was afraid of all the people and the D.S. was the Lady of the Nombril and there was champagne and music and I was glad for a pill of black idol and there were cascades of diamond clouds crashing over a mountain of emerald the spray of the clouds flew off like sea-gulls and there were silver stars done up in red ribbons and a giant crane swinging iron baskets of orange suns and there was a catapulting through tunnels of delirium into a bed of fire.

28. Diamond Necklace for C!

March 1. Flew to Croyden to get the diamond necklace (a thousand dollars saved by having it sent over and going over to get it in England) and drank down my flask of Cutty Sark Whisky and flew back to Paris—the Bird in Flight above the bric à brac of life—the diamond necklace around my neck like a chain of fire—and we are the first generation to get our feet off the ground we leave the ground we fly we soar we catapult into Sun while the engines roar ya-hoo ya-hoo ya-hoo ya-hoo and the wind hurricanes and we balance on the breast of the sky like a diamond on the breast of a woman and I see the sun through the whirling propellor wheels whirling whirling and I see the land below she is the mistress of the sun her hair is a black forest her eyes are lakes her arms are the roads her legs the rivers her smile is a village her breasts are the hills her teeth are the tombstones of a cemetery her nose is a locomotive snorting white puffs of smoke towards the sun her heart is a red factory her draperies the undulating folds of the fields the channel is her bathtub the sun her desire the sun covers her with gold, kisses the hills which are her breasts, burns away the shadows of her hair.

March 3. In February drank only red wine except for one glass of champagne in the middle of the month—a gold sun on a string of red stars but to-day drank sherry and champagne and a glass of Cutty Sark and Hart Crane appears and talks about sailors and hurricanes and about the Bridge and about how Otto Kahn gave Crane money so that he could write the Bridge and to-day Short Stories by Kay Boyle is being completed by the Black Sun Press and again I say that Kay Boyle is the greatest woman writer since Jane Austen.

4. Monday—a grey day and I go for my walk (I have a wonderful walk it takes forty minutes) along the quays from the foot of the Rue des Saints-Pères down along the real quays (not up along the bookstall quays) under the bridges the Pont Neuf the Pont St-Michel the Pont de l'Archevêché the Pont de la Tournelle until I come to the new bridge connecting the Isle St-Louis with the Quay de la Tournelle then back again and there are barges and tug-boats and cobblestones and queer people (no bourgeois here) and up above on the quays the roar of traffic—a real walk and much the best walk in Paris—Four o'clock and a glass of Cutty Sark then with C to see Joyce on a little cul de sac street off the Rue de Grenelle and he was sitting in a chair in the middle of a small salon with the French translation of Ulysses (vient de paraître) at his feet—his wife sat opposite him on the sofa—there was his son there was his daughter in a blue sweater—he spoke to them in Italian—there was the proprietor of the Trianon Restaurant where he has eaten for eight years there was a rug presented to him by Marie Monnier which symbolized the rivers in Anna Livia Plurabelle—there was the dining room where he and I and C talked about editing a fragment of his Work in Progress the Apologue and Fable of the Mookes and the Gripes—and we suggested that Picasso might do a portrait of him to go in the book. We stayed an hour and he showed us the carpet woven by Marie Monnier and he showed us his picture by Wyndam Lewis (I like the Becat one we saw at that exhibition two or three years ago much much better) and we talked about Borsch the oculist who died last month and about MacLeish (who had sent Joyce a case of wine for Christmas) and we met his son and his daughter (in a blue sweater) and he talked of his suit-case full of note books and he remembered the Anabase I had sent him two or three years ago and he kept asking do you think Picasso will do my portrait and then he talked to us of his Work in Progress [*of how the first part was retrospective of how the second part represented shadows of how the third part is what takes place in sleep and the fourth part which was going to take place in an inn or something like that I did not quite understand. And now for the contract with Sylvia Beach*].

9. Built a bonfire and burned eighty copies of Red Skeletons a rotten book. There were four copies left and these we shot full of bullet holes—they made a very nice target. Took forty-eight photographs to-day I like taking pictures very very close up I took a picture of C's right eye of her mouth of the sun shining down her throat of the tip end of her breast (bout de la mamelle) of the toes of her left foot Etcetera and to-day races on the donkeys and to-day I read Tamburlaine "Threatening the world with high astounding terms. And scourging Kingdoms with his conquering sword".

March 13. C goes to see Baker the clairvoyant he tells her without asking any questions that she was born in 1892 that she has been married twice (two children by the first marriage) that it is important for her to be faithful to me that I like a girl whose first name began with a C [(Constance)] that I AM[1]* a genius but difficult to live with but that in the next three years she is going to harvest the seeds she has sown during the difficult years that she likes a man whose first name begins with A [(*Armand*)] that I have not begun to write the things that I AM[1] going to write that she will live to be seventy-seven.[2] Good Omens.

14. The Count for luncheon—it was his seventy-ninth birthday (he was born before Rimbaud) and we had a cake for him and we opened a bottle of champagne and to-day I read a critical essay on Blake of his resolve to soar (which was natural to him) and not to walk (which was unnatural and repulsive) and of how he was an exceedingly impulsive and in a certain sense a violent man—always vehement and unmeasured. I am influenced most by the Fire-Princess, by Rimbaud, by Blake, by Aknaton, by Van Gogh, by Marlowe.

15. D. H. Lawrence for luncheon and we disagreed on everything. I am a visionary I like to soar he is all engrossed in the body and in the mushroom quality of the earth and the body and in the complexities of psychology. He is indirect. I am direct. He admits of defeat. I do not. [*He is commonplace. I am not. He is unthoroughbred. I am thoroughbred. He was "seedy" looking how I hate the word "seedy". I guess he is a sick man I forgive him a great deal because of* The Plumed Serpent *but I can see no excuse for writing* Lady Chatterly's Lover. *That is why*] he is here in Paris to try to get someone to publish *Lady Chatterley's Lover.* There have already been several pirated editions both in France and in America where Lawrence doesn't get one cent of benefice. An editor who can do that is a skunk. Lawrence stayed until four attacking my visionary attitude but my fort withstood the bombardment and I marshalled my troops and sallied out to counter-attack all of which took time so that I was not able to go out to the opening of the flat races at Maisons Laffite where I wanted to see the Lady of the Gold Horse and watch The Arrow win at seven to one I had a thousand on her to win.

18. Out to the races at Saint-Cloud a warm orange sun of an afternoon and I lost on Irish Marvel (second) whom I should not have played (I was persuaded by the bookmaker—one should never listen to anyone unless it is to a Rimbaud or a Blake) and I lost on Mauretania (second) and while the Lady of the Gold Horse ran around looking at horses and betting I sat in the

---

*Notes for Volume Three begin on p. 289.

sun on a bench way off down the lawn and continued to read the essay [*by W. M. Rossetti*] on Blake ("his attitude was always that of an inspired seer—the thing was so because he saw it so and he saw it so not by a bodily and argumentative eye but by a spiritual and intuitional one") stopping every half hour to gaze into the Sun and to look through my field glasses at the horses as they swept round the last curve and supper with the Lady of the Gold Horse and black idol and gold champagne.

March 19. I have begun to go down to the boat again—wonderful atmosphere and Frans is doing a portrait of Erik Doll (Erik Doll was standing on the deck in a top hat when we arrived—he had been to a funeral or was it a wedding) and May was sewing a lace pantalon and there was red wine and remains of the duck we had had for supper the other night (I forgot to say what a mad time we had at the Grand Ecart the Lady of the Gold Horse never looked lovelier) and Frans introduced me to a friend of his called Sim who writes dime novels (five novels a month—he dictates them) and I sat at May's desk and wrote a letter to the Fire-Princess.

20. I lose five thousand francs on the races (Sun-Goddess, Silkiness, La Simonetta, Princess Mad, Red Sun) and I go to the boat to drink champagne with May (we played the graphaphone) and when I got home a letter from Sylvia Beach to say we can have the Joyce (we are going to sign the contract on Monday) and this evening just before starting out for the Moulin (C and I and Frans and May) the Zorn Etching I have looked and looked for for so long arrived from London It is Jacqueline the Grey Princess.

Valkulla

25. Read again Une Saison en Enfer "Et à l'aurore armé d'une ardente patience nous entrerons aux splendides villes".

26. Foch's Funeral. At ten o'clock C and I went down to the Boat and persuaded Frans to crank up the little scooter (May refused to come said she was too timid—she stuck her blonde head out the window and waved goodbye). We scooted down to the Pont de l'Alma and tied up to the rive gauche and climbed up an iron ladder on the quays. C and Frans climbed up on a pyramid of gravel while I spent twenty minutes persuading a workman to let me climb to the top of an iron crane (une grue I think they call it in French). He absolutely refused not even for fifty francs would he let me. But he weakened for a hundred and so it was I climbed to the top clinging to the iron girders of the crane there was no ladder and I was frightened and felt dizzy. I remember hearing people in the crowd shouting bravo plus haut plus haut. And here I clung precariously higher up than the tops of the trees with a splendid view looking right down on the bridge. All around there were people on the quays on the streets on the bridge in the tree-tops on the tops of taxicabs on the roof tops cannon were firing salutes somewhere there was a blare of trumpets then appeared the head of the cortege and there were

French infantry with bayonets flashing in the Sun but soon there was fog and the lamps were lit on the bridge and then appeared the English Grenadiers with their red uniforms and their black busbies and there were mounted Spahis the horses' tails knotted with crêpe bows and there were Czecho-Slovakian troops and Italian troops and the clergy in their scarlet robes and Foch's horse riderless covered with a black pall studded with silver stars and then came the artillery caisson carrying the coffin which was draped with the French Flag and as it passed out of sight I said to myself this is the end of the war and it began to grow cold and my legs were cramped by the iron girders and I was glad to get down again my suit ruined by black grease and my hands and face black as a negroes. And so in the scooter back to the foot of the Rue des Saints-Pères where Frans left us. And I would rather have seen the Arrival of Lindberg than the Funeral of Foch. But I would rather be Rimbaud (if I had to be someone else which I would hate "the utter impossibility of any one soul feeling itself inferior to any other soul"—Edgar Poe) than either of these two.

March 27. With C to see Joyce. It is definitely decided that our Black Sun Press is to bring out the three fragments from the Work in Progress. He showed us the corrections and additions he is making since it came out in Transition I hope that Picasso can be persuaded to do a drawing of Joyce but I doubt it [3] [*he is almost inaccessible*] (C went to see Christian Zervos this morning and he told her that Picasso is going through a "crise morale" and that he won't see even his best friends). [I also hope that Sullivan will write an Introduction] Joyce seemed very blind and he knocked into the tea table trying to show us the painting of his father by an Irishman called Thohey who has also painted Joyce and his son. He said that a woman who had translated Virginia Woolf into French wanted to translate this Work in Progress but that after ten minutes she was convinced of the impossibility of such an undertaking. Joyce then asked me to read aloud one of the passages we are going to edit "Can you not do her, numb? asks Dolph, suspecting the answer Know. I cont, ken you, ninny? asks Kev, expecting the answer guess" whereupon Joyce explains this passage and I realize how ignorant I am from the scholastic point of view and how sane a writer is Joyce. He spoke of Roth that skunk who published Ulysses altering the text and paying Joyce nothing and telling the public he had paid him a large sum of money (I am glad to hear he is in prison) and he spoke of XYZ (he didn't say his name) an American publisher who appeared one day from America with a cheque made out to Joyce and a book which he said he had printed at his own expense containing the Work in Progress as far as it had gone and that he had had it copyrighted in his not Joyce's name. He must have felt very cheap when Joyce declined his offer. Joyce was very nice and signed our copy of the first edition of Ulysses in the magnificent blue binding and as we were leaving he asked if he couldn't do it up in a package so he brought out some pink wrapping and we did it up, and took it home with us. I liked the painting of his father I liked the way Joyce pronounced the word "stick" and I liked most the flash of triumph when C asked him how much he enjoyed doing this new work, the same flash of triumph as when one is sleeping with a woman one loves, the same flash of triumph when one bets high on a horse and sees him gallop past the winning-post a winner, and to-day Red Sun won (that is his stable companion won) and I won ten thousand francs. Almost enough to pay for Valkulla.

March 29. The D. H. Lawrences come out to the Moulin. He wanders in the field picking flowers. I pray from my sun-tower into the setting sun. Caresse plants tulips. Freida (Mrs. Lawrence) walks in the wood. At suppertime in front of the fire I played the graphaphone James Joyce reading aloud from Ulysses and after listening to it Lawrence said Yes I thought so a preacher a Jesuit preacher who believes in the cross upsidedown. And how he hated the Empty Bed Blues. And how he was shocked when I gave a dissertation in favor of la morsure in love-making. We disagree on a great many things but I am not afraid to attack and attack and my firetroops are alive and furious—no mercy shewn to the wounded no prisoners taken no fort left standing.

30. A basking in the sun and a wandering through the woods. Frieda and Lorenzo in the yellow donkeycart C astride the little donkey I on foot. And the return to the fire and little or no attacking or counter-attacking and the Lawrences described their life in New Mexico on the ranch and their life in Australia on the sea-coast and their life in the villa near Florence. Apparently if he ever goes back to England he will be put in prison (on account of Lady Chatterley's Lover) and in New York there have already been three pirated editions of this book they even forge his signature—too disgusting but the book itself is so poor that I have very little interest in its fate. Not like The Ladybird.   Not like The Plumed Serpent. [4]

31. Easter, and Lawrence and I drove over in the car to Chantilly to look at Gin Cocktail and Sunstroke and at suppertime around the fire he began to talk of a new unpublished book of his called The Escaped Cock about the wanderings of Jesus after his resurrection and of how he met a priestess of Isis in a little temple on the coast of Phoenicia and how they lived together and how this is the missing link in the history of the Christ and C and I are excited and we offer to bring this book out at our Black Sun Press and all the candles burned low and guttered and went out and we looked into the redgold of the fire and it was like a conspiracy.

April 1. In to Paris and I read Une Saison En Enfer and I believe that Rimbaud is the greatest poet of them all—bow down ye Shelleys ye Keatses ye Byrons ye Baudelaires ye Whitmans for you have met your Master and I am glad the first quarter of the year is over—if we can hold the pace it will be a good year.

2. Made my Last Will and Testament.

April 3. Exhausting [5] day. D. H. Lawrence appears to be sculpted by Caresse. Frieda appears with Aldous Huxley and the typewritten sheets of The Escaped Cock and there is a discussion about Joyce. C and I pro-Joyce Lawrence and Huxley anti-Joyce and I proclaim the Word itself the Word is a talent of gold but it is a friendly discussion this time (no need to call out my shock-troops) and there was tea and glasses of sherry and then C and I rushed off to the lawyers on the Place Vendôme where we met Joyce and drew up the contract for us three to sign. How I despise lawyers—they waste so damn much time and their bird-brains are spotted with technicalities. Afterwards Joyce went with C to the Black Sun Press (he didn't want to meet Lawrence—said his eye hurt him—he is very timid) and I went home and the Jolases appeared and we discussed the future of transition [and I agree to stand back of it and to become an associate editor and our] policy to be based on Une Saison En Enfer, a policy of revolution of attack, of the beauty of the word for itself, of experiment in painting, in photography, in writing, of a tremendous campaign against the Philistines, of explosions into a Beyond, and then we all four went to Pruniers to eat oysters and drink anjou and to-day I won eighty dollars on Narcotic and four hundred dollars on Fire-Crest.

4. Party with the Countess baccardi cocktails champagne black idol and the coming home along the river in the rain. Little Barbara-Jane to carry up the staircase in the rain.

5. S V R C arrives from America (he is looking younger than ever) and Lord L arrives from London and after luncheon we all go to Patou's where S V R C buys C a dress—we all drank free Gin fizzes at the bar and I felt better but I mustn't take any more of those opium pills they play hell with one and the model known as Helen of Troy was there (we asked her out to the Moulin) and Ginetta by Gin and Miss Etta appeared she was just back from Spain where she had been in the bull-ring with Del Monte and there were dresses and dresses and dresses only about one out of twenty attractive (like people) and I spent most of the time reading in a book S V R C gave me about the Sun-Gazer who sits all day glaring at the blazing sun whose fiery rays have burned out his eyes long years ago "Each morning as I floated down the sacred stream I saw this sun-gazer being carried down the steps to his accustomed place on the Dasashwamedh Ghat. His brothers placed him down gently—he could not walk as his legs had withered away from years of inactivity—and turned his face towards the East. Slowly he opened his eyes to greet the morning sun as it raised its burning head over the temple tops of the Holy City here he remained the whole day with his wide staring eyes fastened on the blazing sun without once turning them away or closing them for an instant until the dying disc had sunk once more below the horizon. He had been doing this for fifteen years".

6. Hargreaves breaks all records five fillings in fifteen minutes and a signing of the Joyce contract and a going away in the car to the country—a luncheon at the Gargantua C and I SVRC Lord L and the soi-disant Helen of Troy and much drinking of red wine and the Countess arrives in her yellow Hispano and we all go to the Moulin for walks to the Poteau de Perthe and polo on the donkeys and for me prayers from the suntower into the setting Sun.

April 7. Gin-Cocktail races at Longchamp twenty-five horses ran and although he ran in fourth place until the last turn he finished nowhere and I lost on Gin-Cocktail and on Kantar and on Palais Royal and on Morning Sunny and on Torchbearer and to-night in Leaves of Grass I read "O you and me at last—and us two only" and this is I burning into the Goddess of the Sun.

9. Nina for tea. She also like Constance asked if the picture in the silver frame (of the Fire-Princess) was my sister because we look so much like each other. But when she saw who it was she began to criticize the way her hair was done. I took the picture and walked out of the house. [This is the end of Nina.]

10. After an attempt last year and another one this year I finally launch myself into Walt Whitman and am rewarded for after reading over a hundred pages neither good nor bad I come to this Poem which expresses exactly how I feel towards those who love me

"Whoever you are, holding me now in hand,
Without one thing, all will be useless,
I give you fair warning, before you attempt me further,
I am not what you supposed but far different.
Who is he that would become my follower?
The way is suspicious—the result uncertain perhaps destructive
You would have to give up all else—I alone would expect to be your Sun-
God, sole and exclusive,
Your novitiate would even then be long and exhausting
The whole past theory of your life, and all conformity to the lives around
you would have to be abandoned;
Therefore release me now, before troubling yourself any further
—Let go your hand from my shoulder
Put me down, and depart on your way."

[11. My new book I shall call Torchbearer]

15. Joyce here to correct proof sheets from 5-9. We had an enormous electric light bulb so that he could see. In the middle of the session the fuse blew out. I took a great many notes. The New Word the deformation and reformation of old words is as exciting as a horse race which reminds me that to-day I won on Argonaute.

19. A sun-bask naked on the de Geetere boat. I feel like a target pierced by the arrows of the Sun. At cocktail hour Joyce appeared. He would not accept one. Said his favorite drink was Muscadet white wine. We didn't have any. More correcting of proof sheets. The four cardinal points of the Work In Progress are the thunderclap the marriage by auspices the burial of the dead the divine providence. Joyce is stimulating and I feel the disc of my mind whirring out a glory of sparks. As he was going downstairs I showed him the skeleton and asked if he was superstitious. Only of deaf-mutes he said. He always asks where Narcisse is. We keep him locked up in the bathroom because I think he makes him nervous. I remembered to give him the Dictionary of Old English Slang. After which a hurried getting dressed for dinner and a rushing out in the car to get S V R C and so to Carlos' C and I S V R C Evelyn and Carlos and another woman. Much too much vodka. Just before midnight C and I to the Jungle to drink gin fizzes and dance to good jazz.

April 20. C's birthday. Four orchids. We rush to Joyce's I feeling like hell from the vodka and gin fizzes and all morning we correct proof sheets with him. He showed me Max Eastman's Essay called the Cult of Unintelligibility in the April Harper's. I shall answer it in the next number of transition. More taking of notes, more amazement at the Mind of Joyce. At one o'clock to the Moulin, I trembling like an aspen leaf (fever and chills). Sat by the fire all afternoon except for a struggle to the Poteau de Perthe and a climb to my Sun-Tower where C and I drank a little bottle of champagne in the setting sun. This as a prayer for her happiness on her birthday—and for Always.

23. Cocktail Party for S V R C. About fifty people. I still feel very weak . . . I did not drink anything. Difficult for me not to drink when other are drinking. Sat in front of the fire in the bathroom with Pepo. He brought us back from the Argentine a magnificent fur designed in the shape of the sun the centre in light fur then two circles of dark fur and rays of white and black fur. C C C at the party. Never saw her looking worse so different from the afternoon we kissed goodbye in Bodega's. She has been loosing heavily at the races. Women are wretched gamblers.

30. S V R C leaves. We had luncheon Chez Fouquet's and afterwards went to see Napoleon's Tomb—he never misses that visit—then to the Gare Saint-Lazare where we drank goodbye on the platform in a little bottle of Napoleon Brandy smashing the glass for good luck when we had finished. And so another goodbye (life is a procession of goodbyes) and the last quick flash of a look and behold I am out in the centre of the whirlwind of the street.

May 1. Your ears are the tiny slippers for the feet of my voice. This is the beginning of a poem I have begun and out to the races with Carlos. I win on Camors I lose on Eversharp and I come home and take a hot bath and get into bed to begin my essay on the Moderns. I shall call it Observation Post.

3. C spends the morning with Picasso I with Joyce. Picasso told her he wouldn't do a portrait of Joyce because he never did portraits any more but

that sometime he would do a drawing for the Black Sun Press. He showed her his latest paintings and told her that she could see those beach scenes painted at Dinard in the summer of 1928 at Rosenberg's. He also said that he and Madame Picasso would come out to the Moulin for the bull-fight. Before C left he went to get his child to bring him to see Narcisse. C said that as she went downstairs the entire Picasso family were leaning over the bannisters waving goodbye. [*Joyce or Picasso which would I rather be?*] Joyce this morning was feeling very poorly—he had been working terribly hard on the three fragments for the Black Sun Press, he has a cold, he is nervous because his daughter is dancing this afternoon in a public performance at the Femina and he has to go to it. He has added a multitude of corrections one of which took him three days to write. This has even Flaubert beaten. A difficult mathematical sentence with the clue at the end (the word Finish to show that the words in the sentence are of Finnish derivation). [*I shalln't go into details as all this work I refer to in Observation Post—The life C and I are leading is most stimulating*]

May 4. En repos at the Moulin C and I are a little like the shock troops in the War who were often en repos because they often attacked.

5. Ivresse at 18-1 finished in a dead heat with Souk Ahras at Longchamp and I won 9000 francs. But il faut dire that I lost on Soleil and on Herakles and on Golden Arrow and on Eversharp. However plus five for the day is not bad. Did not see the races as we came in from the country straight to the house where I found a letter from MacLeish which made me glad because he said nice things about Transit of Venus and praise from a man like MacLeish means something I should rather have a sincere word from him than a thousand and one laudatory effusions from the average critic for the average critic always reminds me of the man who said that he was never intensely excited (sexually) except when a spectator at a funeral. I quote from M's letter "I think you have got hold of something valuable in Transit of Venus I think also that the valuable thing you have got hold of (and this is almost always the case) is a by-product of the thing you were most after. To be precise I am not convinced that your device of the incompleted phrase is what you want. It gives you some good effects but it is very voulu. On the other hand you hit upon a kind of true brevity in those and other poems. And that brevity is signed with your name. Thus in Nor Look Behind. And Last Contact regardless of anything is a good poem. I mean on any scale. And passages I think beautiful are in the end of Eventuate, the fine Shakespeare run of Forecast, the magnificent second phrase of We Are One. There are of course others. These most. I think you have learned the smell of your own flesh. I think you should be well satisfied with where you are going". (The Sun).

6. Finished Observation-Post and went with C to see Brancousi The Bird in Space The Torse de Jeune Femme. The Tête de la Princesse X . . . which the French authorities refused to allow to be shown. The bastards! It was raining. I was a little frightened having to ask him if he would do another picture for the Joyce book (the one he has done is not enough in advance and therefore takes away from the preface by Ogden and the text). He was very nice about it said he hated to do things to order and that he had thought we meant him simply to draw a likeness of Joyce but that if given absolute freedom he would create a new thing. Much shaking of hands and C and I out through the rain to Rosenberg's to see the Picasso's Ninety thousand francs he wanted for the two beach scenes (the girls playing at ball and the men playing at ball) and he would not sell them apart. Il a raison. When I think of some of the women I know spending this amount at the dressmaker's or some of the men I know spending this for a bigger and better touring car I think they are not so wise as they think. Well Harry then why don't you buy them yourself. For one and only one reason because it would hurt my father's feelings so much if I were to sell any more stock I would rather own these two pictures than any paintings I know. They represent Picasso at better than his best—they are as chaste and naive as a religious painting by an Italian primitif and they have the freshness and erotic innocence of a poem by Cummings. They are as certain of enduring as a Shakespeare play or a painting by Leonardo and I should rather have them than a painting by Leonardo and I say this is no spirit of detracting from Leonardo. Afterwards we went to Cuvillier to buy Joyce a bottle of Irish Whisky then I walked home with Narcisse down along the quays in the rain while C went off to Ronald Davis' to buy the first edition of Rimbaud's Saison En Enfer for my birthday next June.

May 7. Yesterday I lost on Tornado to-day on Heliotaure but I am still ahead for the year (I love horse-racing) and this afternoon I went to take photographs of the Foire in front of the Invalides and I paid one franc to see a woman whose mother slept with an ourang-outang (she was covered with coarse hair and monstrous welts—she kept combing the hair on her legs with a red comb I was alone in the tent and felt very self-conscious) and another franc to see a liontamer insert his head between the jaws of a lion while a man beat on a drum and the crowd applauded. Quel métier! And at eight to Cuvillier to meet C C C (the first time since our quarrel) and we drank baccardi cocktails and talked about horseracing and later on drank a bottle of champagne.

8. C went to Reims to visit La Marquise and I stayed in bed all day (it was raining dehors) putting my note-books in order and preparing for future poems. Got up at six and went to the bar in the Rue du Bac to read on the ticker that Mad Queen was beaten and so across the Tuileries to Bodegas and a glass of champagne and so to the movies with La Jeune Fille du Relieur. She is not sortable. Still raining when I got home.

9. To Longchamp to bet on Amor in the second race couldn't find the bookmaker anywhere and hadn't a sou in my pockets so I had to go through the painful ordeal of seeing Amor at four to one win by two lengths. Hells-

Shadows of the Sun

bells! Went over to the pelouse and lay in the grass in the Sun and took some good (at least I hope they are good) photographs and took tea with CCC at the Cascades and took her home and took a hot bath. Then Joyce arrived with the final corrected proof sheets of the Ondt and the Gracehoper with his bon à tirer written across the top page [*and I showed him the name of the English publisher in 1799 called Joyce Gold*] and C arrived from Reims (Bourdé who wrote La Prisonnière and Arthur Rubinstein were out there) and we all three sat around the fire and talked about the Mookse and the Gripes and the Ondt and the Gracehoper

May 10. To the Bank. To the Coiffeur's Revenez dans dix minutes so I sat at that bar across the street sideways from the Nain Blue and drank a bock in the Sun. The loveliestyoungestgayest girl in black her skirts up to her knees walked past I tossed off my bock left three francs and turned into a greyhound She was about twenty yards ahead and was walking with another (unattractive as far as I could see) girl. As I was about to accost her I saw a man appear from nowhere and begin to talk to her. He apparently knew both girls so there was rien à faire. But she was too pretty to abandon so I followed them up the Rue Cambon. They went into the restaurant on the corner of the Rue Cambon and the Rue Mont Thabor so I went in and stood at the bar and drank another beer. They began to eat so I went back to the Coiffeur's (Rue Saint-Honoré) and met the coiffeur coming out for luncheon. He said he thought I had forgotten to come back. I did not tell him I almost had. I had my hair cut then went back to the Cambon Mont Thabor restaurant. They were still there. I ordered a beer and waited (it was time to go home to luncheon but I would not abandon my pursuit—signed Casanova). At 1.10 they ordered their coffee. At 1.20 they asked for the addition. At 1.30 they walked out the Rue Mont-Thabor door and turned the corner up towards the Rue de Rivoli I twenty yards behind. Imagine my surprise when I saw the meek bespectacled young man doff his hat kiss their hands ("I Kiss Your Little Hand Madame"—graphaphone record) and disappear through a doorway. I caught them at the Rue de Rivoli and speaking to the Blonde in Black asked them if one day they would also care to take luncheon with me. Peut être chez Voisin? We had reached the Rue Saint-Florentin before she smiled and said yes. Quand? Jeudi prochain. So we she and I shook hands and they went down the Rue Saint-Florentin I across the Rue de Rivoli to hail a taxi and rush home (à suivre). At five in the car with C to the Moulin. We stopped near the Abattoires I for beer she for white wine so the trip was very refreshing and it was nice to see the new donkeys the ânesse we shall call Eclipse and so out to the Pôteau and then I climbed to the top of my Sun-Tower and with certain prayers lit my new pipe and smoked it towards the setting sun gold bokhara cramoisy grey fire and at supper time watched through the round window the red gold round sun go down behind the black trees *carrying my inner fire with it I actually felt myself disappearing in the Sun Perfection.*

1929

May 11. Read in the Kabala of Numbers (Sepharial) that I is the symbol of the Sun   it is my number. It is the letter I. It is an Arrow "It symbolizes manifestation, assertion, the positive and active principale. It represents the ego, self-assertion, positivism, egotism, separateness, selfhood, isolation, distinction, self-reliance, dignity, and rulership. It is the unit of life, the individual. It is the O made manifest." From eleven to noon basked in the Sun on the Sun-Tower taking into my heart the fire and madness of noon and in the afternoon donkey-races and four hours of work putting these Shadows of the Sun à jour and to-day the workmen (I gave them a bottle of wine) finished laying the bricks in the swimming pool.

12. Rushed in from the Moulin to get to Longchamp for the first race to bet on Tornado but someone claimed her before the race so she did not run. Bet on Cheval de Troie instead who won at six to one (at least his stable companion won) and it was a grey spring afternoon and there were many people and I wandered around under the trees smoking my pipe and looking at the girl who always dresses in black hat and white gloves and who always sits reading her programme under the tree and at last (I say at last because I have seen her for six weeks now) I decide to talk to her so I went up and sat down beside her and spoke to her and she didn't answer so I waited and spoke to her again and again no answer but the third time she turned her head half around and said Yes to a question I had asked her about a horse So we talked about horses for ten minutes and then it began to rain and I got up and smiled a goodbye at her and she acknowledged it with an imperceptible nod of the head and I saw CCC wandering around under a blue umbrella she was dressed in pink and brown with a brown hat and she had lost two thousand francs on Cri de Guerre and I saw D[rosso] his face pale as the whitest white (the result of black idol) and I saw Pantall who said Gin Cocktail might win on Saturday and saw Melchior de Polignac and the Prince G[uy de Polignac] who seemed surprised because I had no hat on (thank Christ I don't wander around like a perfect ass in a top hat the way he does with one foot in the grave) and I left and came home and drank a glass of Cutty Sark and took a hot bath and went to bed and wrote out lists of words: Amor, Arrow, Amon-Ra, Arctic, Aztec.

13. Lost again on Mad Queen she can't seem to win and went to the Black Sun Press to see our workmen begin to "tirer" the Mookse and the Gripes and came home and wrote a letter to D H Lawrence [I don't see why Curtis Brown hasn't sent us the first half on the Escaped Cock] and went to bed and discovered in the Kabala book that according to the date of my birth 4 June 1898 whose sum is 27 whose sum is 9 my number is 9 which stands for freedom energy keenness acumen zeal penetration fever fire. This is very pleasant.

14. Joyce here to correct final proof sheets on the Triangle. He loves to talk about his work and if ever the conversation goes off at a tangent he always coaxes it back to the Work in Progress. He is very shy almost like a schoolboy at times blushes squirms about in his chair is eager for praise laughs a lot. Never pedantic so that even when the subject matter is way over our heads it still remains interesting. And he says amusing things. For instance he compares the Gripes to an octopus and a plate of tripes à la mode de Caen. Himself he compares to a trapezist who has accomplished a difficult acrobatic feat and then is called upon to perform this feat again and again and again. I liked the way after he had signed the bon à tirer for the Mookse and Gripes how he thought of another word and rushed over to the Black Sun Press in a taxicab to change it. Still another proof of his seriousness.

May 15. I see Joyce who has still another sentence to add to the Triangle (quand il n'y en a plus il y en a encore) and I go to see Brancousi who gives me the abstract portrait of Joyce and I take the abstract portrait of Joyce to show to Joyce and he has great difficulty in seeing it and Stuart Gilbert was there and Mrs Joyce and Miss Joyce and I took the picture to the graveur's and took back the other picture to Brancousi and then went with Croucher to the Bar on the corner of the Rue du Bac to read on the ticker that Elsa de Brabent had lost and while we were drinking our café-crèmes the ticker ticked again and I read that Golden Arrow had lost. Then home to the tea for Frans and May and there were already about twenty people and I hate tea-parties only there was no tea at this one nothing but champagne and C was very pretty in her gold tuxedo set off by the enormous orchid I had given her and more and more people kept stuffing in so I went out and walked around the block. Then back to the party again (I forgot to mention the object of the party which was to show Frans' paintings) and soon Eric arrived with a miraculous blonde. After this the tea-party from my point of view was a success and she (her name is Eva and she is Swedish and she likes Absinthe and Swedish Punch) and I and Eric all dined together Chez Fouquet caviare and caille and then to the Jungle to hold hands and drink whiskey and hear miraculous jazz.

16. Cocktail at the Ritz and at the corner of the Rue Cambon Rue Saint-Honoré I see the little Blonde in Black and we take luncheon together at the little Cambon bar. Her name is Elyane and she has large eyes and long eyelashes and a bouche qui rit ne mord jamais and she is seventeen. She had a girl-friend with her who wasn't bad. The only trouble is they are hardly ever free to go out. What a bore! Went to Longchamp and lost on Lion-Hearted and Saint-Corentin and I didn't play the horse the pretty girl told me to play and it won at fifteen to one and I drove out to the Moulin and walked out to the Pôteau de Perth with C.

17. In to town many aeroplanes overhead and I worked at the Black Sun Press and at six walked over to the Rue Royale to see if I could find Elyane and we went to Prunier together (she had a dreadful girl friend with her) and I drove them out to the Porte Maillot and as she went off she turned and waved goodbye and it is these flashes of communication between two people that are perhaps more important than the actually making love and I drove home and found Mortimer just arrived from America and he gave me the pieces of gold (the Eagle and the Sun) and I went afterwards alone to the Jungle to listen to the jazz and to say hello to the propriétaire's wife and so at midnight home to bed and how would it be to go to bed with Elyane?

May 18. I look at the gold pieces (the Eagle and the Sun) and I begin to read the Book of the Dead and Croucher arrives and we go to the Black Sun Press ensuite to the Viking for cocktails and Eva appears and she and I go to the Catalan but it is very cold and we take luncheon and drink a bottle of the clearest red wine and so to the races at Saint-Cloud getting there just as the horses were coming in from the first race so that we did not see Gin Cocktail run (he was nowhere) and we bet on a horse called Pauline Borghèse who also was nowhere and Carlos and Evelyn were out there and Constance and the Count and Eva and I went way up on top where a clear gold wind blew health and gladness and then we went into Paris to Fouquet's where we found Mortimer drinking a whiskey and soda and he had a letter from the Fire Princess and then to the Montparnasse to leave Eva and so away to the Moulin for donkey races and a walk to the Pôteau de Perthe and a looking westward from the top of the Tower into the Setting Sun I—Five-Grey for the Grey Princess Gold for the Fire Princess Cramoisy for the Cramoisy Queen Bokhara for Bokhara Sunfire.

19. Epithalamiumic braying of donkeys and at noon a donkey-wedding with Sunrise (Castor) for bridegroom and Eclipse for bride and what kicking up of hindlegs on her part what a braying and galloping but what acquiescence once it was inside at which juncture the gate to the courtyard opened. Enter The Prince with P.K. followed by the Rochefoucaulds and Billee Reardon. When the wedding was over we tied the old stagecoach to the back of Sosthenes' new Chrysler car and he pulled us through the woods to the Château not without twice crashing us into a tree and there was a great ringing of bells and a firing off of the cannon from the top of the coach And they all came back to supper at the Moulin and there was a great drinking of cocktails and champagne and after supper G and K took a hot bath together and there was a full moon and at midnight they left Prince George signing GEORGE on the wall and before going to bed the quenching of thirst: champagne arms around and opium.

20. Sun-Bath naked on the top of the Tower and the Kaisers and Crouchers arrived and André Germain and there were donkey races and Prince George and K appeared and Stuart and Croucher and I corrected Joyce proof sheets and then I drove in to Paris to meet Eva at the Viking only she never appeared.

21. Work at the Black Sun Press luncheon with Elyane at the Rue Cambon Bar and at half past five departure for Saint-Dizier correcting Observation-Post and drinking beer on the way down. Not to mention an arrowing into the clean and erotic setting Sun. Saint-Dizier at nine (eleven

years since I drove my ambulance through here during the war) and I go to the Hotel du Soleil d'Or.

May 22. Read from the Book of the Dead, took photographs of the factory smokestacks and of railroad signal-towers, corrected proof sheets and drank beer with Jolas who arrived with Maria at three in the afternoon. We tried to find the bordel Rue des Abattoirs in order to drink champagne but we lost our way and findly took a car back to the station where I just caught the train. Arrived in Paris at nine and took a hot bath and went to the Jungle. As I was leaving C appeared in a racing car with Sosthenes Ganay and Montaudoin and we all went in and drank champagne and danced and to-night I gave Sosthenes the copy of Sylvie in a marvelous binding and with the Gérard de Nerval letters in it.

23. Breakfast an hour late that damned Marguerite is the stupidest woman said she didn't know we were back from the country and then Joyce telegraphed that he had chosen the title for the three Fragments from Work in Progess (Tales Told of Shem and Shaun) then Marcelle came upstairs to bandage my leg which is all swollen from the kick I got from the donkey then a going over my race statistics (I have lost sixteen races in a row) then my daily copying out from the Bible then a reading from the Book of the Dead then out to the races to find that Gin Cocktail can't run any more his leg is so bad and to lose on Saint Corentin (seventeenth in a row) then to buy the pornographic books (My Secret Life) for Marks then to see Joyce here (he was wearing a straw hat, he had lost on Gin Cocktail, he was going to hear some Italian singers, he was wearing a stickpin in the form of a grasshopper) then to take supper with C at Le Doyen (it took them half an hour to get the addition) then a walk home to find a letter from M who is leaving for Greece "La tourterelle que vous poignardâtes" then a pronouncing of the word Ra then an undressing and a going to bed.

24. There is the scene of the weighing of the hearts. Each goddess kneels on the emblem of gold and each has her hands raised in adoration of the Sun-God. Harry + Ra = Harra.

25. Stuart says I look like the Zorn Etching (Valkulla) and I am glad.

26. Stuart works out (he has a good mind Harvard Cum Laude) the anagram for Harry-Caresse Ra's Rays Cheer.

[27. *In to town. I see Elyane. I work with C correcting the Joyce. I write D. H. Lawrence dine with C at Fouquet's.*]

28. Sold $4000 worth of stock enjoy life when you can and had luncheon with C at the Ritz and we all went to the station to meet the Prodigal Son (Sykes) but we got there too late (the stupid man at the bank gave us the wrong hour) and so we went back to the house and there he was and we drank a loving-cup of champagne out in the car in the street then to La Petite Chaise (Percée) and I was in one of my moods and they all went upstairs to eat while I stood in the doorway drinking from an enormous glass of champagne. It was raining and I kept thinking of the Fire-Princess. Then an empty taxi came by and I jumped into it and drove to the Rue du Maréchal-Maunoury and she was sitting up in bed reading the Paris Sport (I lost again to-day on Heliotaure) and we drank white wine whose taste was like fire.

[*May 29. Duomaid telecarb (F P) and I[rene] for tea at the Meurice I was just leaving when she arrived (twenty minutes is my outside limit for waiting) and it is two weeks since I saw her in the Rue Royale and she is very pretty and we drank champagne-cocktails (three each) and then went to the Ritz for some more (two each) then to Le Doyen's (three each) then to the Ballet Russe (very poor) then to the Jungle for gin and dancing (great fun) and they played marvelous jazz and it was hot and alive (I[rene] hot and alive) and C was there with Sykes and there was the proprietaire's wife and I love this madness and then we went for more gin to the Grand Ecart and here we danced and danced and I don't know what time it was when we arrowed out in the car to Versailles the fur rug up over our heads we were sitting on the floor (there was a cold wind) I don't remember very much more a mad goodnight and Auguste saying (nous sommes Rue de Lille Monsieur) and the clock in the bathroom said 4.*]

30. To Patou to watch C try on hats and luncheon with her (Sykes with us) at Le Doyen in the Sun (we had to wait half an hour for the addition) then a hair-cut then to the florist to send orchids then to the little bar in the Rue du Bac to read the race-ticker Amor beaten and White Clover beaten by a nose (damn damn damn) then to the Moulin stopping on the quays to buy two carrier-pigeons (Grey Arrow and Silver Wings) and after supper donkey races on the new race track we have laid out back of the house and to-day I wrote to Marseilles for a python to add to our menagerie.

Race horses: Sunstroke and Gin Cocktail.
Dogs: Narcisse Noir and Clytoris.
Donkeys: Castor Pollux Eclipse Sunlight.
Carrier-Pigeons: Arrowhead and Silver Wings.
Ducks: One Two Three Four Five Six Seven Eight Nine.

31. Telegramme Urgent to Irene and a hot bask (as One) in the Sun and to-day they are letting water into the swimming pool and to-day I finished the Book of the Dead and to-day at the races Heliotaure lost for the seventh time and I am now over nineteen thousand francs behind and it is the end of May and if words were horses the race this month would be a dead-heat between Amor and Râ followed by White Clover Elsa de Brabent Sunstroke and Tornado and this evening the Sun setting back of the moving branches of the trees was a sharp fire into which I arrowed the sharp fire of my soul Sunfire.

June 1. Arrow of the Sunrise and at last at last after Elsa de Brabent had lost, after Saint Corentin had lost making twenty-eight defeats in a row, I read at Chantilly in the Paris-Sport at the Tipperary Bar that Lion-Hearted at 7-1 had won the last race and I am glad and I go to see Sunstroke and then to drink a champagne cocktail at the Manor House, then a mad ride, I at the wheel, back to the Moulin and Nada and her husband (the Marquis of Milford Haven) arrived and Evelyn and Carlos and we drank champagne and then went to bed [*I to dream (not seriously) of Irene*].

June 2. Donkey races. Won 600 francs. Then people began to arrive. Bored and *very* restless. What is it I want? Who is it I want to sleep with? Why do I *hate* society?

[*3. Noon and luncheon with Elayne. 1 o'clock and luncheon with Irene. Which? The Irene party went on well into the night. On the way back from Versailles stopped to see which? The answer is simple, Jacqueline.*

4. Thirty-One.

5. Saw Eva at the Viking Bar.

6. Saw Eva at the Viking Bar.]

[7.] Invulnerability is the word that is ahead this month. Ah! Let us make our hearts invulnerable. And when we have made them invulnerable? Then we must learn that like other combatants the battleship will survive a battle only by her own hard fighting.

[8.] Quiet and grey and all day on top of the Tower wrapped in my polo coat, acquiring a reserve of buoyancy and all day I made armour-plates to make invulnerable the battle-ship of my heart and towards evening people began to arrive [*Eva, Erik, Sykes, Kaiser, Monroes, Mortimer, the young soldier boy, etcetera*] and there was the popping of champagne corks and mad donkey races and jazz records on the graphaphone and [*Noailles*] arrived and was pulled up to the grenier on the rope and there was the firing off of the cannon and [mad words drunkenness and bottle-breaking and rape and riot and] the lights from the cars coming and going [and couples lying on the floor under zebra skins and the young soldier crying because his girl was sleeping with his rival and Gretchen was downstairs choking and someone arrived to give her morphine and I played the graphaphone the same tune again & again & again & at last towards two in the morning] Kaiser and I fired off a barrage, both of us stripped to the waist and there was the flash of the cannon and the acrid smell of powder.

9. Woke up under a zebra skin (it must have been very early as the sun hadn't risen above the trees) and walked out to the Pôteau a little battered from the riot of last night but after a cold bath and breakfast and a jumping about in the sun the compass needle pointed into Sun and on top of the sun-tower C. and I lay naked in the Sun listening to the shouts and cries in the cour below where people were playing ping-pong and riding the donkeys or throwing arrowdarts at the target. More people for luncheon and more champagne and Maisie-Mouse standing on the ping-pong table while we

played a match under the archway of her legs (Whiteknees Arch) while Croucher took moving pictures and the young soldier played the graphaphone. Then a fast drive to Chantilly Mortimer leading the convoy in his Chrysler and drinks at the Manor House and Ukrania wins the Prix de Diane and so back to the Moulin [for donkey-races & drinking]. Hordes of people and a riot and I was angry and told Erik and Montaudin to "enlevez vos putains" and before going to bed a great discussion on the subject of Joyce.

June 10. New Every Morning.

11. Elyane, Eva, Shirley, Miss Carpenter, Alice, Irene, Polia and the Y.S.B. partants probables for the July Derby with Elyane and Alice as favorites.

12. I believe in the eradication of the past (New Every Morning), in the power of the word and the word of power (The word of power which I want to possess is that word the utterance of which shall enable me to recreate myself), in the invulnerability of the heart, in the three great elements of an attack (surprise, rapidity, continuity) in the half sane half insane madness and illuminism of the seer, in the fire and velocity of comets, in the arrows that point to Ra.

13. Good fun with Irene yesterday especially at the Manor House [putting iodine on her shoulder where I had bitten her (we were both tight sherry cobblers and gin fizzes)] but to-day I can hardly remember what she looks like and tomorrow her face will be as empty as the letter O (zero) and to-day there is no sun for basking so I read all of Joyce's Work in Progress from riverrun to Johanahanahana and to-day I exercised the donkeys (SPCE Society for the Prevention of Cruelty to Enemals) and to-day I learned O Carib Isle by Hart and to-day I worked on my new Alphabet Poem.

14. Harry Crosby says: under no circumstances do I wish to be buried in the ground after my death—scatter my ashes to the four winds—I am not of the ground I am of the Sun and to-day is the Bal des 4-Arts but I am glad I am at the Moulin (the party last year was too good to be repeated) [if only we can do everything this way, end our lives this way on the heights] and C appeared from Paris and we walked out to the Pôteau and back and raced about on the donkeys and watched the water pouring into our new swimming pool.

15. Up in the air with Elyane and I mark her next with my sharp teeth and a goodbye at Chantilly (more a badbye than a goodbye as she wanted me to take her back to Paris in the car) and I went to see Sunstroke who races to-morrow and I went to look at a blackboard in a bar to see that Tornado and Golden Arrow had lost and to the Manor House Bar for a gin fizz (no need for iodine to-day) and then back to the Moulin a mile a minute—not fast enough I would like to go as fast as the Sun ten miles a second!

16. Into the New-Pool Grey Morning and the Inner Invisible Sun Virginity.

And there was ping-pong and people arriving and more plunging in the pool and Max Ernst was there and Ortiz and the usual raft of royalty and in the middle of luncheon C and I left and rushed to Chantilly just in time to see our Sunstroke gallop past but he was last and Hotweed won the Prix du Jockey Club (a great horse) and it was a grey afternoon and I felt all inside myself wanting nothing (omnia mea mecum porto) and the Château was grey and quiet and as we left it began to rain and we drank a gin at the Manor House and drove back to the Moulin where we found a great congregation of people and I won three donkey races on Sunlight the last by a nose from Carlos on Eclipse and then everyone departed Parisward and C and I were left alone together. What a relief!

June 17. In to Paris and the Harry Marks' for luncheon and cocktails and champagne and a great talking about the Black Sun Press and $4,000 for The Black Sun Press and the Black Sun Press Joyce is ready to-day (the Tales told by Shem and Shaun) and we drink champagne and talk about books and at five they leave and at half past Mr. and Mrs. W arrive (the intense impression as she arrived at the head of the stairs and came into the Enormous Room and we talk about Joyce and Cummings and Crane and Eliot and Macleish and we drink cocktails and she is very pretty and very very physical and it seems as if all my life I have been waiting for her. Then with C to a cocktail party and we dined at Le Doyens (the stupid French ruin every meal by taking so long with the addition) and walked home along the river and when we got home I found hidden among rose petals and fraises au bois a red tin box from my friend the submarine captain and to-day a black pansy in a white envelope addressed to me but with no word inside. Question-Mark?

18. Ate 44 radishes for luncheon and drove out to the Moulin and undressed and basked in the sun. I want to get as burned as I did last summer at the Lido and to-night the Sun was a frail wisp of burgundy-colored silk to wind about my throat.

19. All day from sunrise to sunset naked on the top of the tower under the hot sun (a point of gold on an enormous blue page) and I rub my body with cocoanut oil and now to-night I am once again a living bronze lean and firedrunken.

20. The clouds this morning are frail wisps diaphanous like Botticelli girls frail as Joyce's Nuovoletta in her "engauzements" and for the first time I feel a gentleness towards these drifting girls who are born in a moment and who are slain in the next by the light bright sword of the wind. Moult m'esbahis de la merveille.

21. I am on my Sun Tower it is approaching noon the Summer Solstice and I am as red as an Indian I am smoking my pipe to the Sun I am naked. My heart toward the world is a heart of stone my heart towards the Sun-Goddess is a Heart of Fire SG + HF = SUNFIRE I SUNFIRE.

1929

It is NOON My Fire Arrows into the Sun Ra Ra Ra Ra
I PENETRATE INTO THE SUN
I AM THE SUN.

June 22. It is a grey day and to-day is shorter than yesterday. The Sun set yesterday at 9.18 to-day at 9.16 (only I couldn't see it set for it was grey) and A arrived with her husband for supper and I fired off the cannon in her honor and it began to rain and we ate supper around the fire and drank champagne and then vodka and A is very physical she excites me to madness and at last here is the ideal combination A = Actress H = Poet.

23. The three great elements in an attack: surprise, rapidity, continuity. Let us attack For even if the attack is a weak one (which it is not) it may be driven home before the defence wakes up to utilise her strength and there is the fur rug in the design of a sun and there is the top of the Tower and there is a danse de feu and there is champagne and the maddest of mad rides to Chantilly and back and there is a firing off of the cannon and more champagne and hordes of people and a climbing out on the roof and a sitting half naked by the fire with a sorceress at my side.

24. Woke up half naked under a zebra skin on the stone floor of the grenier and after going through my rites (Pôteau de Perthe Swimming Pool, Firing the Cannon Top of Tower) we all drove into town—very quiet after the explosions of yesterday and at seven a cocktail party at Bustos (a mêlée de folies de toutes sortes). A was there and back to the house for more cocktails (a great throwing of bottles and glasses down the stairs) and A reappeared and a whole crowd of us to the Coupole and a mad motor ride and a storm at the Crouchers where I was forced to retire to the bedroom where I lay all evening under Caresse's petit gris coat while Constance talked to me and Eva appeared and disappeared and everything seemed blurred and far away and A came up and said goodnight (the eagle and the sun) and she went away and it must have been about four in the morning when C came upstairs to take me home.

25. Cocktail party at Evelyn's and a Liliom scene on a little sofa instead of on a park bench and a goodbye and 3 O's (not yet MO's) and later a surprise and a goodnight. I shall never see eyes again.

26. Grey day and voices sound far away and A has gone and I am alone and invulnerability is being put to the test and this is the grande semaine but who cares . . .

27. Puma = a large feline carnivore.
Sorceress = user of magic arts, enchantress.
Puma + Sorceress = A. Make me like a torch of fire! Awake O Sword!

28. Got up at five in the afternoon after reading notes from the Love Books of Ovid (knowledge is a pre-requisite for profitable employment of fighting strength) and went out to take tea with Madame le Marquise at Les

Ambassadeurs and then back to the house to find Hart Crane back from Marseille where he had slept with his thirty sailors and he began again to drink Cutty Sark (the last bottle in the house) and G.S.W. appeared (how different our attitude towards life) and Evelyn and Carlos appeared and I liked Carlos because he said A liked me and a quiet dinner at Le Doyen S.S.W. and a girl friend and C and I and I is my favorite letter and I my favorite number. Why? Because I is lean and clean and swift and direct as an arrow.

June 29. Bought C a chic modern bathing suit this at Hermes and two sporty automobile rugs one for S. V. R. C. the other for H and C then went to the Tuileries to look at the Oiseau Jaune which has just flown across the Atlantic and I must learn to fly. I am inspired. My soul is a giant aeroplane strong enough to fly across the ocean and sky that separates us from the Sun, a giant eagle to lose myself in the Sun. And this afternoon at the races I read Les Maximes de la Rochefoucauld: "Qui vit sans folie n'est pas si sage qu'il le croit" and I had tea with CCC and then home and Hart Crane was there very drunk (no more Cutty Sark left) and at last he left and so with C to the Ambassadeurs where we saw some horrid Americans
(Z—) but where we ate caviare
(A =) accent on the A.

30. Grand Prix Day and C leaves with Carlos and Evelyn and Narcisse for Cannes while I go to the Grand Prix (my eighth successive Grand Prix) with S and S (Stuart and Stanley) and Hotweed won (a great great horse) and the finish was exhilarating, a neck and a neck and thank Christ the English horse was beaten (he was second) and I lost on Slipper (I bet on her for sentimental reasons) and in the evening to see CCC (she is leaving for Cannes) and while I was waiting for her [*I found that letter I have always wanted back* [the 1923 one] *and I tore it into shreds.*] . . . What a relief!

July 1. Sun Sun Sun I am an arrow thrusting into sun (a diamond arrow fire and sun) and I shout Ra to myself and so to the Moulin for the night and we played the horse game and I went early to bed after drinking a little bottle of champagne looking into the Fire.

2. Departure of guests and I back in the Sun (the acquiring of strength) and I drew pictures with colored crayons (Aerial Mast, Invulnerability, Tarantula, 13, Ra) and Auguste came out with the mail (I can do nothing but think of you) and in the Paris-Sport I read that Soleil at 13 to 1 had won a race (three cheers Ra Ra Ra) and I made 13000 and I am glad.

3. Meteoric [and Meteoric is the leading word].[6]

4. Thought about July 3.

5. Sunstroke is beaten at Le Tremblay but I am thinking of other things car je veux revoir la puma enchantée and I go to the Jardin des Plantes to see the Puma (she only comes out to the front part of her cage at night, so I had

to bribe the guardian who let me in through a gate at the back) and I looked at her for a long long time and she crouched in a corner and whined and she is almost as beautiful as the real Puma who prowls back and forth in the cage of my heart and to-day I read in the Encyclopedia that when caressed pumas purr like domestic cats.

July 6. Clytoris comes in heat so I send Marcelle with her to Cannes so that Narcisse can enjoy a honey-moon and I take two magnums of champagne to Stuart and one of them exploded as I was going through the door of his hotel and I was drenched and we said goodbye (he sails to-night) and I read in the New-York Herald some encouraging facts encouraging because they reveal our generation as a young and fearless and adventurous generation. Lonesome Viking Braves Ocean in foot Open Boat, 115 of 297 West Point 29ers—Ask for Wings, Chicago Berlin Plane Over Great Whales, U.S. Racer Arrives to Shatter French Auto Speed Record, Junkers Aeroplane Crashes at Lido (Five of the Seven Passengers Took The Next Plane To Rome).

7. I begin to read Of Winds by Bacon "in an eastern wind all visible things do appear bigger but in a western wind all audible things are heard further as sounds of bells and the like" and to-day I drank a great many too many dubonnets and to-day I must say I was bored which for me is very, very rare. C is not here. [7]

8. The photographs I took of The Rubber Horse are magnificent. I have had them enlarged and to-day I read in the paper that a bar of gold valued at $100,000 was shipped to New York from Paris. Let each of us ship the bar of gold within ourselves from our Heart to the Sun.

9. Chartres in the morning then to Fontainebleau to see Frans and May and we lay on the boat basking in the sun from noon until sunset when I left and drove my green Voisin in a race against a white Renault into Paris (I was beaten by a length) and Clytoris is back from Cannes where Narcisse was the perfect lover (according to Marcelle) and there is a letter from Kay Boyle to say that Hart Crane is in prison for knocking down a gendarme and there was a letter from C. (when the Sun goes into the C) and there was the Paris-Sport to say that White Clover had won and I went to the Ritz to send a telegram to C and then to the Chicago Inn to eat a large piece of corn bread.

10. To the Black Sun Press (I am doing a second edition of Transit of Venus and a miniature edition of The Sun). Then to take a taxi to see McGowan about Hart Crane. I arrived in front of the Deux Magots and hailed a taxi. Just then McGowan stepped out of the café with Vitrac and a girl called Kitty Cannell. We drove off to the Palais de Justice. It was quarter to one. I had a date with Marks at the Ritz Bar so I rushed off and got him (we drank two cocktails) and brought him back with me to the trial. Hart was magnificent. When the Judge announced that it had taken ten gend-armes to hold him (the dirty bastards, they dragged him three blocks by the feet) all the court burst into laughter. After ten minutes of questioning he was fined 800 francs and 8 days in prison should he ever be arrested again. A letter from the Nouvelle Revue Française had a good deal to do with his liberation. They wouldn't let him out right away so I went with Marks to Le Doyen to eat and to drink sherry cobblers in the sun. We got tight and we went off to see Eugene O'Neill and I went to the bank. On my way back I started off towards the race-ticker bar on the Rue Cambon to see if Tornado had won, but on the way I saw a pretty American girl, so I talked to her and we went to the Ritz for a sherry cobbler (her name was Sheelah—I like it) but I had to rush off to the Conciergerie where I found Vitrac and Whit Burnett. Apparently Hart had been sent back to the Santé so Burnett and I drove over there (we saw a truck run over a cat) and here we had to wait and to wait from six until long after eight (we spent the time drinking beer and playing checkers and talking to the gendarmes). At last the prisoners began to come out, Hart the last one, unshaved hungry wild. So we stood and drank in the Bar de la Bonne Santé right opposite the prison gate and then drove to the Herald office where Burnett got out to write up the story for the newspaper, Hart and I going on to the Chicago Inn for cornbread and poached eggs on toast (Ginetta and Olivares were there and Ortiz) and Hart said that the dirty skunks in the Santé wouldn't give him any paper to write poems on. The bastards.

July 11. I bask in the sun by lying on the hall floor by the dining-room—the only window through which the sun pours. Hart appeared and we talked about The Bridge and I went with him to get his ticket back to New York on the "Homeric" after which I bought and sent a graphaphone to Freida Lawrence and went to the Ritz to meet Marks and we had luncheon in the garden and discussed the Black Sun Press. Later on a sherry cobbler party at Le Doyen with Harry Bull and two girls, then home to write H.M.C. and the Puma.

12. Another basking on the hall floor and Hart appeared rather the worse for wear. He had been up all night in Montmartre. He had all sorts of stars and anchors pinned to his sweater and the dactylo appeared to work on The Bridge and Hart read his poems aloud and declared that there was no greater poet than he and he played the graphaphone and talked of Marseilles and of Roy Campbell of the Flaming Terrapin and I worked at the Black Sun Press and came home to read The Flaming Terrapin.

13. To Git-le-Coeur with a letter and in the car to the Moulin and from 1 until 7 I wrote 7 poems for Transit of Venus and I corrected things for the second edition and in the Paris-Sport to-night I see that I had Velocity at 4 to 1 a produit of Kefalin. (C'est Kefalin qui gagne) and to-night I wish C were here "ayant peur de mourir lorsque je couche seul" and I have tacked the picture she did called "Dormir Ensemble" over the bed and I have been looking at the picture of her (nude) which I always carry in my little black pocket book.

1929

July 14. Naked all morning on The Tower in the hot sun then into Town to see Sunstroke beaten at Saint Cloud. Then home and to bed. I hate holidays.

15. Sherry cobblers in the morning sun (an Egyptian gold point of a sun in an Egyptian sky lapis-lazuli blue—rare for Paris) and the reappearance of the Puma, Puma Sorceress Unfearing Unquestioning.

16. Gold sheft oppne Sun Puma Sorceress Modners Sunfire.
The very danger incurred increased the Sorceress' recklessness and led her to do and dare everything.

17. Iondiule—Desirable—sorcery and magic—hallucinations—gin and ivresse and fire and then I ride alone in the green Voisin (Gus at the wheel) from Paris to Dijon arriving there at one in the morning.

18. C with Narcisse arrives on the Express from Marseilles and away along the road to Paris I stripped to the waist (it was very hot) and wearing my gold necklace and people in the villages shouted à poil, peaux rouges, and heaven knows what and at Avalon we drank cocktails in the Hotel de la Poste where Napoleon spent a night and when we got to Paris we discovered Lord L waiting for us and we all drank gin fizzes and took cold baths and put rouge on our toenails and then we went to Git-le-Coeur where the Sorceress cast her spells over my heart and C and I and Lord L dined at Le Doyen one sherry cobbler two sherry cobblers three sherry cobblers and so home and to bed C lovely looking in her yellow dress and out of her yellow dress and loveliest with her Chanel imitation-ice necklace. I love bracelets and necklaces.

19. Luncheon and afternoon with the Sorceress (we came home in a mad thunderstorm—thunderbolts and flashes of lightning) and after an h and m (haircut and manicure) supper at Le Doyen with C and after innumberable sherry cobblers we stopped at the post office and sent the following cable to the family "please sell ten thousand dollars worth of stock—we have decided to lead a mad and extravagant life" so out in the green Voisin to the Moulin.

20. Meteoric Velocity Madness Sorceress are the four leading words this month a close race and to-day an intense basking in the Sun and towards evening people an Indian Princess (ruined by tortoise-shell glasses) an aviator called Mayer, who had been wounded in the war a Comtesse de Saint Quentin who fell off the grey donkey and hurt her left breast her young lover and a man called Scheck who is learning to swim. Various others. But I stayed up in the grenier playing L'Amour Sorcier to myself on the graphaphone.

21. Morning in the swimming pool and in the afternoon a reading of Bacon's History of Winds (winderful wonderful) an exact strong style containing a synthesis of facts and containing flights of poetry I quote: "All stayed winds (unless they blow from some neighbouring places) are weak

and yield unto sudden winds" and here is a book I should like to edit at our Black Sun Press.

July 22. In to Paris and a day on the chaise longue writing a letter to the family (I quote in part) [8]

[Paris July 23 1929

Dearest Ma and Pa

The cable saying you were shocked and terribly hurt at your selling stock was I suppose perfectly logical (it is so difficult in life to understand people's point of view) and I was afraid you would feel badly but everyone must *must* lead their own lives and what sometimes appears folly on the surface may be underneath wisdom. If it turns out that we have made a mistake why then it will be we who will have to pay for it and if it turns out that we are wise why then it is we who will profit by it. But whether for bad or for good . . . is predetermined . . . I have always believed that everything is predetermined. I am a fatalist. "Whatever may befall thee, it was preordained for thee from everlasting. Whatever happens at all happens as it should." (Marcus Aurelius).]

Perhaps it was the "we intend to lead a mad and extravagant life" that upset you. This should not be taken seriously in the common sense of the words but it should be taken seriously in the true significance of the words. The abyss and swamps of Red Skeletons have been swept clean by the diamond winds of Velocity and Madness. Stagnation is the past. Whirlwinds and Hurricanes are the present and future. Mamma says she fears disaster "what is your life leading you to" I am sure that it is arrowing me into the Finality and Fire of Sun by means of Catapults and Explosions Gold and Sorceresses and Tornadoes I believe in giving to my life new and violent associations and I agree with Jolas there is only one action I can believe in and that is the action that leads me to eternity.

If we appear to you unwise because we like looping the loop and other aerial acrobatics (never forgetting however the directness of an Atlantic Flight) it may be true and there might come a crash but there is no crime in an explosion whereas there is I think a crime in ending life the way so many do with a whimper.

[You feel it is wrong because I refuse to take the questions of money seriously. If you really feel this way, the simplest thing is to leave your money to Kitsa and to her children (as you have already done in a certain sense) who lead the lives you would have them lead.

I spend a great deal of money but I do not consider much of it is wasted. I give gifts to people. I like doing that and helping people to go on vacations and sending books to people and I am having an edition made at the Braille Press for the War Blind and half this is for Caresse so that she can have a good time and buy clothes and develop the Black Sun Press. If I wasted money gambling or sitting in bars drinking or entertaining chorus girls then

I would be entirely or absolutely to blame but as it is I am happy and *living* in the true sense of the word Alive Awake New Every Morning with the Arrow of my Soul pointing to Ra.

Sympathize with us because we are happy, it is more difficult than sympathy for the unhappy and don't be too severe because I cannot seem to take the selling of stock as a grevious fault.

I remember a poem Robbie gave me.

> Do what thy manhood bids thee do
> from none but self expect applause
> He noblest lives and noblest dies
> who makes and keeps
> his self-made laws]

and when we think of the comets and the meteors and the stars and the planets and the Sun all whirling whirling far up above us in the great harmony of the spheres how trivial and ephemeral become dinner parties auction bridge, the editing of books or the investing and selling of stock.

[This is not a mad unbalanced letter. Perhaps even it contains more wisdom than you want to admit and because our life is so totally different from your life it may be impossible for you to understand.]

For the poet there is Love and Death and Infinity and for other things to assume such vital importance is out of the question and that is why I refuse to take the question of money seriously.

[I am really really sorry to feel that you both feel so hurt I seem to have done so much in my life to make you unhappy but perhaps someday I shall have done a fine thing to make you happy.

Harry.]

July 23. The Sorceress and sherry cobblers and orchids and gin and when I got home I fell asleep C came in and threw water over me to wake me up and we went out to dinner at Le Doyen with Carlos and Evelyn C in her yellow dress.

24. Finished a book of pictures thirty drawings in crayon the one of the Puma is the best but where is my Puma-Sorceress to cast enchantments where is her magic and sorcery her love-philtres that intoxicate with the fires of madness?

25. Sykes appears from Finistère I study Divination Magic Witchcraft I write the Sorceress I write a good thing called Illustrations of Madness [*"The inward nerves of my vision are beyond the sentiments of my heart and have no communication with the operations of my intellect. I boast of having effected this in a very complete manner by having caught and distilled certain rays of light from the Sun"*] and to-day I stayed in the house all day "my heart is a madhouse for the twin lunatics of her eyes".[9]

26. I begin to write a thing called Sorcery a twin piece to Illustrations of Madness (I quote item three) "the sorcerer and the sorceress shall cause the stones of the past to vanish into wells, shall cause the present to be the mystic drinking of each other's blood, shall cause the future to be a rapid exchange of lightning" and this afternoon C and I went out for the weekend to the Moulin.

July 27. Carlos and Evelyn arrive bringing with them two letters and the Herald to say that those two fliers are still up in the air (14 days) and Louigi, Carlos' valet, to cook macaroni for us and a graphaphone to play a tune called Broadway Melody and Armand (funny that C and I should both like an A, A and A) arrived with the Mahranee of Coochbehar (Indira of C.B. she signed on the wall) and she is the widow of a Hindou Prince (why didn't she throw herself on her husband's funeral pyre?) and we all played the horsegame and C and I lost a thousand francs and I also lost on the races this afternoon one thousand on Morning Sunny but because of the letters I am glad glad and the duck Gus killed for our supper was delicious and the Broadway Melody was divine. But not as divine as the Pantomime from l'Amour Sorcier.

28. The Sun this morning is a witch's cauldron in which she brews the lovephiltre that will cause the loss of the sorcerer's reason and we play (taking turns at winding the graphaphone) the Broadway Melody from before breakfast until after supper (over one hundred times in all) and the afternoon was grey I had that wonderful interior feeling and just after supper Carlos shot at and perhaps killed the corpse-colored rat who came out of his hole to eat the piece of cheese we had put out for him, and before we left for Paris I tossed the young carrier-pigeon out the bedroom window and this was his First Flight and all the way to Paris it drizzled and we got there about ten to find a boy-friend waiting for C (she had forgotten and he had been there since seven) and she went out dancing with him and I went to bed to think of the Sorceress.

29. I read The Bridge by Hart Crane (damn good) and I begin Aristotle "if in the sphere of action there is some one end which we desire for its own sake and for the sake of which we desire everything else (for me the Sun) it is clear that this must be the supreme good and the best thing of all—and surely to know what this good is, is of great importance for the conduct of life, for in that case we shall be like archers shooting at a definite mark" and to-day Sunstroke lost again and to-day or rather this evening three terrible letters from the family to damn us out for selling the stock with intimations that I need a guardian and that I am wicked and all gone to pieces and heaven knows what else. I became enraged but C quieted me down and at last we went to sleep but where is that damn Sorceress of mine and why hasn't she come back Damn you [come back] you Sorceress!

30. Stayed in bed all day. What else was there to do with the Sorceress away?

1929

July 31. Like other combatants the battleship will survive a battle only by her own hard fighting and Christ only knows my heart has had to fight to preserve its invulnerability (but I can say that it *has* preserved its invulnerability) and to-day the return of the Sorceress and if the Saint Louis fliers have at last come down to earth (after nearly 18 days in the air) I have forever risen off the earth (my feet are no longer upon the ground) and I light a fire in the Enormous Room and it is dark and she is dark (the dark girl on the sofa) and this month the winning word is

Sorceress.

August 1. I definitely decide to learn how to fly. I *do* know how to fly in the *final* and *real* sense of the word that is in the soul Flights to the Sun but now I want to learn also in the Lindbergian sense of the word and I swear on my gold necklace (O Sorcery O Fire O Sun) to add to my names of lunatic and lover and poet the name of aviator for as Shakespeare would say if he were alive these four names "are of imagination all compact" and to-day I read in the White Devil what must be for me prophetic.

> "Of all deaths the violent death is best
> For from ourselves it steals ourselves so fast
> The pain once apprehended is quite past".

2. There is a Sorceress in my Sun.

3. I read aloud the White Devil magnificent and I rank it with Tamburlaine and Hamlet and King Lear:

> "O men
> That lie upon your death-beds, and are haunted
> With howling wives, ne'er trust them! they'll remarry
> Ere the worm pierce your winding-sheet, ere the spider
> Make a thin curtain for your epitaphs".

4. Indira here and Armand and the Duke and Duchess of Nemours and we all played the horse-game and so back to Paris where I read All Quiet On The Western Front (very similar to Les Croix de Bois) and the Duchess of Malfi (not as good as the White Devil) and to-day Sunstroke ran again and was fourth.

7. 1811 brandy with the Sorceress and I read Romeo and Juliet (poet and actress) and Jolas and Kay Boyle here (Sapho Jane Austen Kay Boyle) and they went out for dinner (C and Sykes went too) but I stayed in bed for supper in order to finish Romeo

> "Here's to my love! O true apothecary!
> Thy drugs are quick. Thus with a kiss I die"

and I forgot to say that to-day I had tea at Nina's and that Priscilla was there. She is like the Mona Lisa and she has nice eyes.

Shadows of the Sun

August 8. In the evening gin fizzes color of green and silver and the Sorceress girlish like a young actress feline as a puma she is even more feline and amorous by night and now we are together would that we might vanish together into sleep and . . .

9. A goodnight at one (what an hour to say goodnight) and at 19 Rue de Lille C not back from the Moulin so I took an opium pill and put on a sweater and my polo coat and took a taxi and drove out to the Moulin getting there at about three and no C but the car was there so I went up in the dark to the grenier and fired off the cannon (poet and actress) and as I was coming out into the courtyard in came a car and in it were Armand with C and I was so angry I said nothing and walked across the courtyard without saying a word and said to the chauffeur retournez à Paris and so drove back to Paris (it didn't seem a second no one on the road and the opium pill taking effect) and he let me down at the Pont Saint-Michel (time 4 a.m.) and I went down on the quays and curled up and fell asleep and when I woke up it was dawn the lights were out and the stars dim and I walked home along the quays the stars and the orange house in my mind and after breakfast C appeared from the country and a storm was weathered and I rushed off to the Ritz to meet the Sorceress and a miraculous luncheon gin fizzes and oeufs suzette and coffee ice cream and still the effects of the opium pill and she was lovely and in a girlish dress pink and white and a diamond arrow at her throat and a goodbye and I rushed to Baker the fortune-teller but he has gone away to the country.

10. Il faut se développer il faut pousser plus loin les frontières so Polia once told me and to-day I advance by destroying statistics. This just as I was getting into the car to go to Deauville I had had a gin ginger ale and I ran back and went upstairs and unlocked my desk and tore up pages of statistics who in hell wants to keep track of the number of drinks he has drunk (it ruins drinking) or the number of cigarettes smoked or the number of cold baths taken or the number of sun-baths or the number of orchids sent or the number of times I have made love. Harra-Bourra statistics are destroyed and now Deauville for the beach for baccardis for baccara and to-night I won two hundred dollars at cards.

11. Sunday a grey morning exactly the same sort of a day as a year ago exactly the same scene exactly the same cold bathe in the sea and exactly the same run up the beach exactly the same luncheon at Ciro's exactly the same going to the races and I won on the same race as I won on last year and to-day it was Slipper and I made $300 (I almost put a thousand dollars on him) and how fast the past year has gone the fastest I can remember like a flash of lightning not one vibration of a clock since a year ago and perhaps now I can destroy time as I have destroyed statistics. But this will be harder much more difficult and so to the Casino to lose $200 I made last night and so back to Paris in the car I thinking of the mad aviator (Detroyat) who did those acrobatics this morning over the beach at noon (side-slips tail spins loop the loops and flying upside down) as miraculous a Poem as I have ever seen and to-morow I shall go out to the flying field at Villacoublay and enter my name as a student pilot.

August 12. Sherry cobblers and slippers red and gold and always this damn having to say goodbye and to-day I read Lawrence's The Escaped Cock which we are editing and to-day read poems by B[ravig Imbs]

> "shroud well
> that sanded skull
> lest stars should find an eye
> from which to lust"

but good as this is how can it compare to that mad poem of the aviator yesterday over the beach at noon?

13. I enter my name and pay $400 to the Morane-Saulnier school at Villacoublay in order to learn how to fly and to-day a luncheon with the Sorceress and a supper together (caviare and champagne and clear bright red tomato consommé) and the miracle of sunset into evening and darkness and then the lightning of the lights Autumn is approaching.

14. The telephone to say the Count is dying so we rush up to the Rue Décamps where we find him trying to recover from a terrible attack of pain. If he is to live he will have to be operated on. But he still could talk about the races. A grand old man and because he had lost twenty pounds he had a spiritual look about him ,which was wonderful C and I then drove to Le Bourget where I had to go through a strict medical examination (the doctor asked me if my father was an Indian. This in all seriousness because my body is red gold from head to foot) and when I had received a certificate marked Apte we drove out to the Moulin where I climbed to the top of my tower to bask in the sun and to say prayers into the Sun. I am an Arrow Arrowing Into the Sun.

15. A sun-bask followed by sports: ping-pong rifle-shooting donkey races obstacle races swimming races all this with the children there were six of them then into Paris C and I and half way in I had to tell Gus to get out of the car he was terribly drunk I hope he had a long walk to sober him up and I drove the car into town and we went to see the Count who has somewhat recovered and who was sitting in his study wrapped in a shaggy brown wrapper I should not like to live to be so old.

16. To Deauville Gus driving so carelessly (he must be hung-over to use that horrid word) that I made him sit behind C and I in front and when we got to Deauville at sunset I went down to the beach alone for a swim after which cocktails and cards at the Casino a dinner at Ciros and more playing of cards at the Casino. We have a room at the Normandy on the ground floor over the kitchen so that the floor when we walk on it barefooted feels hot as the sand at noon.

August 17. Lost eleven thousand francs on a stupid horse called Sphinx. Terribly stupid of me and I am angry. My stakes are one thousand francs to win (this is the first time I have varied them for almost four years) and I should stick by them. Also lost five thousand at baccara. This I didn't mind so much. To bed at midnight.

18. When I woke up I felt my gold necklace break. We lay in bed until eleven then to the beach crowds of people and a short swim and a run on the beach and a rush to get ready for luncheon and luncheon at Strassburger's a racing luncheon the Marquis de Llano the Marquis de Brissac the Prince d'Arenberg Etcetera (there was good caviare) then a rush to the races where I was a damn fool not to play New Moon she won at 10 to 1 and I played five thousand on Meeting who lost (my stakes are one thousand francs to win and I should stick by them) but I did recover a little on Pure Gold and C was pure gold pure yellow gold in her yellow jacket and her yellow hat and after the races I drove the car all the way back to Paris C the bride by my side.

19. To the flying field at Villacoublay where I listen to my instructor (Détré) explain certain phenomena of flying and where I watch another student perform on the "rouleur" which is a sort of ground plane one has to learn to manoeuvre over the field before going up in the double control planes and when I got back to town I drank a glass of sherry and went to the bank and then to the Ritz to see the Sorceress more bewitching than ever more feline than ever in black with a red necklace and so to Cartier to have them restring my gold necklace with a slender gold chain then to my lawyers to write out a New Testament.

20. To the flying field where I go up for my First Flight (first that is at the flying school le baptême they call it with the instructor) and afterwards two sessions of work on the "rouleur" then in to Paris where I had a hair cut and rouge put on my nails and I passed Carlos in a taxi by the Nain Bleu and after going to Vionnet to see C (CC) try on her new golden "smoking" I saw Carlos again this time on the Champs-Elysées We went back and got C and went to Cuvillier for cocktails Evelyn appearing very good-looking in black. Later on I saw Priscilla. She seemed to be amused by the rouge on my nails and my black flower. Will Bostonians never accept things naturally? After supper began Melville's Moby Dick "if you come of an old established family in the land of the Van Rensselaers" etcetera and to-day a new burgundy colored carpet for the bathroom.

21. To-day concerned itself with the opening and the closing of a red door—the opening = paradise, the closing = hell, and now I must write again that like other combatants the battleship will survive a battle only by her own hard fighting Invulnerability And that last look of hers. Yes.

22. And that last look of hers.

23. To-day Détré took his hands off the control and I flew the plane for a little while alone after which by car C and I and Sykes to Deauville arriving there at sunset for a swim and a run on the beach Narcisse galloping around me in mad circles the tide way way out, and in front of the mirror put on my gold necklace it should never break now because of the new gold chain (gold does not rot like string) and we dined chez Ciro's and went to the Casino to gamble but we left at midnight to go to bed for we were tired.

August 24. To the beach to Ciro's to the races where I won on Lion-Hearted but lost on other horses to play one name the best to play this one horse a day to play this one horse a day 1000 to win this I think is the best way to bet. But the most important is to disregard advice to make up one's own mind and to stick by one's decisions. Cocktails at Strassburger's where I suddenly began to think of the Girl of the White Polo Coat (I had seen her mother at the races) so I sat down at a desk and wrote her a mad letter while people drank and the man at the piano played jazz and so to the Normandy to dress for dinner and RBS's big dinner at the Ambassadeurs and the eighteen children of China and I smoked for the first time in two years and for the last time in my life a cigar after which into the Salle de Baccara I only had a thousand francs which I staked at one turn and soon I was sitting in place number 1 with my American twenty dollar gold piece the Eagle and the Sun in front of me to bring me good luck and the Duke de Nemours I like him was at the same table and two Hindus and by four o'clock in the morning I had amassed twenty five thousand francs $1000 or fifty twenty dollar gold pieces but throughout all the excitement clear and clean as fire that last look of hers. Yes.

25. Last ocean swim of the year and a short run of the beach there were hordes of people and a hurried horrid luncheon at Ciro's and much stupid betting at the races 1000 is my stake so why the hell not stick to it and I lost heavily (what is most difficult in betting as in other things in life is le contrôle dans le désastre) and I deserved to lose and now I am $2000 (one hundred twenty dollar gold pieces) behind for the year and it is all my own fault but the afternoon was saved by seeing a young girl (fifteen?) dressed in yellow with a yellow hat (yellow is the fashion this year) who had nice eyes and a slender body girlish and sunburnt and clean and I looked at her through my field glasses and forgot my losses but as she was with her mother I could not talk to her so back to Paris in Mortimer's car he and Sykes out in front C and I in the rumble and between Evreux and Nonancourt on that straight straight road we did 88 miles an hour for a short stretch which was the fastest that anyone of us had ever been in a car (Chrysler) and so to the Kilometer 104 where we played at bowls while the supper was being cooked Paris again at midnight.

26. To the flying field and flying in the afternoon the clear wind—no poussière no ugly billboards no traffic jams and to-day I reread Robinson's Tristram a damn good poem no matter what anyone says and it takes courage to attack and bring new freshness to a subject that has been written and written about and to-day I wonder where the Fire-Princess is so long so long since we have seen each other and where is the Sorceress and where is the Queen of Pékin and where the Girl of the White Polo Coat and to-night a nice supper sitting up in bed with the Cramoisy Queen.

August 27. To the flying field and both a morning flight and an afternoon flight and now I begin to see that the Eiffel Tower is a most useful object a lighthouse from which one can take one's bearings and afterwards in to Paris to go with C to see the Count and we went with him for a drive around the Bois and then to the Rue de Civry a little street off the Boulevard Exelmans named after his family and when we had said goodbye to him we went for a baccardi cocktail at Cuvillier's and we saw Evelyn on the Champs-Elysées and then the Veuve Biron selling flowers on the Rue de Rivoli (she said she had dreamt that I was flying) and Mortimer came to supper and to-day a pure-gold letter from the Fire-Princess.

30. Branded my wrist with a black cigarette (the reason is a secret to be kept) and went out to fly and flew and so to the Moulin where I went to bed with a fever I am exhausted what with the heat what with three sessions of Deauville what with the whirlwind campaign what with flying every day.

31. And that last look of hers branded forever into my inmost soul.

September 1. Pheasants in the corn and why did I give away my shot gun I must get another for the little rifle is most inadequate I still have a fever It is very hot. The aviator (Mayer) reappears. He got as far as Russia but could not get through to Pekin. We have much in common the war, girl friends, love of adventure, detachment, drinking, misunderstandings with our families, attitude towards money, restlessness, etcetera etcetera. I lay in the Sun but nevertheless felt like hell C won a shooting contest Afterwards a walk in the woods. Merveilleux saw two village girls. He insisted on showing them one of the donkeys only he didn't notice it was the étalon he had chosen. The étalon got very excited and sniffed the air in that way of his and the girls blushed and looked embarrassed but Merveilleux didn't realize until afterwards what had been going on. Into Paris after supper and I went to say hello to the Lothrops. How can a young married couple stay at the Metropolitan. Of all the dreary places and lousy with Bostonians.

4. I fly almost every day I am beginning to feel better but this hot weather is exhausting—so hot that we actually bought an electric fan I say "actually" for we have intended to buy one for the last three years and it drones pleasantly while we sit up in bed and read Proust I like reading him in English better as I infinitely prefer the English language to the French His style is flawless but there is no freshness no metallic quality no vision.

5. Twice to the flying field I am learning to make "virages". Then into town to go to the dentist no fillings heaven be praised and I pay only three hundred francs it is always five when I charge it it is so much better to always pay things right away so much cleaner I hate things that tend to drag one back like those people whose thoughts drag back to the past and I broke my glasses for the first time in a year and then a second pair right afterwards and to-day I weeded out more books I definitely decide to reduce my library to 1000 volumes so that I can keep it young and alive light-hearted not heavy-buttocked and to-day at the dentists I tore out of a magazine the picture of a panther and I wonder and wonder and I pray to the Sun-Goddess that the young panther shall be mine.

September 6. As I have said before I do not want a funeral. I do not want to be buried in the ground. I want to be cremated. I want my ashes to be taken up in an aeroplane at sunrise and scattered to the four winds. Away with coffins, cemeteries, hearses. Purify me with fire. Take my ashes clean and white ascend above New York at dawn and scatter them to the four winds. Let there be no memorial built for me. Let there be no mourning and lamentation (what have I ever had to do with lamentation). Let there be no funeral marches or hymns unless it be the roar of the aeroplanes. And let there be no remembrance unless of a flag of fire flying aloft in your inmost soul.

7. I finish Swann's Way and begin Within a Budding Grove (A l'Ombre des Jeunes Filles en Fleur) Proust is a great writer as great as Balzac and Flaubert as great as Jane Austen or Fielding or Meredith as great as Tolstoï but because he lacks Vision I cannot compare him with the really great men such as Rimbaud and Blake. Proust's style is impeccable, his mastery of psychology is phenomenal, his humour brilliant but always there is something lacking it is too cérébrale it lacks freshness (how stale Swann's Way is in contrast to the Enormous Room) and it never inspires I should rather have written The White Devil any day than all Proust put together.

8. The story of the carrier-pigeons Arrowhead and Silver Wings the father and mother of the young Silver Arrow who flies to and fro in the courtyard. But the parents we have kept in a cage as the man told us they would fly away to their home in Belgium. To-day however out of curiosity we freed one of them Arrowhead I think. He perched on the white fence for a moment then soared into the air in mad circles higher and higher until suddenly straight as an arrow he flew off towards the North. It seemed mean to keep his wife so we let her go. She flew in mad circles until she had risen to a certain altitude where-upon she also flew off towards the North. We felt quite badly as one does when one loses something which as long as one has it one does not always appreciate. Then too the young one looked so forlorn and alone perched on top of their empty cage. But as we were leaving for the races Silver Wings suddenly swooped down into the courtyard. But Arrowhead never returned and to-day at Chantilly I won on Pearlash. What a wonderful name!

9. Seven orchids because we have been married Seven Years and various rites performed: into the swimming pool a walk to the Pôteau de Perthe a firing off of the cannon and prayers into the Sun from the top of the tower. We took luncheon together at the Ritz—the orange-colored cocktail and the gladness of good fun together. In the afternoon I flew Aviator Poet Lover All for the Cramoisy Queen.

September 10. I keep repeating the name Pearlash to myself. If only her boy-friend Hotweed can win the Saint Léger Stakes as brilliantly as she won on Sunday then I shall be glad for I have played him 100 to win which is the most I have ever put on a horse I am very excited about it I have played him at 6 to 1 and if he wins all the waste months of gambling will be refunded In a day I am taking a thing called Passiflorine to make me less nervous. I continue to read Proust "the culminating point of her day is not the moment in which she dresses herself for all the world to see, but that in which she undresses herself for a man" and to-day C went to Fontainebleau to see Jean de Bossechère he may be going to illustrate The White Devil for us he told C that the most wonderful time of his life was when he was living with a mother and her daughter but that when the mother died (apparently of too much pleasure) he soon tired of the daughter and to-day P appeared for a cocktail he told us of how Indira had made almost a million francs in Cannes at baccara and he told us of a men's party he had given in London where the negro orchestra and the waiters and the guests all raped each other and to-day I wrote a sequence of Maxims on Love which I have called Aphrodite In Flight and to-day (I read in the evening newspaper) that the World's Speed Record was shattered by a Schneider Cup aviator 360 miles an hour or 6 miles per minute!

11. All morning getting more and more nervous about Hotweed is he going to win is he going to win and I think up all the arguments that are in his favor but for every good argument there is always a bad one to counteract it until at last I am so excited (no wonder for it means winning three thousand dollars) that I take three spoonfuls from the bottle marked Passifloreine which seems to have a calming effect but when Armand de la Rochefoucauld and Indira came to luncheon and we all drank Alaska cocktails 2-3 gin 1-3 yellow chartreuse I began to feel stimulated and excited again. After luncheon to see Baker the fortune-teller to see if Hotweed was going to win but he couldn't see me until next Wednesday so I went direct to the little bar at the corner of the Rue du Bac and here on the ticker I read the result the Saint Léger Stakes first Trigo second Bosworth third Horus Hotweed nowhere and so I have lost the hundred pounds and now my betting for the year is minus $2500 Very bad.[10]

12. I fly twice learning how to bank and before coming down Détré executes a series of acrobatics great fun and I saw the Russian prince Prince Carageorgovitch who is also learning to fly (he is always driven out in his coffee-colored Minerva—his chauffeur is like Auguste in that he likes to drink) and when I got home I begin a book that Caresse bought for me called The Art of Flying "Think on the ground first. Before trying anything in the air the pilot should devote thought to it on the ground. If possible let him get into the cockpit of a plane and imagine himself to be in the air flying solo.

Let him visualize difficult situations in flight and think out the correct way to recover from them" all very good advice but where O where is my Sorceress? In my heart? Yes.

September 13. It is Friday the Thirteenth which in the bad old days would have made me nervous as regards flying. I fly twice with Détré learning to do turns. I hope I shall learn to fly cross-country as well as I used to run cross-country many years ago at school. It is still frightfully hot and the electric fan is never given a moment's rest. I lie on the chaise-longue and read Proust or else I write letters or else I weed out books, but this weeding out is about as slow a process as the weeding out of her love-letters by a young woman of fashion for there is almost always some reason however feeble for the not giving away of a book. Still I have reduced the library from twelve thousand to two and that is not bad but I must arrive at a thousand a thousand is such a clean concentrated number.

14. To the Moulin and a long afternoon basking in the Sun and as it sets color of sharp orange and red behind the trees I fire off the cannon symbol of the velocity of my soul catapulting into the Sun and this evening Carlos and Evelyn appeared (the betting is even I think that they will get married) and we all played a card game that they taught us called "Jew" I won.

15. This afternoon in our garden I shot my first pheasant and later on in the day won two hundred dollars from Armand de la Rochefoucauld and the Princess (Indira) playing baccara. After the game I bought from Armand (the pack belonged to him) for $1 the Queen of Hearts and when everyone had gone I burnt it in the fire symbol of her burning up in my heart and we all drank champagne the aviator was there and a literary critic from London and all Indira's children and Erik Doll and Scheck and as we were about to leave for Paris I found a magnum bottle in the corner that was still half full so for good luck I poured it over and rubbed it in my hair as I used to rub sand from the beach into my hair before going back to school only for another and a more sentimental reason that of preserving a few gold grains of that beach which in those days represented all that I knew of happiness and love.

16. By arriving too late at the races I save a thousand francs for our Sunstroke was beaten again (for the sixth time I think or is it the seventh) and by being patient that is by not betting when I wanted to (I refer to Talon Rouge and to Queen Eleanor) I arrive at the last race with no losses but I could not resist the temptation to play Yes Dear the last name on the programme and as the proverb says the last shall be first and she won at fourteen to one only like a fool I did not stick to my thousand francs to win (stake from which I should never vary) with the result that I only won four thousand (I played one hundred to win and nine hundred to place) when I should have won fourteen but thanks to this victory and to the baccara yesterday and to abstaining from several bets in the last week which ordinarily I should have played I have now recovered that 100 lost on

Hotweed. Three cheers! And to-day I added to and revised and hammered into a unity those observations on the aerodynamics of love which I have entitled Aphrodite In Flight.

September 17. I wake up dreaming of aeroplanes and orchids whirling in circles around two figures the Sorceress and the Fire-Princess and it is nine months ago to-day (long enough for me to have had a fire-child) since we have seen each other but my heart still writes sonnets to her eyes my body still blazes into fire at the thought of her and I still look out my library window every day at sunset towards the west and to-night after a thirty-one day drought it began to rain—the sound of the roulade of the rain upon the roof come out of the rain dear Yes Dear into my heart where I shall penetrate you with Fire.

18. The Black Sun Press is editing six books all at the same time (MacLeish's Einstein, the Proust Letters to WVRB, The Escaped Cock D. H. Lawrence, Jolas' Astropolis, Lymington's Iscariot and the Liaisons Dangereuses in two volumes) which makes things too complicated and much too much work for Caresse. Never hereafter more than one book at a time this way is no fun and no one should do work like this unless it is for fun for things done without the element of fun lack spontaneity and must suffer in consequence. This afternoon I flew much improvement said the instructor (Detroyat was up in the air doing acrobatics) after which I went to see Baker the fortune-teller who said he had been sick and couldn't see me for another ten days this is the third time I have been to see him without hearing my fortune told When I got home I found Elisabé cutting in half one of the bookcases and now the library seems lighter I gave him some books for Simone and we drank a dubonnet together Jolas appeared in a new gray (spelt with an "a") suit and we talked about the next number of transition about word lore totality, synthesism, the revolution of the word etcetera after which he departed and C and I went to bed—is there any place more wonderful than bed?

19. Too much fog for flying so I stayed in bed and wrote a thing called New Velocity being several arguments in favor of the Revolution of the Word the rest of the day spent trying to decide whether to go to New York this Autumn I should like to live for a year on top of the Ritz Tower. [*with whom?*]

20. Up in the air but there is a tempest and we are tossed about like a tennis ball but I was not afraid because of a light blue ribbon (taken from her nightdress) which I put this morning in the heart-pocket of my aviation suit.

21. The equinoctial storms and fires are lit in the Moulin and it is a grey autumn day and the leaves are beginning to fall and I took the shot-gun and went out to hunt for pheasant but what I surprised was a young deer not a hundred yards from the house but though I emptied both barrels at him he failed to fall and bounded off like zigzag lightning into the woods. It began to drizzle and grow dark and though I wandered about I saw nothing not even a jackrabbit so I went back to the Mill my polo coat covered with burs ("women are like burs where their affection throws them there they'll stick") and there I found the Aviator in his blue sweater just arrived from Paris with a bottle of 1811 cognac which we proceeded to open and to-day I imagined my eyes into two nests in one is curled the Sorceress in the other the Fire-Princess and when I close my eyes they are my prisoners shut in and protected and all safe from harm.

September 22. In the swimming pool before breakfast I dive into the gold reflection of the Sun. It is eight o'clock in the morning and the water is very cold. A bacon and honey breakfast. At one o'clock alone in the car to Longchamp to play ten thousand francs on Kantar who won easily but I am still two thousand dollars behind for the year. Saw a pretty girl but like the girl the last day at Deauville she was with her mother and I lost them in the crowd stupid of me but I had to place a bet for the Count who is too feeble now to run up and down the stairs and when I looked for her again she had vanished. On the way home stopped at Prunier for oysters and anjou and to buy caviare to take home for supper with C.

23. I practise doing turns "les virages" for half an hour up in the air then to the printers to correct proofs for the Liaisons Dangereuses then home to read in the Paris-Sport that Princess Volante had lost this afternoon then into a hot bath then into bed instead of going to Indira's big dinner party [*which did not prevent C from going so as to see Armand and I suppose that at last the time has come for us to admit that although we love each other we are no longer in love*].

24. C got home at four this morning but I was too proud to ask her anything about the party which must have annoyed her inasmuch as half the pleasure of a party is the being able to talk about it afterwards and this morning I balance the aeroplane of my soul on the diamond wind of the Future. This afternoon to the flying-field. One of the students (Raymond Delair) was killed yesterday afternoon ten minutes after I had left the field— his plane crashed into a tree smashed to atoms. No one very gay to-day and Détré was very quiet although we did do a couple of tail-spins before coming down. When I got home a riot with Caresse and she started to jump out the window [*got half way over the balcony rail.*] It happened so quickly that I hardly had time to be frightened but now three hours later I am really frightened I hope I don't dream about it. Finally a miraculous coming together again and I guess I was jealous (I know damn well I was) and now we are wholly [11] in love again.

25. Slipper is beaten in the Coupe d'Or and I am again $2500 behind on the races for the year I am playing high but it is not exhilarating to lose. Crisp weather with an Autumn Sun and I saw again the girl I had lost at the races last Sunday—very physical dressed in brown but always talking to that old woman—it must be her mother—so that I did not get a chance to talk to her Drank three glasses of champagne with Sykes who also lost Anyone who cannot afford to lose would not gamble this and other time statements such as "the horse races are a problem of self-mastery and self-discipline as much as one in finance" or "the greatest weakness of all gamblers is the tendency to overgamble" or "no mechanical system will ever take the place of judgment" or "any horse can do anything" this last is the truest "any horse can do anything" look at Syblime in the first race at 77 to 1.

September 26. Until quite recently I used to have horrible nightmares but beginning this month there has been a decided change and when I dream which is about one night out of four it is of girls last Sunday of the Sorceress last night of the girl at the races with whom I suddenly found myself in bed I am glad this morning to the flying field and we practised landing "les atterrissages"—crisp autumn morning with the planes twinkling in the sun like stars and a frail ghost of a moon like a white parachute in the sky.

27. Kitsa arrives and as I had prognosticated two years ago on the beach at Saint-Jean she is going to get a divorce and now the poor family will worry about her as they have worried and worry about me only she has caught up now in one fell swoop as I should like to catch up at the races.

28. I fly in the morning sun then in to town to the bank where I saw a racy girl in black to whom I talked (she turned out to be a sort of cousin) and we went to the Ritz for champagne cocktails and before leaving she gave me a tip on the stock exchange (I sent a wire to SVRC) then out to fly again then with Kitsa to Le Bourget to get little Cartier-Bresson then to the Moulin where he and I were arrested by two garde champêtres for having no hunting licence (they sprang out at us from behind a tree and I was so startled I almost shot at them I had my rifle up to my shoulder). After supper everyone went over to the party at the Château but I stayed and played Vagabond Lover on the graphaphone and sat in front of the fire drinking champagne and thinking of fire-princesses and sorceresses until I got quite tight (second bottle of champagne) and I danced and shouted and branded myself with burning coals from the fire (Fanatic) and at last fell asleep under the zebra skin in the corner by the cider barrel.

29. [Everyone fought—too much drinking last night I guess] Armand with the Princess, Carlos with Evelyn [apparently he dragged her downstairs last night and beat her up] C and I. In the afternoon Lady Koo appeared with a Mr. Wang and Mrs. Wang. I liked her jade necklace and she herself was attractive. In to town late in the evening.

30. I fly this time with Van Oast as Détré is away and it is good to change instructors this one is more brutal but I learned more in consequence as I had to do the flying myself—storm clouds rising on the horizon. Then into town to the funeral of Cousin Natalie's husband (the Wretch and I drank

dubonnets first Chez Fouquet so that our heads were reeling round like tops as we entered the church) I felt sorry for the roses on the coffin—how much happier they would have been in the boudoir of some courtesane. Afterwards C and I and Kitsa and the Wretch to the Pont Alexandre-III to see Alain Gerbault's Firecrest and if ever a boat had "soul" this one has. There were crowds along the quays What a morning Flying Funeral Firecrest.

October 1. I fly with the new instructor (a great improvement) but I shall be glad when I can fly alone and to-day the First of October is the day I should like to die only not this year. But I must remember what Jolas said "that time is a tyranny to be abolished".

2. C and I take luncheon at the Ritz with all the Polignacs and the Prince de Monaco. The grouse was delicious. Took Nina to the station (the kissing cousins) and came home to finish A l'Ombre des Jeunes Filles en Fleurs.

3. Luncheon with Lady K, with Lady A at the next table, not to mention Michael Arlen and other quasi-celebrities. The grouse was not as good as yesterday nor Lady K as attractive as on Sunday nor did she wear the jade necklace Jolas (told me to read Rimbaud le Voyant) and the Aviator came to tea We drank sherry and talked about murders and murder cases Then to Prunier for oysters C is physical in her autumn suit ça lui va à merveille.

4. Bought Rimbaud le Voyant but read instead Le Traité du Style (Aragon) very violent very brutal but there are passages qui vaut la peine "que les suicides sont les seuls morts par moi, mais véritablement respectés" and this on surréalisme "mais dans le surréalisme tout est rigueur—rigueur inévitable, le sens se forme en dehors de vous— les mots groupés finissent par signifier quelque chose" which is of great interest.

5. In a criticism of Mad Queen I read "Harry Crosby offers his solution to the decay wrought by civilization in a rebirth through sunstroke" which sums up exactly a point of view of mine which I am glad to have so concisely expressed. Here is an example of synthesis. And at ten to the Gare Saint-Lazare to say goodbye to Cousin Nathalie I brought her a little bottle of brandy concealed in one of those empty books and she was huddled in her seat a poor little black figure with her one eye and her hunch in her back and her small bony wrists but inside a golden light (how Goya would have liked her to sit for him) and I kissed her goodbye (what a lovely journey with that corpse in a coffin for companion) and drove out to the aviation field to fly (prise de terrain et atterrissages) and for luncheon a large piece of bread (the crunching of teeth on the crust) and three glasses of dubonnet after which I flew again—then out to the Mill I driving the car (and how fast one drives after flying) for Auguste wanted to go to a prizefight where a friend of his was fighting and to-day particles of fire under the floor of the brain.

6. A dream last night of pheasants and partridges flying upwards at close range forty or fifty of them and the helpless feeling of not having a gun. However I struck at one with a cane and it fell down and thrashed about until I had beaten its brain into a pulp I also dreamed that Kantar had won but that I had been unable to bet on him because the bookmaker had given up bookmaking to become a policeman I remember bursting in to tears and hunting for Caresse whom I could not find I wake. A plunge in the pool. Three glasses of champagne. Then the Wretch and I start off in the car for Longchamp. We had hardly gone a mile when we saw a group of partridges on the road. I stepped on the accelerator and we ran over one. It thrashed about on the side of the road and I had to take out a screw driver and beat its brain out most unpleasant but what was there to do. A garde-champêtre appeared like an evil spirit I gave him some money and threw the bird into the back of the car. It was not until we had reached Le Bourget that I realized that the killing of this bird was the exact fulfilling of my dream. But the second dream did not hold true for Kantar was beaten by the Italian horse and now I am three thousand dollars behind on the races for the year. After the races Hemingway and his wife (he likes the races as much as I do) came back to the house to drink sherry.

October 7. I fly twice and late in the afternoon the Wretch and I went to Rosenberg's to look at the Douanier Rousseau and at the Van Gogh and at the Picassos I liked best the Van Gogh. Such violence! This is the way I should like to write. Then we went to the Salon des Photographes which was poor except for a miraculous picture of part of a woman's body no head arms or legs just showing the breasts like two mythological suns and of a dazzling whiteness and to-night after supper I kindled the fire to a Book of Dreams which is to be my next book with an Aragon quotation at the beginning "la pureté du rêve, l'inemployable l'inutile du rêve, voilà ce qu'il s'agit de défendre contre une nouvelle rage de ronds de cuir qui va se déchaîner".

8. Joyce appeared to ask us to the anniversary of his silver wedding Many celebrities there in particular Léon Paul Fargue (he came very late and immediately began to eat pink angel cake said it reminded him of young girls cut into pieces) Philippe Soupault young and lean, Gzene, Sylvia Beach Adrienne Meunier looking like a nun, Liam O'Flaherty and a young German writer called Hauser who said to Caresse that she was responsible for his changing his entire opinion of the American nation, Stuart Gilbert and many others. There was Irish whiskey and champagne Joyce sang. He wore a tuxedo with a white carnation in his button-hole. We got home at one.

9. Goops arrives from New York. He drank two bottles of red wine. The Wretch and I went to the Louvre to look at the French Primitifs the Avignon Pièta and l'Homme au Verre de Vin in particular I could feel myself drinking that glass of red wine. This is the first time I have been inside the Louvre for two years I have vaguely attempted to go at least ten times but always seemed to get there at closing time or on a holiday. The Wretch and I went to Sherry's for coffee malted milk-shakes then home across the Tuileries I like New York much better than Paris. Jolas to tea. The aviator to tea Gretchen to tea. The Wretch is very pretty in her white dress.

1929

October 10. A gray day and it began to rain so we all went to the bar at the crossroads and sat and drank champagne until it began to clear up a little when we went back and flew. I love flying after champagne and it was marvelous cold and gray and late autumn and here and there the twinkling of lights being turned on in the houses below us. A hot bath and with C to dine with the Ernest Hemingways. Much good wine and he showed us the book of Goya etchings (Les Désastres de la Guerre) which he picked up for almost nothing in a little village in Spain last summer and he showed us a book of photographs taken on their fishing-trip with Waldo Pierce off Key West one remarkable one of a man's arm (intact) taken out of the belly of a shark. There was a copy of the Police Gazette which I had never read before and which he gave to me (he used to write for it) and he also gave us an autographed copy of his Farewell to Arms.

11. Davis was killed in action eleven years ago to-day. I wonder if Ellen still loves him. No flying to-day—too stormy. I go to the throat doctor Ballerin his name is and he is an expert. Much cocaine and burning irons. Dinner at Prunier with Constance. She "trompéd" me last summer with a pederast. Somehow I don't seem to mind very much. I took her home and she gave me a roulette wheel which I saw on the floor behind some books. It will be nice for the Moulin. Carlos will like it. I keep thinking about the Sorceress.

12. A Saturday. I fly twice then out to the Moulin with Goops. A walk to the Pôteau de Perthe a ride on the donkeys and much cider from the big tonneau.

13. Shot a pheasant from the bath-room window and jumped into the swimming pool (icy cold) and played donkey polo and walked out to the Pôteau and drank a rum grog with Indira and Douglas Fairbanks (he signed on the wall) who wore white spats and an immaculate overcoat. He has nice eyes. We all went over to the Château Indira and D.F. and I on the front seat of the Voisin with the cut-out wide open. I nearly ran the car into the moat coming round the corner and there were a great many people all having cocktails and rum and Mary Pickford was there telling people's fortunes she told me the lines in my hand revealed great health (c'est une précieuse chose que la santé—Montaigne) and she has the tiniest feet (Poem for the Feet of Polia) and we drank and some of us went back to the Moulin. I jumped into swimming pool with all my clothes on and then we left for Paris (after I had been up to my Tower) and we passed the lighthouse of Le Bourget (it is here I hope we can keep our aeroplane) and came into Paris the time being about ten o'clock.

14. I am reading a remarkable book on the Yogi Philosophy of Physical Well-Being and it says to drink two quarts of water every day it says to eat little and to think about what you are eating so that a crust of dry bread becomes as delicious as caviare or alligator pears (which reminds me that to-day we had alligator pears for luncheon which reminds me in turn of the

Girl of the White Polo Coat and how we used to eat alligator pears together
—gold and green as alligator pears) and it says to do deep breathing exercises
and to exercise every day and it speaks of pranic energy and pranic
generation of energy and speaks of the law of rhythm "the swing of the
planets around the sun; the rise and fall of the sea; the beating of the heart
the ebb and flow of the tide. All is in vibration.

October 15. I fly. The Wretch goes out with me and we drink dubonnets
together at the bar at the crossroads. She is very cunning. We go to Prunier
together. A game of baccara after supper. By the end of this month I hope to
fly alone.

16. Nine in the morning and off for Saint Dizier through the fog C and I
and the Wretch and we pick up Sykes the other side of Fontainebleau (at le
Moret where they make the sucre d'orges) and on through Sens and Troyes
and Bar-sur-l'Aube until we came to Colombey-les Deux-Eglises. Here we
found the Jolases and Stuart Gilbert. Red wine and rum and we all departed
(all except Maria) for Saint Dizier. We lost our way in the fog. It was dark
and cold and everyone indoors in the village and no one knew anything. I sat
out in front with the Wretch in my lap. We drove for an hour in the wrong
direction. Finally at about nine we got there cold and hungry but the supper
was wretched. After supper we went across to the Café de l'Industrie to
correct proof sheets for the Autumn Transition and to drink brandy and
wine. My Dreams 1928-1929 aren't bad and Illustrations of Madness is not
bad either. About midnight we went to bed C and I and The Wretch in the
same room.

17. At crack of dawn C and the Wretch leave in the car for Dijon (C is
going to take the Wretch to school somewhere near Chamonix) I waved
goodbye from the window Sykes appeared just after they had left. He had
intended to go with them I poured a large pitcher of cold water over me (this
counts as a bath) and did Yogi exercises and got dressed and went down to
the Imprimerie to correct proof sheets. Jolas there already at work Gilbert
still in bed I don't blame him this cold morning I look at the sky grey and
cold but there is a "horizon" and could fly I hate to miss a day of flying.
There are two blank pages left open for me but I never can write anything on
the spur of the moment unless it is a love-letter and we can't seem to find my
Short Introduction to the Word We telephone to Colombey to have it
dictated over the telephone but we are cut off in the middle of it. A good
meal in a little restaurant Jolas ordered it. Many telegrammes sent off after
luncheon but more to the Sorceress I don't know where she is which is a lie
for she is curled in my heart. At four it begins to grow dark Auguste
exhausted is back from Dijon I put him in the back seat with Narcisse and
Sykes and I sit in front We are off for Paris I drive like the wind and in two
hours we have covered 140 kilometers an average of 70 kilometers an hour.
Pas mauvais. But near Paris there is traffic and we had to slow down. We got
in about eight and I found my Introduction to the Word and sent it back by

express to Saint-Dizier all because I like the word Slipper. A nursery game called Hunt-the-Slipper. A flower called Lady-Slipper. Running in the Gold Cup a horse called Slipper. Drinking champagne out of Her Red Slipper. Her ears two little Slippers for the feet of my voice (see Transit of Venus) From these magic sources the development of the word Slipper in my mind so that it becomes a word internal and therefore as much a part of me as my eyes or heart or mouth or hands.

October 18. Aviation throat operation it rains and C is not back yet and the house is cold and the only thing to do is to crawl into bed and pull the blankets up over my head and go to sleep.

19. C back before breakfast very tired and very pretty any woman who can look pretty after a night on the train is to be felicited and we take a hot bath together and I go out to fly and she goes out to the Black Sun Press. At four off to the Moulin where we find Goops standing in the cour just as we had left him five days ago. He has been making out a list of New York underworld slang words which should be interesting for Transition. I haven't heard from the Fire Princess for so long but she is mine—whether I hear from her or not has really very little importance. All evening Goops plays the graphaphone and the log fire crackles and smoulders and then is bedtime the best time.

20. I win five hundred dollars on Slipper.

21. All day the word Slipper.

22. Acrobatics in the air—a sea of clouds the gold sunray of clouds and he says I have a good eye for tailspins.

23. A grey day with part of the gold won by Slipper I buy a gold wrist watch at Cartiers for I have to have a watch when I go flying and when I get home the letter I have been waiting for for two months The Sorceress.

24. At last a gin fizz again at last a black cigarette again at last her red slippers again at last her mouth again.

25. The Sorceress A Fire The Gold Necklace.

26. A je t'aime de tout mon coeur letter from the Wretch and out to the Mill in a new taxicab our car out of order for Gus got run into again (his eighth accident) and out to the Pôteau with the lantern late at night.

27. My eighth Gladiateur at Longchamp and Ivresse is beaten. So is Yes Dear I translate some more of these damn Proust Letters If they weren't to Cousin Walter I wouldn't think of doing it Croucher arrives from Cannes in a vast red sweater and mud caked sabots. A real man if ever there was one.

28. Gerard Lord of Lymington and harbinger of good arrives no wonder I saw the Sorceress last week no wonder I think of a title for my new book Sleeping Together no wonder I feel that soon there will be a letter from the Fire-Princess I flew to-day Jean de Bosschère came to lunch to-day bringing with them some illustrations he has been doing for the White Devil and to-day Mortimer came to say good-bye and gave us a bottle of very old absinthe No wonder I call Gerard a harbinger of good.

October 29. Panic in the Stock Market (New York) the worst one in the history of the U.S. and shares go down and down and down leaving the speculative shores strewn with the wrecks of more than one man's fortune. That damn United Corporation the girl told me to buy has dropped from 70 to 25 just one example of the general trend SVRC must be at his most nervous I am glad I am not in Boston. It would make an exciting story millions lost in an hour suicides disorder panic.

30. I fly in a rainstorm but there is too much wind and we are forced to land I am hoping for quiet grey days then I shall fly alone I wrote HMC to-day (the eighty-forth letter this year) I translated some more of Proust to-day (almost finished now) I read Rikki-Tiki-Tavi again (for the first time in fifteen years I was not disillusioned) and I did some more work on my book of dreams (for C) Sleeping Together.

31. Letter and a gold eagle and the sun from the Fire Princess I am glad Gold and Fire and Sun.

November 1. Yes the Sorceress and I drive out through the fog singing aloud to myself at the top of my lungs to the Moulin and supper with C in front of the fire and so to bed.

2. From 9 in the morning until 9 at night I write dreams for Sleeping Together when someone said to Whistler how amazing it was that he could paint a picture in ten or twenty minutes Whistler said not at all for in the ten minutes of actual painting is concentrated the experience of ten or twenty years. And so it is with Sleeping Together I have written it all in three or four days but back of it are three or four years of hard work. No people at the Moulin to-day—what a relief for this week-end I want to work.

3. Finished Sleeping Together sixty four dreams (these dreams for C) and I am glad. Shot two pheasants from the bathroom window and rode on the donkeys with C a magnificent race I winning on the little donkey by a short head I to Paris.

4. I fly in the afternoon I refuse to go to America until I have flown alone. A horse called Yes won to-day Good omen C and I went to the Banque de Saint Phalle and bought 100 shares of Calumet and Hekla (we chose this stock because of the C and H) without having any money. We then drank a baccardi cocktail and came home. I go over the dreams. They are funny and fantastic and absolutely individual I am excited.

5. Fog. No flying. Joyce appeared at luncheon time and invited us to come and see him and hear him read aloud from Anna Livia Plurabelle on the graphaphone. Goops here (sober). Transition is out the Fall Number Apparition and Aerotics look well and I like my Illustration of Madness my heart is a madhouse for the twin lunatics of her eyes. [A] And she appears. And we kiss. And she disappears.

November 6. Flying. I am nervous. I wish they would let me fly alone.

7. More flying more wanting to fly alone more hot rum grogs for it is icy cold Glad to get home to a hot bath to a hot fire to a hot bed.

8. It rains—a dark day until the Sorceress appears. Three Roses darkness [12] Yes Pucelle that witch that damned Sorceress It was terrible to have her go but I am damn happy for the word Yes is ringing in my ears and she has given me the letter A.

9. I fly three times but I am not let loose. If I don't fly alone soon I shall go mad I read my letter from the Fire-Princess sitting out on the bank by the brick mill. A large piece of bread and a small bottle of red wine at the bar at the corner then back again to the field to fly. They were taking moving pictures and we sat in the ditch while Détré and Détroyat catapulted over us the wheels of their planes not half a foot over our heads and what a roar from the exhausts. But I did not fly alone to-day and I could almost cry with rage. Goops here when I got back I decide to fly to-morrow Sunday and the next day Armistice Day.

10. I fly four times with Détré twice in the morning twice in the afternoon and now I hope I shall be let loose. To bed at four Goops here he went out to watch me fly and all evening we listened to the graphaphone and drank red wine C is out at the Moulin.

11. Armistice Day. I Fly Alone for the first time at 11 o'clock this morning. [SUN] [13]

12. Storms Happy because I flew alone yesterday at 11 - 11 - 11 - 11.

13. Storms. Mr. Knife and Miss Fork better than the Ladybird or To-Day is Friday, *best* short story.

14. I go to fly in the morning 1 hour at 2000 meters Rum Grogs In the afternoon figure S's [14] Sleeping Together completed.

15. People for tea Jolas Vitrac Alec and Sylvia [Steinert, Cousin] Joe Grew Switz Croucher Goops.

16. Platform party Mauretania Yes A.

17. Aviator and A[ctress]

18. Baccara with C C C finished Beating the Stock Market.

19. Terrific Storm already one day late Wire from Josephine.

20. At sea Wrote to Sorceress.

21. Copied out Sleeping Together for C cold and grey day.

November 22. New York City of Arabian Nights Aeroplane overhead 11 years ago Midnight to Boston Black Cigarette

23. J in the morning sun   gin   public library   H-Y game

24. J at 5 and to Robbies [15]

25. Luncheon   J   at Robbies

26. J

[*27. Motor ride with J   at the house*]

28. Thanksgiving Day dreary luncheon   waiter's dark hand   green glass sliced oranges   to New York   CC

29. Byrd flies to South Pole   Let Us Be Gay   managed Modern Art Van Gogh   Gauguin   Seurat   I like our Room 2702 at the Savoy Plaza I like living in one room more concentrated for the poet and high up 27 stories and the round disc of the Sun miraculous place for the sun-death room of the rising sun. [16]

30. The Sun rises from our window   2702 [17]

December 1. Sun Motored to Cedarhurst with Mortimer to get Caresse dreary scenery ugliest cars weight of Sunday newspaper   back to N Y 2702   love-nest to Rudy Valee   talking pictures   Vagabond Lover

2. J telephones from Boston   J arrives [*from New York   J with H to Detroit*] Wolverine   Fight [18]

3. Detroit Book-Cadillac   Beany [19]   Backer Play   Sun Up   Ghastly Commercial Place   Party at Beany's   actors and actresses   Fisher body [20] girl to bed   madnesses

4. [*Detroit stayed in bed until two   from two to four*] art museum   grey day   *Kolbe* Vlaminck Klee [*to bed again at four*] Moral battle and virginity victory   I'm your little harlot   caviare   game of baccara   I win.

> [Princess Yes
> The Little Yes Princess
> Little Harlot
> Little Animal
> Little Yes] [21]

5. [22] [*12 hours sleep   pillowed in silks and scented down when hushed awakenings are dear much refreshed   oysters for breakfast   J takes her bath   luncheon at speakeasy   J and I and Beamy   cash a cheque   rum in teacups   Mermaid book shop   hot chocolate. With J over the Bridge to Canada and back to the station She sees someone she knows and is upset The Wolverine she cries   many opium pills and all night we catapult through space   J and I in each other's arms visions security happiness*] [23]

1929

December 6. New York   J sick as a cat from the opium   1 West 67 [24]   I see C   I fight with J   I go to bed 2702 with C.

7. Modern Art Gallery   Van Gogh Gauguin Cezanne Seurat   1 Van Gogh still life   2 Gauguin decorative panel   3 Van Gogh room at Arles   J appears all young and sparkling   her eyes goodbye in that grey city. Hart Crane party for H and C   E E Cummings there. [Pack of Cards   I said I like Hearts the best   I drew and I drew the Ace of Hearts the card I wanted] [25]

8. Luncheon with C. H and C in bed. Champagne.

9. And again my Invulnerability is put to the test.

(December 9 1929)

> [One is not in love unless one desires to
> die with one's beloved]

> [There is only one happiness
> it is to love and to be loved] [26]

ADDENDUM

The following fragments among the out-of-sequence entries in the holograph were probably written during Harry's last days, but are undated:

hello Stanley where's that damn girl of mine
hello Stanley where's that damn Harry of mine

.   .   .   .   .

the looking at my wrist watch   one o'clock
seven more hours of happiness

.   .   .   .   .

our mothers don't know what it is to be immoral
Anne said

.   .   .   .   .

Transit of Venus (for Josephine)
Sleeping Together (for Caresse)
(these are the two books I have written which
are damn good the others can go to hell)

Caresse heavily pencilled out the words "for Josephine" on her
typescript of these entries.

.   .   .   .   .

he was operating a service elevator in the hotel at about
10.45 o'clock on the night of the crime and was standing
idle in it on the street floor when his attention was attracted by a man's voice saying 'I'm shot.'

.   .   .   .   .

Sun-Ring
I Fly Alone

Harry and Caresse bought the gold "Sun Ring" in Cairo. He
promised never to remove it. It was found on the floor of the
room in the Hotel des Artistes, smashed.

NOTES

[1] Holograph notebook reads "was."

[2] Caresse died in 1970 at the age of 77.

[3] "but I doubt it"—these words do not appear in the holograph notebook.

[4] The last two sentences do not appear in the holograph notebook.

[5] The holograph notebook reads "Terrific day."

[6] Erased but still legible in the holograph notebook are these words: "The Aerodrome 5:33-8,11 air-cooled Jaguar engines H M A."

[7] The last sentence does not appear in the holograph notebook.

[8] The entire letter is included here, with the sections that Harry omitted enclosed in brackets.

[9] The last quotation does not appear in the holograph notebook.

[10] Harry's looseleaf holograph notebook that contains his diary entries from November 11 to his death also contain a variant entry for September 11, which is reproduced verbatim:

Twin story waiting an evening when there is
no girl friend
Autumn is my lucky time of year
                Hotweed
a great horse   perhaps the greatest French
horse since Ksar
The Herald gives him in their   also begins
with H
always have luck in England   8 - 1   6 - 1
5 - 1 a good sign
he can stand the distance   all right
has only once been beaten for his debut
Perhaps his girl friend   won at Chantilly
and stable-companion
Superstition   H my first name begins with H
will he be scratched
Hot it is a hot day
Esmond the stable in form has worn out Cheval
de Prix and Verdi and they had to buy another
horse to accompany him
Games to games the victory his father
Bruleur a great étalon Eleventh 11 September
cost him two ones   has been   for his
race   Matin Pant all the ground so dry here
not much exercise
do you know what the tracks are like at
Doncaster
hard for a horse to keep his form
fourteen in the race that is a great many
has a French horse ever won the Saint Léger
the English jockeys   many times to box him
and   Games   the way the French did
to Donoghue
all the things I shall do if I win

Shadows of the Sun

pay C   what I owe her
present to Veuve Biron
Marks' present
be able to go to America
have those   The Sun books bound
ask Kitsa to bring over gold pieces
twenty dollars the Eagle and the Sun   500 - 25
gold wrist watch
wine supply
the next class aeroplane licence

how shall I pay for it if I lose
sell Neuremberg Chronicle
perhaps they will dope a horse   perhaps
they will try to bribe the jockey
the waste of months of gambling refunded in a
day   should I have played him to place
in life one must always play to win
thought of the Amateur Gentleman and of the
great horse race
presentiments
Trigo beats Bosworth by a short head
I go to the little bar at the corner of the
Rue de Bac
I could have gone to the Chateau where I saw
Rose Prince win or to the rue Cambon where I
had seen Canadien win
Now Rue du Bac
England fortunate for me this year
Diamonds Aerodrome and now
une plaie d'argent ne tue jamais
I take Passifloreine to calm my nerves
I try to read Proust   quote passage but I
cannot concentrate
I go out to the flying field to take a lesson
I put on my new suit a new black flower
new socks and new necktie
Shall I drink or not
Edward
I visualize Esmond   very serious and competent
brisk inspires confidence
by luncheon time in spite of the Passifloreine
I am high-strung and excited I tell no one
for it might break my luck   I look out the
window I see a yellow taxi with a blue hood
a woman in white with the yellow and blue
sleeve and a white hat the Esmond color   good
omen
I endeavor to control the race by a tremendous
exertion of thought
I try to make him get away with a good start
He must not hold him in too long
his entourage seems to place enormous confidence
in him   but other stables place confidence in
their horses   it is Esmond's year on the
race-track
Lord so and so
look at Pennycomequick   look at Trigo
Everyone fears Bosworth

290

Notes

I go to the bar it is an hour before time
I go out and walk as far as the Pont Royal
Royal bridge the word Royal

I order a hot grog although it is hotter than
hell outside   because hot corresponds to
and g stands for his jockey Games
I resolve to give a tenth of my winnings to
the poor if only I can win
the tricker functions already the races at
Chantilly are being
the Alaska cocktail and the real
it should be Hot   Hotweed not cold
the going to the Fortune Teller's
was going to cable for pieces of gold
throwing a cork (from the Evian bottle)
into the   bucket from the bed and succeeding

Nurenberg Chronicle
so and so wins the first
so and so the second
again the ticker   in the Saint Leger
It is only one   race
Ten for Two   Amor wins   and eight
other
I would have played it
I keep thinking of Pearlace who I believe
to have a great magic influence over   how glad
she will be if he returns as conqueror this
morning's
I have cut out of the paper the name Hotweed
which I carry around with me in my pocket-book
I open my desk to see if my bookmaker's slip
is still there   yes   100 on Hotweed at 6 to 1
I lock my desk
"this voucher must be returned on a receipt
in case of victory"
Transition Hand and Horn
I want to drink another hot grog but if I
drink two he might come in second
One = First
the ticker again the Saint Leger Stakes
tick tick tick tick

Poe and the Law of Averages

see Hemingway book   Race Story
the refusal to buy violets
Fire

now
three hours
more to wait
three hours

then
Armand
arrives for
luncheon
and says that
last week he had dinner
with Franck Castey
the trainer
who said
that the book
was not so good

Fire

291

[11] "wholly" does not appear either in the holograph notebook or in the typescript.

[12] In the holograph notebook the phrase is "Three Roses Madness."

[13] "SUN" is not in the holograph notebook.

[14] The figure S's are figure 8's in the holograph notebook.

[15] Robert Choate, the ex-husband of Harry's sister, apparently encouraged Harry's affair with Josephine.

[16] Harry's description of the room is an out-of-sequence entry placed here by Caresse. She had checked into the room at the Savoy-Plaza Hotel on November 25. Harry joined her on the 28th. (See editor's note on page 226.)

[17] Caresse added the room number, which appears in neither the holograph nor the typescript.

[18] The train to Detroit was called the Wolverine.

[19] Beany was Robert Choate.

[20] The 1930 edition reads "Fisher bodyguard girl," but the holograph is clear. Caresse must have missed the joke.

[21] The poem comes from the out-of-sequence entries.

[22] In the 1930 edition, Caresse omitted the entry after this date and substituted for it this sentence, which does not appear in the holograph: "Thank the Sun for Harry and Caresse."

[23] Related out-of-sequence entries from the holograph notebook:

> 2015   her princess body warm from her hot bath
> slender princess

2015 was their room number at the Book-Cadillac.

> toast rum in tea cups to
>   H the greatest poet
>   J the greatest mistress
>   BB the greatest actress
> Detroit 13-5-12-29 (in a speakeasy)

[24] Stanley Mortimer's address, the Hotel des Artistes.

[25] From the out-of-sequence entries.

[26] The first sentence is from the out-of-sequence section. Caresse used it to end her edition of the diary. But the section continues, as reproduced here. These were the last words Harry wrote. Caresse's edition added "(Tuesday the tenth Harry died)."

INDEX AND SELECTED GLOSSARY

"When I like people immensely," Harry Crosby wrote in an unpublished notebook, "I never tell their names to anyone. It is like murdering a part of them." In *Shadows of the Sun* he extends this protective anonymity to nearly everyone. Even chance acquaintances become "S" or "E" or, at the most explicit, "Lady A."

This index and glossary should minimize his obfuscations. Names are indexed in the form that Harry Crosby most often uses; hence, Josephine Rotch Bigelow is indexed as "Fire Princess" and Constance Crowninshield Coolidge as "Lady of the Golden Horse." These entries are cross-referenced so the reader may use the index without knowing the specific designation Harry employs. When Harry uses the same designation for different people, as in the case of the six he identifies as "C," each is indexed separately as far as possible so the reader can distinguish between them. When Harry uses different names for the same person, each is cross-referenced and indexed after the main entry; hence, the entry for "Lady of the Golden Horse" includes references to "CCC," "Queen of Pekin" and "Star of the East."

Whenever appropriate and possible, brief notes further describe characters. Sometimes these cite passages from Caresse Crosby's *The Passionate Years* (*TPY*) or refer to the Black Sun Press (BSP) or the BSP Archives at Southern Illinois University.

In a few instances the assignment of names to single letters is an educated guess, supported by context or corroborated by evidence from outside the diary.

Harry Crosby was an inveterate listmaker who compulsively recorded names of kings, statesmen, authors, painters and people at parties. These are indexed only selectively. Various minor characters who cannot be confused with anyone else and who appear only once are also omitted. The index contains a few subject listings of unusual interest, including Harry's references to war, suicide, the Bible, flying, to the drugs he used, and to the dreams he had.

Index/Glossary

295

Index/Glossary

Index/Glossary

Index/Glossary

Index/Glossary

Printed April 1977 in Santa Barbara & Ann Arbor
for the Black Sparrow Press by Mackintosh and Young
& Edwards Brothers Inc. Design by Barbara Martin.
This edition is published in paper wrappers; there
are 1300 hardcover trade copies; & 200 numbered
copies have been handbound in boards by Earle Gray.